D0212638

STRAND PRICE
5 00

SILENCE, MUSIC, SILENT MUSIC

Silence, Music, Silent Music

Edited by

NICKY LOSSEFF AND JENNY DOCTOR
University of York, UK

ASHGATE

Published by
Ashgate Publishing Limited
Gower House
Croft Road
Aldershot
Hampshire GU11 3HR
England

Ashgate Publishing Company
Suite 420
101 Cherry Street
Burlington, VT 05401-4405
USA

Ashgate website: http://www.ashgate.com

British Library Cataloguing in Publication Data
Silence, music, silent music
   1. Silence in music
   I. Losseff, Nicky, 1962- II. Doctor, Jenny
   781.2'36

Library of Congress Cataloging-in-Publication Data
Silence, music, silent music / edited by Nicky Losseff and Jenny Doctor.
      p. cm.
   Includes bibliographical references and index.
   ISBN-13: 978-0-7546-5559-6 (alk. paper)
   1. Music–Philosophy and aesthetics. 2. Silence in music. I. Losseff, Nicky, 1962- II. Doctor, Jenny.

ML3800.S543 2007
781.2'36–dc22

2006032282

ISBN: 978-0-7546-5559-6

Printed and bound in Great Britain by TJ International, Padstow, Cornwall
Bach musicological font developed by © Yo Tomita

Contents

List of Illustrations and Music Examples

Cover: *Pilgrim* (1950), etching by Geoffrey Clarke

Notes on Contributors

William Brooks is Professor of Music at the University of York and also Associate Professor of Composition, Emeritus, at the University of Illinois. He has written extensively on American music and especially experimental composers such as Ives and Cage, most recently in two chapters for *The Cambridge Companion to John Cage* and two chapters for *The Cambridge History of American Music*. He is a composer as well as a scholar, and in both domains much of his work is concerned with memory, reference and the relationship between art music and popular culture. His present research is focused on the reception of, and musical settings of, the World War I poem 'In Flanders Fields'; he is also preparing 'an episodic travelogue through American Music' for publication by the University of Illinois Press.

Jan Christiaens studied philosophy and musicology at the Katholieke Universiteit Leuven in Belgium. His PhD in musicology was about the aesthetics of Olivier Messiaen's experimental works (1949–51) and of early serialism, considering especially Karel Goeyvaerts and Karlheinz Stockhausen. Currently, he is a Postdoctoral Research Fellow of the Fund for Scientific Research, Flanders, at the same university, where he is teaching music aesthetics and music sociology. His research interests are twentieth-century music, philosophy of music, Theodor W. Adorno, and religious and spiritual music. He has published on twentieth-century music and music aesthetics in *Perspectives of New Music*, *Dutch Journal of Music Theory* and other journals. His book, *Twelve-Tone Technique and Phenomenology: Use and Abuse of Philosophy in the Writings of René Leibowitz and Ernest Ansermet*, is soon to be published by Koninklijke Vlaamse Academie van België voor Wetenschappen en Kunsten.

Darla M. Crispin is Head of Graduate School at the Royal College of Music. She was formerly a member of the academic studies department at the Guildhall School of Music and Drama, with particular responsibility for co-ordinating postgraduate studies. Darla is Co-Chair of the Association of European Conservatoires POLIFONIA Project 3rd Cycle Working Group, researching the nature of doctoral study within institutions in the European space, and is also active as a member of the NAMHE Executive. A Canadian pianist and scholar, Darla has worked as a solo performer and accompanist in the UK, continental Europe and Canada, specializing in musical modernity in both her performing and her scholarship. Her doctoral work at King's College London, involved a re-evaluation of Arnold Schoenberg's string quartets. A recent article, '"Wine for the Eyes" – Re-Reading Alban Berg's Setting of *Der Wein*', appeared in the Modern Humanities Research Association journal, *Austrian Studies*, in October 2005.

Jenny Doctor's research into the history of BBC music broadcasting has contributed to two books: her own *The BBC and Ultra-Modern Music, 1922–36: Shaping a Nation's Tastes* (CUP, 1999) and Humphrey Carpenter's *The Envy of the World: Fifty Years of the BBC Third Programme and Radio 3* (Weidenfeld and Nicolson, 1996). With Nick Kenyon and David Wright, she has co-edited *The Proms: A New History* (Thames & Hudson) and with Sophie Fuller is currently preparing an edition of letters exchanged by British composers Elizabeth Maconchy and Grace Williams (University of Illinois Press). She is a Senior Lecturer at the University of York.

Coming to academia rather late in life, **Tom Dixon**'s research combines interests in 'early music' with music's philosophical and religious aspects. Pursuing these themes in the thought of the English religious author, Peter Sterry, resulted in an MA thesis (Lancaster University, 2002) and a PhD dissertation (University of Manchester, 2005). He has presented aspects of his research at academic conferences, including invited papers at Northwestern University in Evanston, Illinois, at All Souls' College, Oxford and at a conference on 'Music and Aesthetics' in Venice. Work in progress includes an exploration of the historical, cultural and educational contexts of Sterry's 'musical model', and research on music in the papers of the mid-seventeenth-century 'intelligencer', Samuel Hartlib. He currently holds a temporary teaching fellowship in the School of Arts, Histories and Cultures at the University of Manchester.

Matthew Hill is Associate Professor of Music at Goshen College in Indiana, where he teaches piano, music history and humanities. He has written for *Clavier*, and lectures and presents master classes at the Goshen College Piano Workshop. Matthew has been a guest presenter for the Great Lakes Chapter of the College Music Society and at 'Couleurs dans le vent: Celebrating the Music of Olivier Messiaen', an international conference held at the University of Kansas in 2002. In October 2006 he presented a series of master classes and a recital performance at the Sichuan Conservatory of Music in Chengdu, China; he has performed at the White House in Washington DC, as accompanist for the Wausau Conservatory Choraliers Children's Choir, and has been heard on Wisconsin Public Radio. Matthew has a doctorate in piano performance from the University of Wisconsin-Madison under pianist Howard Karp, and has also studied with the renowned Beethoven interpreter Claude Frank.

Emma Hornby is a Lecturer in Historical Musicology at Goldsmiths College, University of London. She is also Assistant Editor of a New Dictionary of Hymnology project, based at the University of Durham. Emma has close ties with the Irish World Music Centre, University of Limerick. Her research concentrates on the composition and transmission of Western liturgical chant, and on text/music relations in the repertory. Recent publications include her book, *Gregorian and Old Roman Eighth-Mode Tracts* (Ashgate, 2002), and two articles: 'The Transmission History of the Proper Chant for St. Gregory: the Eighth-Mode Tract Beatus uir', in *Plainsong and Medieval Music* (2003), and 'The Transmission of Western Chant in the 8th and 9th Centuries: Evaluating Kenneth Levy's Reading of the Evidence', in the *Journal of Musicology* (Summer 2004). She is currently completing a book on the role of grammar, rhetoric and exegesis in the second-mode tracts.

Ed Hughes is a composer and currently lectures in the Music Department at Sussex University, where he has developed new courses in music and film. He has previously lectured for the British Film Institute Education Department at the National Film Theatre. In the last two years, he has received major commissions from the Brighton Festival and the City of London Festival for The Opera Group. He has written scores for films such as *Battleship Potemkin*, *I Was Born, But...*, *Pacific 231* and *Rain*, as well as work on *Playing a Part: the Story of Claude Cahun* (a documentary by Lizzie Thynne). Previous commissions include *I Fagiolini*, London Sinfonietta, CHROMA, Opus 20 String Ensemble, Bath Camerata, Sinfonia 21, Bath International Music Festival, Bath Film Festival, Schubert Ensemble (for Chamber Music 2000) and Arts Council of England (for New Music Players, which he founded as artistic director). Performances have also been given by distinguished pianists, including Richard Casey, Stephen Gutman, Thomas Adès, Ian Pace and Michael Finnissy. His work is recorded by Opus 20 (DGM label), New Music Players (London Independent Records), the Schubert Ensemble (NMC) and the BMIC (for Unknown Public).

Stan Link is currently the Assistant Professor of the Composition, Philosophy and Analysis of Music in the Composition–Theory Department at the Blair School of Music of Vanderbilt University in Nashville, Tennessee. He teaches music composition, theory, interdisciplinary arts courses and a course on film soundtracks. He has held other academic posts at La Trobe University in Melbourne, Australia, and at the University of Illinois, Urbana-Champaign. Stan holds a Bachelor of Music in Composition and Music History from Oberlin Conservatory, and received his MFA and PhD from Princeton University. Some of his work on film music and sound appears in the journals *Screen* and *American Music*. Further scholarly publications include articles in *Perspectives of New Music*, *Mikropolyphonie*, *Computer Music Journal* and *Music Theory Spectrum*. He is an active composer of acoustic and electro-acoustic music, with musical compositions performed in Europe, Australia and across the USA.

Nicky Losseff is a Senior Lecturer in music at the University of York. She is the author of *The Best Concords: Polyphonic Music in Thirteenth-Century Britain* (Garland, 1994) and the editor, with Sophie Fuller, of *The Idea of Music in Victorian Fiction* (Ashgate, 2004). Her articles and reviews on medieval polyphony, gender and music, and psychoanalysis have appeared in scholarly journals in Britain and America. She is also active as a pianist.

John Potter was a member of the Hilliard Ensemble for eighteen years before taking a position at the University of York, where he is Reader in Music. He performs regularly with Red Byrd, the Dowland Project and the Gavin Bryars Ensemble. He is the author of *Vocal Authority: Singing Style and Iideology* (1998) and editor of *The Cambridge Companion to Singing* (2000), both published by Cambridge University Press. Recent projects have included a history of singing (with Neil Sorrell) and a monograph on the tenor voice. He is currently researching the life and music of the castrato Venanzio Rauzzini.

A UK-Registered Music Therapist, **Julie P. Sutton** is the Head of Training for the Master's in Music Therapy at the Nordoff-Robbins Music Therapy Centre at City University in London, a guest teacher at Leuven University in Belgium and part of the Psychotherapy Centre therapist team led by Lord John Alderdice in Belfast. She has had wide clinical experience over twenty-four years, working in London, Belfast and Dublin, and as a consultant for projects in Bosnia and Belarus. Past research has focused on complex speech and language impairment, Parkinson's Disease, Rett Syndrome, Autistic Spectrum Disorder and psychological trauma. Julie presents her work nationally and internationally, and writes regularly for journals and books; her first book *Music, Music Therapy and Trauma* was published in 2002, and she is currently researching and working on a new book about silence. She is an Executive Committee Member of the UK Association of Professional Music Therapists and a Core Board Member of the European Music Therapy Confederation.

Acknowledgements

The impetus for this book came from the conference 'Music and Silence' that was held at the University of York in October 2003. Of the papers given there, several have found their way in revised form into *Silence, Music, Silent Music*.

We would first like to thank all the authors for their creative ideas, hard work and patience. It was a pleasure to compile and edit this book – first, in finding enthusiastic authors who have curiosity about this unusual topic from diverse points of view, and then in bringing together this collection to launch its exploration in print. We would also like to thank Professor Alain Frogley of the University of Connecticut for his inventive encouragement and inspired thoughts about possible content.

Thanks are due to Heidi May at Ashgate for her assistance and support of this project, and also to Emma McBriarty for her careful work as in-house editor. We are extremely grateful to Stephen Ferre of New Notations Computer Services for his time and expertise in typesetting the music examples. Sincere thanks are due also to the Solesmes Abbey for permission to reproduce the chant examples in Chapter 8.

We are delighted that Geoffrey Clarke was willing to permit his etching, *Pilgrim* (1950), to appear on the cover of this book, and thank him most warmly for this privilege. The image appeared in an exhibition catalogue of Geoffrey Clarke's etchings that was published in 2006; we are grateful to the exhibition curator, Gordon Cooke of the Fine Art Society, and to the printer, Wooter Rummens of Die Keure, for making the image available for our use. We warmly thank Dr Judith LeGrove, cataloguer of Geoffrey Clarke's works, for her rediscovery of the etching and for bringing the catalogue to our attention.

We would like to thank the Music Department at the University of York for its endorsement of the project, both in helping to fund music examples and in providing solid moral support. Nicky would like to thank the University of York for two periods of research leave in 2001 and 2006. The first of these facilitated the initial research for her chapter and the second was used to work with Jenny to complete the editing of the book as a whole. Nicky would also like to thank Gentian Rahtz, for whom the experience of silent music seemed entirely reasonable from the start.

Lastly, Nicky and Jenny would like to thank each other for bringing this book into being; it is unlikely to have materialized without the ideas, work, support and underlying belief in the project that each contributed. It was a profound pleasure to work on it as a team.

Introduction

We do not expect people to be deeply moved by what is not unusual. That element of tragedy which lies in the very fact of frequency, has not yet wrought itself into the coarse emotion of mankind; and perhaps our frames could hardly bear much of it. If we had a keen vision and feeling of all ordinary human life, it would be like hearing the grass grow and the squirrel's heart beat, and we should die of that roar which lies on the other side of silence.

George Eliot, *Middlemarch*

To reach George Eliot's roar on the 'other side of silence' requires a state of mind so finely tuned as to produce a terminal oversensitivity to the mechanics of human life. Yet it also invokes something of the acutely meditative, an alternative to desensitization and a desire to rise above the quotidian that links to other types of transcendence and to stillness. Overcoming the mundane requires an ability to move through sound to silence – a journey Eliot equated with the journey to death.

Like Eliot's undifferentiated 'roar' on the other side of silence, music often functions in philosophical discourse as a metaphor for the unsayable. It is semantically slippery; we can never know its meaning. At best, as an object of fantasy, it might become a discourse of ideas – whether motivic, psychological or narrative depends on the consumer's taste. But it seems strange that in this history of ontological elusiveness, the most obviously intangible aspect of music – its silences – have so seldom been addressed. Music's meanings are obscure, but at least sounds leave traces onto which we can project meaning: a 'something' that both defines and limits what we can say. Silence, in comparison, offers the limitless. It confronts us, perhaps it even 'roars'; in negotiating its hazy boundaries we may meet, head-on, chasms that open up within ourselves. The unsaid and the unsayable – and undifferentiated time – gape before us.

Dictionary definitions of silence privilege its negative qualities: absence of sound, prohibition on speech, refusal to communicate.[1] These negative characteristics reflect a rather narrow European perspective, where silence is too easily equated with the passive, the submissive and the void. The idea that silence can be perceived as a form of communication – expressing reflection, for instance, as it might in Japanese culture – is less widespread in Western social contexts. However, the overarching theme that emerges from this collection of essays is that musical silences are cognitive in the deepest sense. From performers communicating through musical rests and

---

[1] *The Oxford Dictionary of English* gives: 'complete absence of sound … the fact or state of abstaining from speech … the avoidance of mentioning or discussing something'; see 'Silence *noun*', in *The Oxford Dictionary of English*, rev. ed., ed. Catherine Soanes and Angus Stevenson (Oxford: Oxford University Press, 2005), accessed in *Oxford Reference Online*, <http://www.oxfordreference.com>, (accessed 24 March 2006).

composers drawing on meditative silences as fundamental compositional elements, through film sound designers layering and juxtaposing music and its absence, to mystics hearing a silent form of 'music', it is clear that in human perception silence in relation to music does not exist as a vacuum. Perhaps this is why Susan Sontag scorned late twentieth-century modernist art's 'appeals to silence'.[2] Unable to recognize endeavours to abstract music towards silence as generative of the open and non-prescriptive, she instead saw it as ultimately self-annihilating: Sontag did not look beyond silence as absence, thereby confirming her roots as a thinker schooled in European ideas. Embracing silence as a positive, active entity was simply not in her thought spectrum. But then, Western musicians are trained to recognize codes of organized sounds – and Western music curricula do not usually include the reading of silences.

For many composers, silence within their music does not represent a single idea. Silence can stand as the softest kind of music, and it can also exist as the nothingness represented by rests, which the activity of performance must challenge to be alive. There might be a sense of silence that 'is' music unsounded, a kind of ideal condition of music to which a composer's contemplations and compositions might aspire; and there might also be a sense that silence is a sea on which rafts of sounds float.[3] As in film, silence in music may play a diegetic role, a specific part of the action; or silence may be masked by music that in sounding, takes over silence's usual role. At first sight, these ideas stand separately from each other. But, in fact, it is 'the ways in which various silences and hearings of silence point to each other'[4] that may be perceived as significant. Moreover, they meet in the silences that frame occurrences of music, and also in the contextual, often structural, silences within music. What all these silences have in common is their fecundity: they are pregnant with unanswerable questions.

It is tempting to imagine that readings of these silences are easier to grasp the more silences are bound to their immediate contexts. However, as Stan Link has suggested, 'silence is where *we are*, not where it is. ... Our impression of the input and meaning of silence in a musical context is therefore heightened by a sense of transcendence: the ideal silence banishing the real'.[5] The problem with such contextual silences is that they are still temporally bounded by music; when glimpsed, there may not be enough time to transcend the moment before music again interrupts. But sometimes contextual silences do produce those extraordinary moments where everything stops, so that – *what?* – so that *something else* might begin. In these cases, the contextual silences of heard music may bring us face to face with the eternal silences of the

---

[2]   Susan Sontag, 'The Aesthetics of Silence', in *Styles of Radical Will* (1969; London: Vintage, 1994), 3–34.

[3]   Vladimir Jankélévitch, *La musique et l'ineffable* (Paris: Seuil, 1983), trans. Carolyn Abbate as *Music and the Ineffable* (Princeton: Princeton University Press, 2003), Chapter 4 'Music and Silence', 132.

[4]   See Chapter 4 (Link).

[5]   Stanley Boyd Link, 'Essays towards Musical Negation' (PhD diss., Princeton University, 1995), 5–6.

infinite spaces that so frightened the French philosopher, Pascal;[6] but they may also indicate the kinds of silences that have analogies in speech: silences of assent, of contemplation, of trauma. In other words, at the moment of musical silence we may reach into ourselves, but that may be precisely what enables us to 'make a reading' of the music.

Silence and Music

In this book, we've begun to feel our way into a new branch of musicology, in which different disciplines – history, music analysis, psychology, cognition, performance practices, social practices, music therapy, religious studies, philosophy – intersect in considering the multiplicity of relationships that exist between music and silence. We've discovered no model that could guide this process of intersection to full effect, to define what this field might encompass or 'mean'; the essays in this book begin to explore some of the possibilities. By approaching music's relation to silence from different points of view, the essays question the obvious, the invisible. And by looking at the obvious through different lenses, the responses attempt to break through the rather rigid bounds that still confine the field of musicology, often wandering into realms of the personal or spiritual that may embarrass many who protect as paramount 'objectivity' in the discipline. But we strongly affirm this trajectory into the unsayable, remembering the words of Philip Brett:

> Our scholarship always reflects our selves however hard we try to objectify it. The truths we discover and reveal are never so much about a historical situation as they are about our own situations, tastes and perceptions. Once acknowledged, this idea actually facilitates the Platonic search for, and dialogue with, the past and its denizens characteristic of genuine scholarship. And it leads to the further acknowledgment that critical judgments, however 'right' they feel, are only further aspects of the training, personality, associations and predilections of each of us.[7]

Perhaps a reason why engagement with this rich, interdisciplinary field has not been properly initiated before now is because it involves the subjectivity of the personal, the psychological and the spiritual as well as the objectivity of the analytical and theoretical. In moving from sound to silence and back again, the traveller thus challenges not only traditional academic boundaries of discipline, but also those of personal views and beliefs.

Thus, in considering a book on music and silence, we wished to provide both a substantive platform of diverse topics and a variety of perspectives, personalities and

---

[6]   The full passage is from *Pensée* 68: 'When I consider the brief span of my life absorbed into the eternity which comes before and after – *as the remembrance of a guest that tarrieth but a day* – the small space I occupy and which I see swallowed up in the infinite immensity of spaces of which I know nothing and which know nothing of me, I take fright.' Blaise Pascal, *Pensées sur la religion et sur quelques autres sujets* (1665), trans A. J. Krailsheimer as *Pensées* (Harmondsworth: Penguin, 1966), 48.

[7]   Philip Brett, Review of *Letters from a Life: Selected Letters of Benjamin Britten*, vols. 1–2, *Journal of the Royal Musical Association* 119/1 (1994), 145.

approaches. A single volume can only begin the process of opening up and launching this field of study, and we have chosen to do so with twelve interrelated essays. They are presented within the volume in groupings that give alternative views on music and silence in relation to the world around us: (1) the paradox of music evoking silence as a means of perceiving beyond reality, in Olivier Messaien's exploration of spiritual, aesthetic and compositional expression; (2) the power of silence in the context of modern reality, considering the music of Anton Webern, Charles Ives and Tōru Takemitsu; (3) music as silence in the constructed realities of film; (4) music as perceived in altered realities in music therapy; (5) the impossibility of silence in physical reality, considering the music and philosophies of John Cage; (6) performing silences in musical reality, both medieval and modern; and, ultimately, (7) the contemplation of silent music in reaching beyond reality.[8] Despite the relative scarcity of musicological literature that explicitly discusses silence and music to date, the composite bibliography provides both substantial evidence of the 'existence' of this field, and what we hope will prove to be a useful tool for its further interrogation by future scholars.

The Paradox of Music Evoking Silence: the Attempt to Perceive Beyond Reality

It is notable that a number of composers have consciously sought to express their silent contemplations of the spiritual through composed sound: John Tavener, Tōru Takemitsu, Olivier Messiaen and Federico Mompou spring to mind as examples. Their written 'testaments' have similarly arisen through contemplations of silence. Tavener's *The Music of Silence* is replete with references to René Guénon and other philosophers of Nothingness, in his search for 'metaphysical meaning behind the notes', his rejection of modernism in music and his return to traditional social and musical sources as purer means of achieving spiritual expression. Takemitsu's *Confronting Silence* reflects on the historical place of the Japanese aesthetic *ma*, the space and silence between events, in his cultural background, as well as in his musical expressions.[9] Similarly Messiaen explained in written notes that the

---

[8]   The absence of a chapter on the experience of music and silence in relation to hearing loss and deafness may strike the reader as notable; the extensive literature in the fields of medicine and deaf Studies has not been paralleled in any way in musicological literature, after all. Either we could have explored the obvious (Beethoven, Evelyn Glennie – both of whom developed hearing losses after knowing sounding music and whose 'deaf' experience was/is informed by having been part of the world of hearing); or, we could have explored ways in which people who are profoundly deaf from birth experience vibration as music through particular sections of the cortex, by summarizing the medical perspectives currently available. However, after giving it deep thought, we decided that this potentially enormous topic could not be covered in a meaningful way in a single chapter. It is a subject that deserves a book-length study of its own.

[9]   John Tavener, *The Music of Silence: a Composer's Testament*, ed. Brian Keeble (London: Faber and Faber, 1999); Tōru Takemitsu, *Confronting Silence: Selected Writings*, trans. and ed. Yoshiko Kakudo and Glenn Glasow (Berkeley, CA: Fallen Leaf Press, 1995).

seventeenth of his *Vingt regards sur l'enfant Jesu*, the 'Regard du silence', is about the silence–sound paradox, 'each silence from the crib reveals sounds and colours which are the mysteries of Jesus Christ'. Mompou, too, was spiritually inspired to explore music's relationship with silence. Between 1959 and 1967, he composed *Música callada* ('silent music'), a piano work in four volumes on texts of the mystic Catholic explorer, St John of the Cross. This work distilled Mompou's search for purity of expression: like Webern, he found that maximum expression paradoxically led to minimal compositional means.

> This music is silent because it is heard in one's inner self. Restraint and discretion. The emotion remains hidden, and the sounds only take shape when they find echoes in the bareness of our solitude. This music is silent because it is heard inwardly. Restraint and reserve. Its emotion is secret and only takes sonorous form when it finds echoes in the great cold vault of our solitude. I desire that in my silent music, this newborn child, we should be brought closer to the warmth of human life and to the expression of the human heart, that is always the same and yet always being renewed.[10]

Through spiritual questioning and contemplation, each of these composers found himself at that elusive border between music and silence, uncovering silence as the ultimate means of expression and transcendence.

It is easy to dismiss attempts to write music 'that lies on the other side of silence' as at worst insincere, and at best naïve. It can never be more than music, after all. The transcendence claimed by composers such as Tavener, Takemitsu, Messiaen and Mompou is a reflection of a mental state, deeply connected with musical languages familiar from other contexts associated with the introspective or the religious. Such musics might induce a feeling of tranquillity in listeners, or even encourage a 'silence of the mystic', but, it may be argued, they cannot ever reach across to the 'other side', other than as an agency of human transformation (though this might be important enough in itself). However, the idea that music can *express* aspects of the condition of silence is less an act of delusion than one of humility; it acknowledges that all forms of mystical knowledge, however transcendent they appear, must take place through a form of human endeavour that is familiar. Art in itself is neither a direct fruit of transcendent knowledge nor a form of contemplation; but it can be the fruit of that contemplation, since contemplation leads from silence to that which is apprehensible.

Messiaen's exploration of cognitive silence in the 'Regard du silence' is examined in this volume by Matthew Hill (Chapter 2), who studies correlations between musical portrayal and Catholic dogma that Messiaen articulated in prose programme notes

---

[10]   'Esta música es callada porque su audición es interna. Contención y reserva. Su emoción es secreta y solamente toma forma sonora en sus resonancias bajo la gran bóveda fría de nuestra soledad. Deseo que en mi música callada, este niño recién nacido, nos aproxime a un nuevo calor de vida y a la expresión del corazón humano, siempre la misma y siempre renovando.' Federico Mompou, extract from speech made when entering the Academia de Bellas Artes de san Jorge, in *Discurso leído en la solemne recepción pública de D. Federico Mompou: Dencausse el día 17 de mayo de 1952* (Barcelona: Real Academia de Bellas Artes de San Jorge, n.d.), 8.

to his pieces. Hill looks to the Catholic explorer of the mystic and the silent, St John of the Cross, drawing on St John's concept of the 'dark night of the soul' to posit connections between faith, silence and darkness that are useful in understanding how that most paradoxical of endeavours – contemplating silence through sound – can be understood as a piece of theology. The inaudible mysteries surrounding the Christ-child – the silences – revealed something to Messiaen in contemplation, and that revelation took place in sound. The silence from which the music emanates is like the 'night' from which the 'sounds and colours' of the music emerge.

In contrast, Jan Christiaens (Chapter 3) focuses analytically on Messiaen and the paradox of music evoking silence in his interrogation of the early organ work, *Le banquet céleste*. Through this religious piece, to be played during the Eucharist when communicants become at one with Jesus, Messiaen encouraged listeners toward an intense state of 'silent' contemplation, overcoming the sound–silence paradox, Christiaens suggests, with music that would act upon the psychology of auditory perception. From the extreme quiet framing its beginning and end, *Le banquet céleste* gradually shades silence into and away from sound. Harmonic stasis and the acoustic qualities of the organ present sound as static and eternal, while the extremely slow tempo causes listeners to lose their sense of a time framework within which the musical events can be 'placed' in relation to each other. Christiaens relates these effects to the theories of Henri Bergson, who noted that the more events that fill an interval in the present, the quicker time seems to go; the more events that filled similar intervals in the past, the longer they seem to us now. Thus through careful formal, textural and harmonic construction, Messiaen deliberately sought to evoke this intentional fallacy in *Le banquet céleste*: listeners experience stasis and timelessness, to induce contemplation of silence and eternity.

The Invisibility of Silence in Modern Reality

For Messiaen, the dynamic of *pianissimo* could act as a threshold, shading between silence and sounding, a stage on the scale of musical dynamics. For some this 'shading space' is simply and literally the beginning of music's dynamic continuum; but for others, like Messiaen, it might stand for the nexus between human musical practice and the Divine musical universe. Silence thus can be seen to represent music's 'other', in the sense that music exists in 'parallel' to silence.

Industrial developments of Western society in the early twentieth century led remarkably quickly to surrounding landscapes and soundscapes that were unrecognizably altered from the centuries before. In particular, the ubiquity of sound technologies and their products changed the balance between the parallel worlds of sound and silence, leading many, like the Swiss theologian Max Picard, to abhor modern noise, sound media and mechanization. For Picard, it was 'as though the sounds of music were being driven over the surface of silence'.[11] This conception served as a starting point for Jenny Doctor's essay (Chapter 1), which considers

---

[11]   Max Picard, *Die Welt des Schweigens* (1948), trans. Stanley Goodman as *The World of Silence* (1948; repr. Chicago: Regnery Gateway, 1952; facs. repr. Wichita, KS: Eighth Day Press, 2002), 27.

the relationship of silence to music for composers in this modern context. Anton Webern's focus on minute details and moments may be seen as epitomizing this view: music as gesture sounds through the texture of silence. In contrast, for Charles Ives, silence functioned within the sound continuum of 'that human faith melody', and the immensities of life were expressed by tapping into it. But Ives also wondered whether music was actually to be heard, perhaps how music *sounds* is not what it *is*. 'Silence is a solvent ... that gives us leave to be universal',[12] rather than personal and specific.

This conception has similarities with the relationship between music and silence that emerges from the Japanese aesthetic represented in *ma*, 'a "sensually" perceived space'[13] or time between events. For the composer, Tōru Takemitsu, silence did not merely articulate sound structures. Instead, music is either sound or silence; sound, 'confronting the silence of *ma*, yields supremacy in the final expression'.[14] Thus, for Takemitsu the act of composition was a confrontation with silence, which was itself a kind of death. To return to Eliot, 'we should die of that roar which lies on the other side of silence'. The philosopher and musicologist, Vladimir Jankélévitch, also actively explored this conflict between human activity and the 'silence of the eternal spaces'; human presence is a barely audible sigh in infinite space, and human endeavour needs to keep affirming life itself to resist the invasion of nothingness.[15]

Music as Silence in Constructed Realities

This idea of music confronting silence as death, a spiritual, philosophical, private and individual encounter, rather strangely becomes a dramatized, heightened and communal experience within the conventions of commercial film. Stan Link's chapter (Chapter 4) explores diegetic and non-diegetic silences in film scores to examine Hollywood's means of sounding death.[16] As Link reveals, the emotions of death tend to be associated and effected cinematically through different kinds of silences. In the technical construction and recording of silence, a result of digital sound manipulation, post-synchronization and sound effects, it becomes a 'representation', a 'product of contrast', its unnatural quality within the soundtrack pointing inevitably, through decades of film conventions, to death. But Link also shows that it is not silence, nor music, nor dialogue, but *everyday noise* within the soundtrack that allows audiences to enter the filmic world. Recorded ambient noise is the ether in which we can coexist with what we see on screen. Thus, in situations where ambient noise is replaced by music, we may be removed from that world.

---

[12]   Ralph Waldo Emerson, quoted in Charles Ives, 'Epilogue', in *Essays Before a Sonata, The Majority and Other Writings*, selected and ed. Howard Boatwright (New York: W. W. Norton, 1961), 71 and 84.

[13]   Bruno Deschênes, *Aesthetics in Japanese Arts*, <http://www.thingsasian.com/goto_article/ article.2121.html> (accessed on 24 March 2006).

[14]   Takemitsu, *Confronting Silence*, 51.

[15]   Jankélévitch, *Music and the Ineffable*, 131.

[16]   As Stan Link defines it in the film context, 'silence is diegetic, taking place within the world depicted, or non-diegetic, imposed from without'; see Chapter 4 (Link).

Music in film, unless it diegetically participates within the 'reality' of everyday noise, *thus may become a type of silence*, the musical score acting as 'sound without being' within the multi-layered soundtrack.

Ed Hughes (Chapter 5) questions this modern means of constructing complex soundtracks, and the emotional responses that film sound designers aim for them to produce. He returns to the era of silent film to consider the binary effects of music or silence in the early film environment, recalling the power of silence when contrasted with the musical sound continuum. When applying similar principals to sound film, Hughes, like Link, examines scenes in which sound tracks were carefully constructed to deploy the presence or absence of music as a dramatic feature; the tension is enhanced and the perception of passing time altered by the sudden withdrawal or reappearance of music. This quality of filmic 'silence' may include ambient or other sounds, the effect of no music powerful enough to heighten the sense of concentration and drama. Hughes suggests that a carefully discriminate, successive approach to the assembly of aural components has more dramatic potential than the simultaneous, multi-channel mixdowns that have become the norm in Hollywood films. In a world filled with sound, adding more is the obvious answer to creating an impact; but the practice of overloading a soundtrack to heighten emotional content ignores the past art of silencing music, which may have achieved even greater effect.

The Impossibility of Silence in Physical Reality

Mystics such as Peter Sterry and St John of the Cross agree that silence is a pre-requisite for achieving a condition of spiritual contemplation. Yet, John Cage's experience in the anechoic chamber proved that true 'silence' can never exist within human perception: for Cage, silence is a window through which ambient sound might enter consciousness.[17] Theodor Wiesengrund Adorno, writing in 1938, had brought similar ideas to the foreground in relation to listeners' experiences of music through sound reproduction equipment of the time; mediation through technologies was already starting to become a primary means for audience access to music. He considered both the noises of the actual equipment (e.g. the film projector, radio tuning or gramophone needle making contact with the groove) and sounds emitted due to technical imperfections of media themselves. 'This slight, continuous and constant noise is like a sort of acoustic stripe … [music] appears to be projected upon the stripe and is only, so to speak, like a picture upon that stripe;'[18] in other words, the music 'is compromised by a second-order presence, a technological filter whose effects … may function only at the level of the unconscious'.[19] If one

---

[17]   John Cage, 'Experimental Music: Doctrine' (1957), in *Silence: Lectures and Writings* (Middletown, CT: Wesleyan University Press, 1961; London: Marion Boyars, 1978), 13–14.

[18]   Theodor Wiesengrund Adorno, 'Memorandum: Music in Radio', unpublished essay, June 1938, Paul F. Lazarsfeld papers, Columbia University, New York; quoted in Richard Leppert, 'Commentary', in Theodor W. Adorno, *Essays on Music*, selected, with introduction commentary and notes by Richard Leppert, trans. Susan H. Gillespie (Berkeley, Los Angeles and London: University of California Press, 2002), 219.

[19]   Leppert, 'Commentary', 219.

extends this observation to Cage's findings in the anechoic chamber fourteen years later, the question then becomes: if noise is an inevitably *presence*, a 'hear-stripe' that moves into consciousness as conscious sound recedes, does it 'compromise' human experience of silence? Or can this relationship be 'heard' in another way, as a function of human *attention* in the perception of music and silence?

William Brooks (Chapter 6) explores this question in terms of the agreement regarding noise and attention that is 'tacitly' understood by the listener of a performance: the 'conventions of listening' instruct the listener to disregard ancillary sounds in a concert hall, dismiss the static on a radio or ignore the noise produced by imperfections on a sound recording. In Charles Ives's music, silence is cast as an audible *presence*, perhaps to counteract the dangers of noise distracting listeners from the transcendental potential of his musical 'silences'. In contrast, John Cage explores the possibility of composing silence as a featured *absence*. Developing a particular lens drawn from the philosophies of William James and Daisetz Teitaro Suzuki, Brooks considers Cage's *Silent Prayer* (never performed), conceived before the experience in the anechoic chamber, and *4'33"*, composed afterwards. Cage's crisis as a result of his recognition of silence's physical impossibility led not only to a reassessment of listener etiquette, but to an entirely redefined perception of listening, of *attending* to music, silence – and noise – in a way that is *true* to consciousness and the human experience.

Susan Sontag examined Cage's modernist engagements with silence through the gaze of a contemporary critic and discovered not truth, but the aesthetic of the negative, as Darla Crispin explores in her essay comparing Cage's and Sontag's polemical stances with regard to art and silence. In her essay, 'The Aesthetics of Silence',[20] Sontag expressed her fear that the artistic drive towards challenging listeners with the new and different was ultimately destructive: 'Committed to the idea that the power of art is located in its power to negate, the ultimate weapon in the artist's inconsistent war with his audience is to verge closer and closer to silence.'[21] According to Sontag's 'elegiac pessimism', the final achievement of silence would be to obliterate the artwork and the artist. But Cage opposed this in his explorations, which doubled as statements addressing the aesthetics of silence and as artworks in themselves. Realizing that silence could not be experienced as a literal phenomenon, discussions about it had to become metaphors. In *Silence*, the blank, white page becomes a metaphor for silence, the type, text spacing and paragraphing creating a 'visual dialectic' with silence. Cage's statements on the subject became like Zen koans, gaining both clarity and obscurity with repetition: 'I have nothing to say and I am saying it.'[22] For Cage, silence had the potential to make the listener aware, to *attend* to silence, to art, to the sounds all around. Not only was art not obliterated, but the opposite was true: heard through ears attuned outside the Western norm, acknowledging silence enables the realization that 'what one might call art is omnipresent'.

---

[20] Sontag, 'The Aesthetics of Silence', 3–34.
[21] *Ibid.*, 8.
[22] Cage, 'Composition as Process' (1958), in *Silence*, 51.

Performing Silences in Musical Reality

Within music's discourse, silences may be optimized in a psychoanalytical sense when they are read as psychological imperatives, for instance, by considering their impact on an individual's awareness of self. When composers compose silences into musical works consciously, they do not necessarily know why they have done so. And we are wary of making over-facile analogies with, for instance, silence in psychotherapeutic sessions that may indicate some kind of traumatic rupture – times when the client comes face to face with what is unutterable or unthinkable. There are certain works, such as the late Beethoven String Quartet, Op. 132, in which the listener may make strong connections with this kind of broken, traumatized speech, as Susan McClary has noted.[23] Psychoanalytic readings of musical works usually presuppose that composers do not know exactly what they 'meant' by writing in the way they did. Some composed works may bear the weight of the history of Western art music in their constructions; whereas other music may be closer to improvisation, and connections with speech narratives perhaps more obvious. In either case, composers may have a limited awareness of what they are 'working out' through their musical ideas, through their inclusion of silence.

Performers, too, have a role in this psychoanalytical complex. The players of the Beethoven string quartet may each feel a sense of 'singular linearity' that transcends, for them as individuals, awareness of the whole fabric. Performing a single line within a contrapuntal texture may indeed bring an increased sense of individuality: of needing to hold 'my' line 'against' the texture. Thus there is silence within the individual performer as other sounds are rendered 'silent' by close, exclusionary concentration; there may also be silence as the player encounters a rest in his or her part, while the other lines continue to sound. These silences may well not be evident to the listener, who hears the total texture. Historically, performing musicians have been acutely aware of the performativity of silences – of what silences can effect in the musical narrative – and of the importance of directing contextual silences expressively in ways that make interpretative sense. In silences, directions may change; new paths may emerge.

For John Potter (Chapter 8), silences have always functioned communicatively. His account of 'communicative' rests reveal that although silent, they are far from inert. For the story-telling singer, such contextual silences offer opportunities to give the idea of spontaneity and creativity in performance, to give a sense of 'making the story up as it goes along'. And as part of performance rhetoric, from the listener's point of view, there is a reflective element.[24] In communicative rests, listeners can make sense of what has gone before, entering into a creative process of constructing meaning. Thus in performance situations, it is the conspiracy between performer

---

[23]   Susan McClary, *Conventional Wisdom: the Content of Musical Form* (Berkeley and Los Angeles: University of California Press, 2001), 119–33.

[24]   This idea is also explored by Zofia Lissa; see 'Die Ästhetischen Funktionen der Stille und Pause in der Musik' (1962), repr. as 'Stille und Pause in der Musik', in Lissa, *Aufsätze zur Musikästhetik: eine Auswahl* (Berlin: Henschel, 1969), 162.

and listener that opens up dramatic possibilities – that is, it is in the silences that performers and audiences meet.

Listeners may engage with silences to whatever degree they like, depending on how attentively they feel like listening, how actively they are engaging with the material they are hearing, or not at all. In contrast, a performer cannot disengage from whatever it is that silences may force him or her to confront. A work's contextual silences must be actively grasped – which is why the term 'rest' seems so odd, as resting is so completely inappropriate in the circumstances. Even the silences that permit a performer just to 'be' are not passive, since the audience must still be held, and the performer must carry the conviction of being able to do so. For Potter, it is in the silences that performer and audience conspire together in the communicative act.

Before measured silences began to be notated in musical sources in the thirteenth century, the relationship between performer and rest was perhaps not dissimilar to modern experience, but evidence suggests that the text–music–conspirator triangle had a somewhat different configuration. Emma Hornby (Chapter 9) considers the uses of silence in Gregorian chant, the monks of the Benedictine order chanting the entire Psalter together each week as a means of encouraging meditation. The performance involved a pause in the middle of each verse, long enough for the singers to exhale and inhale, each breath providing an opportunity for the Holy Spirit to visit. Beyond the practical necessity of taking in air, the endorphins released by such controlled breathing had a calming and uplifting effect. Thus the monastic community literally 'conspired' together daily in choral psalmody, their performance, particularly in the breathing rests, communing directly with their audience, the Holy Spirit. In contrast, difficult, complex chants were sung by a soloist for the community once or twice a year. The cadences ending each phrase and verse were linked with following silences, which had primarily textual rather than performative functions. However, if the silence was shortened or skipped, the effect added dramatic rhetorical tension, creating a direct engagement between singer and audience. In both choral or solo chanting, resting was inextricably related to breathing, a spiritual silence intended to intensify and clarify communication with auditors, both earthly and Holy.

Silence as Perceived in Altered Realities

Perhaps, many chapters of this volume are preoccupied with silence as an 'object' to be understood in certain ways. While Link's cinematic 'silences' are constructed to evoke death, Hughes makes a plea for soundtracks to cut through modern sound technologies and return to the powerful language of silences more generally. Doctor's textural silences are bounded within the musical context, while Nicky Losseff debates whether there is a category of music that 'exists' as music but silently. Even for Potter and Hornby, performance is a means through which music and its silences may be communicated *to* listeners. Julie Sutton's approach (Chapter 10) differs: she asks that we think of music, and its silences, as a communicative act that unfolds *between* people.

One of the primary differences between music and silence, Sutton argues, is that musical sounds are made and then heard; but musical silences are not made. They are a kind of ether, shared between player and listener. Potter asserts that it is in the silences that performer and listener meet in the creation of a performed drama. In music therapy, Sutton's analysis of the living drama of free improvised duets reveals that both musicians made use of silences at structural points as a means of slowing the overall pace of the music, stimulating affective changes in the performing musicians and their listeners. More significantly, silences have a definite role and function in creating tension; they are not static, but have variety in quality, pacing and impetus. Sutton shows that sounds and silences are meaningful in the ways in which they are experienced between people. This relates to how we acquire an ability to react to sound: we *enter the world* as interactive listeners and as sound-makers. Sutton's work is especially moving because of its implication about music's relationship with silence: silence can offer a space within which the greatest intimacy between composer, performer and listener can be found.

Sutton also examines how subjective experiences of time are a core feature of musical silences. Silences in music appear to alter time – at the very least, they interrupt our perception of the ongoing flow of musical sounds. On the one hand, *chronos* describes time passing in a linear way, as with the beat of a clock. But there is also *kairos*, which relates to a sense of space and a subjective experience of a *lack* of *chronos* – of a time 'out-of-time'. Silence can create an impression of atemporality which erases any sense of movement. Sutton's findings with respect to 'time out-of-time' are thus similar to both Christiaens' analysis of Messiaen, evoking a sense of silence and timelessness through deliberate auditory effects, and Hughes' observations about altered time perceptions in film scores, when music is suddenly withdrawn.

Silent Music Beyond Reality

Music that exists as a type of silence – that is, disassociated from visceral reality – has a strange resonance with mystic perceptions of 'silent music'. Tom Dixon (Chapter 11) questions the 'model' of the seventeenth-century Puritan mystic Peter Sterry, in which music is a medium for spiritual fulfilment on individual and societal levels: through music, the discord of human imperfection would resolve into the perfect harmony of the Divine purpose. Sterry spoke of 'silent music', a music beyond earthly notions of time, space and sense perception, while encompassing all of them. *Musica divina*, music in the Divine mind, is a truly silent music, inaccessible to any of our faculties, yet the source of the music we know in all its manifestations. For Sterry, echoing Plotinus, music became a higher, truer realm of being; and it had the capacity to reflect that ideal realm.

St John of the Cross also seemed to experience a type of 'silent music' that was both a religious and a musical experience, as Nicky Losseff explores (Chapter 12). St John said that his conceptual audition tasted something of a musical condition – revealed to him as a serene and calm intelligence, that enjoyed both the sweetness of music and the quiet of silence, yet without the noise (read: sensuous distraction) of voices. Because he was offered a type of 'music' that did not require degeneration into the body in order to be expressed, he could enjoy a wholly satisfying *musical* experience. Losseff suggests that this type of music had prototypes in other cultures: the Indian treatise *Sangîtaratnâkara* describes both sounding and non-sounding forms of music, and the idea of a 'silent music' also occurs in the Zen koan of the solid iron flute that has neither fingerholes nor mouthpiece. Thus, the idea of 'silent music' is seen by some as an identifiably musical phenomenon, part of a taxonomy of all musics, as well as a symbol for spiritual contemplative experience.

Hill's explication of Messiaen's contemplative process, tracing the trajectory from silence to music, may make Losseff's distinctions between truly 'silent music' and merely 'inaudible music' seem rather precious. As Dixon explains, Peter Sterry may offer a way of blending the two: in ruminations on *musica divina*, Sterry's thoughts included the softest earthly music along with godly, all-encompassing musical thought. Sterry, and others, may have thought that all that takes place within human cognition must be available to the human senses in a form that is intelligible. The difference, then, might be that what Losseff calls 'truly silent music' is apprehended by the mystic in a form that is *not* readily translatable into what we already know; in that sense, it seems almost *non*-cognitive, and the desperate grappling to find a way of spelling out what has been experienced rather misses the point.

There is, in the end, a wealth of difference between the ordered structures of Messiaen's fruits of contemplation and St John's searching prose, with its reliance on linguistic paradox to express the inexpressible. It is as if St John were groping not in a crystallizing sense towards the clarification we associate with sophisticated language, but in a 'regressive' sense to a kind of pre- or non-linguistic experience that defies language: hence, the communicative act of music – and silence – in the purest sense.

We have suggested that silence is deeply cognitive; in the absence of sound, an increased awareness of other senses, both physical and spiritual, seems to be initiated. Paradoxically, cognition of silence is often *re*-cognized as some form of enhanced musical encounter. We are back to St John, whose bride experienced her Beloved as silent music because she 'tasted'[25] spiritual harmony in him; or to Keats, among so many others, for whom melodies are 'sweet'. In the physical experience of the anechoic chamber, John Cage excluded sound and apprehended the impossibility of silence, his nervous and circulatory systems becoming, quite literally, the 'music' of life. And Messiaen: what colour was silence for you? The colour of God? The empowerment that silence offers may ultimately lie in its ability to activate an increased experience of almost anything else – music included, in proximity to which silence confirms its place as both absence and supreme presence. In this way, as the contributors to this volume contemplate silence through words as so many have through music, like Cage we fear not that we have nothing to say.

---

[25]   The main meaning of '*gustar*' is 'to enjoy', and E. Allison Peers translates the passage thus, as reproduced in Chapter 12 (Losseff). Yet the Spanish does give pause here, suggesting that a more nuanced reading is possible. We thank Catherine Duncan for her help with this.

Chapter 1

The Texture of Silence

Jenny Doctor

> The voices blend and fuse in clouded silence: silence that is the infinite of space: and
> swiftly, silently the soul is wafted over regions of cycles of cycles of generations that
> have lived.
>
> James Joyce, Ulysses[1]

In the revised *New Grove Dictionary of Music*, published in 2001, there is no article
on 'Silence'. There is an article called 'Music' this time.[2] There wasn't one in the
1980 edition, the reasoning being that since the entire dictionary embodied music, it
was superfluous to have an article to explain it. But there was much criticism that a
twenty-volume dictionary devoted to music did not specifically define and assess the
term. So it became a point of honour and purpose that Music would be acknowledged
in a concrete way in the revised edition. In fact, Music was the first article to arrive,
well before the rest of the dictionary was even commissioned – and I might well
add that it was the first article to be lost. In his excitement, Stanley Sadie placed the
typescript somewhere, and there were many searches over the next six months as we
tried to find it, tried to find ways to avoid admitting to the author that, now that it
finally existed, this rather significant piece of work had almost immediately vanished
off the face of the *Grove* map.

I found this scenario of Music's arrival and loss amusingly symbolic, even at the
time – but thinking back on it from today's vantage point, it is not nearly as symbolic
as the omission of Silence. You see, amidst all the many noisy discussions about the
content of the revised dictionary, I don't remember there ever being a suggestion that
we include an article on Silence. There was comprehensive lack of recognition of
this term, this concept, this entity as a music-relevant subject, the lack of recognition
itself symbolic of the role Silence plays generally in music-related discourse. And
thinking about it now, after considering, contemplating and confronting various
relationships between Music and Silence over the past few years – and feeling that

---

[1]   James Joyce, *Ulysses* (1936); The Corrected Text, ed. Hans Walter Gabler with
Wolfhard Steppe and Claus Melchior (London: The Bodley Head, 1986), Episode 14, line
1078ff, p. 338. For a recent unabridged reading, see Joyce, *Ulysses*, dir. Roger Marsh,
produced by Nicolas Soames, recorded and ed. by Jez Wells, with Jim Norton and Marcella
Riordan (22 CDs, Naxos Audiobooks NAX30912, 2004).

[2]   Bruno Nettl, 'Music', in *The New Grove Dictionary of Music and Musicians*, 2nd ed.,
ed. Stanley Sadie and John Tyrrell (London: Macmillan, 2001), 17: 425–37.

I'm not yet scratching the surface – I have to wonder: if an attempt were made to capture the concept in a dictionary of music, would silence be defined as music's opposing force or as its consummate, transcendent form?

It is this dichotomy that lies at the basis of my thoughts about music and silence in this essay. I have chosen to explore these musically through the medium of the string quartet, because it encompasses a multi-dimensionality of sound and timbre, as well as an intimacy that encourages textures in which 'the voices [may] blend and fuse in clouded silence: silence that is the infinite of space'.

§

A way a lone a last a loved a long the – riverrun, past Eve and Adam's, from swerve of shore to bend of bay, brings us by a commodius vicus of recirculation back to Howth Castle and Environs.[3]

This celebrated, oft-quoted circular ending–beginning to *Finnegan's Wake* by James Joyce (1882–1941) inspired my initial thoughts in exploring the aspect of music and silence that particularly interests me: the relationship between silence and musical texture. To a large extent, this involves noticing, focusing on and thinking about musical events that are commonplace, so obvious that they often go unnoticed; it requires the acknowledgement of aural spaces that are usually ignored as insignificant.

The monosyllabic sounds of Joyce's concluding text provide a starting point: 'A way a lone a last a loved a long the.' To state the obvious: as an entity in itself, this string of words does not make grammatical sense. Yet space between each pairs of words allows us to glimpse a meaning: 'A way   A lone   a last   a loved   a long   the riverrun.' 'Space between words' meaning: silence. Thus silence plays a functional role here to articulate both a sense of meaning and a rhythm in an otherwise meaningless string of syllables – a single-layer texture of uttered sounds in an undistinguished continuum.

On a larger scale, consider a passage from later in *Finnegan's Wake*, the part in Chapter 8 where two washerwomen gossip about Anna Livia Plurabelle, wife of Humphrey Chimpden Earwicker, whose story has already been told and retold. The text on the page represents another sound continuum, undulating vividly between words and phrases that immediately make sense and those that don't.

Well, you know or don't you kennet or haven't I told you every telling has a taling and that's the he and the she of it. Look, look, the dusk is growing! My branches lofty are taking root. And my cold cher's gone ashley. Fieluhr? Filou! What age is at? It saon is late. 'Tis endless now senne eye or erewone last saw Waterhouse's clogh. They took it asunder, I hurd thum sigh. When will they reassemble it? O, my back, my back, my bach! I'd want to go to Aches-les-Pains. Pingpong! There's the Belle for Sexaloitez! And Concepta de Send-us-pray! Pang! Wring out the clothes! Wring in the dew! Godavari, vert the showers! And grant thaya grace! Aman. Will we spread them here now? Ay, we

---

³   James Joyce, *Finnegan's Wake* (1939; 3ʳᵈ edn, London: Faber and Faber, 1966), 628, 3. Joyce began to write *Finnegan's Wake* in 1922–3.

will. Flip! Spread on your bank and I'll spread mine on mine. Flep! It's what I'm doing. Spread! It's churning chill. Der went is rising. I'll lay a few stones on the hostel sheets. A man and his bride embraced between them. Else I'd have sprinkled and folded them only. And I'll tie my butcher's apron here. It's suety yet. The strollers will pass it by. Six shifts, ten kerchiefs, nine to hold to the fire and this for the code, the convent napkins, twelve, one baby's shawl. ...[4]

This is the text that begins a reading that Joyce gave in August 1929 at a studio in the Orthological Institute in London; and, famously, it was recorded.[5] The words and phrases have meanings as words and phrases, of course; Joyce apparently spent hundreds of hours writing this chapter, filled with symbolism, multiple-entendres, water references and river names; diligent fans have devoted much time ever since to ferreting out even the most obscure textual references.[6] To state another obvious point: this extraordinary recording of Joyce reading with his particular accent and pronunciation immediately clarifies some meanings that may have been obscured on the page.

But listening to the sonority, the music of it, one can derive an entirely different level of understanding. Yet again stating the obvious: through obfuscating usual modes of text communication, Joyce raised the receiver's imagination or consciousness to a new level; this form of communication forces the reader/recipient to find his or her own path of meanings through the passage continuum. In Joyce's own reading, the tone qualities, the counterpoint between his vocal colours and the intermittent spaces, and the diminuendos reducing sounds to silences all contribute toward shaping the sound-syllables into something each recipient comes to understand – even without necessarily comprehending the words. This mental process is analogous to hearing musical settings of texts in languages unknown to the listener and nevertheless deriving meaning from the experience. Through the act of performing this passage, Joyce sculpted the text so that it functioned as texture. When listening to his reading, silence and space play a primary, essential role in permitting the mind to perceive meaning, dividing the landscape into gestures rather than sounds, and using the gestures to discover a way through sonic ambiguity. Silence thus gives meaning here to texted texture.

---

[4]   Joyce, *Finnegan's Wake*, Part I, Chapter 8, 213.

[5]   The recording may be accessed at <http://www.finneganswake.org/joycereading.htm> (accessed 11 March 2006). Joyce's reading continues to the middle of p. 215.

[6]   For example, the James Joyce Society was founded by T. S. Eliot in 1947 at the Gotham Book Mart in New York. An off-shoot is the Finnegan's Wake Society of New York, which meets monthly: 'We read short portions of the text aloud and then discuss them. An advantage of a group is the shared knowledge of the members in interpreting the text ... As the Wake is a circular tale, it does not matter where one starts reading'; <http://www. finneganswake.org/aboutfwsociety.htm> (accessed 11 March 2006).

§

> The silent images of things in the soul bring their silence to the words that are the life
> of the mind. They work silence into the texture of language; they keep it supplied with
> silence, with the original power of silence.[7]

In *The World of Silence* (1948), the Swiss theologian, Max Picard (1888–1965),
found a way to weigh this relationship between silence and sound texture; as this
quotation reveals, in his spiritual quest, Picard gave primary billing to silence. In
the realm of Western art music, silence is generally perceived not as 'the original
power' at the centre of the texture, but at the opposite extreme: its acknowledged
function is to provide the conventional matting, frame and structural delimiters to
ease and define listeners' reception of a performance. There are the obvious framing
silences at the beginnings and endings of movements and entire works, underlined
now by twentieth-century concert conventions, with the dimming of lights, cessation
of audience noise and 'quiet' ambience between movements.

Framing silences also play an important part in the punctuation of musical
structures from the classical era (in the works of Haydn, Mozart and Beethoven, for
example), providing audiences' ears with welcome signposts to make their musical
journeys comfortable and comprehensible. Within the well-defined conventions of
these frameworks, classically built from regular, periodic blocks, silence is of course
often present in the form of structural articulations, rests providing momentary spaces
between the usual two or four-bar phrases, or rhythmic pauses defining the ends of
structural sections. More subtle, perhaps, but no less important is the device, found
for instance in Mozart's movements based on sonata-form, of a dramatic pause at
the end of the development section, marking the moment when the recapitulation
becomes inevitable. The 'silence' in these cases lacks sound, but not motion, the
moment of no-sound carrying forward and raising urgent expectations of what is to
come.[8] In the texture of the Viennese classical tradition, silence functions as more
than a void in sound; in parallel with Picard's observations, 'they work[ed] silence
into the texture of language; they [kept] it supplied with silence, with the original
power of silence'. Silence is thus recognizable as a vital entity within the fabric

---

[7]   Max Picard, *Die Welt des Schweigens* (Erlenbach: Eugen Rentsch Verlag, 1948); trans.
Stanley Goodman as *The World of Silence* (London: Harvill, 1948; repr. Chicago: Regnery
Gateway, 1952; facs. repr. Wichita, KS: Eighth Day Press, 2002), 93.

[8]   A wonderful example of this is found in the first movement of the Piano Concerto
in G major, K. 453, which reaches a dramatic pause on the dominant (bar 224). The piano
briefly skates the surface of the silence with *eingang* filigree; the orchestra responds with
four iterations of the dominant chord, further prolonging the expectation, the stasis – in
effect, the 'silence'. The recapitulation then emerges from this extended pause, with the first
violins alone leading into the main theme. It is interesting to note that at the beginning of
the movement, this theme starts ambiguously, with the violins sounding alone for a bar in an
upbeat-like gesture that teases the ear – is it an upbeat or is it an integral part of the theme? In
the recapitulation (in parallel with the solo exposition), the violins emerge from the expectant
silence with an upbeat to this solo upbeat, with the effect of rhythmically anchoring and
balancing the theme's start.

of this music's soundscape. As the famous dictum observes, 'music is the silence between the notes'.[9]

Haydn, too, was a master of musical texture; the grounding of his compositional style in motivic interplay and development inherently led to varied, contrasting, shifting layers of sound. In Haydn's string quartets, in particular, the composition of which spanned his career, he experimented with the interrelationship of the four voices, the changing possibilities and functions of their roles in relation to each other, and, more important here perhaps, the gradual development of texture as a compositional device. As Haydn became increasingly adept at handling texture, he used it more and more as an *articulating* medium, the distinguishing characters and tensions of different textures in his palette delimiting the structures underlying his compositions. However, he also used texture as an *expressive* medium – expressive in the classical sense of manipulating listeners' expectations of tension and release, of motion and stasis. An option within Haydn's textural spectrum was lack of sound, a conjunction of rests in all voices, and his increasing confidence with this option is evident when it begins to appear as a motivic device. Consider, for example, the beginning of his String Quartet, Op. 71, No. 3, one of the 'public' quartets written in 1793 for public performance during Haydn's second visit to London. Interestingly, he built silences right into the opening ideas, and these fundamental elements, in typical Haydn fashion, then permeate the entire work. As illustrated in Ex. 1.1, the notion of sound opposing silence is boldly introduced as a defining concept in the first bar.

Ex. 1.1   **Haydn, String Quartet in E♭, Op. 71, No. 3, movt. 1, bars 1–14**

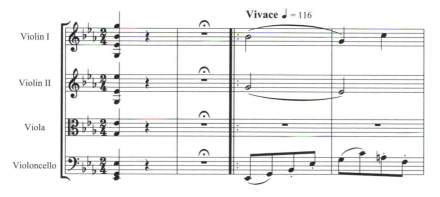

---

9   Neither the origin of this quotation nor the original wording of the phrase is clear. I have seen the quotation attributed variously to Mozart, Claude Debussy, John Cage and Jimi Hendrix. It is likely that they all said it, as have many others.

Following the introduction of the sound-versus-silence motive, the subtle interplay of these opposing elements is worked motivically into the texture in ways so ordinary and obvious as to seem insignificant. Perhaps that is exactly the case – except it is useful here to view this use of silence as an active ingredient, a textural entity in its own right; the rests can thus be viewed as delineating the rhythmic motives and giving the theme its microcosmic cadential character. In the development, Haydn played with this notion, as shown in Ex. 1.2, introducing imitation of the motive between the different parts.

Ex. 1.2   Haydn, String Quartet in E♭ Op. 71, No. 3, movt. 1, bars 136–50

Although the voices perform the rests in their individual lines, the imitation between the parts develops the initial idea, revealing a different aspect of the motive's character: the imitation effectively 'fills in' the rests for a listener hearing the full texture. Thus in this multi-dimensional expression of the motive, the listener effectively hears silence's absence; the listener feels that silence is denied.

§

SHE: *Is it true the music goes on all the time?*

HE: *Yes.*

SHE: *Without cease?*

HE: *Without cease.*

SHE: *It's unthinkable! [Pause.]* ...[10]

Denial of silence is the focus of much of the Western art music canon, the expressive foundation of which requires sound as a basic, essential element. This concept is

---

[10]   Samuel Beckett, *Rough for Radio I* (1961), in *The Complete Dramatic Works* (London: Faber and Faber, 1986; paperback ed. 1990), 267; first written in French (not broadcast); first published in English (1976).

wonderfully illustrated in the string quartets of the British composer, Elizabeth Maconchy (1907–1994). Like Haydn, her music is motivically conceived, but in her case, the intensity of expression resulted in textures woven so thickly as to avoid silence except where absolutely necessary. Maconchy often expressed her view that the historical process of compositional development 'runs like a river in a continuous stream, and one cannot arbitrarily isolate one period from another'.[11] Similarly on a local level,

> in my view, & above all in writing a string quartet – when one is dealing with the very bones of music, with none of the endless variety of colour of the orchestra, or the extra-musical expressiveness of the human voice – everything extraneous to the pursuit of the central idea must be exluded – scrapped. The music is propelled by the force of its own inner logic, and by virtue of this logic every new idea derives from the original premise & throws new light on the whole … This passionately intellectual and intellectually passionate musical discourse is what I seek … to express in music.[12]

Thus in the first movement of Maconchy's Second String Quartet, composed in 1936,[13] the 'river' of music, 'runs in a continuous stream', building without rest to a poignant, intense expectation holding enormous potential. Finally, nearly two-and-a-half minutes into the movement, as shown in Ex. 1.3, potent pauses finally force breaks in the intensity of the sound continuum – perhaps the only way that the columns of sound could possibly shift direction.

Ex. 1.3   Maconchy, String Quartet No. 2, movt. 1, bars 9–18

---

[11]   Elizabeth Maconchy, 'What is Modern Music', unpublished talk, read to Dublin Music Society, 1940, manuscript held at St Hilda's College Library, Oxford.

[12]   Elizabeth Maconchy, 'String Quartet No. 6', unpublished talk, Oxford, 3 February 1952, manuscript held at St Hilda's College Library, Oxford.

[13]   Elizabeth Maconchy, *String Quartet No. 2* (1936) (London: Alfred Legnick, 1959); Maconchy, *String Quartets Nos. 1–4* (*The Complete String Quartets*, vol. 1), Hanson String Quartet (CD, Unicorn-Kanchana DKP(CD) 9080, 1989); reissued in *Complete String Quartets* (CD, Forum FRC9301, 2003).

Reproduced with kind permission of BMG Music Publishing – United Kingdom.

The notion of silence acting upon a musical continuum takes on metaphysical significance in the ideology of Charles Ives (1874–1954). His musical discourse was inspired by his search for ways to express 'that ever-flowing stream, partly biological, partly cosmic, ever going on in ourselves, in nature, in all life'.[14] In particular, Ives searched for the 'ever-flowing stream' expressed in the transcendental philosophies of those extraordinary people who had gathered to live in and around Concord, Massachusetts, in the mid-19th century – Ralph Waldo Emerson, Henry David Thoreau, Nathaniel Hawthorne, the Alcott family and many others who helped to shape American literary thinking of the time. As Ives saw it:

> All around you, under the Concord sky, there still floats the influence of that human faith melody, transcendent and sentimetal enough for the enthusiast or the cynic respectively, reflecting an innate hope – a common interest in common things and common men – a tune the Concord bards are ever playing, while they pound away at the immensities with a Beethovenlike sublimity.[15]

For Ives, musical creation involved connection with that 'human faith melody', that celestial choir singing the common hymns and popular tunes that everyone knows, trying to express the immensities of life by tapping into the underlying continuum of sounds.

This aspiration was the basis of Ives's Second Piano Sonata, subtitled 'Concord, Mass., 1840–1860' (1911–15, with later revisions). Each of the four movements, 'Emerson', 'Hawthorne', 'The Alcotts' and 'Thoreau', captures the essence of its namesake's character, musically reflecting Ives's interpretation of the personalities and writings. The composer verbally supported his musical ideas, which reflected thinking of many years, in his extensive thoughts and notes on the work as a whole and on each movement, published as *Essays Before a Sonata*.

The music is evocative, in places distinctly pictorial, particularly in 'Hawthorne'. All is strongly personal, reflecting Ives's take on each thinker's character and philosophies, and there is a recognizable thread of continuity throughout, the four-note motive of Beethoven's Fifth Symphony 'pound[ing] away at the immensities with a Beethovenlike sublimity'. Thus the opening of 'Emerson' is exuberant, forceful, loud and without rest or closure in its tumuluous ascents and descents. Unbounded by musical conventions of metre, tonality or structure, the music is an expression and depiction of Ives's awed admiration for this

> invader of the unknown – America's deepest explorer of the spiritual immensities – a seer painting his discoveries in masses and with any color that may lie at hand – cosmic, religious, human, even sensous; a recorder freely describing the inevitable struggle in the soul's uprise ...[16]

In contrast, the final movement, inspired by Thoreau, approaches the spiritual immensities in a far more contemplative way, as shown in Ex. 1.4. The ostinato bass

---

[14]   Charles Ives, 'Epilogue', in *Essays Before a Sonata, The Majority and Other Writings*, selected and ed. Howard Boatwright (New York: W. W. Norton, 1961), 71.

[15]   Charles Ives, 'The Alcotts', in *Essays Before a Sonata*, 47.

[16]   Charles Ives, 'Emerson', in *Essays Before a Sonata*, 11.

taps into eternity, the snippets of hymn tunes provide glimpses here and there, punctuated by diminishing presence. Rather than forcing the way ever higher and louder as in 'Emerson', Ives here reduces aural sound in order to *tune in* to the celestial choirs, into the continuum of immortal sounds.

Ex. 1.4   Ives, Piano Sonata No. 2 'Concord, Mass., 1840–1860', movt. 4 'Thoreau', bar 21

*Small notes in piano to be played only if flute is not used.

Reproduced with kind permission of G. Schirmer/The Music Sales Group.

Of course, Ives's famous dictum, 'My God! What has sound got to do with music!'[17] underlines the ultimate destination of this delicate web, the sounds of the ever-flowing stream leading to and dissolving into innate understanding of what is above and beyond.

> That music must be heard is not essential – what it *sounds* like may not be what it is. Perhaps the day is coming when music-believers will learn 'that silence is a solvent … that gives us leave to be universal' rather than personal.[18]

In the essential search for the universal, Ives's ideal sound continuum was in fact epitomized by silence. John Cage later affirmed this view, acknowledging music's power in silence as a conduit to the universal, thus revealing parallel means of hearing through the intensity of the twentieth-century soundscape:

---

[17]   Ives, 'Epilogue', 84.

[18]   *Ibid.* Ives here quotes Emerson, 'Intellect', in *Complete Works*, 2: *Essays, Series 1*, new and rev. ed. (Boston: Houghton, Mifflin, 1894), 319. For further comments on Ives's music and philosophies, see Chapter 6 (Brooks).

I read the essay and in it he [Ives] sees someone sitting on a porch in a rocking chair smoking a pipe looking out over the landscape which goes into the distance and imagines that as that person who is anyone sitting there doing nothing that he is hearing his own symphony. This I think is for all intents and purposes the goal of music. I doubt whether we can find a higher goal namely that art and our involvement in it will somehow introduce us to the very life that we are living.[19]

For Cage, the dissolution of sound within silence to admit the universal symphony brought the idea full circle, right round to art and the universal illuminating the personal.

§

The sound of music is not ... opposed, but rather parallel to silence. It is as though the sounds of music were being driven over the surface of silence. Music is silence, which in dreaming begins to sound.[20]

This shift from music conceived as continuous stream, a texture articulated by silence, to a silence-based foundation from which music sounds represents a significant shift in approach that was characteristic of Western performative arts of the twentieth century. Ironically, this change in perspective was often a response to the significant increase in sound that surrounded those living in twentieth-century Western society. Many reacted to that increase in sound level, and its effect on their creative worlds, through simple negation. Max Picard, for example, abhorred the modern, mid-century world of noise, media and mechanization, taking refuge in silence as a fundamental element at the base of both faith and nature.

Silence was there first, before things. It is as though the forest grew up slowly after it: the branches of the trees are like dark lines that have followed the movements of silence; the leaves thickly cover the branches as if the silence wanted to conceal itself.[21]

As a philosopher and theologian, Picard conceptualized music's relationship to this silent macrocosm, envisaging music as parallel to this base of silence, 'as though the sounds of music were being driven over the surface of silence'.

This conception of silence as a foundation for sound is famously evident in the dramatic works of Irish author Samuel Beckett (1906–1989). Consider the radio plays of the 1950s and 60s, for instance, an especially apt genre, free as it is from the visual dimension of dramatic discourse intended for the stage. The lack of the visual offered a different canvas or mental space to the playwright, enabling audiences' attention to be focused onto 'other' dramatic aspects, parallel dramatic worlds.[22]

---

[19]   John Cage, 'Two Statements on Ives' (ca. 1964–5), in *A Year from Monday* (Middletown, CT: Wesleyan University Press, 1967), 42. The essay to which Cage referred is the 'Postface to *114 Songs*' (1922), in *Essays Before a Sonata*, 120–31.

[20]   Picard, *The World of Silence*, 27.

[21]   *Ibid.*, 137.

[22]   Beckett, *The Complete Dramatic Works*. 'In the fifties and sixties, when the theatre was bound by censorship, much of the experimental and controversial material was performed at clubs. However, since BBC Radio was not bound by the same restrictions, it was particularly

In a highly musical way, Beckett heightened the sense of a linear unfolding of material in the aural plane through the rhythms and counterpoints with which he composed his radio scripts. In addition to words and other sounds in the 'stage' directions, essential to this soundscape is silence, often in the form of '[*Pause.*]', articulating, pacing, interrupting, halting – ultimately controlling the passage of time throughout these texts, as well as the emotional flow. For instance, in the dialogue in *Rough for Radio I* (1961), HE introduces SHE to the wonders of radio, which cannot be controlled except as a binary choice, either presence (sound) or absence (silence). The play uncovers the psychological disturbance represented by another binary choice: the division in creative output between words ('voice') and music:

	[*Pause.*]
HE:	To the right, madam.
	[*Click.*]
VOICE:	[*Faint.*] . . . .
SHE:	[*With voice.*] Louder!
VOICE:	[*No louder.*] . . . .
	[*Silence.*]
She:	And – [*Faint stress.*] – *you* like that?
HE:	It is a need.
She:	A need? *That* a need?
HE:	It has become a need. [*Pause.*] To the right, madam.
	[*Click.*]
MUSIC:	[*Faint.*] . . . .
SHE:	[*With music.*] Louder!
MUSIC:	[*No louder.*] . . . .
	[*Silence.*]
SHE:	That too? [*Pause.*] That a need too?
HE:	It has become a need, madam.[23]

As Zofia Lissa has remarked, music, or in this case dramatic narrative, 'is a process that at a certain moment enters into the silence, then takes its course within it, and with its last sound merges back into it'.[24] In this conception, silence thus shifts from being something that stops action – a silencer, a structural articulator or a frame – to

---

attractive to experimental writers. Radio playwrights found that they did not have to worry about the box office success of their plays in terms of economy or be afraid of offending the kind of mass audience that television attracted, and were therefore free from the self censorship which influenced the other rival institutions. Beckett's plays for radio, too, excluding *Cascando* which was first broadcast by the French radio station ORTF, all originated on the Third Programme'; Stefan-Brook Grant, 'Samuel Beckett's Radio Plays: Music of the Absurd' (Cand. Philol. degree, University of Oslo, 2000), Chapter 1: Background, accessed at <http://www.samuel-beckett.net/ch1.html> (accessed on 30 March 2006).

23   Beckett, *Rough for Radio I*, 268–9.

24   Zofia Lissa, 'Die Ästhetischen Funktionen der Stille und Pause in der Musik' (1962), repr. as 'Stille und Pause in der Musik', in Lissa, *Aufsätze zur Musikästhetik: eine Auswahl* (Berlin: Henschel, 1969), 162. English translation assisted by Irene Auerbach. I am indebted to Darla Crispin for bringing this article to my attention; for further examination of Lissa's ideas, see Chapter 7 (Crispin).

being the main canvas, the *Pauses* active as a primary agent in the narrative while sounds interact over its surface. In this play, Beckett explored the possibility of three non-intersecting psychological continua: streams of music or of words – represented by the two choices of radio programmes – or of the underlying, fundamental state: [*Click.*] [*Silence.*].[25]

This conception of silence as a foundation for sound may be exemplified in music by works of the Austrian composer, Anton Webern (1883–1945). The brief compositions of his atonal period feature extreme concentration of expression through minute focus on the quality of sound. As the composer later recalled:

> About 1911 I wrote the Bagatelles for string quartet, all very short pieces, lasting two minutes; perhaps they were the shortest pieces in music so far. Here I had the feeling that when the twelve notes had all been played the piece was over.[26]

This extreme response to composing is interpreted by many scholars today as 'a direct expression of the crisis that the Viennese triumvirate created for themselves in abandoning tonality'.[27] The others in the 'triumvirate', Arnold Schoenberg and Alban Berg, found their own, very different paths through the crisis, while Webern's expressive miniatures created fleeting soundscapes in which individual musical gestures broke through silence in the most essential way. As Schoenberg wrote in the introduction to the publication of Webern's *Six Bagatelles* in 1924:

> Consider what moderation is required to express onself so briefly. You can stretch every glance out into a poem, every sight into a novel. But to express a novel in a single gesture, a joy in a breath – such concentration can only be present in proportion to the absence of self-pity.
>
> These pieces will only be understood by those who share the faith that music can say things which can only be expressed by music. ...
>
> Does the musician know how to play these pieces, does the listener know how to receive them? Can faithful musicians and listeners fail to surrender themselves to one another?

---

[25]   In another radio play, *Words and Music: a Piece for Radio*, also written in late 1961, Music 'appears', or rather 'sounds', as an individual character (also known as Joe). A nurturing personality, Music woos Words in Beckett's further exploration of the psychology of the creative process; Beckett, *Words and Music*, in *The Complete Dramatic Works*, 285–94. For its first broadcast (BBC Third Programme, 13 November 1962), Music was composed by John Beckett (the author's cousin). When the work was revived for American radio in 1987, Music was composed by Morton Feldman; *Words and Music*, dir. Everett C. Frost, music by Morton Feldman, with Alvin Epstein, David Warrilow and the Bowery Ensemble, part of *The Beckett Festival of Radio Plays* (CD, Everett Review, 1987).

[26]   Webern, lecture (12 Febrary 1932), quoted in Hans Moldenhauer, in collaboration with Rosaleen Moldenhauer, *Anton von Webern: a Chronicle of his Life and Work* (London: Victor Gollancz, 1978), 194.

[27]   Kathryn Bailey, *The Life of Webern* (Cambridge: Cambridge University Press, 1998), 77.

But what shall we do with the heathen? Fire and sword can keep them down; only believers need to be restrained.
May this silence sound for them.[28]

As for Beckett, silence in Webern's work is an expressive force field, a fundamental, essential part of the concentration which stretches to deliver brief notes, as Ex. 1.5 shows, expressing 'a joy in a breath', sounding 'a novel in a single gesture'.

Ex. 1.5   Webern, Bagatelle No. 1, *Mässig*

---

28   Arnold Schoenberg, Foreword to Webern's *Six Bagatelles for String Quartet, Op. 9* (composed 1911–13) (Vienna: Universal, 1924). The *Bagatelles* were first performed on 19 July 1924 at the Donaueschingen Festival by the Amar Quartet (with Hindemith on viola).

The sparse quality of this movement gives an unusual sense of depth to the texture, both when sounding and when silent. This is effected in part by the range of pitches, each sound gesture *noticed* for its place within the pitch spectrum, low and high in some senses more important in performed effect than the actual pitch itself (despite the many analyses of Webern's works of this period that concentrate on pitch alone).[29] As Webern wrote to Berg, 'You must look closely at the instrumentation. You have to imagine very precisely these mixtures and alternations of the various bowing possibilities (col legno, sul ponticello, naturale, etc.)'.[30] Thus the distinctive character of each gesture is effected through the means by which sound emerges from

---

[29]   Compelling pitch analysis readings of Webern's atonal works have been presented, for example, by Allen Forte, in 'An Octatonic Essay by Webern: No. 1 of the "Six Bagatelles for String Quartet", Op. 9', *Music Theory Spectrum* 16/2 (Autumn 1994), 171–95. However, in the short score through which Forte introduced this ten-bar movement, 'dynamics, articulations, and tempo variations have been excluded in order to give the most concise view of the pitch organization of the work' (173). And although there is a section entitled 'Surface Features of Op. 9, No. 1', it effectually dismisses the non-pitched qualities of the work's sounds: 'Many of the external aspects of this movement will be familiar to students of Webern's atonal music: the absence of obvious repetitions of longer pitch formations and, correspondingly, the scrupulous avoidance of traditional themes and motives, the extraordinary attention accorded dynamics, mode of attack, and rhythmic articulation, and the carefully notated expressive changes of tempo … In addition … are the registral extremes' (174). Needless to say, the silences are not mentioned, except briefly in terms of rests articulating form.

[30]   Webern, letter to Alban Berg, 23 May 1913, quoted in Moldenhauer, *Anton von Webern*, 191. Sound may be produced on a string instrument in a variety of ways, including: '*naturale*' bowed tones, the harsher, less focused quality of bowing near the bridge (*sul ponticello*), playing with the wood of the bow (*col legno*), rapid rearticulations, back and forth with the bow on the string (*tremolo*), bouncing the bow on the string (*spiccato)* or plucking the strings

and interacts with silence. In conjunction with pitch placement, this close attention to the quality of each sound – its level of dynamic and accent as well as its means of sound production – enables the gesture to remain distinguishable within the multi-dimensional texture. Or, from a different point of view, 'may this silence sound for them': different layers of silence may be heard to interact expressively as Webern's musical utterances briefly and distinctively sound in their different characters. The sense of silence/sound texture is clearly articulated both linearly, within each instrumental line in two dimensions, and conjunctively, as a string quartet in three.

After a failed performance of an early manifestation of these string quartet movements, Webern, in a letter to Schoenberg, tried to verbalize their essence:

> First a word: angel. From it comes the 'mood' of this piece. The angels in heaven. The incomprehensible state after death.[31]

§

> Hasn't art been the human creature's rebellion against silence? Poetry and music were born when man first uttered a sound, resisting the silence.[32]

The Japanese composer Tōru Takemitsu arrived at a not dissimilar sound world to Webern in his contemplations of sound and silence, though the journey there was entirely different. Another composer who committed his thoughts as well as music to paper, Takemitsu wrote a series of essays that was published in English as *Confronting Silence*.[33] This collection contains his ruminations as a composer who trained and worked within the mid- to late-twentieth-century Western art music tradition; however, he had reached a crisis in his engagement with the Western compositional world and thus was re-visiting, re-'searching', his background in relation to Japanese culture and Eastern aesthetics and philosophies:

> I wish to discard the concept of building sounds. In the world in which we live silence and unlimited sound exist. Painstakingly I wish to carve that sound with my own hands, finally to reach a single sound. And it should be as strong a sound as possible in its confrontation with silence.[34]

A fundamental cultural difference that Takemitsu negotiated derived from his deep grounding within the Japanese aesthetic *ma* – the space or time between events.

---

in various ways (*pizzicato*). *Spiccato* and *pizzicato* both produce non-*legato* (unconnected) articulations; thus their characteristic sounds 'contain' silences by definition.

[31] Webern, letter to Schoenberg, 24 November 1913, quoted in Moldenhauer, *Anton von Webern*, 192.

[32] Tōru Takemitsu, *Confronting Silence: Selected Writings*, trans. and ed. Yoshiko Kakudo and Glenn Glasow (Berkeley, CA: Fallen Leaf Press, 1995), 17. I am indebted to Noriko Ogawa for her evocative explanations of Takemitsu and his music, as well as for her expressive and discerning performances.

[33] *Ibid.*

[34] *Ibid.*, 6.

It is not an abstractly calculated space, as is conceived by Westerners, but rather a sensory … a 'sensually' perceived space … For art lovers, it is that space between oneself, while perceiving, and what is being perceived in the flow of time. … In music, *ma* refers to the silence between musical phrases, as well as how each of the phrases is performed.[35]

An example may give an idea not only of the physical idea of space or time between musical events, but also the nature of such 'rests', active yet lacking the Western sense of intentionality: 'Unlike a European bell that peals the hours, a Japanese bell (although used for the same purpose) is struck with so much time spent between each striking that it finishes ringing far after the hour.'[36] Such Japanese sound spaces are not communicative in the sense of sounds and rests performed in Western art music, or even communing in the sense of the breathing rests performed in Christian chanting,[37] though the latter may perhaps have been executed for a similar higher purpose. It is indeed spiritual motion that is the aspiration behind performance spaces within Japanese sound events, and this is of fundamental significance to *ma*. The spaces inspire an entirely different conception and approach not only to the physical passing of time during their unfolding, but to the sounds themselves, which in their concentrated, essential form reduced for Takemitsu – as for Webern – to individual sound events.

The external and internal world is full of vibration. Existing in this stream of infinite sound, I thought that it is my task to capture a single defined sound.

In its complexity and its integrity this single sound can stand alone. To the sensitive Japanese listener who appreciates this refined sound, the unique idea of *ma* – the unsounded part of this experience – has at the same time a deep, powerful, and rich resonance that can stand up to the sound. In short, this *ma*, this powerful silence, is that which gives life to the sound and removes it from its position of primacy. So it is that sound, confronting the silence of *ma*, yields supremacy in the final expression.[38]

Thus for Takemitsu, silence did not serve merely as mediator, articulating structures of sound; instead, there was an essential merging of the two polarities.

Yet, in contrast to the thought processes that led Webern to miniaturism in his atonal works, for Takemitsu sound reduction was a concentration, a way of finding essential meaning within the complex sound continua underlying his compositional sphere.

To me the world is sound. Sound penetrates me, linking me to the world. I give sounds active meaning. By doing this I am assured of being in the sounds, becoming one with them. To me this is the greatest reality. It is not that I shape anything, but rather that I desire to merge with the world.[39]

---

[35]   Bruno Deschênes, *Aesthetics in Japanese Arts,* <http://www.thingsasian.com/goto_ article/ article.2121.html> (accessed 24 March 2006).

[36]   Noriko Ohtake, *Creative Sources for the Music of Toru Takemitsu* (Aldershot: Scolar Press, 1993), 54.

[37]   See Chapters 9 (Potter) and 8 (Hornby).

[38]   Takemitsu, *Confronting Silence*, 8, 51.

[39]   *Ibid.*, 13.

As we've already seen, Ives's search for a way to articulate glimpses of the essential meanings to life – derived as much from the simplicity of hymn tunes as from the incomprehensible complexities of Emerson's thoughts – led him to conceive, comprehend and compose an ever-flowing stream, a texture of celestial sound. Takemitsu too sought to make sense of an ever-running 'stream of sounds':

> This is not only an impressionistic description but a phrase intended to contrast with the usual method of constructing music – that of superimposing sounds one on another. This is not a matter of creating new space by merely dividing it, but it does pose a question: by admitting a new perception of space and giving it an active sense, is it not possible to discover a new unexpected, unexplored world?[40]

This stream, this 'riverrun, past Eve and Adam's, from swerve of shore to bend of bay, brings us by a commodius vicus of recirculation back'[41] – back to James Joyce and on to conclude with a composition inspired by Joyce's *Finnigan's Wake*, Takemitsu's string quartet *A Way A Lone* (1981).[42] As Ex. 1.6, from the beginning of the work, illustrates, this quartet is not about individuality of voices; instead the voices sound together, closely spaced in a homophonic texture of gestures: the bowing, the shaping of the phrases, the breaths of sound together phrase utterances, carefully enunciating meaningful gestures within the sonic stream.

Ex. 1.6   Takemitsu, *A Way A Lone*, bars 1–13

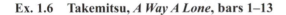

---

[40]   *Ibid.*, 7–8.

[41]   Joyce, *Finnegan's Wake*, 3.

[42]   Tōru Takemitsu, *A Way A Lone: for String Quartet* (Mainz and New York: Schott, 1982); another version of the work is for string orchestra, *A Way A Lone II* (Mainz and New York: Schott, 1981). Takemitsu also wrote a piano concerto inspired by *Finnegan's Wake*, *Riverrun* (1984).

It is indeed paradoxical that Takemitsu – who would seek 'that single sound which is in itself so strong that it can confront silence', and would conclude that 'sound, in its ultimate expressiveness, being constantly refined, approaches the nothingness of that wind in the bamboo grove'[43] – should nevertheless find inspiration in the voluminous verbal world of James Joyce. Did the mysteries and complexities of Joyce's language with its multiplicity of meanings, its puzzles, its pure sounds and gestures – and of course the mental spaces between – paradoxically balance the simplicity of Takemitsu's creative ideal? Was the sonority of Joyce's text, with its ability to lead the reader to a different level of understanding or consciousness, perhaps congruent in some way to Takemitsu's search within the sound-stream for 'a new perception of space ... a new unexpected, unexplored world'?

---

[43]   Takemitsu, *Confronting Silence*, 52, 51.

Perhaps the Joycian qualities noted earlier influenced this unlikely attraction: the way Joyce read from *Finnegan's Wake* is remarkably similar to how Takemitsu 'carved' the textures of silence and sound in *A Way A Lone*, his quartet gestures tapering into sound and away into silence. Silence punctuates the sounds, but equally, in Takemitsu's phrase, the sound 'punche[s] beautiful holes in that space',[44] an ever-flowing exchange in which the 'resonance', the texture of that silence – of *ma* – 'gives life' to the sounds.

Once again recalling Picard's words, in the texture of silence,

> The silent images of things in the soul bring their silence to the words that are the life of the mind.[45]

---

[44]   *Ibid.*, 32.
[45]   Picard, *The World of Silence*, 93.

Chapter 2

Faith, Silence and Darkness Entwined in Messiaen's 'Regard du silence'

Matthew Hill

The monumental *Vingt regards sur l'Enfant-Jésus* of 1944, by Olivier Messiaen (1908–1992), is a musical-mystical compendium of twenty piano pieces that evoke the mysteries of faith associated with the birth and infancy of Christ. For each piece in the *Vingt regards*, Messiaen affixed within the published score[1] a short, poetic verbal preface directly below the title, in parentheses with written in thoughtful pauses (…). These short verbal 'meditations' focus attention on an aspect of faith expressed through the music. In addition to these prefaces, Messiaen eventually wrote lengthier programme notes for each of the *regards*, often found as liner notes for recordings.[2] These more elaborate commentaries explain each piece's structure, Messiaen's unique compositional techniques, and the connection he sensed between music and colour.

Messiaen attached verbal commentary to his religiously inspired music in his desire to portray musically elements of his Catholicism. In an interview with Claude Samuel, he explained the relationship between some of his music and his faith:

> The first idea I wanted to express, the most important, is the existence of the truths of the Catholic faith. I have the good fortune to be a Catholic. I was born a believer, and the Scriptures impressed me even as a child. The illumination of the theological truths of the Catholic faith is the first aspect of my work, the noblest, and no doubt the most useful and most valuable.[3]

The *Vingt regards* were also inspired by works of visual art, theology and poetry. Messiaen's prefatory notes listed several writers whose theological or poetic

---

This chapter is based on my dissertation: 'Messiaen's *Regard du silence* as an Expression of Catholic Faith' (DMA diss., University of Wisconsin–Madison, 1995).

[1]   Olivier Messiaen, *Vingt regards sur L'Enfant-Jésus* (Paris: S. A. Durand Editions Musicales, 1944).

[2]   Olivier Messiaen, liner notes to his *Vingt regards sur L'Enfant-Jésus*, Yvonne Loriod (Messiaen's wife), piano, recorded 1973 (CD, Erato 4509-91705, 1993, digitally re-mastered from original analogue recording).

[3]   Olivier Messiaen, *Music and Color: Conversations with Claude Samuel*, trans. E. Thomas Glasow (Portland: Amadeus Press, 1994), 20.

reflections were influential,[4] including St John of the Cross, Dom Columba Marmion's *Le Christ dans ses mystères* and Maurice Toesca's *Les douze regards*.[5] According to Nigel Simeone's investigation of Messiaen's diaries, there are 'numerous references to the *Vingt regards* and to a very closely related project which evolved in parallel – the provision of twelve pieces ("Douze Regards" to use Messiaen's description) as incidental music for a radio broadcast, written to accompany poems by Maurice Toesca about the Nativity'.[6] Robert Sherlaw Johnson explained in reference to Marmion and Toesca that 'these last two writers have spoken of the "Regards" of the Shepherds, of the Angels, of the Virgin and of the heavenly Father'.[7] Moreover, in the preface to the *Vingt regards*, Messiaen noted that he followed 'the same idea' while 'adding sixteen new "Regards"'.

Messiaen's use of the word *regard* throughout this work is suggestive. *Regard*, meaning 'look' or 'gaze', seems to imply an outward process rather than an interior experience. However, it is not uncommon to see the word, translated in reference to Messiaen's work as 'meditation', 'adoration', or 'contemplation'. Norman Bryson provides the following lexical background for it:

> The etymology of the word *regard* points to far more than the rudimentary act of looking: the prefix with its implication of an act that is always repeated, already indicates an impatient pressure within vision, a persevering drive which looks outward with mistrust (*repondre sous garde*, to re-arrest) and actively seeks to confine what is always on the point of escaping or slipping out of bounds. ... its overall purpose seems to be the discovery of a second (re-)surface standing behind the first, the mask of appearances.[8]

Bryson presents more than the exterior activity of looking; the word *regard* suggests an intensity of interior grappling, a type of persistence that is always looking beyond appearances for something more hidden. Johnson also understood *regard*, specifically as used by Messiaen in the *Vingt regards*, with similar overtones of meaning: 'the sense of the word *regard* in this work involves contemplation as well as the more literal meaning "gaze". It is essentially a contemplation of the mysteries involved in the subject of each piece as well as of the child Jesus'.[9] Messiaen's *regards* move beyond musical representations of scenes or ideas relevant to the Christian faith,

---

    [4]   Messiaen, general introduction to *Vingt regards sur l'Enfant-Jésus* (1944); see also Robert Sherlaw Johnson, *Messiaen* (Berkeley: University of California Press, 1975), 71.

    [5]   Columba Marmion (1858–1923) wrote meditative reflections, *Le Christ dans ses mystères* (1919*)*, translated by Mother M. St Thomas as *Christ in His Mysteries* (St Louis: B. Herder Book Co., 1939). *Les douze regards* were, at the time of Messiaen's *Vingt regards*, unpublished poems about the Nativity of Christ by Maurice Toesca (1904–1988).

    [6]   Nigel Simeone also explains that 'Toesca's poems, under the title *La Nativité*, were eventually published in 1952 by the Paris firm of Sautier'; see liner notes to *Vingt regards sur L'Enfant-Jésus*, Steven Osborne, piano (CD, Hyperion A673512, 2002). See also Toesca, *Les douze regards* (1944), pubd as *La Nativité* in Michel Ciry, *La Nativité: eaux-fortes originales* (Paris: Marcel Sautier, [1952]).

    [7]   Johnson, *Messiaen,* 71.

    [8]   Norman Bryson, *Vision and Painting: the Logic of the Gaze* (New Haven: Yale University Press, 1983), 93.

    [9]   Johnson, *Messiaen*, 71.

there is a 'gazing in' that experiences 'interiorly' through music the mysteries to which Messiaen's verbal prefaces allude.

As Messiaen the composer used music to contemplate the mysteries of faith, the 16th-century Spanish Carmelite mystic and poet, St John of the Cross (1542–1591), used poetry and subsequent commentary to evoke the mysteries of the divine in such works as *Subida del monte Carmelo* ('The Ascent of Mount Carmel'), *Noche oscura* ('The Dark Night'), *Cántico espiritual* ('The Spiritual Canticle') and *Llama de amor viva* ('The Living Flame of Love').[10] José C. Nieto explains the relationship between St John's poetry and his commentaries:

> This temporal order of poetry over prose is why he [St John of the Cross] is known as the poet of mysticism par excellence. It was only later that he interpreted his poems in a systematically mystical way. Thus, John's commentaries on his poetic writings, in which he interpreted the poetic expression of his mystical experience, are what give his poems a mystical value which would have otherwise probably been missed by their readers. In fact, it was to make sure that his readers interpreted his poems in a mystical rather than in a profane sense that he entered into exegetical analysis of them.[11]

The Ascent of Mount Carmel explores the poetic metaphor of the 'dark night' used in the poem 'The Dark Night',[12] which entails the process by which the believer can ascend the hidden path by faith that leads to union with God. This cannot be fully grasped in words, and through the *analogy* of faith as a 'dark night', understanding or knowledge of this means towards divine union can be imparted. St John explained the meanings of such analogies by combining poetry with criticism, which directed the reader's interpretative process. In *The Ascent of Mount Carmel*, St John's annotations were an interpretive pathway to the poetry, which in turn conveyed a mystical journey of faith. This is comparable to Messiaen's contemplation through music, the mysteries of faith suggested by his verbal prefaces to the *Vingt regards*. Messiaen imparted a mystical language to his musical prose that intentionally directed a listener's understanding; heard independently of their titles and accompanying prefaces, Messiaen's intended meanings for these pieces would be lost.

Music Contemplating Silence

> (Silence dans le main, arc-en-ciel renversé … chaque silence de la crèche révèle musiques et couleurs qui sont les mystères de Jésus - Christ …)

---

[10]   See *The Collected Works of St John of the Cross*, trans. Kieran Kavanaugh and Otilio Rodgriguez (Washington DC: ICS Publications, 1991): *The Ascent of Mount Carmel* 113–349, *The Dark Night* 358–457, *The Spiritual Canticle* 469–630, *The Living Flame of Love* 638–715.

[11]   José C. Nieto, *Mystic, Rebel, Saint : a Study of St John of the Cross* (Geneva: Librairie Droz, 1979), 22.

[12]   *Noche oscura*, or 'The Dark Night', is the poem upon which St John of the Cross bases two of his theological treatises on prayer, *The Ascent of Mount Caramel* and *The Dark Night*. See *The Collected Works*, 50–52. See also the first two stanzas on p. 50 (below).

(Silence in the hand, upside down rainbow ... each silence from the crib reveals sounds and colours which are the mysteries of Jesus Christ...)

Messiaen's preface to 'Regard du silence'[13]

This chapter will explore Messiaen's musical contemplation of silence in the 'Regard du silence', the 17th of the *Vingt regards*. Messiaen created a paradox: audible music that contemplates silence. Yet the paradox we first expect – sounding music *representing* the absence of sound – was not Messiaen's aim. Rather, according to Messiaen's prefatory text, the 'Regard du silence' is a contemplation of silence *through* musical sound. Messiaen's musical contemplation presents a unique triangular relationship between faith, silence and darkness: the music that reveals the mysteries of Christ in 'each silence' can be likened to faith, a type of 'knowledge of unknowing'. St John of the Cross refers to faith as a 'dark night' because the complete reality of the divine transcends human reason. In this *regard*, Messiaen conceived of movement from the music's silence to the audible 'silences' from the crib, which he further described as like the emergence of 'colours' from the 'night'.[14] I will examine whether this can be understood as being analogous to discursive meditation, where words and ideas emerge from quietude. Moreover, his conception of these 'sounds and colours' as revealing impalpable mysteries is similar in wordless contemplation to the idea that the divine light is communicated through the darkness of faith. Throughout this essay, meditation and 'infused' or 'mystical' contemplation shall be understood in the sense that St John of the Cross used them, referring either to the use of the senses or to an experiential knowledge, infused by divine grace, that transcends the senses.[15] The music that contemplates silence is analogous to faith – and *acts* of faith such as meditation or contemplation – and examining such analogies will help reveal how faith, silence and darkness intermingle in this *regard*. Here my interest is not to draw attention to Messiaen's religiosity, but to illuminate a musical 'epistemology' of faith that includes the music, Messiaen's descriptive title and his prose. To better understand the knowledge of 'faith' revealed in this *regard*, this chapter will also explore relevant theological principles through the apophatic mystical theology[16] of St John of the Cross as presented in his major treatise on contemplation, *The Ascent of Mount Carmel*. In either St John's understanding of

---

[13]   Messiaen, preface to 'Regard du silence', in *Vingt regards sur L'Enfant-Jésus* (1944), 128.

[14]   In his programme notes, Messiaen wrote: 'where the music seems to emerge from silence like colours emerging from the night'; see the liner notes for the 'Regard du silence', in *Vingt regards sur L'Enfant-Jésus*, (CD, Erato, 1993). The full quotation (in French and English) appears later in this essay.

[15]   St John explains in *The Ascent of Mount Carmel*, Book 2, Chapter 14: 'It should be known that the purpose of discursive meditation on divine subjects is the acquisition of some knowledge and love of God ... What the soul, therefore, was gradually acquiring through the labor of meditation on particular ideas has now, as we said, been converted into habitual and substantial, general loving knowledge [contemplation]. This knowledge is neither distinct nor particular, as was the previous knowledge'; see *The Collected Works*, 191–2.

[16]   An 'apophatic' mysticism stresses the ineffability of God and faith as being 'darkness' to human reason with knowledge gleaned through 'unknowing'. Earlier examples of this

faith or Messiaen's musical contemplation of silence, the intellect needs something that the sense faculties are unable to provide. We enter a 'dark night'.

Faith

Faith is a theological virtue of the intellect,[17] an intellectual assent. It does not present information to the intellect in tangible form, but only in obscurity. Faith makes it possible to believe in something with certainty without fully possessing that belief in an intellectually concrete manner. According to St John of the Cross:

> Faith, we saw, affirms what cannot be understood by the intellect.... faith is the substance of things to be hoped for and that these things are not manifest to the intellect, even though its consent to them is firm and certain. If they were manifest, there would be no faith. For though faith brings certitude to the intellect, it does not produce clarity, but only darkness.[18]

The writings of St John explore the contemplative assent to the divine, the ultimate goal of which is union of the soul with God. For St John there is an essential likeness between the virtue of faith and the quality of divinity; faith is *connatural* to the divine and therefore is the proper means to this union. Divine essence is completely unlike the essence of any created creature. Before an assent to the divine is possible, there needs to be a means through which created creatures can operate, and for St John, this means must have this essential likeness. Because of this connaturality between faith and the divine, faith can be the means by which the soul, operating as an intellectual assent, can enter into union with God.

Faith is always informed by love, which is the theological virtue of the will. Charity or love is that virtue which transforms the lover into the beloved. Through the will the soul becomes more similar to the divine. The greater the similarity, the more easily the intellect – moving through faith and informed by love – participates with God. Because of the soul's desire to become more like the divine, the will, working in charity, *negates* that which is contrary to the divine. This purgation brings about an emptiness or void in the intellect, which St John refers to as 'darkness', because charity is directed towards that which reason cannot empirically grasp. Moreover, this assent of faith is also 'darkness' because it follows a mystical or *hidden* pathway to the divine. Faith does not present divine truths to the intellect as an understood substance. Divine truths, revealed through faith, become an object of belief that lacks clarity. By faith in the intellect and love in the will the believer is led to what St John of the Cross says is 'a higher knowledge of God' or a 'mystical theology, meaning the secret wisdom of God'.[19]

---

approach include St Gregory of Nyssa (4th century), Pseudo-Dionysius (5th century) and the anonymous 14th-century text, *The Cloud of Unknowing*.

[17]   For a summary of the theological virtues, see St John of the Cross, *The Ascent of Mount Carmel*, Book 2, Chapter 6, in *The Collected Works*, 166–7.

[18]   St John of the Cross, *The Ascent*, Book 2, Chapter 6, 166–7.

[19]   St John of the Cross, *The Ascent*, Book 2, Chapter 8, 176.

St John of the Cross also implies another type of faith, or trust, between word and world. Such a trust assumes a 'real presence'[20] that insures meaning for verbal discourse. Faith, then, is necessary to give meaning to symbols, metaphors and analogies. It is a 'hermeneutical end-stopping'[21] mechanism that creates boundaries to give readers an interpretive focus. For St John, this focus is directed only to the revealed truths of faith as sanctioned by the Catholic Church. Vincent Brummer explains that 'we do not, however, have this truth at our disposal. What we do have is merely our human attempts at conceptualising this truth'.[22] St John's faith is an assent to a divine essence that transcends all human knowledge. This 'real presence' creates a void of 'unknowing', something that language can grasp at, yet never hold. Christian theology uses language to reveal such articles of faith as: 'God is three persons, yet one', or 'Christ is both completely God and completely man'. In positing such truths, this theology, by faith, assents to un-provable assumptions that are never under dispute. The concepts such statements express, though made through language, cannot be completely understood as empirical realities.

The philosopher Max Picard believed, 'the sphere of faith and the sphere of silence belong together',[23] and he continued, explaining that the 'mystery' of the incarnation is itself enshrouded in silence:

> This event is so utterly extraordinary and so much against the experience of reason and against everything the eye has seen, that man is not able to make a response to it in words. A layer of silence lies between this event and man, and in this silence man approaches the silence that surrounds God Himself.[24]

The 'mystery' of Christ lies in a silence that no formulation can approximate. Faith accepts the ineffable mystery that silence signifies, silence being the chasm that exists between the believer and the divine. Perhaps the 'Regard du silence' can be understood as an expression of the layer of silence that 'surrounds God', a musical response to the mysteries of faith. In the 'Regard du silence' we can *hear* the music, but not the inaudible 'mysteries' that 'each silence' contemplates. In the crib these

---

[20]   In *Real Presences* (Chicago: University of Chicago Press, 1989), George Steiner borrows the term 'real presence' from Catholic sacramental theology, which in this context refers to the mystical presence of Christ in the Eucharist. Steiner uses this term when he considers that the meaningfulness of textual interpretation is ensured by its 'presence'. He posits: 'any coherent account of the capacity of human speech to communicate meaning and feeling, is, in the final analysis, underwritten by the assumption of God's presence. I will put forward the argument that the experience of aesthetic meaning in particular, that of literature, of the arts, of musical form, infers the necessary possibility of this "real presence"', 3.

[21]   Another phrase borrowed from George Steiner, where a text 'can mean this and this, but not that'; Steiner, *Real Presences*, 44.

[22]   Vincent Brummer, 'Philosophy, Theology, and the Reading of Texts', *Religious Studies* 27/3 (1991), 462.

[23]   Max Picard, *Die Welt des Schweigens* (Erlenbach: Eugen Rentsch Verlag, 1948); trans. Stanley Goodman as *The World of Silence* (London: Harvill, 1948; repr. Chicago: Regnery Gateway, 1952), 227.

[24]   Picard, *The World of Silence*, 227.

'silences' surround the Christ-Child, and, for Messiaen, 'each silence' revealed the awe-inspiring experience of 'sounds and colours'.

Sound and Colour

> I am all the same affected by a sort of synaesthesia, more in my mind than in my body, to see inwardly, in my mind's eye, colors that move with the music; and I vividly sense these colors, and sometimes I've precisely indicated their correspondence in my scores.[25]

Messiaen saw colours while hearing music. For Messiaen sounds produced colours, and his synaesthetic responses were often the catalyst toward an assent of faith. As he explained:

> Colored music does that which the stained-glass windows and rose windows of the middle ages did: they give us dazzlement. Touching at once our noblest senses: hearing and vision, it shakes our sensibilities into motion, pushes us to go beyond concepts, to approach that which is higher than reason and intuition, that is to say FAITH.[26]

Messiaen's synaesthesia related to sonorities as chords, rather than to keys or particular pitches. As he explained,

> one cannot talk of an exact correspondence between key and color; that would be a rather naïve way of expressing oneself because, as I've said, colors are complex and are linked to equally complex chords and sonorities.[27]

These sonorities are constructed from the pitch-class formations found in his 'modes of limited transposition'.[28] According to Jonathan Bernard, four specific modes – 2, 3, 4 and 6 – had strong connections to colour for Messiaen.[29] Because the composer's synaesthesia was consistent in his pairings of colour with particular modal constructs,

---

[25]   Messiaen, *Music and Color*, 40.

[26]   Messiaen, quoted in Almut Rössler, *Contributions to the Spiritual World of Olivier Messiaen*, trans. Barabara Dagg and Nancy Poland (Duisburg: Gilles and Francke, 1986), 65.

[27]   Messiaen *Music and Color*, 42. Theorist Jonathan Bernard also states: 'For Messiaen we know that it was harmony, specifically *chords*, that produced the response'; Bernard, 'Colour', in *The Messiaen Companion*, ed. Peter Hill (London: Faber and Faber, 1994), 205.

[28]   Unlike major and minor scales, which have twelve transpositions each before they are replicated, the 'modes of limited transposition' are scales constructed in such a manner that they replicate themselves with only a few transpositions. As these 'modes' are transposed successively up semi-tones (e.g. if based on C, then transposed up to C# D, D# etc.) the original set of pitches will reappear at some point before the upper octave is reached (e.g. C an octave higher). The first 'mode of limited transposition' is the whole-tone scale, which is reproduced after two semi-tone transpositions. For a listing of these modes, see Paul Griffiths, *Olivier Messiaen and the Music of Time* (Ithaca: Cornell University Press, 1985), 38–9.

[29]   Jonathan Bernard, 'Messiaen's Synaesthesia: the Correspondence Between Color and Sound Structure in his Music', *Music Perception* 4 (1986), 45. See also Bernard, 'Colour', 208–9.

Bernard explained that Messiaen 'was able to evoke colours consciously through his compositional choices'.[30] Thus Messiaen's synaesthetic responses to sound could directly influence his chord constructions. As he stated, 'I do indeed try to translate colors into music; for me, certain sound complexes and sonorities are linked to complexes of color, and I use them with full knowledge of this'.[31]

Bernard categorized three basic types of colours that Messiaen saw in his music:

> The first type is monochromatic: simply 'green' or 'red', for example. The second type is also of uniform hue, but more complex than the first: two colors are mixed as one might find them blurring into one another at the edges of the bands of a rainbow. These are given hyphenated names, such as 'blue-orange' or 'grey-rose'. The third type includes combinations of varying complexity, ranging from simple pairs of colors ('grey and gold') or triplets ('orange, gold, and milky white'), which conceivably are produced in turn by successive chords; to parallel or vertical bands of three colors simultaneously, of apparently more or less equal strength; to effects involving a dominant color flecked, striped, studded, with one or more others.[32]

The sonic landscape for the 'Regard du silence' must have been a highly colourful experience for Messiaen.[33] This *regard* uses transpositions of 'colour modes' 2, 3, and 4 to create a musical design, certain to have strong colour associations, colour connections that Messiaen would experience as a source of 'dazzlement' that moved him into the orbit of faith. Listeners may not share such synaesthetic reactions to the music, or may have very different colour responses. Listeners do, however, have access to the music, which for Messiaen stimulated such unique, stained-glass-type colour responses. Perhaps the music itself, when understood in conjunction with his verbal commentary in both his preface and programme notes, was also meant to push beyond the tangible.

From Darkness and Silence to 'Silences' that Contemplate Faith

Messiaen's triangulation of faith, silence and darkness in the 'Regard du silence' is musically structured in three distinct sections: an Introduction, two middle 'strophes' and a Coda. The composer commented on the opening in his programme note:

---

[30]   Bernard, 'Colour', 205–6.
[31]   Messiaen, *Music and Color*, 41.
[32]   Bernard, 'Messiaen's Synaesthesia', 44.
[33]   Messiaen's musical contemplation of divine mysteries often corresponded with his synaesthesia, but it is debatable whether he intended the listener to be led toward God through a similar union of sound with colour. All allusions to colour refer to Messiaen's own experience, not to an intended effect for the listener. Bernard suggested that listeners may be able to enter, albeit with difficulty, into Messiaen's synaesthesia by identifying the colours Messiaen spoke of while hearing the modal constructions, if one 'is prepared to do some homework'. Bernard presented the possibility of 'the development of facility with the modes [of limited transposition] at the keyboard, along with the development of sensitivity to absolute pitch for the sake of recognizing the different transpositions of each mode'; Bernard, 'Colour', 216.

Méme canon rythmique par ajout du point que dans la cinquième pièce: 'Regard du Fils sur le Fils' – mais avec une autre musique. La partie proposante use d'un ostinato de dix-sept accords en mode 3⁴. La partie répondante (celle dont les durées sont pointées) use d'un ostinato de dix-sept accords en mode 4⁴. Après cette Introduction où la musique semble sortir du silence comme les couleurs sortent de la nuit, deux Strophes.

Like the one in the fifth piece – 'The Adoration of the Son by the Son' – the rhythmic canon heard here is formed by the addition of dots to the notes of the lower part, it is, however, based on different material. The top part consists of a seventeen-chord ostinato, in mode 3⁴, while the similar ostinato of the lower part is written in mode 4⁴. Following this Introduction – *where the music seems to emerge from silence like colours emerging from the night* – are two Strophes. [34]

Messiaen's comments about the opening, in conjunction with his verbal preface (quoted earlier), offered two meanings for 'silence', each suggestive of the entwining of silence with darkness. The primary way by which silence is understood is as analogous to faith, because in 'each silence' the mysteries of Christ are revealed. These 'silences' are audible as 'sounds and colours' that correspond in the Introduction to the two seventeen-chord ostinatos. These chords are akin to 'colours emerging from the night' or as music emerging from silence. The translation of 'each silence' into audible chords offers ideas of these 'silences' as tangible – something that can be held 'in the hand', as audible 'silences' ('musiques'), and as something visible – an 'upside down rainbow' or 'colours'. This imagery allows us to understand how Messiaen may have experienced this music, which was an experience that catapulted him toward faith. However, the fundamental nature of faith, made audible by the music, is inaudible to reason: 'each silence' points to the complete *otherness* that resides within the darkness of faith.

A second connotation for silence is as the absence of sound. This meaning may be read from Messiaen's description of the music in the Introduction. In his programme notes, he explained the opening as the place 'where the music seems to emerge from silence like colours emerging from the night'. This 'where' is the 'natural silence' that acts as the context for the music itself. Thus each audible 'silence' also emanates from its own silent background. Messiaen's brief sojourn into this meaning for silence, as the absence of sound, did not contradict his contemplation of silence as 'sounds and colours'. This allusion to music's own silent fabric 'colours' his meaning for 'la nuit', 'night', as the *absence* of colour – it might more appropriately be translated as 'darkness'. The initial point of departure for those 'silences from the crib' that make audible the mysteries of faith is itself shrouded in darkness.

The experience of colours proceeding from darkness, and of music sounding through the fabric of silence, can be likened to the experience of words arising from the natural silence of meditation. Similar to Messiaen's description of the opening of this *regard*, meditation itself often proceeds from a quietude. John F. Teahan calls

---

[34]   Messiaen, liner notes for 'Regard du silence', in *Vingt regards sur L'Enfant Jésus* (CD, Erato, 1993), original French 18, English translation 35 (no translator named); emphasis added. I have made one alteration by showing the translation of *la nuit* more literally as 'the night', rather than 'the dark' as in the original translation.

this 'shallow silence', when 'normal desires are forgotten, and ordinarily powerful emotions are pacified. This condition, in which one maintains awareness of ordinary identity and individuality, frequently occurs during successful meditation practice'.[35] Meditation is an act of faith that makes use of discursive reason – to the extent to which it is possible – to reflect upon scripture or a particular divine mystery with the aid of concepts and images. Karol Wojtyla (Pope John Paul II) defines discursive meditation as:

> acts of knowledge and of love wherein the intellect and will function with the aid of the lower sense faculties. Meditation is thus characterized by the activity of the senses, and when it is directed to the consideration of revealed truths, the soul receives them so far as they are perceptible to the senses and the imagination.[36]

The mysteries of faith are formulated in conceptual terms in discursive meditation, just as the 'Regard du silence', through its cognitive structure, meditates on the mysteries of faith revealed in the 'silences'. In the Introduction, the 'silences' that surround the Christ Child, made audible by the music, are akin to the beginnings of discursive reason, where concepts and images are intelligible to the intellect. The opening chords as 'sounds and colours' emerge from music's own silence, analogous to the 'thoughts' and 'intuitions' of meditation. These highly chromatic chords as 'silences' are articulated in a type of 'shallow silence', as may possibly be inferred from the very quiet dynamic, *ppp*. The rhythmic canon of the two seventeen-chord ostinatos, one in each hand (to which Messiaen referred in his note),[37] lends this music a sense of 'intellection', analogous to the use of reason in discursive meditation. The Introduction is never forced or volatile, and its happening in time is calmly organized by the rhythmic canon between the hands.

Meditation makes use of the senses to arrive at a fuller understanding of the contents of faith. Messiaen's synaesthetic experience of 'sounds and colours' also makes use of sense perception to reveal awe, wonder and adoration in the presence of the impalpable 'silences' of Christ. His comments in the programme note regarding the middle strophes reveal the array of colours he sensed:

> Première Strophe. Plusieurs registres, plusieurs intensités, plusieurs colorations, en 'litanie harmonique' sur les notes: sol, fa. On y entend des 'accords à renversements transposés', des 'accords à résonance contractée', le *Thème d'accords* concentré (toutes notes simultanées), des oppositions de couleur entre le mode 3^3 (bleu et vert), le mode 2^2 (mauve et rose dans l'aigu, or et brun dans le grave), le mode 4^4 (violet veiné de blanc), et des arpèges contraires à mains croisées qui frémissent délicatement comme des toiles d'araignée. Vers la fin de la Strophe, le *Thème d'accords* combiné avec lui-même

---

[35]   John F. Teahan, a Thomas Merton scholar, introduces two 'types' of silence, 'shallow' and 'deep', in 'The Place of Silence in Thomas Merton's Life and Thought', in *The Message of Thomas Merton*, ed. Brother Patrick Hart (Kalamazoo, MI: Cistercian Publications, 1981), 93.

[36]   Karol Wojtyla, *Faith According to St John of the Cross* (1948), trans. Jordan Aumann (San Francisco: Ignatius Press, 1981), 152.

[37]   This canon mathematically organizes the two ostinatos in such a way that the right-hand chord pattern repeats three times, while the left-hand ostinato is heard twice.

en mouvement rétrograde et droit, la rétrogradation faisant résonance et réverbération du mouvement droit, comme deux arcs-en-ciel dont l'un entoure l'autre. La deuxième Strophe use des mêmes matériaux que la première, avec quelques changements.

In the first Strophe there are several different registers, several intensities, several bands of colour – forming a 'harmonic litany' on the notes G and F. This section includes 'chords of transposed inversions', 'chords of contracted resonance', a concentrated version of the *Theme of Chords* (all the notes being sounded simultaneously), contrasts of colour between mode 3^3 (blue and green), mode 2^2 (mauve and pink in the treble, gold and brown in the bass) and mode 4^4 (violet, veined with white) – as well as contrary-motion, crossed-hand arpeggios, which quiver with the delicacy of cobwebs. Towards the end of the Strophe, the *Theme of Chords* is combined with itself in both its original and its retrograde forms – the retrogration adding reverberation and resonance to the original (like two rainbows, one encircling the other). The second Strophe is based on the same material as the first, but with certain changes. [38]

The references to colour, such as 'blue and green', 'mauve and pink in the treble, gold and brown in the bass', and 'violet, veined with white', in addition to the image of 'two rainbows encircling one another', suggests the dazzlement of Messiaen's experience. The sound-colours that he sensed were his personal synaesthetic responses; however, the music itself expresses dizzying effects with its collage of colours and musical sounds. The G–F motive harmonized by different chromatic chords (which Messiaen mentions in his note) heralds in the first strophe at an audibly louder dynamic. This motive resonates through repetition, as one might hear the successive invocations of a 'litany'.[39] Messiaen's use of the term 'strophe' applies to the internal structure of this middle section, which repeats itself with a few changes. Towards the end of each strophe, Messiaen employed the 'Theme of Chords'[40] and the simultaneous sounding of its retrograde, causing 'reverberation and resonance'. He explained his vision at this musical juncture as 'two rainbows, one encircling the other'. Though this musical landscape was for Messiaen a glittering array of colours, as in discursive meditation, a sense of structure was maintained, organized by the 'strophic' form. Throughout these two parallel 'strophes', there are many changes of register, texture, dynamic intensities and rhythm that musically portray the dazzlement of Messiaen's sound-colours.

For Messiaen, this stunning array was not an end in itself; the materiality of the music pushed beyond its sonic structure toward the immateriality of faith. This is analogous to the movement from the use of conceptual reason to infused contemplation. The intellect participates actively in its own reasoning, based on

---

[38] Messiaen, liner notes for the 'Regard du silence', original French 18–19, English translation 35–6 (no translator named).

[39] The composer explained a 'harmonic litany' as 'a melodic fragment of two or several notes repeated with different harmonizations'; Olivier Messiaen, *Technique de mon language musical* (Paris: Leduc, 1944); English trans. John Satterfield (Paris: Leduc, 1956), 53.

[40] Messiaen used four musical themes that recur in various *regards*. He called these the 'Theme of God', the 'Theme of Mystical Love', the 'Theme of the Star and the Cross' and the 'Theme of Chords'. This last theme is wholly musical and has no extra-musical connotation.

the input it receives from the sense faculties. However, a *complete* understanding of the divine is incapable of being communicated to the believer through sensory knowledge; all concepts or images of God are infinitely separated from the divine. The concepts within the language acts of discursive reason cannot fully signify the 'mysteries' that such concepts express. Therefore dissatisfaction slowly ensues and the intellect, still moved by grace, desires to go beyond discursive reasoning. Eventually there is a movement, by faith, towards mystical or infused contemplation, where concepts and images give way to a mystical 'knowledge' of an un-definable perception of God. Wojtyla, in his analysis of this type of knowledge for St John of the Cross, explained:

> As regards the object contemplated, there is some knowledge of it, but it is also obscure, confused and general; in fact the perfection of contemplation is measured by the imperceptibility of the object, its lack of any particular form in which the intellect can naturally come to rest.[41]

Infused or mystical contemplation in its most strict sense is an awareness or knowledge of God that lies outside the boundaries of language, images and concepts. The *meaning* presented to the intellect is ineffable. Contemplative activity is always beyond analysis and description – it is the certain knowledge of unknowable obscurity. One approaches the unapproachable essence of the divine, but no understanding is accorded to the intellect. Mystical contemplation can only be experienced, but nothing meaningful can be said of the divine truths imparted to the soul. Contemplation is 'silent' because language cannot speak of it. It can only be arrived at through 'faith' because no idea can aspire to the 'unknowing' reality of God, and contemplation is 'darkness' because its meaning transcends reason.

The movement from meditation to mystical contemplation often journeys from the quietude of silence to language acts utilizing concepts and images, to more passive moments whereby the intellect through grace transcends reasoning to rest in the darkness of faith. Similarly, Messiaen experienced 'sounds and colours' that acted to dazzle the senses of hearing and seeing, and did so in order eventually to transcend the senses. Just as transcending the senses in meditation means entering the 'darkness' of contemplation, finding where within the 'Regard du silence' we can 'hear' what it means for music to contemplate mystically the mysteries of Christ in 'each silence', in the *truest sense,* is beyond possibility. Infused or mystical contemplation cannot be communicated in any way through the senses.

However, Messiaen's prose for the closing Coda suggests several correspondences with what has been said of contemplation:

> La Coda reprend la polymodalité de l'Introduction, dans le registre suraigu, en alternant les accords entre les deux mains: musique multicolore et impalpable, en confetti, en pierreries légères, en reflets entrechoqués.

---

41   Wojtyla, *Faith According to St John of the Cross*, 157.

The Coda returns to the polymodality of the Introduction, alternating the chords between the two hands in the top register of the keyboard: this is multi-coloured and intangible music – music of confetti and delicate jewels, with colliding reflections.[42]

This music is 'multi-coloured' but also 'impalpable' or 'intangible' as, similarly, the infusion of divine grace in contemplation is connatural to God's *brilliance* yet 'darkness' to conceptual reason. Messiaen expressed the intangibility of this music by relating it to 'confetti' – which is often numerous in appearance and difficult to hold – and with the image of 'delicate jewels' that must be handled with great care. Like 'confetti' or 'delicate jewels' the mysteries of Christ are numerous and ineffable, and in the darkness of infused contemplation these 'mysteries' are too delicate for the language acts of reason to possess.[43]

The music that Messiaen *saw* as 'multi-coloured' and sensed as 'intangible' brought back a condensed version of the opening chord constructions. The Coda is of contrasting rhythmic character compared to the previous sections. Juxtapositions of conflicting rhythms and the use of rhythmic canon have been replaced by an even rhythmic flow of chords – also 'numerous' – alternating between the hands; in accordance with Messiaen's image, these portray 'confetti' and 'colliding reflections'. Messiaen pointed out that these alternating chords are heard in the 'top register' and that the music continues to ascend and transpose itself upward. Accordingly this shift in register will affect the music's shading. Messiaen explained the relationship between register and colour in his music:

When I move the same chord from midrange up one octave, the same color is reproduced shaded toward white – which is to say, lighter. When I move the same chord from midrange down an octave, the same chord is reproduced, toned down by black – which is to say, darker.[44]

For Messiaen, music became 'lighter' as sounds ascended upward. As the colours became 'lighter' and more transparent, Messiaen made audible a gradual slowing and quieting of the music that seemed to approach silence itself. As Peter Hill observed: 'The remarkable Coda fuses rhythmic stillness with these glinting colours as the harmonies of the earlier canon circle in even semiquavers, with a long diminuendo to the edge of silence.'[45] This is akin to the movement toward the darkness of

[42]   Messiaen, liner notes for the 'Regard du silence', original French 19, English translation 36 (no translator named).

[43]   In *The Spiritual Canticle* (an earlier poem and mystical commentary by St John of the Cross), St John explained the 'numerous' and ineffable mysteries of Christ with his analogy of the 'high caverns in the rock/which are so well concealed' (from Stanza 37). St John's commentary: 'They are so well concealed that however numerous are the mysteries and marvels that holy doctors have discovered and saintly souls understood in this earthly life, all the more is yet to be said and understood. There is much to fathom in Christ, for he is like an abundant mine with many recesses of treasures, so that however deep individuals may go they never reach the end or bottom, but rather in every recess find new veins with new riches everywhere'; *The Collected Works*, 615–16.

[44]   Messiaen, *Music and Color*, 64.

[45]   Peter Hill, 'Piano Music I', in *The Messiaen Companion*, 101.

contemplation, where one seems enveloped by the 'silences' that surround God – the 'silences' of faith that lie beyond hearing because they cannot be apprehended by conceptual reason. Max Picard's idea that 'silence is never more audible than when the last sound of music has died away',[46] well describes how the 'Regard du silence', which originally arose from silence to make audible 'each silence from the crib', now recedes towards silence, as colours evaporating into God's ineffable light.

The 'Dark Night' of Silence

As we've seen, Messiaen's contemplation of silence entailed two meanings for 'silence', first as *absence* or *negation* of sound and, second, as an audible expression of the mysteries of Christ, which Messiaen experienced as 'sounds and colours'. We can understand St John's use of the metaphor of a 'dark night' in the opening stanzas of his poem 'The Dark Night' in two corresponding ways. First, as the process of asceticism that puts the senses to sleep in mortification of natural desires – a process that entails the *negation* of all that is not of the divine. Second, as the 'darkness' produced in the intellect by the excessive light of faith.

The first two stanzas of 'The Dark Night' are as follows:

En una noche oscura,	One dark night,
con ansias, en amores inflamada,	fired with love's urgent longings
¡oh dichosa ventura!	– ah, the sheer grace! –
salí sin ser notada	I went out unseen,
estando ya mi casa sosegada	My house being now all stilled.
A oscuras y segura,	In darkness, and secure,
por la secreta escala disfrazada,	by the secret ladder disguised,
¡oh dichosa ventura!	– ah, the sheer grace! –
a oscuras y en celada,	in darkness and concealment,
estando ya mi casa sosegada.	my house being now all stilled.[47]

St John provides the reader with this summary for the first stanza:

In this stanza the soul desires to declare in summary fashion that it departed on a dark night, attracted by God and enkindled with love for him alone. This dark night is a privation and purgation of all sensible appetites for the external things of the world, the delights of the flesh, and the gratifications of the will. All this deprivation is wrought in the purgation of sense. That is why the poem proclaims that the soul departed when its house was stilled, for the appetites of the sensory part were stilled and asleep in the soul, and the soul was stilled in them.[48]

---

[46]   Picard, *The World of Silence*, 27.

[47]   St John of the Cross, 'The Poetry', in *The Collected Works*, 50–51.

[48]   St John of the Cross, *The Ascent*, Book 1, Chapter 1, 119.

In the first stanza, 'dark night' refers to the mortification of sense appetites by which 'My house' – the sense faculties of the contemplative – was 'all stilled'. Wojtyla explains this meaning for 'night':

> The reason for using the term 'night' is that, just as night designates the privation of the light by means of which objects are visible to us, so metaphorically it signifies the privation of the psychological light whereby naturally desirable objects are presented to the appetite and thus stimulate a desire for them.[49]

This process is *purgative*, in which one is conformed, 'fired by love's urgent longings', to God's will by a detachment from all that is not of the divine through a deprivation of sense appetites. This purgation *darkens* the desires of the senses (which St John says are 'stilled' and 'asleep'), so God alone can be heard, the quieting of the appetites of the senses necessary for infused contemplation.

Similarly, Messiaen's initial movement towards 'sounds and colours' originated in the 'stillness' of music's 'own house'. His use of 'la nuit' was similar to St John's use of the word in Spanish, 'noche', which denoted the same quality for 'night' as darkness. Just as Messiaen used 'la nuit' to imply the *absence* of colour – which in musical terms paralleled music's own *silence* – St John used 'noche' to refer to *the negation of all that is not God*. This is the purgation necessary before one can 'hear' God by faith. As the 'night' of music's silence makes possible the expression of 'each silence from the crib' that are the 'mysteries of Jesus Christ', the calming of the appetites by the 'night' of the senses prepares the soul, by grace, for the divine indwelling. This purgation, by 'the sheer grace!', transforms the sense faculties so everything within the soul is centred upon the love of God. Similarly, this *regard*'s silent surface is *transformed* by 'sounds and colours', the music itself, to make audible Messiaen's gazing into the 'silences' of Christ.

The meaning of 'darkness' in Stanza 2 is closely aligned with what has been said of the act of faith in infused contemplation. Faith, an assent of the intellect, being the proper means to union with God, follows a dark or hidden path. In this stanza, the 'secret ladder' is faith. It is secret 'because all the rungs or articles of faith are secret to and hidden from both the senses and the intellect'.[50] The type of knowledge that faith imparts to the intellect is one of 'unknowing'. St John explained, 'the intellect knows only in the natural way, that is by means of the senses'.[51] However, faith 'informs us of matters we have never seen or known, either in themselves or in their likenesses'.[52]

At first glance, Messiaen's expression of the mysteries of faith 'in each silence' as 'sounds and colours' significantly contrasts with St John's understanding of faith as a 'dark night'. Upon closer scrutiny, when looking more specifically at *why* faith is for St John of the Cross 'darkness', we find a strong connection with Messiaen's 'sounds and colours' that push towards contemplation of the mysteries of Christ.

---

[49]   Wojtyla, *Faith According to St. John of the Cross*, 97.
[50]   St John of the Cross, *The Ascent*, Book 2, Chapter 1, 154.
[51]   *Ibid.*, Chapter 2, 157.
[52]   *Ibid.*, Chapter 3, 158.

Faith, the unknowing knowledge of God, said St John of the Cross, is the 'excessive light of faith', a 'thick darkness' to our intellect.[53] To human reason, faith is darkness, but for St John of the Cross, faith is connatural to God, which means that faith contains within it something of the unapproachable and 'dazzling' light of the divine. St John of the Cross explained why this divine light produced darkness:

> The sun so obscures all other lights that they do not seem to be lights at all when it is shining, and instead of affording vision to the eyes, it overwhelms, blinds, and deprives them of vision since its light is excessive and unproportioned to the visual faculty. Similarly, the light of faith in its abundance suppresses and overwhelms that of the intellect.[54]

When St John spoke of faith as 'darkness', he spoke in terms of how human reason *perceives* faith. In essence, faith in its truest reality is a super-natural brightness, the light of God, which is blinding to reason. Messiaen's idea of 'sounds and colours' carries with it similar connotations. Christ's divine nature was for Messiaen the dazzlement of 'sounds and colours' that pushed beyond the senses. Further, Messiaen's experience of the closing Coda was perhaps an ineffable, inwardly visual experience of colliding colours made intangible by excessive light as the music ascended to the extreme upper registers of the piano. Yet the divine in its purest reality will always be to finite reason an experience of *otherness* that is darkness to the intellect.

§

Acts of faith such as discursive meditation and mystical contemplation, the metaphor of faith as a 'dark night' and Messiaen's 'Regard du silence' are all modes of 'unknowing knowledge' that entwine faith, darkness and silence. For Messiaen, 'each silence' could be made sensible through a musical landscape where its 'sounds and colours' communicated the ineffable mysteries of Christ, just as faith communicates what is beyond conceptual or empirical understanding to the intellect. Messiaen's *regard* evokes sounds from the natural silence of the music, which are likened to colours emerging from darkness, akin to the emergence of thoughts in the quietude of meditation. The music, which provoked Messiaen's synaesthetic colour responses, depicts the dazzlement of 'sounds and colours' through a changing musical fabric of differing registers, intensities, rhythms and textures. For Messiaen, 'sounds and colours' move the senses beyond the material toward the immateriality of faith. The chords that originally signified the emergence of 'sounds and colours' are by the close of the 'Regard du silence' described by Messiaen as 'multi-coloured' and 'impalpable'; analogously, the intellect moves beyond the use of reason and in infused contemplation rests in the 'dark night' of faith. Messiaen's music assents to the darkness of faith through a glittering herald of sounds that make present the mysteries of Christ – mysteries that are evoked as audible 'silences', but whose contents, the essence of God in the flesh as an Infant, are impalpable 'silences' to the mind's ear.

---

[53]   *Ibid.*, Chapter 3, 157.
[54]   *Ibid.*, Chapter 3, 157.

Chapter 3

Sounding Silence, Moving Stillness: Olivier Messiaen's *Le banquet céleste*

Jan Christiaens

Sounds in Time versus Silence and Timelessness

Among the fine arts, music has always been considered a privileged medium when it comes to expressing philosophical or religious ideas. Throughout the history of music aesthetics, music's immateriality has been interpreted as a warrant of its ability to reach the transcendental realm. The music philosophies of Augustine, Schelling and Schopenhauer – to name but a few – are a case in point. In the sixth book of De Musica, Augustine describes how music can foster man's detachment from the material world and his ascent to God. This is possible, Augustine continues, due to the numerical nature of music, which it shares with the material world – created and ordered according to number, as well as with God: the immaterial source of all number and order.[1] Friedrich Schelling (1775–1854) held a similarly ambivalent view of music. While its sound-material makes it belong wholly to the material world, it is at the same time the most abstract and spiritual artform. In its temporal dimension it presents pure movement, the becoming of things, in short the very essence of reality.[2] In *The World as Will and Representation*, the primary work by Arthur Schopenhauer (1788–1860), music is identified, as it was by Schelling, with the very being of the world – which is, according to Schopenhauer, the Will.[3] Artforms other than music only furnish representations of Ideas, which are themselves copies of the Will. Thus the arts are in fact a copy of a copy of the essence of the world. Music is given a unique position among the arts, since it penetrates the Will itself. Therefore, Schopenhauer could paraphrase the famous dictum of Gottfried Wilhelm

---

[1]   Cited in James McKinnon, 'The Early Christian Period and the Latin Middle Ages: Introduction', in *Strunk's Source Readings in Music History*, rev. ed. Leo Treitler (New York: W. W. Norton, 1998), 113–14.

[2]   Edward Lippman, *A History of Western Musical Aesthetics* (Lincoln: University of Nebraska Press, 1992), 218–24.

[3]   Lippman, *A History of Western Musical Aesthetics*, 229. See also: Arthur Schopenhauer, *Die Welt als Wille und Vorstellung* (1819, rev. 1844), trans. E. F. J. Payne *The World as Will and Representation* (Indian Hills, CO: Falcon's Wing Press, 1958; repr. with minor corrections, New York: Dover, 1966), 255–67, esp. paragraph 52.

Leibniz in the following way: 'Music is an unconscious exercise in metaphysics in which the mind does not know it is philosophizing.'[4]

In all these views, music was conceived as a more powerful philosophical instrument than verbal language, as an insurmountable gap was perceived between words and transcendental reality. Not only in philosophical reflection about music, however, was this topic developed. Many composers also have developed individual kinds of music, albeit intuitively, that aim at expressing higher truths. The twentieth-century composer, Olivier Messiaen (1908–1992), explicitly created his music with this aim. He had a clear awareness of the particular power of music:

> Most of the arts are unsuited to the expression of religious truths. Only music, the most immaterial of all, comes close to it. … In a certain sense, music possesses a power that is superior to the image and the word because it is immaterial and appeals more to the intellect and to thought than the other arts.[5]

The religious truths mentioned by Messiaen are dogmas of the Roman Catholic faith. The titles of his religious works put us on the trail of his preferred 'truths'. *La Nativité du Seigneur*, *La Transfiguration de notre Seigneur Jésus-Christ*, *L'Ascension*, *Messe de la Pentecôte*, *Méditations sur le mystère de la Sainte Trinité*, to name but a few. These titles read as a theology of glory, for they all have one feature in common: they deal with the glorification of Christ as the Son of God. Messiaen's music is fundamentally determined by his preoccupation with translating into music this fusion of the divine and the human, of the eternal and the temporal.

> The first idea I wanted to express, the most important, is the existence of the truths of Catholic faith. I have the good fortune to be a Catholic. I was born a believer, and the Scriptures impressed me even as a child. The illumination of the theological truths of the Catholic faith is the first aspect of my work, the noblest, and no doubt the most useful and most valuable – perhaps the only one I won't regret at the hour of my death.[6]

Generally speaking, this preoccupation with Catholic faith gave birth in Messiaen's oeuvre to two opposing styles of music. On one side of the spectrum, there is a kind of exalted, dazzling music, rhythmically complex, usually in a rather fast tempo, with loud dynamics and a bright, extensive instrumentation. This is the kind of music with which Messiaen wanted to celebrate the greatness and the splendour of these religious dogmas.[7] On the other side stands a kind of music characterized by a very slow tempo, very soft dynamics, harmonic stasis and a silent, contemplative

---

[4]   Schopenhauer, *The World as Will and Representation*, 264. Leibniz's dictum reads: 'Musica est exercitium arithmeticae occultum nescientis se numerare animi' ('music is an unconscious exercise in arithmetic in which the mind does not know it is counting').

[5]   Olivier Messiaen, *Music and Color: Conversations with Claude Samuel*, trans. E. Thomas Glasgow (Oregon: Amadeus Press, 1994), 27, 29.

[6]   Messiaen, *Music and Color*, 20–21.

[7]   Good examples of this type of music are the second of the *Trois petites liturgies de la Présence Divine*, the last of the *Vingt regards sur l'Enfant Jésus*, and 'Dieu parmi nous', the last part of *La Nativité*.

atmosphere.[8] It is this type of music that will be dealt with here, in the example of its prototype, Messiaen's first published organ work, *Le banquet céleste*.[9]

In this composition Messiaen, then twenty years old, had already reached an astonishing mastery in bringing about a sense of immateriality, silence and timelessness. The score's biblical inscription leaves no doubt as to his religious associations with this piece: 'Those who eat my flesh and drink my blood abide in me, and I in them' (*John* 6, 56). With these words of Christ, St John the Evangelist is referring to the Eucharist. According to Roman Catholic theology, the consecration of the host and the wine during the Eucharist renders Christ really present in the shape of bread and wine. Thus the faithful consumption of the host and wine would lead any who so believed to abide in Christ.

With *Le banquet céleste*, intended for performance during communion, Messiaen wanted to intensify the atmosphere of silent contemplation he associated with communion. His strategy for doing this, in this piece as elsewhere, was to extract characteristics from the religious content that were general enough to allow for a musical translation. In this organ piece, to my mind, these characteristics are silence and timelessness. On the one hand, they touch the core of the attitude of the faithful during communion, for the contemplation of the presence of Christ during communion – that is the presence of the Eternal in the temporal world – usually happens in silence. On the other, silence and timelessness are concepts general enough to serve as aesthetic guidelines for composing music. By starting with these common elements, Messiaen tried to tune his music to the religious content, or, at least, to create the appropriate atmosphere to accompany the Roman Catholic ritual of communion.

Still, the question remains: is music capable of evoking this silence and timelessness, and the religious dogmas for which they stand? The composer himself seemed to have doubted this, as he indicated in the above quotation that music, thanks to its immateriality, merely 'comes close' to expressing these truths.[10] By connecting the degree of immateriality of the arts with the capability of expressing religious content, Messiaen seemed to admit that that which gives art its very objectivity and existence – a certain degree of materiality – at the same time prevents it from fulfilling what for him was its deepest function, namely the expression of religious truths. Although he stated that music is the most immaterial of all arts, its residuum of materiality seems to be incongruent with the religious truths he preferred.

---

[8] As Jonathan Harvey noted: 'Although I believe this "stillness" can be found in all great music, there are occasions when composers make us especially aware of its presence'; Harvey, *In Quest of Spirit: Thoughts on Music* (Berkeley and Los Angeles: University of California Press, 1999), 67. *Le banquet céleste* certainly represents such an occasion, since Messiaen directed creative energy towards bringing about an awareness of stillness and timelessness.

[9] Olivier Messiaen, *Le banquet céleste: pour orgue* (Paris: Alphonse Leduc, 1934); nouvelle éd. (Paris: Leduc, 1960). Other well-known examples include the two *Louange* movements from the *Quatuor pour la fin du temps*, 'Le baiser de l'Enfant-Jésus' from *Vingt regards sur l'Enfant Jésus*, and 'Prière du Christ montant vers son Père', the last part of *L'Ascension*.

[10] See footnote 5.

As an art consisting of sounds organized in time, music has little in common with the heavenly visions of silence and timelessness that played such an important role in Messiaen's music. 'I aspire toward eternity, but I'm not suffering while living in time, all the less so since time has always been at the centre of my preoccupations.'[11] In interviews, Messiaen repeatedly insisted on his 'desire to stop time'.[12] Paul Griffiths rightly discerned this desire to be 'the generative and fundamental substance of Messiaen's music'.[13] Moreover, this aspiration towards a certain kind of stasis is closely connected to another of Messiaen's preoccupations: creating a kind of music that bathes in silence. In *Le banquet céleste*, the sounds seem to emerge almost imperceptibly from the silence surrounding them. In short, Messiaen's theological music confronts us with a paradox: sounds moving in time are being used as an evocation of a silent eternity.

So the question becomes: how did Messiaen go about securing his object? The above quotation again contains a hint, for besides noting music's immateriality, Messiaen praised the fact that it appeals more to the intellect and to thought than the other arts. Here he gave us a clue to his compositional strategies: it is not so much the music as such, i.e. as a temporal art, as the way in which it acts upon the psychology of auditory perception that is the action field of Messiaen's theological music. This is an aspect, however, that is regularly disregarded in Messiaen scholarship.[14]

Yet the composer's preoccupation with the impact of his music on audiences was not to be misunderstood. For instance, in the foreword to *Quatuor pour la fin du temps*, Messiaen clearly indicated how he wanted to bring the listener closer to eternity and infinity.[15] In analyses of his own works, contained in *Traité de rythme, de couleur et d'ornithologie*, as much attention is devoted to the intended impact of the music as to technical analysis of it.[16] In the case of Messiaen's theological music, this preoccupation is more than merely a solicitude for communication common to all composers. As will be shown below, Messiaen perspicaciously manipulated the parameters of his musical language in effective ways, so that it was seamlessly tuned to secure the intended effects on his audience.

Thus this investigation into key concepts within Messiaen's theological aesthetic – silence and timelessness – will pass through analytical examination of *Le banquet céleste*. Even lacking knowledge of Messiaen's prefatory words to the score, there may be a certain consensus about the atmosphere in which this piece bathes: it brings

---

[11]   Messiaen, *Music and Color*, 34.

[12]   Antoine Goléa, *Rencontres avec Olivier Messiaen* (Paris: Slatkine, 1984), 64.

[13]   Paul Griffiths, *Olivier Messiaen and the Music of Time* (London: Faber and Faber, 1985), 17.

[14]   For instance, in Ian Darbyshire, 'Messiaen and the Representation of the Theological Illusion of Time', in *Messiaen's Language of Mystical Love*, ed. Siglind Bruhn (New York: Garland, 1998), 33–51. The author focused exclusively on the symbolism of Messiaen's compositional techniques, without taking into account their intended effects on human perceptive faculties.

[15]   Olivier Messiaen, Foreword to *Quatuor pour la fin du temps* (Paris: Durand, 1941), 2.

[16]   See for example the discussion of *Mode de valeurs et d'intensités*, in Olivier Messiaen, *Traité de rythme, de couleur et d'ornithologie* (Paris: Alphonse Leduc, 1996), 3: 125–31.

about an impression of slowness bordering on timelessness, stillness, silence and, if you wish, contemplation. Below, I shall analyse the ways in which the work's harmonic, formal and textural lay-out contributes to bringing about this impression. My aim is to show that Messiaen's later comment about the piece – 'a very charming, tender, soft and spring-like piece that has nothing extraordinary about it'[17] – is too modest a statement to do the work justice.

Stasis and/as Silence

Music as an evocation of silence: it's hard to imagine a stronger paradox. As such, it is closely related to the theological paradox that most fascinated Messiaen: the dogma of the incarnation of God in Christ, the fusion of the Eternal with the temporal. Messiaen's predilection for such paradoxes stems from the fact that they contain a 'charming impossibility', a feature on which he built his most innovative compositional techniques.

> First of all, I must speak to you about a phenomenon that, if I may say so, has dominated my whole life as a composer and that in my first treatise I called, perhaps a bit naively, 'the charm of impossibilities'. I always thought a technical process had all the more power when it came up, in its very essence, against an insuperable obstacle. This is exactly the case in my three principal innovations: modes of limited transpositions, non-retrogradable rhythms, and symmetrical permutations.[18]

The impossibility dealt with here, that of evoking silence in music, is not an insuperable obstacle. If silence were to be understood as total absence of sound, there would be no possibility whatever to evoke silence in music. But silence is not just absence of sound, or emptiness. Besides this evident physico-acoustic definition, silence can also mean a certain quality in the mind of the listener, brought about by a specific acoustic atmosphere in the music.[19] As such, silence stands for a definite kind of presence rather than absence.

There are three main strategies Messiaen used to organize this presence in *Le banquet céleste*, so that an impression of silence is brought about in the mind of the listener. First, the beginning and ending of the piece seem to emerge from and flow back into silence in a very natural way. The first bars are in a *pianissimo* dynamic, to which Messiaen added *lointain, mystérieux* ('from afar, mysteriously') as a performance indication. Thus the piece does not start with a clear-cut caesura between silence and sound, but rather from a desire to continue the preceding silence. Also in the final bars, it is as if Messiaen leads the music back into its natural biotope of silence. From bar 18 onwards, the organ sound is gradually decomposed by the systematic elimination of organ stops, until at the end only a very soft sound

---

[17]   Messiaen, *Music and Color*, 118.

[18]   *Ibid.*, 47–8.

[19]   See Thomas Emmerig, 'Stille in der Musik und der "leere Raum" in der Zeichnung', *Musiktheorie* 19/3 (2004), 213–14.

remains.[20] In doing this, Messiaen in effect realized a radical shift in perspective. Whereas in traditional music, sound is the central paradigm and the starting point of composers' creative activity, in many twentieth-century compositions there seems to be a shift towards silence or at least a desire to approximate it musically.[21] Messiaen's *Le banquet céleste* is an early example of this tendency, which would later, in the music of Morton Feldman, Luigo Nono, Arvo Pärt and others, become prominent. In this kind of music, silence is the starting point. It is the continuum surrounding the composition, the silent totality in which the sounding composition emerges as an island in a sea of silence. As I've shown, in *Le banquet céleste* this emergence hardly disturbs the quiet of the sea.

Messiaen's second strategy for creating an impression of silence for the listener involved the acoustic qualities of sound. It is no coincidence that he composed this piece for organ, for the modern organ is one of the few instruments that enable a completely immovable and static sound. Since its sound production is not directly dependent on human agency, as with bowed, struck or wind instruments, its produced sounds do not have the inflections or irregularities typical of these instruments, nor are they limited in time or in dynamics by respiration. Due to their static and timeless qualities, organ sounds are entirely appropriate for evoking religious ideas. Put another way, because of its constancy, an organ sound has a kind of inherent silence that is absent in sounds produced on bowed, struck or wind instruments. In this respect, the imperturbable constant flow of soft sound in *Le banquet céleste* contributes to the evocation of silence. It also shows that a composer does not have to write many rests or *fermata* symbols to evoke silence, since in *Le banquet céleste* there is an uninterrupted flow of sound throughout. In fact, this continuous flow paradoxically adds to the creation of a silent atmosphere. For just as silence is total and all-encompassing – otherwise it is not silence – in *Le banquet céleste* the sound continuum is 'total' and all-encompassing, effective in evoking the total coverage of silence.

In addition to these aspects of volume and sound production, there is, thirdly, a more inherently compositional strategy for creating a sense of silence in music. This strategy amounts to a radical changing of so-called 'intentional listening'. By this term, I mean the mental acts that enable a listener of a piece of music to follow and to re-execute on an intellectual level the inherent logic of the tone-relations. Intentional listening is to a large extent conditioned by tonal music, since this is the repertoire with which most people are familiar. As I will show in the analysis below, in *Le banquet céleste* Messiaen deliberately played upon these tonal expectations with a view to creating a kind of 'intentional silence'. When the obvious grammatical frame for intentional listening fails in part, the listener is guided towards other experiences. Messiaen organized the features of the piece so that intentional listening based on tonal expectations (harmony, form, texture, tempo, speed etc.) was brought to silence.

---

[20]   Notice that in this respect, the final bars of *Le banquet céleste* are similar to Haydn's *Farewell Symphony*. In the last bars of the Finale, Haydn also gradually decomposes the orchestral sound by letting the players go off stage one by one.

[21]   Wilhelm Seidel, 'Stille', in *Die Musik in Geschichte und Gegenwart*, 2nd ed., ed. Ludwig Finscher (Kassel: Bärenreiter, 1998), 8: 1760.

Generally speaking, he did this by approximating musically the typical dynamic and structural qualities of silence.

Franz Schubert's Lied, *Meeres Stille* (1815), is a good example of this kind of strategy. In order to represent the stillness of the sea, Schubert wrote a piano accompaniment with very soft, arpeggiated chords, to be played in a slow tempo and at an utterly regular pace. In its stillness and stasis – the dynamic and structural qualities of silence – this music tried to approximate stillness in sound. Notice how in the word 'stillness', meaning quiet as well as immovability, the relation between silence and a corresponding structural quality merges.

Thus music that aims to represent an atmosphere of silence might similarly take into account these general structural features, transposing them onto a compositional-technical level. The challenge for Messiaen in *Le banquet céleste* was to create a kind of music that in its stillness and stasis created the appropriate atmosphere to accompany what for Catholics is the high point of Eucharist: the silent contemplation of Christ during communion. Since the forementioned qualities of silence are incarnations of conceptions of time, it was in this direction that Messiaen focused his creative energy.

Harmony and Form in *Le banquet céleste*: the Transfiguration of Teleology in Theology

It is significant that Messiaen designed his own modal scale-system, with a view to the realization of a certain conception of time. In the traditional scales of tonal music the sequential tones of the octave have hierachical relationships to each other. The implied relations of tension and resolution have a quality of temporal articulation that contribute to a strong sense of linearity. In classical and romantic music, the degrees of these tonal scales are attributed certain harmonic functions. A triadic chord built on the fifth degree, for instance, has an inherent harmonic tension that seeks resolution in the triadic chord on the first degree, the tonic. In this system of goal-oriented functional harmony, a linear and progressive time concept is articulated by short and long-term cadential goals that underlay the foundations of compositional structures.

In contrast to tonal hierarchies, Messiaen's modes involve symmetrical organizations of the tones of the octave. Modal music, as the most important alternative to tonality, does not have a linear force, since a mode is simply a tone-supply, without implicit hierarchical relations between the tones. Composers often use modal scales to suspend linear time, or to draw attention to inherent sound qualities and colours, as in so much of Debussy's music. Messiaen created seven modes, each of which is organized symmetrically, built upon a repeating unit. Because of their symmetry, these modes avoid the goal orientation of the tonal system.

> When a mode divides the octave symmetrically, … it becomes a musical expression of suspension in space. Here music is not symbolizing; it is itself a form of prayer, a means

for experiencing unity. It is not a code for pointing *to* something; rather, it seems to have an inner feeling *of* something.[22]

Furthermore, Messiaen's modes cannot be transposed as distinct entities on every degree of the scale, as in tonal music. Since each is built on a repeating unit, the pitches of the original mode reappear after a limited number of transpositions. That's why Messiaen called them the 'modes of limited transposition'.[23]

In *Le banquet céleste*, Messiaen used his favourite mode of limited transposition – the second – shifting constantly between its first (2.1) and second (2.2) transpositions (see Ex. 3.1).[24]

Ex. 3.1   Mode 2, in its first (2.1) and second (2.2) transpositions

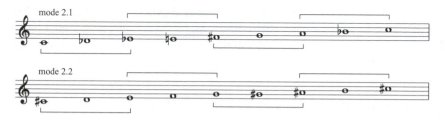

The symmetrical construction of this mode, with its repeating unit of a minor third, lends it not only tonal instability, but also its static character. In his *Traité de rythme, de couleur et d'ornithologie*, Messiaen insisted that his modes of limited transposition should not be understood and perceived analogously to modal or tonal scales, for they do not bring about an organization of musical time and space.

> The modes of limited transposition have no tonic nor a dominant. They have no initial nor a final tone. They are not to be understood as a musical space, as is major tonality. They are not a certain order of tones, as is a twelve-tone series. They are colours, harmonic colours.[25]

Whereas major and minor tonalities organize musical space and time in a hierarchical way, articulating a linear, teleological, concept of musical time, Messiaen's modes of limited transposition have no analogous gravitational power. His modal system deliberately avoids all linear and teleological features of tonal music. Instead, Messiaen wanted to establish what he called a 'tonal ubiquity':[26]

---

[22]   Harvey, *In Quest of Spirit*, 71.

[23]   For a more detailed account of the modes of limited transposition, see: Olivier Messiaen, *Technique de mon language musical* (Paris: Alphonse Leduc, 1944), 85; and Antony Pople, 'Messiaen's Musical Language: an Introduction', in *The Messiaen Companion*, ed. Peter Hill (Oregon: Amadeus Press, 1995), 17–31.

[24]   For further details about this 'modulation from one mode to itself', see Messiaen, *Technique de mon language musical*, Chapter 17.

[25]   Messiaen, *Traité de rythme, de couleur et d'ornithologie*, 7: 51.

[26]   Messiaen, Preface to *Quatuor pour la fin du temps*, 1.

there is no hierarchy, no before and after, only an eternal Now of harmonic colours. Still, of all the modes of limited transposition, the second has the most points of contact with tonal functional harmony. The tone-supply of the second mode allows for four major chords (see Ex. 3.2), all of which Messiaen used extensively, though stripped of their tonal-gravitational power.

Ex. 3.2   Mode 2 chords

In *Le banquet céleste*, Messiaen deliberately used two transpositions of the mode, allowing him to play upon its inherent ambiguity. On the one hand, the mode favours tonal relationships, since there are tonic–dominant relationships between the first and second transpositions (see Ex. 3.3a). On the other, the tonal relationships are distorted by augmented-fourth relations, Messiaen's preferred relations within each transposition (see Ex. 3.3b).

Ex. 3.3   (a) Tonal and (b) augmented-fourth relations between the first (2.1) and second (2.2) transpositions of Mode 2

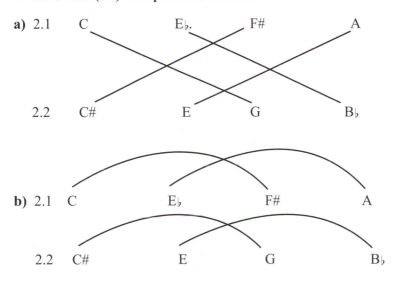

In this way, Messiaen preserved a reminiscence of tonal-functional harmony, while at the same time disturbing it by the most powerful means at his disposal, the tritone – or, as it was in the middle ages, the *diabolus in musica*.

But far from disturbing the celestial banquet, this devil in fact contributes to the unearthly atmosphere of it. A closer look at the harmonies in bars 1 to 3 will make my point clear (see Ex. 3.4).

Ex. 3.4   Messiaen, *Le banquet céleste,* **bars 1–3**

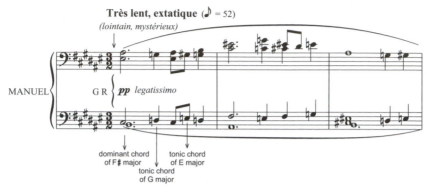

Reproduced with kind permission of Alphonse Leduc & Cie, Paris, owners and publishers for the world.

In the first bar, there are three main harmonies, which can be read as a dominant chord of F# major, a tonic chord of G major and a tonic chord of E major. Note that between the fundamental notes of the first two chords – C# and G♮ – there is an augmented-fourth relation. The tonal resolution of the first chord is only heard at the beginning of the second bar, with a tonic chord of F# major. But here again, Messiaen inserted an augmented-fourth relation, that is between the fundamental notes of the first and second chords of that bar: F# and C♮. Thus the tonal relationships played between the bars are neutralized by the strongest possible non-tonal interval – the augmented fourth – played within each bar. Moreover, since the tonal relationships between chords are never heard within the same bar, and since the tempo of this piece is extremely slow, it is rather difficult for the listener to perceive in sound the tension–resolution relation.[27] Thus, by playing deliberately on the harmonic ambiguity of the second mode of limited transposition, Messiaen lends the long-held chords of *Le banquet céleste* a static, non-developmental character. They are, as John Milson states, 'so pregnant with potential harmonic movement, yet so frozen in time'.[28]

The tempo-indication for the piece adds further to this effect. In the first edition, Messiaen wanted it to be *extrèmement lent* ('extremely slow'). Apparently, his point was not clear enough, for the performances he was able to hear struck him as being played too quickly. Therefore, in the second edition (1960), he not only added a metronome mark ($\mathsf{J} = 52$) and changed the tempo-indication – *très lent, extatique* ('very slow, ecstatically') – but also changed the metre from $\frac{3}{4}$ to $\frac{3}{2}$. When the piece is played at the specified tempo, it is perceived as uncommonly slow. The effect is that musical events belonging to the same time-frame cannot be perceived

---

[27]   In conversation with Claude Samuel, Messiaen assessed the presence of tonal elements in his music as follows: 'Some of my works contain tonal passages, but they are precisely blended with those modes that color them and ultimately have little importance'; in Messiaen, *Music and Color*, 49.

[28]   John Milson, 'Organ Music I', in *The Messiaen Companion*, 63.

as such because of the extremely slow rate at which they are presented. The first chord played at the correct tempo lasts for some seven seconds! Thus, the harmonic destabilization is joined on the temporal level by a perceptual destabilization. By virtue of their slowness, the chords are perceived as self-sufficient icons of eternity rather than as moments in a linear development.

When discussing the theological impact of this piece, only these two aspects (static harmony, extreme slowness) are usually mentioned. Paul Griffiths, for instance, concludes that 'right from the first, and even quite decisively, Messiaen abandons the attunement to measured progress that had been a feature of almost all Western music since the Renaissance'.[29] It seems to me that this is only partially true, as on the formal level there are features attributable to the classical concept of measured progress, as I will now show.

Le banquet céleste can be segmented into three parts, each containing an exposition of the main theme. But whereas the first exposition takes four bars, the second and the third take seven and fourteen bars respectively. This is due mainly to the sequential development of certain motivic cells of the main theme. Not only the segmentation, but also the general dynamic evolution betrays a rather traditional formal concept, with its curve of increasing and decreasing (see Ex. 3.5).

Ex. 3.5   **Messiaen, *Le banquet céleste,* dynamic motion in each exposition**

	bar numbers	dynamic markings
1st exposition	1 to 4 (=4 bars)	*pp*
2nd exposition	5 to 11 (=7 bars)	*peu à peu p* (b. 5) *cresc.* (b. 8) *mf* (b. 10) *peu à peu f* (b. 10-11)
3rd exposition	12 to 25 (=14 bars)	*f* *dim. poco a poco* (b. 20) (pedal) *mf* (b. 21) (pedal) *p* (b. 22); (manual) *pp* (b. 22) (pedal & manual) *pp* (b. 25)

Although the formal organization of the piece suggests a traditional concept of linear time, this is not the impression the listener has when hearing the music, for two reasons. First, the formal segmentation is presented at such a slow pace that the actual proportions between the three segments cannot possibly be perceived adequately. Second, and more importantly, Messiaen designed the texture of the piece in such a remarkable way, that human auditive perception is steered quite prescriptively towards an impression of timelessness and silence. Since it is in this dimension that Messiaen's visionary qualities reveal themselves most clearly, I shall dwell on it a little longer.

---

[29]   Griffiths, *Olivier Messiaen and the Music of Time,* 33.

Messiaen's Intentional Fallacy: Putting a Generous Deceit on the Listener

It is no coincidence that the first chapter of Messiaen's magnum opus *Traité de rythme, de couleur et d'ornithologie* is devoted entirely to the philosophy of time.[30] To Messiaen, time was not only the most wonderful creation of God, it also constituted an aesthetic and compositional *crux*. For in large parts of his *oeuvre*, the desire to stop time and to create a sense of timelessness was his primary preoccupation. To gain an adequate understanding of how Messiaen brought about this sense of timelessness, it is important to have some idea of the prevailing ideas in this first chapter.

The French philosopher Henri Bergson (1859–1941) makes frequent appearances in this chapter. Bergson convincingly showed that the classical concept of time – the one-dimensional, abstract time of Isaac Newton's mechanistic physics – could not do justice to multi-faceted time experience.[31] In fact, Bergson reacted against the Kantian parallelism between time and space, a parallelism that amounted to a spatial hypostasis of time.[32] According to Bergson, this spatial view of time could not capture the true nature of time experience, since it projected spatial categories such as homogeneity and successivity onto time, and by so doing obscured the true nature of time experience. In order to put an end to this spatial contamination of the time concept, Bergson introduced the concept of *durée vécue* ('lived duration') to indicate subjective time experience. As such, it is not homogeneous, but heterogeneous, to be determined not quantitatively but qualitatively, not abstract but concrete, and not objective but subjectively variable. Thus, Bergson made a distinction between the objective, scientific time concept (clock-time) on the one hand, and the subjective experience of time on the other. As an 'immediate given of human consciousness',[33] this subjective experience of time could no longer be considered as an *a priori* schema of transcendental subjectivity, as Kant thought. On the contrary, the 'lived duration' was immanent to its own content, and as such constitutive for human subjectivity.

According to Bergson, the subjective experience of time or duration may vary according to its very content, i.e. according to what exactly takes place in a certain interval of time. Bergson's analysis put into words a very common experience indeed. The same interval of time may be experienced as passing by quickly or, on the contrary, slowly, according to circumstances taking place in that interval of time. When, for example, you have to wait five minutes in the station and you're bored, time will be experienced as passing slowly. When, on the other hand, you're at a party, the same five minutes will generally be experienced as passing quickly. Such an analysis of time experience as a variable, heterogeneous flux proved food and

---

[30]   Messiaen, *Traité de rythme, de couleur et d'ornithologie*, 1: 5–36.

[31]   Henri Bergson, *Essai sur les données immédiates de la conscience* (1889), 6th ed. (Paris: Quadrige, 1997), 68–74.

[32]   In the transcendental aesthetic of his *Critique of Pure Reason*, Kant stated that time and space are the two fundamental perceptual schemata of man; see Immanuel Kant, *Critique of Pure Reason* (1781), trans. Norman Kemp Smith, rev. 2nd ed. (Basingstoke: Palgrave Macmillan, 2003), 67.

[33]   The formulation comes from Bergon's title, *Essai sur les données immédiates de la conscience* (see note 31 in this essay).

drink to a composer whose primary occupation was to play upon the subjective time experience of his audience. For Messiaen, then, a musical time experience could be steered, according to the concrete musical circumstances with which a certain time-interval was filled.

Messiaen cast this Bergsonian analysis into two laws of time experience, the second of which was particularly pertinent to musical time perception.[34] The first law states that in the present, the more events that fill a certain time interval, the shorter it seems to us (and *vice versa*). The second law pertains only to a retrospective appreciation of a time interval. As such, it is the inversion of the first law and reads: in the past, the more events that filled a certain time span, the longer it seems to us now. According to Messiaen, only the second law pertaining to a retrospective appreciation of duration applies to the perception of musical time. In this respect, he was perfectly in keeping with Bergson's own analysis of 'lived duration'. Bergson stated that this 'lived duration' – that is, the continuous flux of actual states of mind – is experienced as belonging to the immediate past.[35]

The Bergsonian opinion that time perception varies according to circumstances was at the core of the music theory of André Souris (1899–1970), a Belgian composer and music theorist, whose name is prominent in the 'Time' chapter of Messiaen's treatise. Messiaen cited abundantly from Souris' article entitled 'Notes sur le rythme concret', which dates from 1948.[36] In it, Souris applied Bergsonian time philosophy to the experience of musical time, by showing how a concrete musical texture shapes its own musical duration.

> We experience that musical duration is not at all a chronometrical duration, and that music does not take place in a pre-existing physical time, but that it generates its own time, which is stretched out, contracted, coloured and qualified by the music.[37]

Souris indicated quite precisely which musical elements could modify time experience: the mode of attack, dynamics, octave position and instrumentation. A short mode of attack with a rather strong dynamic and high octave position contribute to a stretching

---

[34]   Messiaen, *Traité de rythme, de couleur et d'ornithologie*, 1: 10. In fact, Messiaen copied these laws from a philosophy textbook by Armand Cuvillier, *Précis de philosophie: classe de philosophie* (Paris: Armand Colin, 1953).

[35]   This idea is only implicitly present in the *Essai sur les données immédiates de la conscience*. In *Matière et Mémoire* (1896), Bergson expressed it explicitly: 'If one considers the concrete present, as it is lived and experienced by human conscience, then it appears that this present for the most part exists in the immediate past. ... Our perception, however momentary it may be, consists of an innumerable amount of remembered elements. In fact, every perception already is a remembrance'; quoted in Mike Sandbothe, *Die Verzeitlichung der Zeit: Grundtendenzen der modernen Zeitdebatte in Philosophie und Wissenschaft* (Darmstadt: Wissenschaftliche Buchgesellschaft, 1998), 89–90.

[36]   André Souris, 'Notes sur le rythme concret', *Polyphonie* 2 (1948), 4–11; repr. in Souris, *Conditions de la musique et autres écrits* (Bruxelles and Paris: Editions de l'Université de Bruxelles, 1977), 241–7. All further references are to the original journal article.

[37]   *Ibid.*, 6.

out of the subjective time-experience.[38] Messiaen eagerly adopted these insights into (musical) time experience, as they coincided with his preoccupation with creating a sense of timelessness in his music. Bergson's philosophy of time, and the music-theoretical interpretation of it by Souris, corroborated Messiaen's conviction that musical time was not a homogeneous abstract; on the contrary, in every new composition a new experience of time was generated by the specific parametric modalities of the music.

It is astonishing that some twenty years before Souris' article, Messiaen intuitively shaped the musical texture of *Le banquet céleste*, with a view to its religious bearing, according to principles later to be espoused by Souris. Of the organ registration prescribed in Messiaen's score, the *voix céleste* ('celestial voice') is the most remarkable stop.[39] Within this heavenly banquet of sounds, the celestial voice holds pride of place, as it has a characteristic sound that floats over the listeners. The *voix céleste* yields a soft string tone, which is intended to be combined with another soft string stop, such as *salicional* or *viola da gamba*. Although the *voix céleste* has the same pitch as the other stops, it is intentionally tuned slightly off-pitch to produce mild beats with another rank, thus generating a gentle tremolo-effect. It is often used to give a light, wavering, otherworldly quality, a heavenly voice indeed.

This hovering effect is further intensified by the highly un-idiomatic use of the pedal, from bar 12 onwards. Strangely, the pedal gives up its bass function as support for the shifting harmonies. Instead, Messiaen coupled it to the registration of the third manual, the so-called *positif*. The pedal thus produces actual sounds from a combination of high stops (*flute* 4', *nazard* 2 2/3', *doublette* 2' and *piccolo* 1'), pitched between one and four octaves higher than the notated sound. Only in the final bar does Messiaen use a normal pedal registration (*bourdon* 8', *soubasse* 16' and *bourdon* 32'), though the bass supports a dominant-seventh chord that does not resolve. So even here at the end, the pedal part is in a certain sense floating.

The staccato use of the high pedal sound from bar 12 onwards is of particular interest here, because it prefigured Souris' ideas about the variability of rhythm-perception (see Ex. 3.6).

---

[38]   Souris does not mention instrumentation, because 'the variations concerning the diverse instruments are too manifold and too subtle to be generalized'; *ibid.*, 6.

[39]   Although this stop was initially found mainly on organs of the French organ-builder, Aristide Cavaillé-Coll (1811–1899), it was later adopted by organ-builders all over the world. The organ of Sainte-Trinité, the church in Paris where Messiaen served as organist, was built by Cavaillé-Coll.

Ex. 3.6   Messiaen, *Le banquet céleste,* **bars 12–13**

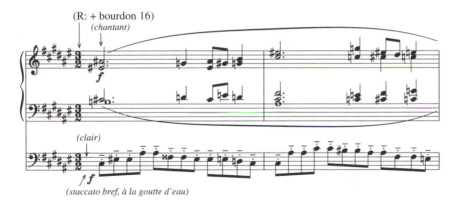

Reproduced with kind permission of Alphonse Leduc & Cie, Paris, owners and publishers for the world.

In this pedal part, Messiaen introduced one of his most experimental organ sonorities, the *staccato bref, à la goutte d'eau* ('short staccato, as waterdrops'). This un-idiomatic use of the organ pedal has baffled many Messiaen scholars. John Milson, for example, questioned: 'What this texture is meant to signify in a piece called *Le banquet céleste* Messiaen never explained, yet its oddness somehow seems justified in music that asks us to ponder the unfathomable.'[40] Paul Griffiths did not mention the pedal part at all, while for Aloyse Michaely the dripping staccato sounds represented the blood drops of Christ on the cross.[41] To my mind, this interpretation reads too much into Messiaen's composition. Moreover, I think that Messiaen's music should be interpreted not so much as a literal imitation of extra-musical ideas, as a presentation of these ideas in and through the music itself. A reference to Messiaen's preoccupation with musical time and its perception may offer some help here.

Starting at bar 12, the staccato pedal tones sustain the third exposition of the theme, which is the longest of the three. From earlier comments about the formal lay-out of the piece, it follows that Messiaen composed an objective slowing down of the rate at which the music unfolds (see Ex. 5). In addition to this objective feature, other aspects play on subjective experience of the music, and by so doing also contribute to an impression of slowing down. The staccato pedal part has characteristic features that, according to Souris, contribute to a stretching out of subjective time experience. To begin with, it has a short mode of attack, poetically specified, as noted above, as *staccato bref, à la goutte d'eau*. Second, the dynamic marking is *forte*, to which Messiaen added the prescription *clair* ('clear, bright'). Third, the octave position of the actual sounds is between one and four octaves higher than the notated sounds.

40   Milson, 'Organ Music I', 63.

41   Aloyse Michaely, *Die Musik Olivier Messiaens: Untersuchungen zum Gesamtschaffen* (Hamburg: Karl Dieter Wagner, 1987), 500.

Finally, the long, sustained chords in the manual are filled by the quavers in the pedal part, affecting the time perception of this passage. Thus the time-span of the exposition theme is filled with more musical events than during its first or second soundings, when there were no short pedal notes but only long, held chords. For me, it is the effect of all these textural peculiarities on the perception of musical duration that gives the odd pedal texture of *Le banquet céleste* its true signification. Thus, in accordance with Bergson's analysis of time experience and the laws of perception derived therefrom, Messiaen achieved a stretching-out of the subjective perception of duration using purely textural means.

Stillness and Timelessness in Music: a Charming Impossibility

To a certain extent, Messiaen's later comment about *Le banquet céleste* – 'a very charming, tender, soft and spring-like piece that has nothing extraordinary about it' – is accurate. For, as Roger Nichols argued, it is indeed tempting to describe this piece as a small work.[42] It is only 25 bars long, and it consists of three quasi-identical statements of a rather simple theme. But the effect on the listener is far from small. By ingeniously casting the harmonic, formal and textural lay-out of *Le banquet céleste*, the twenty-year-old Messiaen continues to force his listeners to rethink their notions of sound and time. As such, the piece reads as a motto of Messiaen's aesthetic and compositional stance: pursuing charming impossibilities that continue to cast their spells on listeners.

---

[42]   Roger Nichols, *Messiaen* (London: Oxford University Press, 1975), 9.

Chapter 4

Going Gently: Contemplating Silences and Cinematic Death

Stan Link

Silence and Stylized Murder in *Road to Perdition*

Death will be here soon enough. Before its arrival we already hear its approach …

> John Rooney and his bodyguards leave O'Neill's bar. They step into the rainy night and move toward their waiting car. Rooney knocks on the window to alert the driver, who isn't responding. Dead already. Just as recognition of what is about to happen sinks into Rooney's face, from further up the street come the flashes of a machine gun. Rooney's men all turn and fire into the shadows. Useless. The hail of bullets out of the darkness is matched only by the relentless rain. Rooney's men are each mowed down in turn – one by one by one. Only Rooney himself has been left untouched. Motionless and with his back to the gunman, he remains clutching the car door handle, now standing in a field of bodies. As rain continues to sheet down, Michael Sullivan approaches out of the darkness, gun at his side. Standing face to face with Rooney, Sullivan remains silent. Rooney's last words, 'I'm glad it's you', break the tacit look between them. Sullivan points the gun from waist level and fires off a medium burst, point blank.

After many viewings, I still find this scene from director Sam Mendes' *Road to Perdition* (2002) hauntingly poetic beyond its brutal content.[1] There is already abundant tragedy in the narrative of Sullivan's need for revenge against his former boss, friend and father figure. Perhaps my reaction can be written off as susceptibility to manipulation. Violent destruction is being made not only presentable, but spectacular. Maybe I've bought into that. But to some degree, the sensuousness of all cinema, even the most austere, feels like manipulation. This may be film's real medium. When I think about this scene, it is indeed surface and presentation, more than the narrative events, that provide an overwhelming share of the poignancy. Examining violence in cinema, Stephen Prince described an historically escalating

---

[1]   *Road to Perdition*, directed by Sam Mendes, cinematography by Conrad Hall, screenplay by David Self after the novel by Max Allan Collins and Richard Piers Rayner, film score by Thomas Newman, supervising sound editor Scott Hecker, foley mixer Lane Birch; with Tom Hanks, Paul Newman, Jude Law, Tyler Hoechlin and Jennifer Jason Leigh, 117 minutes (Dreamworks Pictures, 2002).

'stylistic amplitude' – the ways in which the spectacle of a violent event may be expanded, extended or intensified through editing, multiple points of view, close ups and so on.[2] John Rooney's murder is, in that sense, at a very high 'stylistic amplitude'. The events are not documented photographically as much as seen and painted by an eye and hand given over to impressionistic sensuality.

The stylization is only partially visual, however. Elements such as slow motion, camera angles, editing and lighting indeed play a significant role. But Rooney's violent death is not only visibly amplified, it is aurally lyricized. As beautifully as the cinematography of the glistening street paints an image of loss and regret, the scene's most touching energy surfaces in the invisible fluidity of a precisely calculated soundtrack. Rain sounds provide the warming background radiation for an explosion of violence. The downpour prepares and envelopes the scene well before Rooney and his men step into the night. As they walk to their car, however, the sound of rain dies out, leaving the storm's image behind as a mute witness. Inaudible also is Rooney's voice, along with those of his men. The machine gun aimed at them flickers away, briefly lighting Sullivan's corner of the street, but remains unheard – just like the revolvers answering back. Rooney's men make no sound as they are hit, none as they fall, none while they die. Rooney is still. Sullivan's footsteps on the stones of the street make no sound as he approaches. As the cinematic world floods with vengeance and blood, its sounds, speech and noises have drained away. They aren't just 'inaudible', however, a word implying they are still there simply lurking below perceptibility. Sound is instead just gone – excluded – and its absence becomes the most moving part of the experience for me. Silence is style, but is also an emotional core. With Prince's term turned paradox, silence becomes an unlikely 'amplification' of violent deaths: 100 decibels of soundless bloodshed.

The noise of rain fades gradually back in to swaddle the resignation of Rooney's last words along with the blazes of Sullivan's lethal response. The sound of the scene is wholly unrealistic, and it is especially these moments of its going and coming that reveal its artifice. In clarifying the status and 'fidelity' of sound recordings, Rick Altman noted that they 'do not reproduce sound, they represent sound'.[3] This is all the more true of a scene such as this, a product of digital sound manipulation, post-synchronization and sound effects foley work. We must remember that silence too can be a recording, and that the irreality of a soundless image is an aural fabrication that can only be meaningfully understood as a 'representation'. Silence is a construction at once technical and subjective. 'Construed as representation', Altman continues, 'sound inherits the double mantle of art. Simultaneously capable of misrepresentation and of artistically using all the possibilities of representation, sound thus recovers some of the fascination lost to its reputation as handmaiden of the image'.[4] And yet, *Road To Perdition*'s trick also seems strangely authentic. Even if it wouldn't sound like this, the scene feels affectively almost as though it *should*. Why?

---

    [2]   Stephen Prince, 'Guns and Cameras: From the PCA to the Passion of the Christ', talk given at Vanderbilt University, 30 September 2005.
    [3]   Rick Altman, 'Four and a Half Film Fallacies', in *Sound Theory, Sound Practice*, ed. Rick Altman (New York: Routledge, 1992), 40.
    [4]   *Ibid.*

It is certainly tempting to make a direct connection between the silence of the world and the impending nothingness of death. As a child trying to imagine death, I would stop my ears as tightly as I could, thinking that absolute silence must be what it 'sounded' like. The complete loss of self and senses were only imaginable through silence. Cinematic silence may likewise be an indirect 'representation' of death, but one providing a direct perceptual experience as well. The slow motion dissection of killing in *Road to Perdition*, however, quickly discourages an overly simple equating of silence with death. The most glaring disqualification is that the scene as a whole is far from silent. As the sound of rain fades, a thin veneer of a desolate, wind-like drone takes its place. Over that, we hear the crystalline varnish of composer Thomas Newman's airy piano scoring – sounding somewhere between a hesitant melody and the remnants of a harmonic skeleton. Rooney's brogue falls onto this rarefied atmosphere like a dried leaf. And the tearing reports of Sullivan's gun stop short the glacial motion of the piano score. In all, the scene is much more sound than silence. We don't go long without the music, speech or noises that usually stock a scene. But their power is somehow inverted, magnifying the most unrealistic feature of the presentation: the unheard world around us. As Michel Chion wrote, 'silence is never a neutral emptiness. It is the negative of sound we've heard beforehand or imagined; it is the product of contrast'.[5] The converse is true as well. Speech and music occur, but with their comfort and familiarity scrambled by even the temporary withdrawal of noise. The musical background is laid bare. Speech violates. Far from being mere witnesses to a silence acting on its own, music, speech and sound are hired accomplices. Silence reorganizes everything around itself.

I suggested that we know death will visit. How? The unnatural silence predicts the end for John Rooney, but it is similarly connected with fatality, dying and deathlike experiences in many films. To be sure, not all cinematic death is marked by silence, and likewise not all marked silence is death. In *Hear No Evil* (1993), the main character's hearing impairment is represented through silence. In *All That Jazz* (1979), silence becomes a sign of a director's intense nervousness and concentration during a script reading. In *Papillon* (1973), silence supports a near-death hallucination. The technical effect in *Road to Perdition* is common enough, and it may be that variations on silence's association with death have simply become refined into a cinematic code, or even a cliché. But identifying a filmic shorthand for death still doesn't explain how it works, grafting itself seamlessly onto the narrative. How do we understand or accept silence's expressive values? As a composer, I have long been interested in the significance of silence in music.[6] Silence in film is constructed somewhat differently, however. Within the soundtrack's layering, it may not be silence *in* music, but the silence *of* music that matters. Likewise, muted speech and the absence of noise may each become *a* silence among and within both other sounds and silences alike. And as we may respond to speech, music and sound

---

[5]   Michel Chion, *L'audio-vision: son et image au cinéma* (1990), ed. and trans. Claudia Gorbman as *Audio-vision: Sound on Screen* (New York: Columbia University Press, 1994), 57.

[6]   Stan Link, 'Much Ado About Nothing', *Perspectives of New Music* 33/1–2 (Winter/ Summer 1995), 216–72.

each on a very different basis, their absences are probably not equivalent. A linguistic silence is not the same as the silence of the natural world, nor of a musical ensemble, nor of a machine. And, of course, it matters whether silence is diegetic, taking place within the world depicted, or non-diegetic, imposed from without. In all, the reinforcement of death with some kind of silence is not likely a simple declarative statement couched in quiet. It is a negotiation inflected by all of a film's elements.

Silence and Loss of Being in *The Jazz Singer*

> Jack Robin takes the stage at Coffee Dan's restaurant. Singing the last verse of 'Dirty hands, dirty face', he pulls up the collar of his suit jacket, acting the part of a weary man returning home, hunched against the cold. His beloved son runs to greet him. '… but to me he's an angel of joy!' The audience at Coffee Dan's bursts into applause as Jack Robin throws his arms open, both letting go and holding on to the last note.

Even without connecting them directly, *The Jazz Singer* (1927)[7] clarifies a greater share of the bond between silence and death than many more technologically sophisticated soundtracks. Though celebrated as the first narrative talking feature, the film's most engaging implications for cinematic death aren't rooted in hearing Al Jolson's character singing and speaking. Instead, one of the most significant moments for me comes as Jack Robin's last note in 'Dirty hands, dirty face' is received with applause. It's not that we hear Jolson, but that we hear his *audience* responding. We have heard music in the film's narrative before – the young Jakie's musical numbers in the saloon and his father's service as cantor in the synagogue. The musical numbers are clearly 'representations'. There is scant correlation between the acoustic situation of the music suggested by the screen images and what we actually hear. The music is right, but the sense of its physical environment seems mismatched or missing.

It's not the quality or character of the acoustic context in the Coffee Dan scene, but the fact that there is one at all that matters most. In the absence of more intimate acoustic and visual integration, a chasm may open up. The distance between the boy Jakie and his saloon audience sounds unbridgeable. Likewise, the cantor and his celebrants sing into an insatiable void. Like no other, this film makes clear that *noise* more than speech or song informs our sense of contact with, and placement *in*, a diegetic world. Claudia Gorbman noted that 'it seems hardly accurate to call the bulk of *The Jazz Singer*'s score *nondiegetic*, since the film constructs no consistent diegetic sound space to which to oppose non-diegetic music'.[8] Moving beyond such filmic issues, however, the stakes are higher still. Perhaps the most concise summation of ambient noise's power comes from the seventeenth-century metaphysical poet, John Donne. 'I throw my selfe downe in my Chamber', he wrote, 'and I call in, and invite, God and his Angels thither, and when they are there, I neglect God and his Angels, for the noise of a Flie, for the rattling of a Coach,

---

7   *The Jazz Singer*, directed by Alan Crosland, screenplay by Samson Raphaelson, Vitaphone sound; with Al Jolson and May McAvoy, 88 minutes (Warner Bros., 1927).

8   Claudia Gorbman, *Unheard Melodies: Narrative Film Music* (Bloomington: Indiana University Press, 1987), 47.

for the whining of a doore.'[9] During prayer when he aspired to sail on pure spirit, pure thought, Donne found himself anchored to his physical environment by the slightest aural disturbance. Noise betokens the profane and the mundane. It trades interiority for open experience and physical contact. As a distraction, noise works by attracting us to its source. In drawing us out of ourselves the value of noise becomes nothing short of the world itself, becoming a vital function for creating the illusion of a realistic narrative world in *The Jazz Singer*. Ambient sounds enworld screen characters and us. 'You ain't heard nothin' yet', says Jack Robin famously before his next number. But we *have* heard nothing, and plenty of it. In fact, it is more akin to *nothingness*. For most of *The Jazz Singer*, there is little sense in speaking of a quiet or unquiet 'world'. There is simply no *place* at all – nowhere to be. For that fleeting moment at the end of 'Dirty hands, dirty face', however, Jolson's voice finds itself contained *in* something. Music exists within a whole that both emanates and absorbs it. That is, music is part of a physical setting much like our own, and has, momentarily at least, somewhere that it resides and from which it emerges.

The Jazz Singer's jolting oscillations between the silent and talky become more compelling to me than the story itself – and more poignant. Jack's father returns to interrupt the extended sound scene with his mother. At his incredulous arrival during Jack's singing of 'Blue skies' he shouts his command to 'Stop!', and the film instantly reverts to silent cinema. Alan Williams noted that 'it seems one of the most momentous spoken words in all of sound cinema, wrenching the film out of its most developed music-with-speech sequence and back into the traditional discourse of "silent" cinema. It is as if the older man is also saying stop to the sound recording machines, and they obey'.[10] But it feels as though something far richer and deeper than a tenuous foray into the age of sound has been torn away – something bordering on the metaphysical. The sense of loss is overwhelming, feeling like the withdrawal of a world almost in its entirety. The film's greatest power to me lies precisely in its uncomfortable and incomplete technological advancement. As few films entirely of either the sound or silent era could, *The Jazz Singer* reveals the deepest experiential investment in sound: a sense of being. Williams captured the effect best when describing the film's jumps from the sound to silent discourses as 'almost *physically painful*, and from the latter to the former as liberating, like a chance to *breathe anew*'.[11] Noise not only constructs the world, but a physical, bodily existence within it. The lack of sound in pre-sound cinema is of course not merely 'quiet' or even 'silence' in any ordinary sense, but a kind of auditory non-being.

Without torrents of rain and gunfire in *Road to Perdition*, the removal of noise withdraws us from the world. 'Soundless' is quieter than quiet, deeply annihilating to a mode of our existence. The implication of death is clear, though it is not just a

---

[9]   John Donne, sermon 'Preached at the Funeral of Sir William Cokayne, December 12, 1626', repr. as Sermon No. 10 in *John Donne's Sermons on the Psalms and Gospels*, ed. Evelyn M. Simpson (Berkeley: University of California Press, 1991), 226.

[10]   Alan Williams, 'Historical and Theoretical Issues in the Coming of Recorded Sound to the Cinema', in *Sound Theory, Sound Practice*, ed. Rick Altman (New York: Routledge, 1992), 131.

[11]   *Ibid.*, 130 (emphasis added).

symbol. Sound's non-existence points indirectly to its significance not only to the film's world, but beyond, into ours. Noise is not merely a way of situating screen characters in *their* place, but is a perceptual anchor for us as well – both relative to the film world and to *ours*. Noise is an ether in which we exist, and can coexist with that which we see in film. Making us real to ourselves, noise informs our locatedness and marks a boundary between self and surroundings. Literally making *sense* of space – its distances, directions and surfaces – noise gives it a corporeal imprint. Likewise, noise renders physical the passage of time. Sound thus encourages us to inhabit film just as we inhabit our own surroundings. Banish noise, and primary evidence of the universe itself – its fingerprint, so to speak – is wiped away, erased with our ability to be *there*. So, unlike stopping my ears as a 'dead' child, silence is not simply a deprivation of the senses, but allows me to experience the very death of *being*. As Chion might describe it, silence may become 'a bridge to total emptiness'.[12]

If silence predicts death in film, it is therefore not merely that of screen characters, but our own. Much of silence's power, then, derives from the persistence of image and narrative in the absence of sound. They go on heedlessly. Stanley Cavell described film's 'automatism' as 'the experience of the work happening of itself'.[13] This notion of film as 'automatic world projection' clearly informs our relationship to a cinematic world that has been silenced. Going on without us, without our *being* there, a silent street's indifference resides in its hardened, purified visibility, its glassed-in images. What may remain to be heard – the score – is a sound *without* being. Itself dislocated, music lacks room for us, lacks the capacity to place us *there*. We cannot reside *within* it as we do noise. We cannot speak of music in a scene such as that in *Road to Perdition* (or those like it) without involving the absence of sound, and conversely cannot understand the scene's silence while avoiding music's complicity. Without noise, music remains as a sound that *contains* nothing, and as such its effect and meaning are no longer separable from that of silence. Instead, music becomes another kind of absence, a sounding one, by intensifying the feeling that the world has become unreachable and, for us, uninhabitable. Thus the silence of sound becomes not only withdrawal from the world, but withdrawal *of* the world, which has receded to a point just beyond our touch. Silence is not only an aspect of the filmic automatism Cavell ascribed to all film, but one fulfilling its near metaphysical impact as well. 'A world complete without me', Cavell wrote, 'which is present to me is the world of my immortality. This is an importance of film – and a danger. It takes my life as my haunting of the world, either because I left it unloved or because I left unfinished business.'[14] This is, perhaps, the quiet power and wonderful efficiency of Thomas Newman's music for the scene. The score embodies the brittleness of an event unfolding behind a window, a crystalline image with its empty, transparent austerity made audible. To whatever extent we look to film for experiences we cannot have, surely silence places our own demise within the space and span of our lives. The absence of sound kills us, and yet we automatically remain as witness.

---

[12]   Chion, *Audio-vision*, 58.
[13]   Stanley Cavell, *The World Viewed: Reflections on the Ontology of Film* (1974), enlarged ed. (Cambridge, MA, and London: Harvard University Press, 1979), 107.
[14]   *Ibid.*, 160.

Sacred Silence in *Apocalypse Now*

> Willard surfaces from the water, face illuminated by a flash of lightening. A crowd is gathering for a celebration. A large bovine is moored to a stake. Willard slips past into the ancient rooms Kurz has made his living area. Kurz delivers one of his philosophical addresses to soldiers over a field radio: 'Their commanders won't allow them to write "fuck" on their airplanes because it's obscene.' Willard strikes. Outside too, the first blow falls across the neck of the animal. Another, and another. Inside, Willard hits again and again. Sparks fly as his next blow glances off a stone pillar. Kurz staggers, feebly trying to escape – not quite able, and yet not quite wanting to. Willard keeps up with forehands and swirling windups culminating in upward smashing blows. Outside, they have cut half way through the beast's neck. Kurz falls to the stone floor. Struck in the flanks, the animal falls to its knees – more blows as it rolls to its side in the dirt. His work done, Willard finally emerges again, standing framed in the doorway. Kurz breathes his last: 'The horror. The horror.'

Confronted with such forceful images in *Apocalypse Now* (1979),[15] we may hardly notice that the world goes soundless between Willard's first blow and Kurz's dying words. In fact, it hardly seems to matter. Thunder peals the scene at either end, and The Doors' apocalyptic anthem, 'The End', rises from its place alongside the storm to become the soundtrack's overwhelming totality. All told, the tableau is in fact quite loud, but in its 'heart of darkness' crouches a profound silence. 'The End' seems to be there less as something to hear than as an extension of visual spectacle into the auditory realm – a sounding image. Hearing nothing of the deadly blows, no human or animal distress, no clanging of blades on bone or stone, the noise of activity is exsanguinated.

Though its use of sound in connection with death is technically akin to *Road to Perdition*, differences in *Apocalypse Now*'s narrative, imagery and musical material appear to demand disparate interpretations. *Road to Perdition*'s use of music reinforced its superficial quietude. The sparse piano texture is very intimate. Climaxing after Jim Morrison's booming baritone, on the other hand, *Apocalypse Now*'s soundtrack behaves as though bent on obliterating the silence it artificially establishes. 'The End' not only comments on the scene, but replaces the energy of its missing sound. Amplifying the scene's brutality, 'The End' is music made noise, and noise turned to violence.

Still, part of me can't help but be relieved not to have been subjected to the actual sounds of chopping slaughter, blunt trauma and lives ending. Claudia Gorbman noted that 'diegetic sound with no music can function to make the diegetic space more immediate, more palpable'.[16] It follows, of course, that music can assuage the

---

[15]   *Apocalypse Now*, directed by Francis Ford Coppola, screenplay by John Milius and F. F. Coppola after Joseph Conrad's *Heart of Darkness*, cinematography by Vittorio Storaro; music by Carmine Coppola and F. F. Coppola, also by The Doors ('The End') and from Richard Wagner's *Die Walküre*; with Marlon Brando, Martin Sheen, Robert Duvall, Dennis Hopper and Harrison Ford (Zoetrope/United Artists, 1979).

[16]   Gorbman, *Unheard Melodies*, 18.

realism thrust upon us by sound itself.[17] Almost seamlessly, 'The End' in *Apocalypse Now* rushes up to mitigate the severity of realism while still preserving its relentless emotional and visceral intensity. A more penetrating question, however, is not in how violence destroys silence, but in how silence transfigures violence.

The visual explicitness tends to anchor the deaths of both Kurz and the animal in reality. Indeed, director Francis Ford Coppola's footage of an actual animal slaughter reveals the theatricality of mere real-*ism* simply by placing it side by side with the real. But without their appropriate sounds, both deaths have already escaped mundane limitations. It is not mere relief from 'the horror' that silence offers, but transcendence. That is, soundlessness doesn't just soften reality – it overcomes it, leaves it behind. There is a folk expression in German for those strangely synchronized moments of silence punctuating even the liveliest group conversation: *Ein Engel fliegt durch das Zimmer*. Meaning literally that 'an angel is flying through the room', the saying has silence responding to the divine. Similarly, it is telling that we are said to *observe* rituals and often watch and remain silent in the presence of actions connecting the metaphysical with the mundane. Although there may come moments when music, speech or other noise is called for, sacred rituals, settings and feelings (such as Donne described) more often elicit stillness. A sense of 'reverence' seems seldom associated with amplitude. As such, silence also becomes a way of *participating* in a sacred setting or in the process of sacralization.[18] Such stillness is therefore far from passivity. Instead, it is an active transformation of social and individual behaviour reflecting engaged consent and assistance to transcending the mundane. Indeed, it may be that silence itself effects this alteration by performing the work of reforming ordinary space. It is therefore not simply that silence *responds* to sacred presence. In abandoning mundane noise, enworldedness and being, the silenced film world *is* sacred. The soundless image offers a transformed space, one of transfigured reality. This brings to mind Mircea Eliade's concept of *hierophany*, i.e. when 'something sacred shows itself to us'.[19] That the experience of hierophany in *Apocalypse Now*'s silent images is mechanically produced and enforced makes it no less a sacred space. Indeed, it may serve to heighten the effect. With hierophany, Eliade wrote, 'we are confronted by the same mysterious act – the manifestation of something of a wholly different order, a reality that does not belong to our world, in

---

[17]   An excellent, if gruesome, test of this can be found in listening to the shower scene in Hitchcock's *Psycho* without the musical sound track – a feature on DVD releases. Without Bernard Herrmann's score, the sheer 'nakedness' of the slashing and stabbing sounds, along with the screams, is all the more shocking for its physical reality. The 'immediacy' of this diegetic space, as Gorbman called it, is almost unbearably tactile.

[18]   This is not, of course, to suggest a single relationship to silence that cuts across all beliefs. For a study in contrasting statuses of silence and religious participation, for instance, see Daniel N. Maltz, 'Joyful Noise and Reverent Silence: the Significance of Noise in Pentecostal Worship', in *Perspectives on Silence*, ed. Deborah Tannen and Muriel Saville-Troike (Norwood, NJ: Ablex Publishing, 1985), 113–37.

[19]   Mircea Eliade, *The Sacred and the Profane: the Nature of Religion* (1957), trans. Willard R. Trask (New York: Harcourt Brace Jovanovich, 1959, 1987), 11.

objects that are an integral part of our natural "profane" world'.[20] The hierophany of a silenced film image is the revelation and manifestation of a 'sacred reality'.

Coppola's visual and narrative intertwining of the two slaughters is not subtle, perhaps over-literalizing its metaphor. The soundtrack, conversely, not only leaves more to the imagination, but relies on it. The twin offerings are wrapped in the same sacred transfiguration of silence. And again, music amplifies and focuses the effect of this silence. Also existing outside the mundane world, the sound-without-being of the apocalyptic non-diegetic music, 'The End', complements the hierophany of soundlessness. Silencing profane sounds and overwhelming the image with out-of-world music during the presentation of sacrificial slaughter not only depicts its sacred significance, but enacts it. The film itself becomes a kind of ritual. Cinematic silence raises its deaths into a sacred space, with images conversely – literally – projected into our profane space of spectatorship. This cinematic hieraphony goes well beyond 'stylistic amplitude'. We watch Kurz die, our participation marked both by our own silence and that constructed on our behalf by the film. If 'The End' serves to make the visual spectacle audible, silence performs the even greater slight of hand of vanishing the entire scene of action. The silent, aural stylization of Kurz's death is an amplification into the invisible – a ritual transubstantiation of narrative realism into myth. Rendered with silenced images, *Apocalypse Now*'s climactic ascension into the sacred space of myth requires an act of negation. Perhaps sound itself is sacrificed. There is an ineluctable 'suspense' associated with its absence, and its return marks our re-entry into mundane physicality. The nature of the represented death matters little, therefore. Whether accidental, intentional or naturally caused, we must remember that a film death has been enacted and displayed for us to see. By excluding sound, cinema makes of any narrative death a rite.

The Quiet Time: Herzog's *Nosferatu*

Death is not on its way. It has already been abundant here for some time. We see down onto the town square. Even from far above the rectangular geometry of a dozen or so freshly made caskets stands out. Smoke rises from several small fires, and small groups of people dot the square. Some are talking, while some appear to have linked arms. Dancing? Lucy Harker makes her way slowly past a dark, cloaked figure, kneeling in prayer over one of several caskets around him. The figure appears as an austere exception. Just beyond this solitary vigil, in front of Lucy, groups of revelers have joined in circle dances around a fire. They half entice, half compel her to join them. Lucy breaks free, stumbling past a large, roaming sheep and into the outstretched arms of yet another merry-maker. She whirls free of him and into the presence of a man with a French horn performing animatedly before two children. Paying him cursory attention, though less to his performance than out of confusion, she wanders into the thick of another dance. This one is accompanied by a fiddler, who later appears playing near a man wrestling a goat. Rats by the dozen clamor at the legs of diners eating tentatively at a table, set formally amidst still more caskets and hundreds more rats. An elegantly dressed man rises and offers Lucy a glass: 'Would you like to drink with us? Be our guest. We all have the plague. For the first time, let us enjoy every day remaining to us.'

---

20   *Ibid.*

As stunning as is this scene from Werner Herzog's *Nosferatu* (1979),[21] attributing its emotionally wrenching appeal to any dramatic suspense or foreboding is difficult. By the time this morbidly beautifully *tableau* appears, the town has already seen dozens of citizens succumb to mysterious causes. The spectator of course knows the death and rats to be associated with the film's title character. But for the inhabitants of the town it has reached the point where their resignation in the face of so much unexplained death can only be expressed through celebration rather than fear and gloom.

The screen world has again gone silent. All the energetic physical commotion produces no sound for the spectator. If the scene is reminiscent of a Brueghel painting, it also resonates with Jacques Attali's characterization of that painter's work, *Carnival's Quarrel with Lent*: 'In this symbolic confrontation between joyous misery and austere power, between misfortune diverted into festival and wealth costumed in penitence, Brueghel not only gives us a vision of the world, he also makes it audible – perhaps for the first time in Western Art. He makes audible a meditation on noise in human conflict, on the danger that festival will be crushed by a triumph of silence.'[22] As with Brueghel's crowded images of human bustle, there is a great deal of implied sound – so much that wants to be heard. But Herzog's scene evokes the stillness of canvas. Accompanied only by non-diegetic music, the frenetic noise of people, footsteps, fire, animals, rats, and abundant on-screen music and dance is subsumed and silent under the elegiac male chorus of the Vokal-Ensemble Gordela's performance of 'Zinzkaro'.

The technical trick of withholding mundane sound invites immediate comparison to other films. And yet, something from similar scenes also seems missing. There is little tension associated with silence here. It builds toward nothing, preparing no particularly significant event. As urgently as Lucy runs through the square, the silence that accompanies her seems not to 'lean forward' into what may come. The withdrawal of sound in a context already so saturated with death might almost seem like overkill, so to speak. Still, hearing silence's voice so clearly within the milieu of *Nosferatu*'s oddly static commotion encourages yet a further reading of its poetic effect. Relative to many other scenes in silenced worlds, the imagery of music-making and dancing not only characterizes our expectations for *Nosferatu*'s soundscape, but focuses them in a peculiar way. Although emanating from the film world as any other diegetic sound, diegetic music does not behave identically with it, especially relative to our perception of time. While mundane noise *reflects* time's passage, musical sound thrusts its own time on its situation, inflecting and reconstructing our sense of its movement. The metabolisms of music only rarely coincide with those of the

---

[21]   *Nosferatu: Phantom der Nacht / Nosferatu the Vampyre*, directed by Werner Herzog, screenplay by Herzog after Bram Stoker's *Dracula*, cinematography by Jorg Schmidt-Reitwein, music by Popol Vuh; with Klaus Kinski, Isabelle Adjani, Bruno Ganz and Roland Topor, two versions filmed simultaneously, in German 107 minutes, in English 124 minutes (Werner Herzog Filmproduktion, Gaumont S.A., Paris, and Zweiten Deutschen Fernsehen, 1979).
[22]   Jacques Attali, *Bruits: essai sur l'économie politique de la musique* (1977), trans. Brian Massumi as *Noise: the Political Economy of Music* (Minneapolis: University of Minnesota Press, 1985), 21.

real world. Instead, musical time may contradict, impose upon or displace real time. Meters, rhythms, pulses and tempi are all explicit means of controlling time's flow on music's own terms. Even with only its automatic, soundless image remaining, music has animated and organized movement around its presence. In offering direct evidence of a well ordered time, the images of live music and dance on the town square acutely heighten perception of the visible world's temporality, in part because that temporality itself has been so deeply intensified. But in withholding the sensual experience, silence displaces us not only from real time, but from an implied musical time as well. We see the world's temporality re-directed, only to be denied access to its replacement.

There is indeed, then, a deeper tension in Lucy's trip through the square. But it is neither dramatic, since it doesn't really bear much on plot movement or characters, nor is it merely the perceptual dissatisfaction of aural expectations raised by the eye. The tension derives from an especially tenuous relationship to time. The removal of both real-world noise and musical sound is the dream-like feeling of walking on ice while wearing hard shoes; there is not enough friction to make progress. We are not anchored temporally in what we see, and the hollowed out image of music almost mocks the effort to be there. Beyond Brueghel, the existential effect of this scene also recalls Gustav Mahler's description of the whirling Ländler Scherzo in his *Second Symphony*: 'If you watch a dance from a distance through a window, without hearing the music, the gyrations of the couples seem strange and senseless because the key element, the rhythm, is lacking. That is how you have to imagine someone who is destitute and unlucky: To such a person the world appears as in a concave mirror, distorted and mad.'[23] In *Nosferatu*, the image of commotion bereft of sound is an image of such a crisis: a world bereft of meaning in which we are unable to participate.

What remains is the music of 'Zinzkaro', hovering above and imposing its own time on the entirety of the experience. The chorus' deliberate pacing deeply contradicts a visual temporality already magnetized around music, and yet offers its own temporal refuge from silence. Imagining the scene with its actual sound and music restored might feel like rejoining the world, re-entering its timeline. 'Zinzkaro' itself would then become an unwarranted and impossible temporal position to take up. Indeed, this is precisely the effect when speech finally breaks the soundlessness. Suddenly revealed is exactly *when* we have been: out of time. The silence of the scene both frees and compels us to take up a position outside of narrative temporality. The sound of 'Zinzkaro' paradoxically holds out the means of actively engaging the promise of that silence. *We* hover.

I have found this scene, its music and its silence, utterly hypnotic for close to twenty years, and have sometimes been puzzled by my own habit of interrupting the

---

[23]   Conversation with Natalie Bauer-Lechner, quoted in Constantin Floros, *Gustav Mahler*, 3: *Die Symphonien* (1985), trans. Vernon and Jutta Wicker as *Gustav Mahler: the Symphonies* (Portland: Amadeus Press, 1993), 63. A useful discussion of Mahler's conception of this scherzo within a music-historical and music-theoretical context can be found here.

film and replaying the scene again and again and again.[24] Viewing and reviewing it this way fulfils some demand the scene seems to make. Repetition enacts the moment's displacement from time. Rewinding: it is already over with. The events have been catalogued, recorded, put away. I retrieve them. Returning now to the question of the scene's lack of narrative tension leads us to an oddly vital aspect of its vivid relationship to its abundance of death. Having so thoroughly abandoned narrative temporality, we watch Lucy's silent trip through the town square as though it has already happened. That is, we are looking *back*. If there is a lack of dramatic tension in the scene, it reflects the inevitability of something that seems already to have occurred. To the extent that silence has the power to transfigure profane space into sacred space, it also manifests sacred time. Although heightened in it, I would not want to say that this silent sense of taking place in an eternal 'past tense' is unique to *Nosferatu*. Having been quieted but not hidden, however, music makes the temporal hierophony of silence more palpable and complete, in turn revealing explicitly what is perhaps more implicit in other similar scenes. Apparently wanting to converge on the 'still', so many silent images are in slow motion. Or is it that so many slow motion images are silent? Once time is untethered, neither the ear nor the eye can abide there. Though technically contrived, silent death is not merely style at all. It is, rather, the very substance of cinema's automatic inevitability. Like photos in an album, silence becomes an eternal retrospective from which any image of the world becomes an image of its own mortality.

The Drama of Silenced Music: *Run Lola Run*

They need 100,000 Marks in 20 minutes or Manni will be killed. So, Manni is emptying the cash registers. Customers and employees of the grocery store are lying obediently on the floor. Lola trains her gun on them to keep them there. 'Beeil dich bevor die Bullen kommen!' ('Hurry, before the cops come.') Manni and Lola flee the store, running a hard left down the side street. Lola is still carrying her pistol in her right hand. Manni holds the red plastic bag with the money in his left hand, pistol in his right. They run rhythmically in step with each other past shop windows and the occasional pedestrian. Lola looks back over her right shoulder, Manni over his left. They turn left again onto another street that is then blocked as the police cars pull up in front of them. They turn back, but more police cars arrive at the intersection behind them. The cops exit their cars, draw their weapons, and quickly take aim. 'Stehenbleiben!' ('Halt!') Manni slingshots the red bag high into the air out of frustration. One of the younger policeman takes his eyes off of his targets, watching the bag instead. His nervous tension seems to be the one pulling the trigger. Already having aimed, his round hits Lola square in the chest, knocking her several steps backwards. She drops to her knees and slumps over to her left. Manni goes limp, drops his gun, and walks the few steps between him and Lola. On her back, she has begun convulsing on the stone road. Manni kneels beside her, looking down at her face. She stares blankly up at him. Not seeing, she is already near death. Her last thoughts start

---

    [24]   Although published too late to consider in the context of this essay, readers may want to consult Laura Mulvey's book, *Death 24x a Second: Stillness and the Moving Image* (London: Reaktion Books, 2006) for an exploration of the relationship between technological media of private viewing and individual spectatorial pleasure.

replaying a conversation they once had: 'Manni? Liebst du mich?' ('Manni? Do you love me?')

As the protagonists flee the grocery store it appears as though nobody will have gotten seriously injured and that the pair might also escape. Indeed, the soundtrack of Dinah Washington singing 'What a Difference a Day Made' in *Run Lola Run* (1998),[25] gives their flight some extra wing. The song's serene lyricism, limpid string accompaniment and lyrics' wry comment on the film's theme of too little time – all lighten Lola and Manni's steps. Lofted by the tune, Lola and Manni glide past in slow motion.

The fate of sound may again be intoning the sound of fate. From under Lola and Manni's feet there is no rhythm of footsteps. The ordinary street traffic around them cannot be heard. But as the pair reach the end of the street, from beneath the surface of 'What a Difference a Day Made', the sound of police cars approaches, and an undulating phrase in the strings coincides eerily with their sirens. Seemingly undaunted, the tune continues to accompany Lola and Manni as they silently turn back. The suppression of street sounds is again effective in isolating and marking the pair for a sudden, dramatic shift of events. Beneath the tune still more sounds of the world tentatively waft through until the imperative of '*Stehenbleiben!*' briefly punctures the bubble of stillness around the fugitives. While their own sounds remain distant, the sounds associated with their coming demise get through almost effortlessly. Still, 'What a Difference a Day Made' floats the scene even as the escape grinds to a halt and Manni launches the red bag. The reassurance of the song's cool demeanor has been misleading. Ultimately, 'What a Difference a Day Made' serves to double the impact of silence. Roaring out after the song's line, 'since you said you were mine', the blast of the fatal shot proves powerful enough to bring even the non-diegetic music itself to an unexpected halt. Speaking almost as forcefully as the sound of the bullet, the sudden cessation of music ripples through the scene as the very sound of interruption.

The expressive distinctions between 'silence' and 'silenced' are put in relief here. There is, of course, the violation of the tune which resonates the physical violence of the scene. But I also find it useful to remind myself of the relationship between music and life here. On the surface, it seems that the tune parallels Lola's life, and that suddenly cutting short 'What a Difference a Day Made' is a metaphor evoking the nature of her end in its suddenness. And indeed, there is much to be said for the 'animating' force of music, which *inspires* – 'breaths life into' – Lola and Manni's escape. Out of breath, so to speak, Lola's run ends.

But there is also, in the most literal sense, a far more important *dramatic* distinction between 'What a Difference a Day Made' and Lola's life. Namely, the former is a whole, while the latter is not. We must remember again that music and real time operate differently. To cut off a song is to cut off something that already has a beginning, middle and end. Existing in real time, on the other hand, Lola's life has

---

25   *Lola rennt / Run Lola Run*, directed and written by Tom Tykwer, soundtrack by Tom Tykwer, John Klimek and Rynhold Heil; with Franka Potente and Moritz Bleibtreu, 81 minutes (X-Filme Creative Pool, 1998).

no such functionally defined trajectory. The ultimate form of her life appears only at the point where it ends. It is only then made into a whole by being given a terminal boundary it didn't yet have. Naturally, we would view her death as tragic, but should not mistake this emotional response for an understanding of time. Silencing the tune violates its self-contained temporality, denying its process of closure and violating a foregone completeness. Barbara Herrnstein Smith's description of closure in poetry is apt here too when she wrote that 'closure allows the reader to be satisfied by the failure of continuation or, put another way, it creates in the reader the expectation of nothing'.[26] This particular nothing arrives unexpectedly, however, and the cessation of 'What a Difference a Day Made' makes clear that silences can feel differently depending on how they arise with respect to closure. Relative to music, the silencing of street noises, for example, rarely feels like much of a shock, in part because such noises have neither a form nor closure to be violated. Like life, noise is not a whole, not a span of an already finalized duration. 'The expectation of nothing, the sense of ultimate composure we apparently value in our experience of a work of art, is variously referred to as stability, resolution, or equilibrium', Herrnstein Smith continued.[27] Conversely, the unexpected nothingness of the silenced tune is unstable. 'What a Difference a Day Made' greatly heightens the impact of Lola getting shot not simply by stopping, but by replacing boundless real time, whose formlessness cannot be interrupted, with a whole whose end before formal closure can only be understood as premature. The relationship of silence to death here is a fatal lack of equilibrium.

In this sense, interrupting the tune underscores Lola's death by dramatizing it. That is, amplifying Lola's demise with the tune's lack of closure removes Lola's life from real time while appearing to inflect it with musical time. Conversely, of course, stopping 'What a Difference a Day Made' with the sound of a bullet suddenly attaches the out-of-world, non-diegetic song to events of the real world – the one of cause and effect, and of real time. The end of non-diegetic music is a triumph of profane time. Silencing music matches one temporality with another – a gesture of *synchronization*. That *Run Lola Run* is also narratively about time – denying it, escaping it, defeating it, altering it – of course heightens the significance of music's interplay with sound in this regard. The largo strings of Charles Ives's *The Unanswered Question* seep into the vacuum left by the absent sound and song after the gunshot. As with Thomas Newman's piano in *Road to Perdition*, this music of silence comes as an unmooring, making the mundane world again seem distant and unreachable. In this instance, however, the film acknowledges this detachment, and Lola defeats her own death, time and closure by returning to a point twenty minutes before. *Run Lola Run* puts into action the sense of 'replay' implied in film silence, using it not simply as a look back in remorse, but as a chance to alter what has already been – to run again. It is telling, of course, that Lola's ultimate victory over time at the film's later climactic moment comes only when she shatters both real world stillness (in the form of a speechless casino crowd) and time (in the image

---

[26]   Barbara Herrnstein Smith, *Poetic Closure: a Study of How Poems End* (Chicago and London: Chicago University Press, 1968), 34.

[27]   *Ibid.*

of a clock) with her own voice. Especially in its suspension, the time of silence is, after all, intimately linked with death through their mutual denial of life's ineluctable forward movement.

Fatally Broken Silence: *The Good, the Bad, and the Ugly*

> In front of the house, Stevens' younger son rides the burro slowly around its counter-clockwise circle, powering the creaking well pump. Spotting a rider approaching from the desert, the boy dismounts and runs toward the house. Reaching the yard, the rider dismounts next to a low, shaded wall. Tethering his horse, he scans the area from beneath a black hat. Neither calling out nor being called to, he approaches the house. Watching mutely from his place in the front doorway, the visitor can see straight through three rooms to where Stevens and the younger son stand framed together at the entrance to a fourth room. Stevens' wife appears with another large bowl of food. Father and son exchange a wordless look and the son takes a place at the table. Stevens shares a silent glance with his wife. Laying her hands gently on the son's shoulders, she signals him to rise and leave with her. Stevens limps to the table, sits, and begins serving himself. Still mute, the visitor approaches, boot heels on stone echoing through the house. Reaching the table, he slowly sits, fixing his gaze on Stevens. Without breaking eye contact, the visitor scoops a serving onto a plate. Himself still wordless, Stevens continues to eat, glancing down only for a split second. The two men continue to regard each other from opposite ends of the table. Stevens asks, 'You're from Baker?' – the first words in the scene. Receiving only a slight and enigmatic smile from across the table, Stevens continues: 'Tell Baker that I told him all that I know already.' The dark visitor finally releases eye contact as Stevens continues to talk.

Making an early but not unexpected exit from *The Good, the Bad and the Ugly*,[28] Stevens will be lying dead along with his older son, shot by 'The Bad' visitor, known as 'Angel Eyes', who has been paid to find him, get information and kill him. We knew it would end this way for Stevens – but not simply from the black hat Angel Eyes wears, or the piercing resolve in his stare. Clearing out voluntarily, Ennio Morricone's score makes ample room for the silence between the two men even before Angel Eyes enters the house. In breaking the silence between them, indeed, in breaking the quiet, wordless tension of the whole scene to that point, Stevens seemed marked to die. Year after year in teaching my course on film soundtracks I stop the film just after Stevens's first line, asking the class, 'What happens next?' 'There's a shootout', comes the response. 'Who wins?', I ask. 'The other guy.' Few students have seen the film, and yet none of them is ever wrong. With dozens of correct answers, it seems like a predictor of considerable accuracy. Violating silence is not the cause of death, but a clear symptom of a fatal condition.

Few seem immune. In the subsequent scene, Angel Eyes then pays a visit to his sleeping patron, Baker. Having crept quietly into Baker's bedroom, Angel Eyes

---

[28]   *Il buono, il brutto, il cattivo / The Good, the Bad, and the Ugly*, directed by Sergio Leone, produced by Alberto Grimaldi, written by Luciano Vincenzoni and Leone, cinematography by Tonino Delli Colli, music by Ennio Morricone; with Clint Eastwood, Lee van Cleef, Eli Wallach and Aldo Giuffrè (PEA/Gonzales/Constantin, 1966).

stands over his bed. Baker startles awake, sees Angel Eyes and, relieved, says 'It's you'. By the end of the scene, however, Baker himself will be dead, shot in the face through a pillow after learning that Stevens had in turn paid Angel Eyes to kill him as well. Following on immediately after this, 'The Ugly', Tuco, finds himself suddenly thrown from a frightened horse, the animal startled by gunshots from bounty hunters. Scrambling for his gun, it seems hopeless for Tuco. 'No. No pistol amigo', says one of the group, 'It won't do you any good. There are three of us'. But by the end of the scene Tuco, who has remained silent, will still be alive. All three bounty hunters will die on the quick and accurate aim of 'The Good' Man With No Name, who shows up not to save Tuco, but to collect the reward himself. Even while outnumbering their enemy, the bounty hunters present the first symptom of death: speaking first.

Within the codes of the Western genre, it is not difficult to gather that talking is a sign of weakness, which itself naturally tends toward dooming the combatant. But how does speech become weakness? There are, of course, traditional gendered conceptions of strength and manhood to consider. To the 'strong silent type' of gunfighter, an excess of speech is emasculating, weakening and perhaps ultimately fatal. But that only trades one set of questions for another. To whatever extent the *symbolic* connection between breaking silence and weakness in conflict becomes reinforced, the *functional* connection may be obscured. Focusing on the vulnerability implied by speech leads us to the wrong question. What happens if we consider the advantage of remaining speechless? Traditional notions of silence often connect it with acquiescence and, especially, passivity. But these relationships are dramatically upended in the Western. Why is silence strength? In his study of silence among the Nigerian Igbo, Gregory Nwoye related this Nigerian folk tale:

> Once upon a time, the kite sent her son to hunt for food. He soon saw a duck with her brood. The young kite swooped down on them and carried off one of the ducklings. The duck stared at him, but said nothing. Meanwhile the kite came back to his waiting mother with his prey. The mother asked him what the reaction of the duck was. He answered that she merely stared at him and said nothing. The mother kite ordered her son to return the duckling to its mother, because her silence forebodes some future action. The son complied. On his way back, he saw a hen with her brood and once more swooped down and carried off one of the chicks. The mother fretted, shouted and cursed. On his return the kite asked once again what the reaction of the hen was. The son replied that she made a lot of fuss. Mother kite ordered her son to prepare the chick for dinner because there is nothing more its mother can do.[29]

The Igbo story encapsulates the possibility of silence as anticipatory – active, rather than weak or passive. And the advantage is not merely symbolic. A broken silence represents not only one combatant's weakness, but frames the other's still unrevealed action. Nwoye's economy of silence among the Igbo seemed to evoke the Western quite nicely when he wrote that while 'silence means assent in most circumstances, in some situations it can imply deferred action. It is generally believed that if one

---

[29]   Gregory O. Nwoye, 'Eloquent Silence among the Igbo of Nigeria', in *Perspectives on Silence*, ed. Deborah Tannen and Muriel Saville-Troike (Norwood, NJ: Ablex Publishing, 1985), 191.

hurts a person and that person keeps quiet, he or she is contemplating an action to take in the future, while a person who vociferates immediately would be unlikely to do much more'.[30] Silence is thus linked to fatality not merely through symbolic weakness, but through strategic and tactical practicalities. Speech becomes a premature or incomplete action. This is borne out most vividly in yet another of the film's shootouts. Tuco seems at his most vulnerable and 'feminized' while in the bathtub. A would-be assailant breaks in on him, with the intention of avenging the loss of an arm that Tuco shot off in an earlier gunfight. Sitting naked in sudsy water, Tuco listens politely to the gunman's protracted rant about learning to shoot with his other hand. Tuco fires the pistol he had concealed under water all along, killing the intruder. Nwoye's dynamics of the Nigerian kite story could again be applied to the Western: 'The story supports the belief that there is a potential and unfathomable decision or action in silence, whereas immediate verbal response to a vexing situation either reveals immediately one's intended line of action, or symbolizes the sum total of all expected action.'[31] Or, as Tuco succinctly puts it while standing over the body: 'When you have to shoot, shoot. Don't talk.'

Toward Cinema and Silence as Speculation

Tuco's laconic advice in *The Good, the Bad and the Ugly* returns us to Michael Sullivan in *Road To Perdition*. In breaking silence, John Rooney signals his own demise. There cannot be a last-second reprieve, as Sullivan's silence still preserves his 'potential action'. Not simply embodying death metaphorically, silence is death held in reserve. Likewise, as Michael Sullivan's gun cuts off even the instrumental underscoring of his final meeting with Rooney, the silencing of music briefly recalls the dramatic exit of 'What a Difference a Day Made' in *Run Lola Run* – a triumph of profane noise. And the ritual soundlessness in *Apocalypse Now* is surely of a piece with *Nosferatu*'s scene of actions taking place while seemingly removed from time. In all, while I have refracted various hues in each of these silences, they remain parts of a spectrum. The sense of a predominant wavelength in any of them depends on the narratives, types of music either silenced or played, particular images and so on. To that extent, there seems less urgency in historicizing silence's amplification of death than in parsing its compelling effect within the immediate cinematic experience. Certainly, a history of stylistic silence and death would be both possible and fruitful. But to function for the spectator, silence's effects must be eminently accessible, experiential and interpretable in real time. The meaning of silence seems as dependent on the spectator – his or her inclinations, which films he or she has seen, their ordering – as on a view of the technique's development. Enriching silence's meaning at all times is its effortless communication with itself across, with and against the currents of the film world and the real world.

By the same token, advancing an overarching aesthetic or philosophical principle for stylistic silence quickly seems disingenuous. Perhaps a unifying concept,

---

[30] *Ibid.*, 190.
[31] *Ibid.*, 191.

metaphysical, semiotic, aesthetic or otherwise, could be argued. It seems, for example, that Cavell's view of automatism could be taken as a cinematic statement of Eliade's hierophony. But such a normalization would create problems of its own. Many of silence's arenas – musical, spiritual, cultural, linguistic, social, sensual – might be understood to make not only complementary, but competing and even irreconcilable, claims. Any existential nothingness or non-being of silence could not, ultimately, be squared with other wagers of a metaphysical sort. Film may bring these into the same space, but it is not their resolution that enhances the power of cinematic silences to vary the theme of death. They do not all point to the same thing. Rather, it is the ways in which various silences and hearings of silence point to each other – claims, contradictions and quarrels included. Therefore, at the risk of leaving them vulnerable to the limits of my own interpretations, I have resisted the urge to encase these instances too leadenly in theory – musical, cinematic, cultural or otherwise. Returning to Rick Altman's characterization of sound recording as 'representation', a fair question becomes 'to what, exactly, does this correspond?' As an image of death, the answer always involves conjecture. Especially in the era of digitally manipulated, post-synchronized sound, the silent amplification of fatalities is already a kind of theory-in-action. It involves a double hypothesis: not only is film style a supposition about silence, its powers and associations, but cinematic silence itself speaks a theory of death.

Chapter 5

Film Sound, Music and the Art of Silence

Ed Hughes

In his 1996 article 'The Silence of the Silents',[1] Rick Altman commented that many writers on film music, at least since Kurt London,[2] have assumed that early cinematic exhibition (c. 1890–1910) routinely employed musical accompaniment. Proceeding from this assumption, Altman argued, writers have speculatively sought to account for the supposed practices of silent film accompaniments in ways that emphasize sociological and psychological need. For example, music continuously accompanied early screenings in order to block out the sound of the projector, or music compensated for the ghostliness of the silent images on the screen. The perpetuation of this tradition of thought in film music studies is evident in the opening paragraph of the entry on film music in the latest edition of *The New Grove Dictionary of Music and Musicians*:

> Early cinematic presentations in the 1890s were an offshoot of vaudeville and show-booth melodrama and, as both entertainment and spectacle, tradition demanded from the outset that they be accompanied by music … As the craze for moving pictures spread, mechanical instruments initially predominated; these helped to drown projection noise and preserved a link with the fairground, but live music became quickly preferred as a better medium for humanizing the two-dimensional, monochrome and speechless moving image.[3]

This summarizes the established view, which Altman described as 'received opinion', that continuous musical accompaniment is typically indicated as co-existing with early film, and is therefore to be regarded as a formative strategy in the founding sensory experiences of cinema.

However, Altman challenged the idea that 'silent cinema was never silent' through research that cites reviews of theatrical showings in the USA between roughly 1904 and 1907. These reveal that performance practices of music to film varied widely; as part of an eclectic package of what we might think of as vaudeville entertainments,

---

[1]   Rick Altman, 'The Silence of the Silents', *Musical Quarterly* 80/4 (1996), 648–718. Later expanded in Altman, *Silent Film Sound* (New York: Columbia University Press, 2004).

[2]   Kurt London, *Film Music: a Summary of the Characteristic Features of its History, Aesthetics, Technique, and Possible Developments*, trans. Eric S. Bensinger (London: Faber & Faber, 1936).

[3]   Mervyn Cooke, 'Film Music', in *Grove Music Online*, ed. Laura Macy, <http://www.grovemusic.com> (accessed 4 January 2006).

films would sometimes *alternate* with musical performances. The assumption of sound's unequivocal association with early cinematographic performances was rejected by Altman as myth.

This is a potentially liberating thought. If it is the case that the first audiences of cinema were often happy with sight-only screenings of film, and that the accompanying silences were neither disconcerting nor sufficiently 'empty' to prompt the need for aural narrative props, then we might usefully revise our preconceptions of early film as necessarily calling for additional media. For although today's viewers may find the gestures and expressions of actors in certain silent films of the 1900s, 1910s and 1920s stylized and remote, this sensation of strangeness may be due to our unfamiliarity with a then well-understood language of movement, and not always to compensation on the part of those actors for a lack of sound.

For the critic Dorothy Richardson, writing in the English journal *Close Up* in October 1927, it was indeed the case that the coming of reproduced sound in the form of 'talkies' was unwelcome – because, far from compensating for a perceived lack, its arrival would banalize the 'essential character of the screen-play'. Sounds are there, she argued, not because of any spirit of experiment or discrimination, but because they are 'easy to produce', and 'more sound is promised as soon as technical difficulties shall be overcome'.[4] In an even stronger invective, Ernest Betts wrote in the same journal in April 1929:

> The real anti-talkie argument is that speech attacks the film's peculiar and individual function, which is to imitate life in flowing forms of light and shade to a rhythmic pattern. That may sound a piece of abstract nonsense, but it is not so when we see Chaplin or Emil Jannings or any other great pantomime artist.[5]

These critics feared the corruption of a unitary and 'complete' visual art-form through the invasion of recorded sound, although admittedly they were more exercised by the onset of speech than of music. Richardson's hint that technology facilitates indiscriminate use of sound is interesting and prescient because it chimes with tendencies in criticism today. Is it too extreme to argue now that contemporary films are drowning in sound; and that film as an art-form is yearning for the condition of silence? Not for at least one contemporary critic:

> What I miss in films is silence, not only as a neutral medium, or even for its powers of contrast, but for the things from which music is debarred. There are things that only silence can express ... Silence and music have coexisted in films in a thousand different ways in the past, and music is the loser when silence dies.[6]

If one can even temporarily empathize with this critical direction, then the density of modern multilayered soundtracks is thrown into relief, particularly when compared

---

[4]   Dorothy Richardson, 'Continuous Performance 4: a Thousand Pities', *Close Up* 1 (October 1927), 60–64; repr. in *Close Up, 1927–1933: Cinema and Modernism*, ed. James Donald, Anne Friedberg and Laura Marcus (London: Cassell, 1998), 168.

[5]   Ernest Betts, 'Why "Talkies" are Unsound', *Close Up* 4 (April 1929), 22–4; repr. in *Close Up 1927–1933*, 90.

[6]   Adam Mars-Jones, 'Quiet, Please', *Granta* 86 (Summer 2004), 249.

with the dominant pursuit of narrative coherence on-screen. The contemporary commercial film soundtrack is the latest culmination in a long negotiation between uncritically accepted generalized codes of meaning, which Adorno and Eisler called 'rules of thumb',[7] and the dramaturgical need for sound to punctuate and frame the unfolding of narrative.

The aural complexity (the simultaneous delivery of a range of musical and non-musical elements) made possible through contemporary technology is both a fascinating and troublesome aspect of late twentieth- and early twenty-first-century narrative films. Particularly notable is the widespread exclusion of significant silence, whether literal through the muting of soundtrack, or ambient, meaning the aural presence of natural sound. Claudia Gorbman has defined the former as 'nondiegetic silence' and the latter as 'diegetic musical silence'.[8]

Of course, there is rarely a 'natural' soundtrack conveying unadorned 'location' sounds; the soundtrack is almost invariably compiled at the sound design stage as part of the editing process. Perhaps because of the ease with which layers of sound can be organized and manipulated spatially, and in the absence of informed choices being made, one sometimes encounters an almost baroque extravagance of aural elements, many of which may seem redundant, particularly when compared with the (admittedly very differently intended) aural classicisms of mid-twentieth century directors such as Robert Bresson and Alfred Hitchcock.

In recent work, the technological ease and facility with which ever more layers and channels of sound can be achieved has allowed this tendency to perpetuate itself into a fashionable, self-conscious decadence, rather than to resolve or clarify itself in a reformed practice. These latter-day, richly woven aural tapestries are manifestations of a product, the contemporary commercial film, which emanates from an industry predicated on collective entertainment values. In this context there is a tension between the inevitable tendency to homogenize means of musical and sonic expression in order to achieve maximum accessibility, and the need to retain some semblance of the individual and hierarchical principles of sonic structure that support the film's narrative articulation. It is interesting to trace the emergence of the modern event-laden and multi-layered soundtrack through a series of early examples which range between musical continuity and fragmentation.

Entr'acte (1924)[9] and *Rain* (1929)[10] are short, silent, experimental films made by European artists on the cusp of the soundtrack era. Being conceived and constructed

---

7   [Theodor Wiesengrund-Adorno and] Hanns Eisler, *Composing for the Films* (New York: Oxford University Press, 1947), 3.

8   Claudia Gorbman, *Unheard Melodies: Narrative Film Music* (London: BFI, 1987), 18. Implicit in the concept of 'diegetic musical silence' is that the presence of music on a soundtrack is normative.

9   *Entr'acte*, silent film, directed by René Clair, screenplay by Francis Picabia adapted by Clair, cinematography by Jimmy Berliet; with Francis Picabia, Marcel Douchamp, Man Ray, Jean Börlin, Inge Frïss, Darius Milhaud, Erik Satie, Georges Auric etc., 22 minutes, black and white (1924). Satie's score is discussed fully in Martin Miller Marks, *Music and the Silent Film* (New York: Oxford University Press, 1997), 167–85.

10   *Regen / Rain*, silent film, directed and written by Joris Ivens and Mannus Franken, 12 minutes, black and white (CAPI Amsterdam, 1929).

outside studio conditions, they have little to do with narrative and the establishment of commercial norms. They are indeed also very differently conceived films: *Entr'acte* is the work of a surrealist, whereas *Rain* reads like a cross between a study in light and a city-symphony film-poem.

For all their differences, though, these two films share that decade's striking commitment to the invention and uncompromising occupation of new visual languages; and their special relationships with music have enabled them to retain vitality, and to continue to pose questions about film and discontinuity, and continuity and music. *Entr'acte* was originally shown with music by Erik Satie, at the Théâtre des Champs Elyseés in Paris between two acts of the ballet *Relâche* (also with music by Satie). *Entr'acte* is now associated definitively with Satie's score, and parodies the model of continuity – in which the spectator is held in the absurdist thrall of unremitting sound and picture. *Rain* has much more open and controversial, but nevertheless rich, associations with music; its fast moving, inventive and on occasion virtually abstract images of rain falling on Amsterdam are suggestive of discontinuity in the aural domain – of a powerful tension between music and silence, a debate opened up by the several retrospectives scorings of this film over succeeding years.

When Satie wrote *Cinema,* his score to *Entr'acte,* he embraced an extreme form of continuity based on repetition. The music confronts and exposes the mechanistic basis of cinema. Silence is expunged from this manic cabaret and synchronization is assured through the simple expedient of repeating each formulaic passage until the next visual cue is attained. But as Martin Miller Marks has commented, music shares with the images a discontinuity embedded within continuity:

> The film's fast-paced movement is mirrored by the music's quick tempo and unflagging momentum. The fragments of music are as discontinuous, and as subject to unpredictable recurrences, as the images they accompany.[11]

The endlessly repeating dance patterns and vexatiously simple rising and falling scale patterns parody the mechanical basis of the art form – until Jean Börlin bursts through the screen in the closing ironic end-title shot and the music abruptly ceases; the machine has been disrupted and its mechanisms have fallen silent. This is a paradoxical version of musical continuity – one which is breathless and as absurd as the images themselves.

Questions of continuity, discontinuity and silence persist in discussions of Ivens' silent film *Rain* (1929), which Hanns Eisler scored in 1941 and used as the basis for an analytical appendix to *Composing for the Films.*[12] Eisler's score consists of a theme and fourteen intricate atonal variations. Lou Lichtveld had already written

---

[11] Marks, *Music and the Silent Film*, 174.

[12] Adorno and Eisler, *Composing for the Films*, 148–52. Eisler published the score as *Vierzehn Arten, den Regen zu beschreiben*, Op. 70 (1941, 'Fourteen ways of Describing the Rain'), for flute, clarinet, violin/viola, cello and piano; new ed., ed. Manfred Grabs (Leipzig: Edition Peters, 1976).

    The sound print of *Rain* made by Eisler was lost, but has recently been reconstructed by Johannes Gall; the restored version will be issued on DVD with a new German-language

a score for this film in 1932 at Ivens' request,[13] and his work has been described as 'impressionistic'[14] – presumably because of the passages for harp which mimic the action of raindrops falling on oildrums and water surfaces; Eisler does much the same with his dissonant piano clusters. Both scores are continuous and in that sense (alone) conform to the silent film orthodoxy that musical accompaniment should move from beginning to end without a break. The film itself verges on the abstract in its depiction of effects of chiaroscuro, mist under bridges and city forms. It also moves very fast when shown at the standard mechanical speed of 24 frames per second. The film and its relationship with music continue to provoke debate, while at least one of Ivens's contemporaries believed that it should only be experienced silently.[15]

When I came to score this film myself in 2001,[16] I adopted a much slower than standard rate of projection (18 frames per second) and integrated silences of up to twenty-five seconds between sections. Although the composition has since been adapted for standard projection speeds, my memory of the first live performance of the score was of a beauty in the silences magnified by the aural and visual flow around them.[17]

In contrast to silent film, the condition and role of music and silence in sound film obviously become more complex. The binary status of music in silent film, either present or absent, cedes to a new relationship mediated by electronic 'mixing', between sound design (the organization of all sound elements) and music 'cues'. This complex relationship is critically implicated in the creation of space for silence, which is now even more necessary (or should be, in my view) as an organizing and clarifying agent for a film's structure.

If, then, the complexity of sound in film leads one to regard its elements as essentially dissonant, at least in terms of functionality (dialogue, diegetic sound, diegetic music, non-diegetic music, and silence), it becomes clear that unconsidered

---

translation of the book: T. W.Adorno and Hanns Eisler, *Komposition für den Film* (Frankfurt am Main: Suhrkamp, 2006).

[13] This was the first sound version, scored for flute, string trio and harp. I am grateful to André Stufkens, Director of the European Foundation Joris Ivens, for access to the Lichtveld version of *Rain*.

[14] Berndt Heller, 'The Reconstruction of Eisler's Film Music', *Historical Journal of Film, Radio and Television* 18/4 (1998), 544.

[15] For example, the French filmmaker Germaine Dulac, commented that *Rain* is itself a 'moving symphony, with harmonies, chords, grouped in various rhythms, consonance and dissonance' and that therefore music is superfluous; in 'Holland and the Visual Ideal', article in Henri Barbusse's magazine *Monde* (12 January 1929); reported by André Stufkens in *European Foundation Joris Ivens Newsletter* No. 6 (November 2000), <http://www.ivens.nl/newslet6.htm#rain> (accessed 25 March 2006).

[16] Ed Hughes, *Light Cuts Through Dark Skies* (York: University of York Music Press, 2001), scored for flute, clarinet, violin, cello and piano; commissioned 2001 by Bath International Music Festival.

[17] I have described working on my score at greater length in 'Scoring "Rain": A Contemporary British Composer's Perspective', in *European Foundation Joris Ivens Newsmagazine* No. 11 (November 2005), 26.

mixing is potentially problematic. One solution to this is to resist continuous musical 'underscoring' in the classical manner of Max Steiner (in films such as *King Kong* and *Gone With The Wind*), and instead to mount and frame sonic elements in selective and sequential fashion on the audio track. By creating and controlling musical space, diegetic musical silence is able to operate at a heightened structural and expressive level.

A good example of such handling of sound, controlled in a way that contributes directly to narrative and dramaturgy, is found in Jules Dassin's film *Rififi* (1955).[18] This is the story of a heist on a Parisian jewellers led by an ex-convict, Tony le Stéphanois. Intriguingly, in *Rififi*, the sound track is constructed with great care, and the 'dissonant' or conflicting elements are deployed in order to maximize psychological tension.

The overture music to the titles contrasts two types of music: George Auric's urgent orchestral music, emblematic of the action and drama of the heist itself, is cut with the languid saxophone melody of the night-club music, which grounds the narrative in the *noir*-ish atmosphere of post-war Paris. In the sense that the overture music anticipates themes which follow in the movie, it is a conventional beginning. What follows, however, in terms of aural structure, is not. There are five clear sonic phases leading to the critical midpoint of the movie:

1. **Diegetic sound**. To 29:00. Dialogue, city sound, night club music.
2. **Non-diegetic music** (1). 29:00 to 33:32. A four-and-a-half minute sequence depicting preparations for the heist, told primarily in visual terms. No dialogue, limited sound effects, and the foregrounding of Auric's non-diegetic orchestral score. The association of the urgent repeating rhythms of the orchestral score with action is reinforced with a *fugato* during the taking of an impression of the lock to the target building's door. While selected footsteps are recorded on the soundtrack, dialogue exchanges are actually mimed, thus ensuring the uninterrupted primacy of Auric's neo-classical score, and of musical time, which effectively compresses an important series of actions and informs the lead-up to the heist itself.
3. **Diegetic musical sound**. 33:32 to 41:10. A relaxation of tension with the brief restoration of 'normal' club music sounds.
4. **Non-diegetic music** (2). 41:10 to 44:38. As the criminals gather in order to enact the heist, Auric's score works itself up to a frenzy, climaxing on a rising chromatic motive played in unison on xylophone, flutes and tremolando strings (Ex. 5.1):

---

[18]   *Rififi / Du rififi chez les hommes*, dir. and written by Jules Dassin, after a novel by Auguste Le Breton, cinematography by Philippe Agostini, film score by Georges Auric; with Jean Servais, Carl Möhner, Robert Manuel, Jules Dassin, Marie Sabouret and Janine Darcey, 115 minutes, mono, Western Electric Sound System, black and white (Indusfilms/Prima/ Société Nouvelle Pathé Cinéma, 1955). Information on sound films has been derived from *The Internet Movie Database*, <www.imdb.com>.

Ex. 5.1   Georges Auric, *Rififi*, chromative motive before heist

5. **Diegetic musical silence**. 44:38 to 1:08:21. The heist itself – depicted in visual terms, and with the symbolic withdrawal of non-diegetic music. The depicted events of the heist are understood to take several hours, but their compression into a sequence lasting 23:43 is almost unbearably tense, precisely because we, as the audience, are acutely conscious of the significant absence of music. There is no musical underscore to assuage what seems like a very long sequence in cinematic time. The 'silence' that is achieved here is of a special quality because the preceding four phases directly manipulate and contrast narrative modes through the dissonant elements available to the soundtrack. This 'silence' emphasizes and dramatically underscores the diegetic need for wordless communication and intense concentration.

Another classic sound treatment also illustrates the power and lucidity of what one might call the successive approach to the assembly of aural components in a narrative soundtrack. This is a scene in *Once Upon a Time in the West* (1968),[19] in which a family is brutally gunned down by bandits. For several seconds there are shots of landscape before the murderous action by unseen hands. Here the soundtrack is neither muted, nor 'ambient' or 'realistic' in the manner of straightforward diegetic musical silence. These agonizing seconds are drawn out by the presence of sound eerily and selectively emphasizing occasional details in the static landscape (such as a flock of birds rising up from bushes). After the killings, as the bandits approach their victims, Ennio Morricone's laconic and merciless music surges forward, vanquishing the preceding 'silence'. The aural montage is selective, successive and marked by a precision and control equalling that of the images. In particular, the careful timing and the equal weight given to silence and music imbue the scene with formidable dramatic power. One's expectation of underscoring patterns is subverted first by music's withdrawal, and then again by its sudden and shocking presence in the perceptual foreground.

If *Rififi* and *Once Upon a Time in the West* illustrate 'successive' construction in the aural domain, one might turn to the 1990s for instances of a very different model, heir to the innovations in sound technology forged by George Lucas and Dolby in the 1970s. For example, in *The Silence of the Lambs* (1991),[20] modern multi-channel mixdowns and the greater dynamic range of recording techniques

---

[19]   *C'era una volta il West / Once Upon a Time in the West*, dir. Sergio Leone, written by Dario Argento, Bernardo Bertolucci and Leone, cinematography by Tonino Delli Colli, film score by Ennio Morricone; with Henry Fonda, Charles Bronson, Claudia Cardinale, Jason Robards and Gabriele Ferzetti, 165 minutes, mono (Rafran–San Marco, 1968; (USA) Paramount, 1969).

[20]   *The Silence of the Lambs*, dir. Jonathan Demme, screenplay by Ted Tally, after the novel by Thomas Harris, cinematography by Tak Fujimoto, film score by Howard Shore, sound designer Skip Lievsay, production sound mixer Christopher Newman; with Anthony

clearly take principles of composition, mixing and editing as established in classical Hollywood practice to a level of previously unimagined sophistication. However, the soundtrack in many ways continues to work within, rather than against, classical premises. In the opening sequence, for example, shots of a forest in subdued lighting are accompanied by orchestral music in a neutral major key tonality; as the camera picks up and then tracks the protagonist Agent Clarice Starling as she jogs through the forest, the music changes key to E minor, and a slow theme is heard which emphasizes the flattened-sixth scale degree, e.g. the final C in Ex. 5.2:

Ex. 5.2   Howard Shore, *The Silence of the Lambs*, theme from opening sequence

This is one of two key harmonic moments that have the effect of giving depth to this character. Such harmonic changes denote impending drama; and the Wagnerian-style emphasis on the sixth scale degree shades the understated atmosphere of tension and expectation. Thus far the music conforms with the concept of referential narrative cueing in classical film music practice.

However, this same sequence is markedly different from the Leone example in its simultaneous presentation of aural elements. The music is overlaid by sounds of the forest (footsteps, birds fluttering past etc.); and the use of a stereo or multichannel audio output significantly widens the aural field. The successive model of aural construction of a sound track, with its classical control, is now replaced by the simultaneous paradigm. At this point in the film it is absolutely crucial that the viewer remains captured within the cinematic experience – becomes a compliant viewing subject – because any conscious attempt to analyse the experience will render it totally implausible.

In other words, the visual track of Jodie Foster running through the forest is fine, but the simultaneous presence of forest sounds and music is potentially problematic and more confusing than the highly controlled successive montage discussed in *Once Upon a Time in the West*. For while the soundtrack to *The Silence of the Lambs* bristles with ambient aural information, the earlier soundtrack arguably displays more discrimination in its deployment of limited, indeed ritualized, aural resources. The Leone film is both more theatrical, and more artificial, in its handling of silence and music, and yet also more credible than Skip Lievsay's soundtrack which, in its simultaneous fusion of musical artifice and naturalism in a complex 'sound design', sacrifices much of the potential power of diegetic silence. The elements of sound design gain from separation, individual crafting and careful handling, rather than continuous simultaneous deployment.

Hopkins, Jodie Foster, Scott Glenn and Ted Levine, 118 minutes, Dolby Surround sound (Orion Pictures, 1991).

As a result, where silence in the *Once Upon a Time in the West* sequence is indicated within an extremely limited and focused array of sounds, on occasions in *The Silence of the Lambs* where the effect of silence would be dramatically transformative, so-called 'underscore' music is actually used to block out or obliterate excess ambient sound. A good example of this occurs at approximately thirty-eight minutes into the film. Starling is taken to view a recent murder victim and encounters the sexist gaze of a provincial police officer. In the background there is bland organ music from an unseen chamber organ, motivated by the laying out of the victim in the chapel of rest. The chamber organ is performing stock phrases in B♭ major, overlaid by ambient sound. Starling enters the chapel of rest and slowly approaches the body. As she does so, she is thrown back in time to the memory of approaching her dead father as a little girl. The overwhelming shock of this sudden involuntary memory is matched by a very sharp cut (reinforced by a tonal shift of a tritone) from bland, ambient, chamber organ sound to a version of the opening orchestral music, again in E minor and again emphasizing the flattened-sixth scale degree. All ambient sounds are obliterated. Music (rather than silence) now stands for intense mental activity – in this case the internalizing of the past and the silencing of the external present. Then with almost classical symmetry, a door opens and Starling is thrown back into the present; the multi-layered ambient music and noise of the soundtrack recommence.

Modern digital film soundtracks are complex tapestries. Because sound designers use sophisticated electronic mixing techniques, the tendency to confuse the essentially 'dissonant', or conflicting, elements of the soundtrack has grown, resulting in perceptual overload. Nowhere is this clearer than in the ubiquitous exclusion of silence. The structural properties afforded by silencing, both metaphorically in the withdrawal of an expected element such as non-diegetic music, and literally in the form of muting, have declined. The resulting strategy of continuous and simultaneous presentation of elements through mixing has been further thickened by 'surround' textures in order to create a state of truly uncritical immersion. If film music is today in some cases generalized and lacking in individual character, this may in part be due to its use, in the digital model, to purge an overloaded soundtrack to achieve heightened or expressionistic effects, where formerly silence would have had the same or greater impact.

Chapter 6

Pragmatics of Silence

William Brooks

These comments are grounded in the music and writings of the American composers John Cage and Charles Ives and in recent (re-)readings of passages by and about William James, American philosopher and founder of modern psychology. I do not wish to claim that there are direct links between these figures, though I will briefly address that possibility below. Nor do I wish even to claim that James's intellectual influence extends to Ives or Cage – though that too may be the case. Rather I want to explore silence and its opposite (but what *is* its opposite?) in a reflective, personal way: these are my own thoughts, offered in the end without justification and without promises – efforts, in keeping with James's own introspective method, to consider silence within the self, in a domain beyond negation, and to find the actions it invites.

Introduction

It was one of John Cage's favourite anecdotes; he was, he remarked, 'constantly telling it'.[1] I offer here the version from what was arguably his most influential essay, 'Experimental Music' (written in 1955), the second item in *Silence*.

> There is no such thing as an empty space or an empty time. There is always something to see, something to hear. In fact, try as we may to make a silence, we cannot. For certain engineering purposes, it is desirable to have as silent a situation as possible. Such a room is called an anechoic chamber, its six walls made of special material, a room without echoes. I entered one at Harvard University several years ago and heard two sounds, one high and one low. When I described them to the engineer in charge, he informed me that the high one was my nervous system in operation, the low one my blood in circulation. Until I die there will be sounds. And they will continue following my death. One need not fear about the future of music.[2]

Shall we parse this passage? It falls into three parts: three related assertions; an account of an experiment; and an admonition. Each suggests a line of thought, and

---

[1]   John Cage, 'How to Pass, Kick, Fall, and Run' (1965), in *A Year from Monday* (Middletown, CT: Wesleyan University Press, 1967), 134.

[2]   John Cage, 'Experimental Music' (1955 [not 1957]), in *Silence* (Middletown, CT: Wesleyan University Press, 1961), 8.

so I offer a discussion in three sections, each loosely linked to one of the parts of Cage's anecdote.

Part I

> There is no such thing as an empty space or an empty time. There is always something to see, something to hear.

Two assertions, seemingly parallel: a rhetorical flourish, perhaps, in which the author rephrases a statement to emphasize it.

But the two statements, strictly speaking, are *not* parallel. 'There is no such thing as an empty space or an empty time' is a metaphysical assertion; it concerns the nature of things. It seems to run counter to common sense: as children, after all, we learn that space *is* empty, void, without form. And so, surely, is time – or else how is it that we *fill* our days? Cage's proposition challenges the 'facts' about things. It tells us that space and time have unsuspected attributes: they are what they are, not what we think they are.

The second sentence – 'There is always something to see, something to hear' – is about observation, about attention. It describes the activity of a mind, a *consciousness*. It can be true *whether or not* the first assertion is true; it stands apart from metaphysical speculation. Suppose there *were* an empty space or an empty time; nevertheless, the second sentence says, we cannot *experience* this. The fact of observation, simple attention, puts something there; if we attend to nothingness, nothing itself becomes something.

Such an assertion recalls Zen koans, and of course Cage constantly acknowledged his indebtedness to Zen and especially to the lectures and writings of Daisetz Teitaro Suzuki. But it is also resolutely *empirical*; it insists that studying *what is* necessarily entails studying *what is seen, what is heard*. It does not *equate* the two; this is not an idealist speaking; on the contrary, here and elsewhere Cage rejoiced in all that was external to him, in the abundant and variegated otherness that is not the self. That we know only what we see, what we hear, does not imply that all is imagined. Cage's assertion asks that we be slaves to neither habit nor will; because the universe is larger than our imagination, he posited, it enlarges our experience: there is *always* something to see, something to hear.

Cage's empiricism, then, rests neither on mind in itself nor on the universe in itself; it requires the intersection of the two – their 'interpenetration', he might have said in later years. It is this interpenetration that the two sentences create, in their apparent identity but actual difference: it is this interpenetration that is properly the subject of Cage's essay – and of his music. And it is on this interpenetration that Cage's most celebrated musical proposition rests: *silence*, the musical equivalent of 'empty space' (an 'empty music') is – regardless of its metaphysical attributes – an experience, not the absence of one.

Cage reached this position only after many years' work as a composer and performer. From the start he was concerned with the limits of the *musical*: he scrutinized on one hand the boundary between music and noise and, on the other, that between music and silence. With respect to noise he soon concluded that no sounds were intrinsically unmusical. In an early lecture, 'The Future of Music: Credo', he famously wrote: 'I believe the use of noise ... to make music ... will continue and increase'; and nearly twenty years later he explained that 'noises are as useful to new music as so-called musical tones, for the simple reason that they are sounds'.[3] His position had been anticipated by earlier thinkers, such as Luigi Russolo, Charles Ives and Edgard Varèse – who, Cage wrote, 'fathered forth noise ... into twentieth-century music'.[4] Noise caused Cage no difficulty.

Silence was more problematic. The received aesthetic regarding silence was that it marked an *absence*: it was useful, compositionally, precisely because there was nothing to hear. It had recognized functions, which Cage once summarized thus:

> Silence was the time lapse between sounds, useful towards a variety of ends, among them that of tasteful arrangement, where by separating two sounds or two groups of sounds their differences or relationships might receive emphasis; or that of expressivity, where silences in a musical discourse might provide pause or punctuation; or again, that of architecture, where the introduction or interruption of silence might give definition either to a predetermined structure or to an organically developing one.[5]

To these I would add that silence also served as an *accent*: when there was *nothing* where there should be *something*, the absence, the silence, was a matter 'of note' – something to which one attended, about which one *felt*.[6]

In Cage's early works, noisy though they might be, silence plays exactly these roles. Consider, for example, the opening of the second Sonata from *Sonatas and Interludes* (1946–8), shown in Ex. 1.[7]

---

[3]   John Cage, 'The Future of Music: Credo' (1940 [not 1937]), in *Silence*, 3; 'History of Experimental Music in the United States' (1959), in *Silence*, 68. The former is dated 1937 in *Silence*, but the date is rightly 1940. See Leta E. Miller, 'Cultural Intersections: John Cage in Seattle (1938–1940)', in *John Cage: Music, Philosophy and Intention, 1933-1950*, ed. David W. Patterson (New York and London: Routledge, 2002), 54–6.

[4]   John Cage, 'Edgard Varèse' (1958) in *Silence*, 84.

[5]   John Cage, 'Composition as Process' (1958), in *Silence*, 22.

[6]   Each of these functions is explored (implicitly) in other essays in the present collection. For silence as accent, for example, see Chapter 1 (Doctor); for silence as punctuation, consider Chapter 8 (Hornby); for silence as expressivity, see Chapter 9 (Potter).

[7]   John Cage, *Sonatas and Interludes* (1946–8) (New York: Henmar Press, 1960), 9.

Ex. 6.1   Cage, Sonata II, bars 1–14

The empty $\frac{3}{8}$ bars can be thought of as architectural, to use Cage's term; they 'give definition to a predetermined structure'. The crotchet rests in bars 2 and 3 separate groups of sounds; they contribute to 'tasteful arrangement'. And the quaver rests in bars 7 and 8 enhance 'expressivity' by providing 'punctuation'. Finally, the quaver rest that opens bar 4 is, I would say, an accent – acknowledged by Cage, in effect, in the turn and articulation applied to the following sound. Whereas in all previous phrases quavers had occurred in pairs, marking the pulses of the underlying meter, here the sounded pulse is absent; and that absence is notable, a *something* (not a nothing) to which a listener responds with a *feeling* (of surprise, imbalance, puzzlement … – there are many possibilities).

At the same time that Cage was applying these conventions, however, he was moving toward a more distinctive view of silence. Well before the *Sonatas and Interludes* were complete, he had come to believe that 'the underlying necessary structure of music is rhythmic'.[8] By 'rhythmic' Cage meant simply the use of metric notation to measure time: 'structure', he explained a decade later, 'was a division of actual time by conventional metrical means, meter taken as simply the measurement

---

8   John Cage, 'Defense of Satie' (1948), in *John Cage*, ed. Richard Kostelanetz (New York: Praeger Publishers, 1970), 83.

of quantity'.[9] And it was *silence* that required that structure be conceived this way: 'of all the aspects of sound … duration, alone, was also a characteristic of silence'.[10] Or, writing later, 'silence cannot be heard in terms of pitch or harmony: it is heard in terms of time length'.[11]

Note that *this* silence is actually 'heard', in Cage's formulation. Yet at the same time it 'cannot be heard'; it has no amplitude (or pitch, or harmony). But it is no longer the case that there is 'nothing' there; Cage wanted this silence to be a *something*, something that is *there* but is not sound. If, as before, silence is an absence, we are asked now to hear that absence in itself, for what it is, not merely as a marker by which sounds are distinguished or arranged.

So many paradoxes, so many contradictions! But I can find no way to avoid them, save by metaphor. Silence is a ribbon, a track, a stream, upon which sound-events are etched, play, float. More practically, silence is the blank tape upon which sounds are recorded, the empty file waiting for data.[12] We can attend to that tape, to that stream; we can notice them. And when we do, they become things in themselves – in the case of silence, things to be *heard*.

But in 1948 the convention was to *not*-attend to silence, to time. Rather it was assumed that these exist to be filled – the one with 'music', the other with 'activity'. And indeed, Cage himself filled his 'structures' with 'material'; though silent proportions were planned in advance,[13] the 'music' consisted of the artful disposition of sounds.

The problem was to shift the listener's attention away from the 'music' and to the empty field of 'silence' on which the sounds had been placed. How could a composer accomplish that? Cage was fond of citing Satie and Webern as predecessors, claiming that they too had built their compositions from lengths of time.[14] But even if that was true, neither had successfully demonstrated how to attend to *silence*.

A more plausible forbear was Charles Ives, who created a sounded 'silence' explicitly in two experimental works from 1906: *Central Park in the Dark* and *The Unanswered Question*.[15] Ives later linked the two pieces as *A Contemplation of a Serious Matter* and *A Contemplation of Nothing Serious*; for both, sometime in the

---

[9] Cage, 'Composition as Process', 19.

[10] *Ibid.*

[11] Cage, 'Defense of Satie', 81.

[12] Cage thought of music in such technological terms even before tape was in use (though optical sound on film was available). In 1940 he noted mischievously that 'any design repeated often enough on a sound track is audible. Two hundred and eighty circles per second on a sound track will produce one sound, whereas a portrait of Beethoven repeated fifty times per second on a sound track will have not only a different pitch but a different sound quality'; Cage, 'The Future of Music: Credo', 4.

[13] *Sonata II*, for instance, is built of structural units of $1\text{-}1/_2$ and $2\text{-}3/_8$ semi-breves in length.

[14] See, for instance, Cage, 'Defense of Satie', especially 81.

[15] Ives's pieces were first played as a pair on 11 May 1946 in a well-publicized concert at Columbia University's McMillan Theatre in New York. It is quite possible that Cage was present; he and Merce Cunningham gave a concert at Hunter College the very next night. See David Patterson, 'Appraising the Catchwords, c. 1942–1959: John Cage's Asian-Derived

1930s he amplified and extended the sketchy comments on his manuscripts into full-blown programme notes.[16]

About *The Unanswered Question* Ives wrote, in part, 'the strings ... represent "The Silences of the Druids – who Know, See and Hear Nothing"'. And, about *Central Park*, 'the strings represent the night sounds and silent darkness'. In each piece, the 'silence' of the strings is broken by other instruments. These depict, in *The Unanswered Question*, 'The Perennial Question' and the hunt for 'The Invisible Answer'; and, in *Central Park*, 'sounds from the Casino, ... street singers, ... pianolas ...'.[17]

In these works, then, for Ives like Cage, silence is a continuity onto which sounds are placed, a canvas on which musical 'stuff' appears. But Ives creates his 'silence' by means of *sounds*; this really *is* a 'heard' silence. The strings can function as silence – can *be* silent – only because of the implied relations between the 'silent' and the 'heard': it is the sounded difference that allows silence to be *felt*.

In both works the foreground material – the 'music' – is highly characterized. In *Central Park* it is largely derived from daily life at the time: popular songs, marches, dance music. In *The Unanswered Question* it is newly composed but equally distinctive: a single 'question' is repeated by a solo trumpet, seemingly without variation, while a quartet of winds 'answers' with contrasting or related material.[18]

The 'silences' also differ. In *Central Park* a ten-bar phrase made of chords of stacked intervals moves irregularly up and down, as shown in Ex. 2. It is played ten times, without change, during the composition's duration. This 'silence' marks the passage of time in equal, unvarying units; it functions exactly like Cage's 'rhythmic structures,' measuring out the continuity upon which 'sounds' are placed.[19]

Rhetoric and the Historical Reference of Black Mountain College' (PhD diss., Columbia University, 1996), 287.

[16]   James B. Sinclair, *A Descriptive Catalogue of The Music of Charles Ives* (New Haven: Yale University Press, 1999), 102–4, 128–30, 589.

[17]   Ives, *The Unanswered Question* (1906), ed. Paul C. Echols and Noel Zahler (New York: Peer International, 1984), [10]; *Central Park in the Dark* (1906), ed. John Kirkpatrick and Jacques-Louis Monod (Hillsdale, NY: Mobart Music Publications, Inc., 1973), [31].

[18]   In the 1906 version, the trumpet plays exactly the same phrase seven times. In a revised version from the 1930s, two phrases alternate, differing only in their final note. The motivation for Ives's changes can be argued, but it seems clear that the final notes differ at least in part to avoid consonances with the strings: that is, that the differences clarify the *relations* between the question and the silence, not the 'question' itself.

[19]   In *American Experimental Music, 1890–1940* (Cambridge: Cambridge University Press, 1990), 61–2, David Nicholls points out that the 10 x 10 structure of *Central Park* even anticipates Cage's own 'square-root' formula, in which the proportions of the parts echo the proportions of the whole.

Ex. 6.2   Ives, *Central Park in the Dark*, bars 1–10

[typeset]
Reprinted by kind permission of Mobart Music Publications.

In *The Unanswered Question*, the string music suggests a hymn or chorale, with correct voice-leading, passing tones and ornamental notes, and something that might be a melody in the upper parts. The slow tempo and uncertain cadences make for rather static phrasing, but after thirteen bars the material reaches a conclusion and – as in *Central Park* – is repeated.

However, the repetition occurs only once; thereafter the musical 'silence' only *appears* to recur. Ives actually varies the material, though even to an experienced listener the effect is of cyclic recurrence. There seems to be no particular reason for the choices made: why this variation rather than another? Why shorter here, longer there? In *The Unanswered Question*, then, 'silence' is ever-changing: time passes not in unvarying units, but in a perceptual flux, a continuum of alternatives.

I am tempted to account for these different kinds of time, these different silences, by Ives's programmatic descriptions. *Central Park* is an urban work, after all; it takes place in, and is about, New York City: a grid of equally measured squares; an artificial space, a set of coordinates upon which events take place, are located. And in Ives's portrait, the events that are placed into the 'silence' of the strings are city events:

> some 'night owls' from Healy's whistling the latest or the Freshman March – the 'occasional elevated', a street parade, or a 'break-down' in the distance – [sounds] of newsboys calling 'uxtries' – ... a fire engine, a cab horse runs away ...[20]

The Unanswered Question, in contrast, is not physically situated; at the very least it occurs in an unspecified rural landscape, but more likely its space is that of the imagination. And the imagination, for Ives, is both 'natural' and constructed: it is emphatically not a product of the city, nor even of the countryside; rather it is intrinsic to *experience* in the broadest sense. In the imagination, in *experience*, time is a continuum, not a grid; and this continuum, this stream, flows at different rates at different moments, shaped by consciousness.

Floating upon the imagination is *memory*; upon the stream's surface are played out games of re-assembly, recall and return. In Ives's composition the 'question' is constant (even though it may vary); the 'silence' is ever-changing (even though it appears constant). The answers, manifold and metamorphic, arise from the intersection of the question – of the *memory* of the question – with the desire for change. Answers are born both from habit – the same question, again and again – and from resistance to habit: new answers, but constructed of the same 'stuff' – ultimately, the stuff of the question.

In both these pieces, then, Ives presents silence not as emptiness but as substance, as sound – in one case made up of discrete, repeating units, in the other case as an ever-changing continuum. Upon this sounded silence he places the music and the noise – the sounded *sound*. These are differentiated from the silence by the relations they contain, which stand in relief against the sound-qualities of the silence.

Thus, in *Central Park* the 'sounds' are either triadic and familiar ('music') or irrationally complex ('noise'). Neither of these qualities can be found in the 'silence', which is non-harmonic and constructed systematically of equal-spaced intervals. In *The Unanswered Question*, these fields are reversed: it is the silence that is triadic and familiar, while the questions and answers are erratic and atonal. The workings of both pieces rely upon the listener to construct a difference, a *relation*, between the 'music' and the 'silence' – to *hear* 'silence' when the 'music' stops, even though in 'fact' the sound is continuous.

---

[20]   Ives, *Central Park in the Dark* [31].

In summary, when silence is truly an *absence*, as it is in Cage's *Sonatas and Interludes*, it is one-dimensional, monochromatic: it occurs only when sounds have not yet been specified (composed), or when they have ceased. Its meaning is narrow and specific: silence tells us that the music is *not there* yet; or it tells us that the music has ended, or been removed, or displaced.

When silence is a *presence*, as for Ives, it is itself a composed, sounded continuity. Silence is *there*, but only because it is, in effect, not silent; rather it is constituted from a music that differs crucially from that music that constitutes the 'sounds' (the questions and answers, the snatches of city life). It offers an alternative to 'sound'; and because it is itself composed and sounded, its meanings are manifold and varied, like those of any music.

But can one compose silence itself? Can one – returning to Cage's third assertion – '*make* a silence'? By 1955 Cage had his answer: 'try as we might … we cannot'.[21] Earlier, however, he was not so sure. In a series of pieces in the 1940s, well before the *Sonatas and Interludes*, Cage struggled to 'make a silence', to compose continuities in which empty durations would themselves become objects of attention: *presences*, not absences, but (unlike Ives) presences *without* sound.

A good example is *Experiences*, a piece that exists in two versions. First performed in January 1945 to accompany Merce Cunningham's dance solo by the same name, the initial version was scored for two pianos; the second part of Cunningham's dance was accompanied by music by Livingston Gearheart. In 1948 Cage adapted the melody to his part, creating *Experiences II* for unaccompanied voice; this then replaced Gearheart's music for the second part of the dance.[22]

In its vocal form, *Experiences* is as close to a Romantic *lied* as Cage ever wrote; the text, a sonnet by e. e. cummings, is an unrestrained love-lyric that Cage fit elegantly to the pre-existing melody. Even though the text was added later, there is every reason to assume the score was meant in part as a gift, an expression of the composer's feelings towards the dancer, who by then had become his life-long partner.

And now, good reader, I must ask your assistance in the first of two small experiments. Ex. 3 offers bars 64–100 from *Experiences II*, containing the third and longest of three substantial silences in the score. Please, can you find a musician to sing or play this example for you? For present purposes the instrument (or voice) doesn't matter; all that's necessary is that the melody be performed lyrically, at the given tempo, without hesitation – and especially that the bars of rest (86–91) be performed exactly and without impatience. Please don't play the example yourself – and don't read the score during the performance! Just *listen*.

---

[21]   Cage, 'Experimental Music', 8.

[22]   John Cage, with Robert Dunn, *Catalogue* (New York: C. F. Peters Corp., 1962), 11, 20. The two-piano version of *Experiences* was given on the dance concert at Hunter College, 12 May 1946, that followed by one day the première of Ives's two 'contemplations'; see note 14, above. See also David Patterson, 'Appraising the Catchwords', 280, 298–9.

Ex. 6.3   Cage, *Experiences II*, bars 64–100

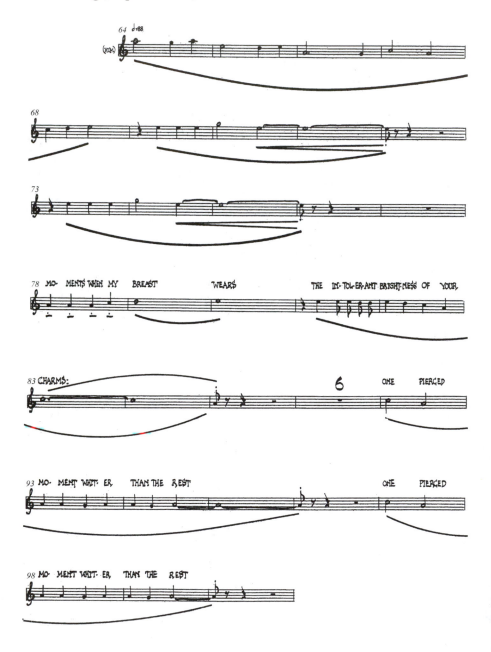

Now. The question is: what did you 'experience', what did you *do*, during the performance of that music? Did the silence serve any of the purposes Cage described (and which we observed in Ex. 1)? Was it there to arrange, to punctuate, to structure?

(I added 'accent' to the list, but perhaps we can rule that out immediately.) Or perhaps it was there for all three of these purposes? Or for more??

This, alas, is a monologue, and I cannot hear your reply. I can only offer my own answers – in the hope not that we agree, but that the differences between us will prove illuminating.

We must recall that the music was meant to accompany a dance, and that certainly none of us have experienced the music with the dance before us. Perhaps the silences were filled with activity; perhaps there were dramatic or narrative reasons for them.[23] However, Cage happily transferred most of his early dance scores to concert halls or recordings, and for this experiment we can treat *Experiences* as a concert work.[24] Hearing the music thus, it seems to me that all the 'useful ends' Cage described might apply perfectly well: the silence certainly does separate phrases, thus aiding in the 'tasteful arrangement' of the melody; quite possibly it contributes to expressivity, providing 'pause or punctuation'; it may 'give definition' to a musical structure.

Moreover, silence is explicitly invoked in the text – 'silence moulds such strangeness as was mine a little while' – and a silence, an unmeasured time, is also implicit in the opening line: 'it is at moments after i have dreamed …' The silences that partition the music, then, might be explained by conventional practices of word-painting (although we must remember that in this case the text was added to a score already composed).

But what strikes me most is that for all these purposes the silences are unnecessarily *long*; far briefer pauses would have served at least as well. Indeed, for some of the purposes one would think that a briefer silence might have been *better*. As it is, for instance, the musical phrases are so far separated that to some extent a listener's ability to observe 'differences or relationships' is actually impaired.

What is the effect of these long silences? Now our answers become personal indeed: for me, their length invites consideration (listening, true experience) of silence *in its own right*, independent of its possible function in the sounded continuity. I cease to wait for the next sound and I simply *hear* the silence; it becomes a 'theme', a musical presence exactly like the melodies that precede and follow. As such – as a presence – it has its own meaning, its own expressivity. If I had to describe this in words, I would offer terms like 'quietude', 'contemplation', 'solitude', 'fullness'. Recall Ives, just for a moment: his two *contemplations*, with an 'unanswered question' leaving, at the end, 'the "Silences" … heard beyond in "Undisurbed Solitude"'.[25] Indeed, by the

---

23   Paul Van Emmerik notes that similar silences in *Credo in Us* (1942) were there to accommodate spoken texts; see 'An Imaginary Grid: Rhythmic Structure in Cage's Music Up to circa 1950', in *John Cage: Music, Philosophy, and Intention*, 229.

24   Indeed, the Henmar Press publication of *Experiences II* (published 1961) contains instructions regarding transpositions that make sense only in the context of concert performance.

25   Ives, *The Unanswered Question* [10]. Cage once described his *Amores*, a piece different from but related to *Experiences*, as concerned with 'the quietness between lovers';

end of *Experiences II*, it is *silence* that has become the 'melody'; the sung phrases appear within it like reflections in a stream.

The silences in *Experiences*, then, are among many attempts Cage made in the 1940s to *express* something. His discovery at that time, I suggest, was that in some circumstances *only silence* could express what he wished; sounds would not do.

Arguably the most extreme instance of these attempts was a piece Cage didn't write but which he titled *Silent Prayer*. He described this project, somewhat whimsically, in a lecture given at Vassar College in 1948:

> I have … several new desires ([which] may seem absurd, but I am serious about them): first, to compose a piece of uninterrupted silence and sell it to Muzak Co. It will be 3 or 4½ minutes long – those being the standard lengths of 'canned' music – and its title will be *Silent Prayer*. It will open with a single idea which I will attempt to make as seductive as the color and shape and fragrance of a flower. The ending will approach imperceptibility.[26]

What is one to make of this account? Is this Cage the neo-Dada? (He was, after all, now fast friends with Marcel Duchamp and had for years been devoted to Satie and his contemporaries.) Or is this Cage the satirist, taking on bourgeois culture as he had in the wartime work *Credo in Us*? Or is this John Cage, as he tells us, quite serious?

The description of *Silent Prayer*, like the intention, is ambiguous. It was, Cage wrote, to 'open with a single idea'; was this to be a *sounded* idea, or was the idea itself to be silent? And the ending was to 'approach imperceptibility'; but if the silence was to be uninterrupted, what would do the approaching?

Possibly – just possibly – Cage meant the 'uninterrupted silence' to be framed by sounds, thus inverting the usual convention: the 'music' is soundless; the 'silence' before and after is sounded. And possibly – just possibly – the intention was serious, even profoundly so: the framed silence was to be *expressive*, just like the silences in *Experiences*.

What might *Silent Prayer* have expressed? This was a time of crisis for Cage, in which both his personal and his aesthetic lives were being reshaped. The personal crisis led him to Jung and 'the integration of the personality'; the aesthetic led him to 'oriental and medieval Christian philosophy and mysticism'.[27] The latter Cage also described in his 1948 lecture:

> To what end does one write music? Fortunately I did not need to face this question alone. Lou Harrison, and now Merton Brown, another composer and close friend, were always ready to talk and ask and discuss any question relative to music with me. We began to read the works of Ananda K. Coomaraswamy and we met Gita Sarabhai, who came like an angel from India. She was a traditional musician and told us that her teacher had said that the purpose of music was to concentrate the mind. Lou Harrison found a passage by Thomas Mace written in England in 1676 to the effect that the purpose of music was to

---

see 'A Composer's Confessions' (1948), in *John Cage, Writer: Previously Uncollected Pieces*, ed. Richard Kostelanetz (New York: Limelight Editions, 1993), 40.

[26]   *Ibid.*, 43.

[27]   *Ibid.*, 41.

season and sober the mind, thus making it susceptible of divine influences, and elevating one's affections to goodness.[28]

Quite possibly, then, *Silent Prayer* was meant to 'concentrate the mind', to make it 'susceptible of divine influences', to elevate 'one's affections to goodness'. The extremity of the crisis required an extreme solution: only through 'uninterrupted silence' could Cage accomplish his intention.

But Cage never wrote *Silent Prayer*, and to our knowledge it never moved beyond a concept. Expressive silence, it seemed, was intrinsically problematic. Indeed, by this time Cage had come to doubt the possibility of expressive communication in any form. *The Perilous Night* (1944), a piece into which Cage 'had poured a great deal of emotion', had been described by a critic as resembling 'a woodpecker in a church belfry'. 'Obviously I wasn't communicating this [emotion] at all', Cage concluded; and he continued, 'if I *were* communicating, then all artists must be speaking a different language, and thus speaking only for themselves.'[29] He amplified this later: 'no one was being understood at that time. Each composer worked in a different way and no two composers understood what each other said. Sometimes, when I wrote a sad piece, half the audience would laugh.'[30]

Ives had described a similar condition a quarter-century earlier: 'A theme that the composer sets up as "moral goodness" may sound like "high vitality" to his friend, and but like an outburst of "nervous weakness" or only a "stagnant pool" to those not even his enemies. Expression, to a great extent, is a matter of terms, and terms are anyone's.'[31] For both Ives and Cage, then, expressivity of any kind was highly unreliable, if only because of the irremediable differences between individual listeners.

But there was a second problem. Music is fragile; listening is easily disrupted – by a sneeze, a passing train, the sounds from the next room. Quiet, simple music – the melody in *Experiences*, for instance – is even more fragile, since it does not insist on the listener's attention; and *silent* music is the most fragile of all. In the silences of *Experiences*, to which one is asked to attend with full emotional commitment, any sound is a potential intrusion.

Listeners are taught to disregard ancillary sounds. Silences in music invoke a tacit agreement: anything that might be heard is not really *there*. The listener stipulates, at the composer's request, that at such times there is *not* something to hear, and the empty moments in the music invite the contemplation of this possibility – 'a

---

[28] *Ibid.* David Patterson explores the relationship between Coomaraswamy and Cage in 'The Picture That Is Not in the Colors: Cage, Coomaraswamy, and the Impact of India', in *John Cage: Music, Philosophy and Intention*, 177–215. For further information on Thomas Mace, see Austin Clarkson, 'The Intent of the Musical Moment', in *Writings Through John Cage's Music, Poetry, and Art*, ed. David W. Bernstein and Christopher Hatch (Chicago: University of Chicago Press, 2001), 78–9.

[29] Calvin Tomkins, *The Bride and the Bachelors: the Heretical Courtship in Modern Art* (New York: Viking Press, 1965), 97.

[30] Quoted in Joan Peyser, *Boulez* (New York: Schirmer Books, 1976), 59.

[31] Charles Ives, *Essays Before a Sonata* (1921), in *Essays Before a Sonata, The Majority, and Other Writings*, ed. Howard Boatwright (New York: W. W. Norton, 1961), 8.

contemplation of a serious matter', in the phrase Ives applied to *The Unanswered Question*.

Ives protected his silences by filling them with composed sounds, which the listener hears but understands (Ives hopes) as 'silent'. The quiet, highly characterized string textures in Ives's two 'contemplations' invite an extraordinary attentiveness, a state of listening in which all extraneous sounds are ignored; and the extent to which that happens is a measure of Ives's success: silence becomes a way of listening, not an acoustic verity.

But Cage took a far riskier path: his silences were naked, unmediated. In his expressive music he did all he could, compositionally, to prepare them: in *Experiences*, for instance, the text, the melody, the rhythm all prepare the listener for the cessation of sound. Hence, although the silences there are not short, it is perhaps still possible for them to be *heard*, to be expressive – that is, possible for a listener to disregard whatever acoustic intrusions might occur.

But what would happen during the silence in *Silent Prayer*? Cage was an empiricist; if he had been truly serious about composing 'uninterrupted silence', he would have tried out the idea. And he would have found, perhaps, that into an unprotected silence of that length external sounds would inevitably intrude; the conventions of listening, the pretence that something perfectly audible isn't really *there*, couldn't be maintained.

Hence *Silent Prayer* was problematic on two counts. First, the 'silence' would certainly not be *silent*. Noises would intrude; the experience would be imperfect; the listener would be distracted. And second, like any expressive music, it might not actually convey Cage's intentions; it might be more likely to amuse or irritate than to sober and quiet the mind. The question was: was it the first failure that gave rise to the second? If one could *truly* experience 'silence', would the mind be quieted? Were the *circumstances* to blame?

And so, I suggest, Cage entered the anechoic chamber – an instrument, in effect, within which he hoped *Silent Prayer* could be performed. He expected to encounter a perfect silence; he hoped thereby to find a way to sober and quiet his own *very* active mind. But to his surprise he was distracted; he heard sounds. These, it emerged, were inevitable: he made them himself. There was no such thing as silence; there was no instrument on which his piece could be played. Perfect, expressive silence was an acoustic impossibility.

What then?

There, for the moment, let us leave Mr Cage, listening to his nervous system and his blood in operation. While he contemplates that silence filled with sound we shall pay a short visit to another, different, very active mind – that belonging to William James.

Part II

I assemble what is convenient to me, and I read (or re-read) James's writings and some writings about him.[32] But this reading is *purposeful*; I am filtering, assessing, integrating what I encounter in order that it be brought to bear in the discourse already begun – which concerns silence, and Cage, and Ives. What follows, then, is in no way a full representation of James's thought. Quite probably it is not even a *true* representation, from other readers' perspectives; in their views I will seem to excise, re-present, distort the substance of James's work.

But I write the foregoing not merely as a disclaimer or apologia, but rather as an illustration of an activity that all of us undertake, more or less continuously, in our ruminations as well as our day-to-day business. And this activity is precisely the subject of James's analysis: what happens, he asked, when consciousness acts upon the undifferentiated flood of sensation that impinges, ever-changing, on a sentient being? What is it that such a being *makes* of this flood, and how does it make it? And how does it determine what is *true*?

From a Jamesian perspective, then, this essay is the subject of its own analysis; and one method for testing its truth is to examine whether it accounts for its own existence. I leave that test to you – but I leave it as a request, not just a theoretical alternative. Thinking about *thought*, that is to say, requires thinking about thinking; and *that* thinking I must ask each of you to do, independently: a reflexive, circular activity, it would seem, that is wholly self-contained, inaccessible to others, who can do no more than to set down a record of their own circulations.

James

William James was born in 1842 and died in 1910. That makes him a near-contemporary of Charles Ives's father (1845–1894), and of John Cage's grandfather (1857–1923). We have three generations here, then, unrelated biologically but – in my view – constituting something like a kinship of thought. I might expect each individual to be shaped by the circumstances of his time; I expect differences. But I am looking for links as well; and I begin (as did James) with the concrete.

James's first training was in medicine, in the science of the body. He entered medical school at Harvard in 1864 and received his degree in 1869. But he never practised as a doctor; instead, three years later, he began a teaching career at Harvard by offering courses in physiology and anatomy. In 1875 he began teaching psychology, which then became the focus of his academic career. From 1880 his

---

[32]   My reading is centred on James's own prose, of course; an excellent collection of extracts is to be found in *The Writings of William James: a Comprehensive Edition*, ed. John J. McDermott, rev. ed. (Chicago: The University of Chicago Press, 1977). Ralph Barton Perry assembled many of James's letters, linking them with illuminating commentary, in *The Thought and Character of William James*, 2 vols. (Boston: Little, Brown, 1935). My favourite introduction to James remains Jacques Barzun's affectionate, probing volume, *A Stroll with William James* (Chicago: The University of Chicago Press, 1983). Biographical details that follow are drawn from Perry and Barzun.

Harvard appointment included philosophy, and thereafter it becomes difficult to distinguish between the two fields: James's philosophy was, in large part, the study of consciousness; and his psychology, more introspective than experimental, was preoccupied with what it means to *know* something. Both, however, remained grounded in the empirical; James's ultimate appeal was always to *experience*, to the interaction of a consciousness with its surroundings.

All this followed a rich and complex youth in the company of his father and his brother Henry. The elder James (also Henry), with restless feet and a restless mind, took his sons back and forth from the United States to Europe; William acquired a daunting command of several European languages, though unlike his brother his life and thought remained centred in America.

Henry senior was a close friend of Ralph Waldo Emerson, though his own thought was more argumentative, less literary, than Emerson's. A letter from Henry to Emerson, written when William was seven, seems curiously suggestive regarding not only his son's later work but also the transcendent position Emerson would assume in American culture:

> It seems to me the authorial vocation will not be so reputable in the future as in the past. If, as we are promised by all signs, the life which has hitherto glistened only in the intellect of men shall come down to their senses and put on every palpable form, I suspect the library will fall into disuse, and men will begin to believe that the only way for each to help the other is to live one's own life. Your own books suggest this conviction incessantly. I never read you as an author at all. Your books are not literature but life, and criticism always strikes me, therefore, as infinitely laughable when applied to you.[33]

The next generation of thinkers would come to terms with Emerson in divergent ways. For Ives he took on Promethean stature:

> We see him – standing on a summit at the door of the infinite, where many men do not care to climb, peering into the mysteries of life, contemplating the eternities, hurling back whatever he discovers there – now thunderbolts for us to grasp, if we can, and translate – now placing quietly, even tenderly, in our hands things that we may see without effort.[34]

Ives went on to explain how Emerson worked, using language not unrelated to that used by both Jameses (father and son):

> Emerson reveals the lesser not by an analysis of itself, but by bringing men towards the greater. He does not try to reveal, personally, but leads, rather, to a field where revelation is a harvest-part – where it is known by the perceptions of the soul towards the absolute law. He leads us towards this law, which is a realization of what experience has suggested and philosophy has hoped for.[35]

---

[33]   Henry James to Ralph Waldo Emerson, 31 August 1849, quoted in Perry, *The Thought and Character of William James*, 1: 58.

[34]   Ives, *Essays Before a Sonata*, 12.

[35]   *Ibid.*

However, Ives cautiously admitted, '[Emerson's] very universalism occasionally seems a limitation. Somewhere here may lie a weakness, real to some, apparent to others; a weakness insofar as his revelation becomes less vivid – to the many, insofar as he over-disregards the personal unit in the universal'.[36]

It was precisely 'the personal unit in the universal' on which William James's work was focused. Not surprisingly, he had his doubts about the absolute (and, implicitly, about Emerson's philosophy):

> Whereas absolutism thinks that ... substance becomes fully divine only in the form of totality, and is not its real self in any form but the *all*-form, the pluralistic view which I prefer to adopt is willing to believe that there may ultimately never be an all-form at all, that the substance of reality may never get totally collected ... and that a distributive form of reality, the *each*-form, is logically as acceptable and empirically as probable as the all-form.[37]

And then, in an astonishing passage, James situates philosophy itself in the context of the absolute:

> The absolute and the world have an identical content. The absolute is nothing but the knowledge of [the world's] objects; the objects are nothing but what the absolute knows. The world and the all-thinker thus compenetrate and soak each other up without residuum. They are but two names for the same identical material, considered now from the subjective, and now from the objective point of view ... We philosophers naturally form part of the material ... The absolute makes us by thinking us, and if we ourselves are ... believers in the absolute, one may then say that our philosophizing is one of the ways in which the absolute is conscious of itself.[38]

And this James will not accept. If there *is* an absolute, he argues, it is incommensurate with the world as it is experienced *individually*.

> As the absolute takes me ... I appear *with* everything else in its field of perfect knowledge. As I take myself, I appear *without* most other things in my field of relative ignorance. And practical differences result from its knowledge and my ignorance ... We are invincibly parts, let us talk as we will, and must always apprehend the absolute as if it were a foreign being.[39]

That passage comes from nearly the end of James's life, when he had become – in the popular mind, at least – more philosopher than scientist. But he began his career as a psychologist; and in that domain, too, his contributions rested fundamentally on an unequivocal insistence on *pluralism*. He studied individuals not in an attempt to describe a universal human condition, but precisely to define the nature of *difference*, to celebrate the very irreducibility of each person's understanding:

---

[36]   *Ibid.*, 17.

[37]   William James, 'A Pluralistic Universe', in *Essays in Radical Empiricism; A Pluralistic Universe* (New York: Longmans, Green, 1943), 34.

[38]   *Ibid.*, 37.

[39]   *Ibid.*, 39–40.

In this room – this lecture-room, say – there are a multitude of thoughts, yours and mine, some of which cohere mutually, and some not. They are as little each-for-itself and reciprocally independent as they are all-belonging-together. They are neither: no one of them is separate, but each belongs with certain others and with none besides. My thought belongs with my other thoughts, and your thought with your other thoughts. … Each of these minds keeps its own thoughts to itself. There is no giving or bartering between them. … Absolute insulation, irreducible pluralism, is the law.[40]

And pluralism, total and undifferentiated, is also the condition from which each consciousness starts. In one of James's most celebrated passages, he described the newborn's perception of the world as 'one great blooming, buzzing confusion'.[41] But his point was not merely that the world is teeming with variety; his observation was that *discrimination* – the acts by which a consciousness partitions the 'confusion' into manageable units – was fundamental to human existence, and that discrimination was accomplished by each of us separately and individually. There are no archetypes, for James, no absolute categories; there are only descriptions of things and relations between them, and these descriptions and relations are products of consciousness, of each *individual* consciousness.

Stein

Throughout his life James was a teacher, much beloved by his students. Gertrude Stein was his pupil, and his 'irreducible pluralism' provided the challenge for the first phase of her writing:

I became very interested in resemblances, in resemblances and slight differences between people. I began to make charts of all the people I had ever known or seen, or met or remembered … I began to be sure that if I could only go on long enough and talk and hear and look and see and feel enough and long enough I could finally describe really describe every kind of human being that was or is or would be living. I got very wrapped up in this. And I began writing The Making of Americans.[42]

Crucial to Stein's project was the evolution of her own consciousness in time. 'If I could only go on long enough and talk and hear and look and see and feel enough and long enough', she wrote; and indeed her life's task became 'to go on and to keep going on and to go on before'.[43]

James had famously described consciousness as a 'stream of thought' that was constantly changing: 'Experience is remoulding us every moment, and our mental reaction on every given thing is really a resultant of our experience of the whole

---

    [40]   William James, *The Principles of Psychology* (New York: Henry Holt, 1890; repr. New York: Dover, 1950), 1: 225–6.

    [41]   *Ibid.*, 1: 488.

    [42]   Gertrude Stein, 'The Gradual Making of the Making of Americans' (1934), in *Selected Writings of Gertrude Stein*, ed. Carl Van Vechten (New York: The Modern Library, 1962), 245–6.

    [43]   *Ibid.*, 250.

world up to that date.'[44] In this, too, James was a catalyst for Stein, whose writing again and again offers something that might be what it was before but is in fact not ever quite the same. And the writing project on which she embarked is unending, if only because each of us can take it up at any time; and each of us necessarily brings to it something different:

> When I was working with William James I completely learned one thing, that science is continuously busy with the complete description of something, with ultimately the complete description of anything with ultimately the complete description of everything. If this can really be done the complete description of everything then what else is there to do. We may well say nothing, but and this is the thing that makes everything continue to be anything, that after all what does happen is that as relatively few people spend all their time describing anything and they stop and so in the meantime as everything goes on somebody else can always commence and go on. And so description is really unending.[45]

James

James takes description, the drawing of distinctions, to be the starting point for thought, for consciousness, for life itself. Through experience the mind accommodates the world; it makes of the world's confusion a collection of entities and relations: 'If we start with the supposition that there is only one primal stuff or material in the world, a stuff of which everything is composed, and if we call that stuff "pure experience", then knowing can easily be explained as a particular sort of relation towards one another into which portions of pure experience may enter.'[46] James is an empiricist, then; knowledge derives from experience, not the other way around.

But James does not stop there. Rather, he asks: is that into which the 'portions of pure experience' enter – that is, consciousness – something that itself stands apart from experience? To answer affirmatively would be to reinstate a kind of dualism: there is mind and there is the world. They stand in a fixed relation, and in that relation one or the other is contained: either the mind is in the world, which brings us back to the absolute; or the world is in the mind, which brings us to idealism. James is resolute, and he answers negatively; rather, he insists, consciousness is itself experience, subject to its own relations and made of the same 'stuff' as all the rest. James sets down his thesis in italics:

> *Experience, I believe, has no such inner duplicity; and the separation of it into consciousness and content comes, not by way of subtraction, but by way of addition* ... [A] given undivided portion of experience, taken in one context of associates, [plays] the part of a known, of a state of mind, of 'consciousness'; while in a different context the same undivided bit of experience plays the part of a thing known, of an objective 'content'. In a word, in one group it figures as a thought, in another group as a thing. And,

---

44   James, *The Principles of Psychology*, 1: 234.
45   Stein, 'The Gradual Making of the Making of Americans', 255.
46   William James, 'Essays in Radical Empiricism', in *Essays in Radical Empiricism; A Pluralistic Universe*, 4.

since it can figure in both groups simultaneously we have every right to speak of it as subjective and objective both at once.[47]

The world and the self interpenetrate, in fact; consciousness is not a thing, but a kind of relation, brought into being at the moment when content and knowledge intersect.

In *The Principles of Psychology*, James had famously insisted that relations between objects were themselves part of the stuff of experience, handled by the mind exactly as it handled objects or attributes:

> If there be such things as feelings at all, *then so surely as relations between objects exist in rerum naturâ, so surely, and more surely, do feelings exist to which these relations are known.* ... We ought to say a feeling of *and*, a feeling of *if*, a feeling of *but*, and a feeling of *by*, quite as readily as we say a feeling of *blue* or a feeling of *cold*. Yet we do not: so inveterate has our habit become of recognizing the existence of the substantive parts alone, that language almost refuses to lend itself to any other use.[48]

Now he insisted that *that which relates*, not merely that which is related, nor even the relations themselves, is part of the same 'stuff'. James employs psychology to trump the assertions of philosophy; or, alternatively, he offers a philosophy that circumscribes psychology. James assumes a position that is not merely empiricist, but *radically* so.

The waters are becoming deep indeed, but let me offer one last raft to help keep us afloat – James's own summary, written late in life, of the essence of his position. I'm hoping that it will resonate in the silences to come, when we return to John Cage in his chamber:

> Radical empiricism consists first of a postulate, next of a statement of fact, and finally of a generalized conclusion.
>
> The postulate is that the only things that shall be debatable among philosophers shall be things definable in terms drawn from experience. ...
>
> The statement of fact is that the relations between things, conjunctive as well as disjunctive, are just as much matters of direct particular experience, neither more so nor less so, than the things themselves.
>
> The generalized conclusion is that therefore the parts of experience hold together from next to next by relations that are themselves parts of experience.[49]

Suzuki

James became something of a celebrity in his lifetime. He wrote voluminously and persuasively for the lay public; his lectures were widely attended; his writings were disseminated broadly through American culture at many levels. James and

---

[47]   *Ibid.*, 9–10 (emphasis in original).

[48]   James, *The Principles of Psychology*, 1: 245–6 (emphasis in original).

[49]   William James, *The Meaning of Truth: a Sequel to 'Pragmatism'* (New York: Longmans, Green, and Co., 1909), xii–xiii; excerpted in *The Writings of William James: a Comprehensive Edition*, 136.

his pragmatic philosophy, though often simplified and misrepresented, so pervaded American thought during the first half of the twentieth century that virtually no creative mind was unaffected. Moreover, James and pragmatism were claimed as quintessentially American: with his insistent pluralism, his preoccupation with *experiment*, his skeptical and radical empiricism were associated precisely those attributes of American ideology – multiplicity, autonomy, resourcefulness – that were threatened by the closing of the frontier and the forced internationalism of World War I. And it was precisely those attributes that underpinned the popular perception of American 'experimental' composers, figures like Ives and Cage.[50] The true affinity between James and Cage, however, is attributable less to ideology than to psychology; both men were in essence *observers* who took themselves as their subjects, finding the fullness of self, of silence, that others had overlooked.

Among James's close readers was Paul Carus, writer, editor and publisher of the journals *The Open Court* and *The Monist*.[51] Carus and James were often at odds, even though *The Monist* was one of the few journals to champion the writings of Charles Peirce, James's close friend and fellow empiricist. Carus devoted himself in part to promoting the understanding and discussion of Buddhist thought in America, and in 1894 he invited a young Japanese scholar, Daisetz Teitaro Suzuki, to join him. Suzuki wrote, translated and edited for Carus; and, probably through Carus, Suzuki encountered the writings of Peirce and James. Suzuki remained in America until 1909, and then returned to Japan; but in 1951 he returned on a lecture tour, joining the faculty at Columbia University from 1952 to 1957.[52]

James had placed 'pure experience' at the centre of his radical empiricism, and Suzuki took this concept to be a link between Zen and current Western philosophy. He brought the idea to the attention his close friend, the philosopher Kitaro Nishida;[53] and as he pursued his own attempts to bring together Oriental and Western thought, Suzuki returned repeatedly to James (and Peirce), sometimes even echoing James's very turns of phrase:

> Tasting, seeing, experiencing, living – all these demonstrate that there is something common to enlightenment-experience and our sense-experience; the one takes place in

---

[50] The relationship between James and American culture – and specifically American *arts* – is a central subtext of Barzun's *A Stroll with William James*.

[51] Carus' life and work is discussed in Harold Henderson, *Catalyst for Controversy: Paul Carus of Open Court* (Carbondale: Southern Illinois Press, 1993).

[52] The relationship between Suzuki and James is discussed in Austin Clarkson, 'The Intent of the Musical Moment', and in an unpublished paper by Ed Crooks, 'The Cageian Sublime', delivered at *Hung Up on the Number 64: International Conference on John Cage*, Huddersfield University, 4 February 2006. The more general relationship between James and Buddhist thought has been treated in a number of sources; a useful introduction, with an excellent bibliography, is by David Scott, 'William James and Buddhism: American Pragmatism and the Orient', *Religion* 30 (2000), 333–52.

[53] David A. Dilworth, 'Suzuki Daisetz as Regional Ontologist: Critical Remarks on Reading Suzuki's *Japanese Spirituality*', in *Philosophy East and West* 28/1 (January 1978), 110–13n. For the relationship between Nishida and James see Matao Noda, 'East-West Synthesis in Kitaro Nishida', *Philosophy East and West* 4/4 (January 1955), 345–59.

our innermost being, the other on the periphery of our consciousness. Personal experience is thus seen to be the foundation of Buddhist philosophy. In this sense Buddhism is radical empiricism or experientialism.[54]

A later exchange of views over several issues of *Philosophy East and West* culminated in 'A Reply' to Van Meter Ames's article 'Zen and Pragmatism'.[55] In this Suzuki echoes James's analysis of consciousness and finds a close parallel in Zen:

> When we have an experience, say, when I see a flower and when I begin to talk about this perception to others or to myself, the talk inevitably falls into two pans: 'this side' and 'that side'. 'That side' or 'the other side' refers to the flower, the person to whom the talk is communicated, and what is generally called an external world. 'This side' is the talker himself, that is, 'I'. Zen takes up this 'I' as the subject of its study. What is 'I'? That is, who is the self that is engaged in talking (or questioning)? … As long as 'I' am the talker, 'I' am talking about me not as myself but as somebody who stands beside or opposite me. The self is an ever-receding one, one who is forever going away from the 'self'. … The talking is always about something, never the thing itself. However much one may talk, the talking can never exhaust the thing. … To be more exact, perhaps, the self cannot be understood when it is objectified, when it is set up on the other side of experience and not on this side. This is what I mean by 'pure subjectivity'.[56]

James

James might have been distressed by Suzuki's use of the phrase 'pure subjectivity'; he was very careful in applying his own phrase, 'pure experience'. Nevertheless, in his thought, as in Suzuki's, the place of the subject was somewhat problematic. If we encounter the world as a 'blooming, buzzing confusion', and if in response we draw distinctions, create differences, how does it happen that our judgements cohere with those by others? What enables us to escape from our 'subjectivity'? How can we evaluate the relations between our judgements and whatever we take to be the world? What can we use to test the *truth* of our decisions, our actions?

We cannot appeal to a hierarchy of truth; that (again) leads back to the absolute. Nor can we remove ourselves from the act of deciding; radical empiricism requires that we take ourselves as part of the 'confusion' – no more, no less. In these straits, confronted with the seeming impossibility of testing any judgements, including his own, James resorted to the only external verities he had admitted into his psychology: space, and time. He had finished his *Psychology* with a chapter boldly titled 'Necessary Truths and the Effects of Experience', and there he had addressed this matter directly. '*Time- and space-relations*', he wrote,

---

[54]   Daisetz Teitaro Suzuki, *Mysticism: Christian and Buddhist* (London: George Allen & Unwin, 1957), 48.

[55]   Van Meter Ames, 'Zen and Pragmatism', *Philosophy East and West* 4/1 (April 1954), 19–33.

[56]   Daisetz T. Suzuki, 'Zen and Pragmatism – A Reply', *Philosophy East and West*, 4/2 (July 1954), 167–8.

are impressed from without ... Things juxtaposed in space impress us, and continue to be thought, in the relation in which they exist there. Things sequent in time, ditto. And thus, through experience in the legitimate sense of the word, there can be truly explained an immense number of our mental habitudes, many of our abstract beliefs, and all our ideas of concrete things, and of their ways of behavior.[57]

I can put this in another way: whatever there is, is proximate to something else; and whatever happens, happens before and after other events. These assertions are taken as given – the only absolutes, really, that James would accept. And it is on these assertions that James relied for his test of truth, to which he gave the name 'pragmatism'.[58] He asked that any proposition, any course of action, be considered not in itself but with respect to its consequences. That is, truth was to be a particular kind of relation between parts of experience that are associated in time or space (always remembering that *ideas*, *relations* are themselves 'parts of experience'):

> [Truth] means nothing but this, *that ideas (which themselves are but parts of our experience) become true just in so far as they help us to get into satisfactory relation with other parts of our experience*, to summarize them and get about among them by conceptual short-cuts instead of following the interminable succession of particular phenomena. Any idea upon which we can ride, so to speak; any idea that will carry us prosperously from any one part of our experience to any other part, linking things satisfactorily, working securely, simplifying, saving labor; is true for just so much, true in so far forth, true instrumentally.[59]

This conception of truth has important consequences for our understanding of the relations inherent in memory, in habit, in past and future. The pragmatic method allows us to test truths concerning the *futures* we distinguish, and their relations, as well as those concerning objects (and their relations). And from the futures thus selected, from the truths thus verified, we make, we re-make, our pasts. 'When new experiences lead to retrospective judgments, what those judgments utter *was* true, even though no past thinker had been led there. ... The present sheds a backward light on the world's previous processes.'[60]

Furthermore, the pragmatic method offers a ruthless test for determining relations between propositions. If two propositions, two courses of action, have no discernable difference in their consequences, they are equivalent, and to dispute about them is foolish. Indeed, from James's perspective they are simply *not different*, regardless of appearances: 'There can *be* no difference anywhere that doesn't *make* a difference elsewhere – no difference in abstract truth that doesn't express itself in a difference

---

[57]   James, *The Principles of Psychology*, 2: 632 (emphasis in original).

[58]   James took care always to acknowledge Charles Peirce's role in establishing 'pragmatism' as a useful term. Peirce had introduced the word in 1878, applying it strictly to the relations between language and thought. James accepted his argument and built upon it to formulate his own, more general ideas; see William James, *Pragmatism* (1907; Amherst, NY: Prometheus Books, 1991), 23–4.

[59]   James, *Pragmatism*, 28 (emphasis in original).

[60]   *Ibid.*, 98.

in concrete fact and in conduct consequent upon that fact, imposed on somebody, somehow, somewhere, and somewhen.'[61]

Finally, pragmatism allows its test to be applied to itself; indeed, it requires that this happen. Since the true is, James writes, *'only the expedient in the way of our thinking'*,[62] pragmatism admits the possibility that the 'expedient' will be, from time to time, absolutism, or monism, or any of a dozen systems of thought to which pragmatism is usually opposed. But these thoughts, these systems, are applicable, are true, only so long as they are efficacious.

> The truth of an idea is not a stagnant property inherent in it. Truth *happens* to an idea. It *becomes* true, is *made* true by events. Its verity *is* in fact an event, a process: the process namely of its verifying itself, its veri-*fication*. Its validity is the process of its valid-*ation*.[63]

Everything, then, is subject to change; and the test we apply in evaluating the possibility of change is pure experience. When we encounter something that runs contrary to our known 'truths', pragmatism offers an opportunity to remake *truth* rather than to deny experience. Pragmatism both invokes and repudiates the past; it is fundamentally a philosophy of stipulations, a philosophy in the subjunctive mood. 'Let it be the case that ...', begins the pragmatist argument; and the experience that is in the future at the time of the utterance becomes the test of the utterance when that utterance is in the past.

Part III

We left John Cage in the anechoic chamber, in a condition somewhat like that of William James's hypothetical baby: thrust into a new world, senses fully alert, ready to make sense of the 'blooming, buzzing confusion'. But there is a difference, of course: Cage was not a baby; he brought to the chamber a lifetime of experience; and on the basis of that experience he expected no buzzing, no confusion. Yet buzzing he heard, and confusion may well have followed.

What would he do in response to this unexpected experience? To whom might he turn for advice or guidance?

Not to William James, I think; though Cage surely knew *of* James, and quite possibly had read James, there's no indication that James figured directly in his thought, then or ever.[64]

And probably not to Gertrude Stein, James's student, though Stein was clearly important to Cage. In Cage's *Living Room Music* (1940), movement 2, he had used

---

[61]   *Ibid.*, 25.
[62]   *Ibid.*, 98 (emphasis in original).
[63]   *Ibid.*, 89 (emphasis in original).
[64]   Joan Retallack has, however, repeatedly linked Cage with James's fellow pragmatist John Dewey; see her 'Poethics of a Complex Realism', in *John Cage: Composed In America*, ed. Marjorie Perloff and Charles Junkerman (Chicago: University of Chicago Press, 1994), 242*ff*; and also 'Introduction: Conversations in Retrospect', in *MusiCage: Cage Muses on Words, Art and Music* (Hanover and London: University Press of New England, 1996), xxiv.

Stein's text 'The World Is Round';[65] and he reported adopting her prose style at college, with mixed results: 'At Pomona College, in response to questions about the Lake Poets, I wrote in the manner of Gertrude Stein, irrelevantly and repetitiously. I got an A. The second time I did it I was failed.'[66]

But Suzuki is a possibility. The difficulty here is that we do not know exactly when Cage visited Harvard – and further, that the details of Cage's encounters with Suzuki are still somewhat uncertain. Cage himself gave two contradictory dates for the Harvard experience in a single, late source. 'In the late forties ... I went into the anechoic chamber ... ,' he wrote; but a few sentences earlier he also reported attending Suzuki's classes 'in the late forties.' Suzuki did not lecture in New York until 1951, and his course at Columbia University in New York did not start until spring of the following year, so clearly Cage's memory has played him false on this occasion. A few pages later, however, Cage described the first 'happening', given at Black Mountain College, North Carolina, in the summer of 1952. Later that summer, he noted, he was in Rhode Island; and 'from Rhode Island I went on to ... the anechoic chamber at Harvard'.[67] This is more probable; and in this case, Suzuki's first course of lectures, given the previous spring, would have been very much on Cage's mind.

In any case, as Cage listened in the chamber, his direct connection with William James was oblique at best. Nonetheless, I suggest, his experience and his response were quintessentially Jamesian: pragmatic in their method and effect, and of import equally to psychology and philosophy.

In the early chapters of *The Principles of Psychology*, James considered two essential and intertwined phenomena: attention and habit. It is because we are capable of *attending* to certain matters while ignoring others, he argued, that the 'teeming multiplicity of objects and relations'[68] can be reduced to the sensations that constitute pure experience:

> Millions of items of the outward order are present to my senses which never properly enter into my experience. Why? Because they have no *interest* for me. *My experience is what I agree to attend to.*[69]

But every act of attention, every declaration of interest, shapes the future; each contributes to the set of *habits* by which each consciousness manages daily life. And a habit, once ingrained, 'diminishes the conscious attention with which our acts are

---

[65]   He evidently set other texts in even earlier works now lost; see John Cage, 'An Autobiographical Statement' (1989), in *John Cage, Writer*, 238.

[66]   John Cage, 'Preface to *Indeterminacy*' (1959), in *John Cage, Writer*, 75–6. Cage's story is strikingly reminiscent of one that Stein told about herself and William James, in which she declines to write an examination paper and is given 'the highest mark in his course'; see Stein, *The Autobiography of Alice B. Toklas*, in *Selected Writings of Gertrude Stein*, 74–5.

[67]   Cage, 'An Autobiographical Statement', 241, 243. See also David Patterson, 'Appraising the Catchwords', 141–4.

[68]   James, *The Principles of Psychology*, 1: 224.

[69]   *Ibid.*, 1: 402 (emphasis in original).

performed'.[70] Thus attention both shapes and is shaped by habit and, more broadly, by all that a consciousness has learned. Indeed, wrote James,

> men have no eyes but for those aspects of things which they have already been taught to discern ... *the only things which we commonly see are those which we preperceive*, and the only things which we preperceive are those which have been labelled for us, and the labels stamped into our mind.[71]

It follows that habits change only when attention is brought to bear on objects or relations that were previously not of interest. It is possible for interest to be stimulated externally; attention can be 'called to' something. But it is also possible to build a habit of attending to matters not yet 'labelled'; it is possible to build a habit of breaking habits.

For John Cage, attention was a matter of interest from the beginning. A talk written in 1937 advocated 'attentive listening to music', by which Cage meant attending to sound rather than to theories or descriptions: 'Curiosity as to labels, the desire to identify and pigeon-hole a pleasure, [has] separated us from the real job of listening to the whole thing, the rich continuous music.'[72] As a composer he sought to draw his listener's attention to sounds habitually overlooked: 'I used noises. They had not been intellectualized; the ear could hear them directly ... Noises, too, had been discriminated against; and being American, having been trained to be sentimental, I fought for noises.'[73] And he was forthright about the ways in which musical dogma had constrained attention: 'Our common answer to every criticism must be to continue working and listening, ... disregarding the cumbersome, top-heavy structure of musical prohibitions.'[74]

The sounds Cage heard in the anechoic chamber were not new to him; generated by his own body, they had been available to his consciousness for years. But they had not formed part of his *experience*; his habit was to disregard them. He had to some extent repudiated the labels, the preperceptions, that he had been taught regarding music. To do this, he had attended to *silence*, and he had written music designed to draw a listener's attention to silence. But he had not repudiated the preperceptions associated with silence itself. Attending to silence had meant, for him, attending to an *absence* and thus disregarding sounds actually present at that moment. Thus he had directed his attention elsewhere, away from his nervous system, his circulation and all the other ancillary sounds that 'silence' actually made audible.

In the anechoic chamber, however, Cage invoked his habit of attending to attention, a habit meant to challenge the habits that diminished his attention. He asked, as he had before, 'what can I attend to?' – and found that the answer was not a *nothing*, not an *absence*, as he had expected, but two rather ordinary sounds:

---

[70]   *Ibid.*, 1: 114.

[71]   *Ibid.*, 1: 443–4 (emphasis in original).

[72]   John Cage, 'Listening to Music (1937)', in *John Cage, Writer*, 15, 19.

[73]   John Cage, 'Lecture on Nothing' (1950), in *Silence*, 116–17. In *Silence* the date is given as 1959, but it is now well established that Cage first delivered this talk in 1950; see, for instance, Patterson, 'Appraising the Catchwords', 351, and Chapter 3, pp. 126–79, *passim*.

[74]   John Cage, 'Goal: New Music, New Dance' (1939), in *Silence*, 87.

'one high, and one low'. He had a choice: he could cleave to his preperceptions, disregarding these two sounds in order that he experience 'silence' as he had before – a condition in which it is stipulated that no sounds occur and which (he hoped) would 'quiet' the mind; or he could disregard the preperceptions and attend to the sounds. He chose the latter.

As a composer it then became incumbent upon him to draw the attention of others to the sounds that he had found, as he had to noises earlier. But these sounds were *inside* him, inaccessible to others; James's 'irreducible pluralism' was indeed 'the law'. All that he could do was to offer an imperfect analogy to his own experience – an analogy without an anechoic chamber, since his listeners would be elsewhere; and without his own body.

And now, good reader, we come to the second small experiment. Could you ask your previous collaborator (or another, if necessary) now to perform *4'33"*? There have been extensive discussions about performance alternatives in this, Cage's 'silent piece'; for our purposes I suggest a version that very much resembles the original. Ask your performer to indicate the beginning and endings of three movements with some appropriate and simple action: opening and closing the lid to the keys on the piano (as David Tudor did); or removing and replacing a mouthpiece cap; or moving out of and into the 'rest' position for an instrument. Let the performer make no sounds intentionally during the periods of silence; and as before, let the performance be *simple*, without impatience or hesitation. (It's not as easy as it sounds! By all means allow your performer to rehearse, if necessary, but not in your presence.)

And again the questions will be: what did you 'experience', what did you *do*, during that music? Did *these* silences serve any of the purposes Cage had described in 1958? Did you experience them in the same way as the silences in *Experiences*? Once again I will not hear your answers, of course; once again I can only offer my own response, hoping not for agreement but for discovery.

The three silences (the three movements of the piece) last 30", 143" and 100", respectively. Shall we listen?

My own experience has ended. I can report that the fans in this room produce a quite complicated drone that I hadn't noticed previously. Someone's shoes seem to stick when they are lifted from the floor. I thought those distant rattles were a computer keyboard, but now I'm not so certain. There is a high, faint whine that seems to be in my ears themselves. At one moment I was briefly aware that I had exhaled audibly.

That is, I heard sounds. I did not hear *silence*. I did not choose to disregard what occurred in order to attend to an absence; I attended to what was present. Perhaps some of the sounds I have reported were audible to me alone (recall James's 'irreducible pluralism'); but some, I would think, would have been audible to other listeners as well. But *none* of those sounds were the sounds that John Cage heard. His composition does not offer me an expression of his experience, as the aptly-named *Experiences* is meant to do. It offers me a *pragmatic* method to test my preperceptions; it offers me a chance to change my habits.

And because, in the context of this paper, *4'33"* is one of a series of musical examples, I am also offered the opportunity to apply the pragmatic method both to certain *utterances* (musical compositions) and to my experiences of these. In particular, I can compare the hypothetical *Silent Prayer* and the very real *4'33"*. Are the consequences of these, of my *experience* of these, the same? If so, then they are, pragmatically, the same composition.

Silent Prayer contains a framed silence, an expressive silence. Knowing what I do about Cage's thought in 1948, I understand that I am to *not-attend* to sounds that may occur. I am, in fact, to attempt to continue to disregard them, to stipulate *silence*, as before. And if I cannot disregard them – which, I suggest, is what Cage discovered in his initial experiments with that piece – then *Silent Prayer* is a failure: it is not *useful* (one of Cage's favourite words) for my purposes. It is not 'expedient', James might write; it is not *true*.

Because it is not *true*, and because, I believe, Cage understood this, *Silent Prayer* was never performed. Instead, after the experience in the anechoic chamber, Cage wrote *4'33"*. And *4'33" is true* – not because its description differs, but because the facts of its performance, of my experience, *change* things. If I, the listener, attempt to disregard the sounds that occur, I find I cannot; and that discovery – precisely analogous to Cage's own discovery – precipitates a crisis. I can accuse the piece, I can accuse Cage, of failure – but where does the failure reside? Cage has prescribed *nothing* – quite literally *nothing* – and has asked me to listen to it. And the *nothing* thereby has become *something*: the failure, then, is in my purpose, in my desire to retain *nothing* – to 'keep silence' – not in the *something* that is there. *4'33"* leads to a new discovery, a new assertion about the world. I find, in Cage's phrase, that 'try as we may to make a silence, we cannot.' This assertion and the new relations it implies can guide me into and through a new stream of experience; they offer a way out of the impossibilities represented by *Silent Prayer*. They are *useful*; and hence *4'33"* is *useful* – not expressive, not good, not beautiful: *useful*.

In sum, the pragmatic method is implicit in the very experience constituted in *4'33"*. Cage's 'silent piece' is *non-sense* (*non-sensation*) if approached from the absolute, or from idealism, or from other positions that demand fixity in the universe of relations. It is *sense* (*sensation*) only to a pragmatist; and the *silence* it proposes, which inevitably and always contains sound, is a pragmatist's silence.

In at least one source Cage asserted that there was a direct, causal link between his experience in the anechoic chamber and the composition of *4'33"*. In 'An Autobiographical Statement' the second of the two chronologies took Cage from Black Mountain College through Rhode Island to Harvard, where he 'heard that silence was not the absence of sound but was the unintended operation of my nervous system and the circulation of my blood'. 'It was this experience', he continued, 'and the white paintings of Rauschenberg that led me to compose *4'33"*.' But then, once again, the chronology goes seriously awry: the 'silent piece', Cage asserted, had been described 'in a lecture at Vassar College some years before when I was in the flush of my studies with Suzuki'.[75]

The 'Vassar lecture' is 'A Composer's Confessions', in which Cage described *Silent Prayer*. But he was certainly not studying with Suzuki then; Suzuki would not return to America until two years later. Nor, I have argued, is a description of *Silent Prayer* in any sense a description of the 'silent piece' (*4'33"*).

If we set these errors aside, however, a possible chronology emerges. The last event in which Cage participated at Black Mountain College was a performance of the *Sonatas and Interludes* on 16 August 1952. Two weeks later, on 29 August, David Tudor gave the first performance of *4'33"* at Woodstock, New York. If we take Cage at his word, the Harvard experience must have taken place some time in the two intervening weeks, and the composition of *4'33"* was an immediate response to that experience.[76]

In two weeks, then, Cage's universe – his *experience* – had been wholly transformed. The question then became: what now?

Recall William James, again: 'The present sheds a backward light on the world's previous processes.' If the 'silence' of the anechoic chamber was filled with sound, it must have been the case that all previous silences were also filled with sounds – sounds to which Cage had not attended. And since music, too, is filled with sounds, the pragmatic test tells us that any difference between the two (music and silence) *cannot* depend upon the presence of sound. Sound is not suitable to 'verify', to 'validate', the ideas of music or silence; if sound is to be the criterion, music and silence are identical.

Another test, another criterion, was therefore needed, and Cage proposed *intention*. In 1958, after he had summarized the conventional uses of silence ('tasteful arrangement', 'expressivity', and so forth), Cage continued:

Where none of these or other goals is present, silence becomes something else – not silence at all, but sounds, the ambient sounds. The nature of these is unpredictable and changing. These sounds (which are called silence only because they do not form part of a musical intention) may be depended upon to exist. The world teems with them, and is, in fact, at no point free of them. ... There are, demonstrably, sounds to be heard and forever, given ears to hear. Where these ears are in connection with a mind that has nothing to do,

---

[75]   Cage, 'An Autobiographical Statement,' 243.

[76]   David Patterson supplies the dates of 16 and 29 August in 'Appraising the Catchwords', 340. In Larry Solomon's article "The Sounds of Silence" (http://solomonsmusic.net/4min33se.htm), he asserts, but without evidence, that Cage returned to New York after Black Mountain and that Cage encountered the anechoic chamber in 1951. Peter Dickinson interviewed David Tudor on 26 July 1987, when Tudor described the links between the first version of *4'33"* and the compositional method for *Music of Changes*. Tudor's account is consistent with the chronology I propose but does not confirm it. To verify my hypothesis it will be necessary to trace Cage's movements in the two intervening weeks, something not yet done. (See *CageTalk: Dialogues With and About John Cage*, ed. Peter Dickinson, Rochester, N.Y.: University of Rochester Press, Woodbridge: Boydell & Brewer, 2006. My thanks to Professor Dickinson for supplying me with a copy of this interview in advance of publication.)

that mind is free to enter into the act of listening, hearing each sound just as it is, not as a phenomenon more or less approximating a preconception.[77]

How like James this is! The world 'teems' with sounds; the 'act' of listening is burdened with 'preconceptions' (James writes 'preperceptions'); only by freely 'entering into the act of listening' – that is, by choosing to *attend*, by taking an *interest* – can habits, habituated goals, be changed.

And in the passage that follows Cage's description of the anechoic chamber – the excerpt quoted near the beginning of this essay – we can again hear James's voice:

> One need not fear about the future of music. But this fearlessness follows only if, at the parting of the ways [*the pragmatic test*], where it is realized that sounds occur whether intended or not, one turns in the direction of [*one attends to*] those he does not intend. This turning is psychological and ... leads to the world of nature [*of pure experience*], where ... one sees that humanity and nature, not separate, are in this world together [*that parts of experience hold together by relations that are themselves parts of experience*].

The key, indeed, is in the final, reflexive assertion. Cage proposed that we, we listeners, *attend to attention*: that we notice *that* we are noticing, not merely *what* we are noticing. The inclusion of the self in the universe of experience is, for Zen, a path to selfless-ness. For James it was implicit in pragmatism and the recognition that truth is neither willed nor absolute: 'truth *happens* to an idea'.

For this kind of attention Cage reserved the word 'discipline', and he asked, repeatedly, that his listeners, his readers, act in a disciplined manner. Discipline then becomes, for all practical purposes, an application of the pragmatic method: attend to the act of attending in order to challenge the habits, the preperceptions, from which your experience is built.

In the end – conceptually, aesthetically and biographically – the forty years of work that followed all rest on Cage's encounter with silence in the anechoic chamber. The immense and complex body of his later music and thought relied upon relations that came into being when Cage examined, attended to, the *presence* that he found there. What he created thereafter is not a metaphysics of sound, nor an aesthetics of music, nor even an ethics of listening.

It is a pragmatics – of silence.

---

[77]   Cage, 'Composition as Process', 22–3.

Chapter 7

Some Noisy Ruminations on Susan Sontag's 'Aesthetics of Silence'

Darla M. Crispin

Susan Sontag's 'Aesthetics of Silence' (1967) is a work that leads us to important questions about theories of modernism, especially about the role of silence in art and in the modernist/post-modernist debate.[1] The essay was written forty years ago in New York City – a noisy metropolis, which was, and is, paradigmatic of so much that typifies the modern; but it was written by a critic whose stance reflected a gathering doubt that modernism's impact could truly oppose the 'determining power of history'.[2] Sontag viewed the American appetite for constantly creating the new with an undercurrent of sober retrospection that has led the cultural historian Sohnya Sayres to call her an 'elegiac modernist'.[3] The motivation behind Sontag's examination of silence was largely related to her re-appraisal of literary criticism and of the place of certain works of literature in the modernist category. By implication, Sontag reassessed her own work in the essay, and applied her analysis of silence as a corrective.

Although Sontag's 'The Aesthetics of Silence' concentrates on literature, her references here, and elsewhere in her writings, to the composer John Cage make one aware that her questions have promising applications to music and to issues of musical modernism. The book, *Cage–Cunningham–Johns: Dancers on a Plane,* which catalogues a project in which works of the composer, the choreographer Merce Cunningham and the artist Jasper Johns were displayed side-by-side, has an extensive preface by Sontag, in which Cage's influence is not only apparent on the level of form, but also of content.[4] It is possible to apply Sontag's arguments more broadly, considering the relationship of silence to time, to the process of individual development and, specifically, to the compositional credos of certain composers and thinkers.

---

[1]   Susan Sontag, 'The Aesthetics of Silence', in *Styles of Radical Will* (1969; London: Vintage, 1994), 3–34.

[2]   Sohnya Sayres, *Susan Sontag: the Elegiac Modernist* (London: Routledge, 1990), 1.

[3]   *Ibid.*

[4]   Susan Sontag, 'In Memory of their Feelings', in *Cage–Cunningham–Johns: Dancers on a Plane*, ed. Judy Adam (1989; London: Thames and Hudson in association with Anthony d'Offay Gallery, 1990), 13–23. A section of Sontag's contribution to this collection, entitled 'Silence', makes reference to one of Cage's favourite subjects, mushrooms (21).

In various strands of twentieth-century modernism within the arts, especially those contemporaneous with the First World War, the search for the new has been accompanied by, and often manifested in, a conscious attempt to obliterate the traditional. Although the act of obliteration was often noisy, its immediate consequence was to conjure up the prospect of a space, a silence, a void. Consider the deafening silence that resonates at the end of the litany of renunciation, read out by the poet Louis Aragon (soon to be one of the key members of the Surrealists) during a meeting of Dadaists at the Salon des Indépendants on 5 February 1920:

> No more painters, no more writers, no more musicians, no more sculptors, no more religions, no more republicans, no more royalists, no more imperialists, no more anarchists, no more socialists, no more Bolsheviks, no more politicians, no more proletarians, no more democrats, no more bourgeois, no more aristocrats, no more armies, no more police, no more nations, in fact enough of all these imbecilities, nothing more, nothing more, nothing, NOTHING, NOTHING, NOTHING.[5]

While the Dadaists contemplated this void with an exultant nihilism, others strove to fill it immediately with something novel, however makeshift. The poet Guillaume Apollinaire made the search for 'a new language / about which no grammarian of whatever language will have anything to say',[6] the theme of part of his poem 'La victoire'. But his quest for new sounds quickly turned into the willing acceptance of grunts and obscenities as substitutes for traditional poetic language:

> We want new sounds new sounds new sounds
> We want consonants without vowels
> Consonants that emit dull farts
> Imitate the sound of a spinning top
> Bubble continuously with a nasal sound
> Click your tongue
> Use the dull sound of someone eating impolitely.[7]

Like others of his later generation, but more completely than most, Cage was more relaxed in his contemplation of the void and content to inhabit it, examining the possibilities of the space itself. It was Sontag's view too that, in the case of literary

---

[5]   'Plus de peintres, plus de litterateurs, plus de musicians, plus de sculpteurs, plus de religions, plus de républicains, plus de royalists, plus d'impérialistes, plus d'anarchistes, plus de socialistes, plus de bolcheviques, plus de politiques, plus de prolétaires, plus de democrats, plus de bourgeois, plus d'aristocrates, plus d'armées, plus de police, plus de patries, enfin assez de toutes ces imbecilities, plus rien, plus rien, rien, RIEN, RIEN, RIEN'; Maurice Nadeau, *Histoire du surréalisme* (Paris: Éditions du Seuil 1964), 48.

[6]   '... d'un nouveau language / Auquel le grammairien d'aucune langue n'aura rien à dire'; Guillaume Apollinaire, 'La victoire', in *Calligrammes: poémes de la paix et de la guerre, 1913–1916* (Paris: Éditions Gallimard, 1925), 180.

[7]   'On veut de nouveaux sons de nouveaux sons de nouveaux sons / On veut des consonnes sans voyelles / Des consonnes qui pètent sourdement / Imitez le son de la toupee / Laissez pétiller un son nasal et continu / Faites claquer votre langue / Servez-vous du bruit sourd de celui qui mange sans civilité'; Apollinaire, 'La victoire', 180.

criticism at least, this was often 'a vigorous, tonic choice'.[8] In order to trace more clearly how her ideas can be seen as relating to musical issues, I would like to create a 'dialogue between two silences' in which Sontag's essay is read alongside Cage's collection of lectures and writings, *Silence*, thereby exposing the accords and resistances that appear.[9] My aim is not only to create a sense of how Sontag's and Cage's ideas relate, but also to reconstruct some aspects of the debate about modernism that were taking place in America in the late 1960s.

A warning needs to be borne in mind here: Cage's textual utterances are just as liable to be 'composed' as his music. Reading *Silence*, one needs to be aware that the 'truth content' of the texts is subject to the same laws of chance, the same zest for experimentation and play, as in the more obviously 'musical' works. Indeed, this collection of texts may be seen as an extension of Cage's ideas of chance performance and silence into the realm of words. Arthur J. Sabatini summarizes the contradictions inherent in the very particular process of reading demanded by Cage's writings:

> For readers of John Cage, nonreading is a consequence of reading, just as listeners to his music encounter silence. Cage's later writings distil and rarify the performance of writing/reading to a point of utter density, a black hole within which all the physics of the Cagean universe simultaneously hold true and are questionable. For both Cage and readers, nonreading is reading's dumb show: a performance that verges on meaning where signs are ultimately themselves, isolated, yet as full as Cagean silence.[10]

So, the literal nature of my own constructed 'conversation' needs to be approached with some scepticism. Although Sontag's essay writing appears to be influenced by Cage's example in the variation of section lengths and the repetition of certain phrases, her prose remained essentially conventional in its concern to convey meaning. However, her detailed questioning uncovered the multi-faceted nature of what appears to be a simple absence of sound. Silence, she said, can be considered in relation to theories of origins, in terms of social choices and necessities, as a function of the musical, literary and visual art spheres, and as an adjunct to faith or wisdom traditions. But Sontag's point here was not about faith itself, but about the paradoxical connection of elected silence with spiritual ambition, something that she brought back into the sphere of art, her central concern.[11]

Consider her evaluation of the 'mythic view' of silence:

> In my opinion, the myths of silence and emptiness are about as nourishing and viable as might be devised in an 'unwholesome' time – which is, of necessity, a time in which

---

[8]   Sontag, 'The Aesthetics of Silence', 10. Sontag also considers these 'tonic choices' at length in the collected essays, *Against Interpretation and Other Essays* (1967; London: Vintage, 1994), and *On Photography* (1977; London: Penguin Books, 1978).

[9]   John Cage, *Silence: Lectures and Writings* (1961; London: Marion Boyars, 1978).

[10]   Arthur J. Sabatini, 'Silent Performances: On Reading John Cage', in *John Cage at Seventy Five*, ed. Richard Fleming and William Duckworth, *The Bucknell Review* 32/2 (Lewisburg: Bucknell University Press; London: Associated University Presses, 1989), 91.

[11]   'Underneath what looks like a strenuous modesty, if not actual debility, is to be discerned an energetic secular blasphemy: the wish to attain the unfettered, unselective, total consciousness of "God"'; Sontag, 'The Aesthetics of Silence', 14.

'unwholesome' psychic states furnish the energies for most superior work in the arts. Yet one can't deny the pathos in these myths.[12]

In spite of this grudgingly accepting view of myth advanced in the latter part of her essay, Sontag began by discussing the problem of the demystification of myth, which she associated with 'the incorrigible survival of the religious impulse. [She wanted to] enliven the debate about absolute art by heading off religious encapsulation'.[13] She denounced the myth of art's absoluteness, which makes art the 'enemy of the artist, for it denies him the realization – the transcendence – he desires'.[14] Transcendence, for Sontag, was a state beyond realization; this may account for the pathos that she identified in the myths of silence and emptiness, and the relative tolerance with which she viewed them.

An even more important feature of Sontag's essay writing is her mistrust of the device of metaphor. This is most clearly demonstrated in her book, *Illness as Metaphor*, which deals with problems of perception faced by those with cancer.[15] Sontag discussed the difficulties associated with coping with *illness*, the real, physical disorder, and *sickness*, the metaphoric beliefs that one develops about the illness, which, Ken Wilber has suggested, are often societally-based.[16] In a similar vein, in 'The Aesthetics of Silence' she asked the reader to reassess the metaphors associated with silence. While acknowledging that stripping silence of metaphor is ultimately problematic, she asserted her view that metaphor is a compromise. The fall from transcendence to metaphor is a principal concern for her. The transcendence myth about art

> installs within the activity of art many of the paradoxes involved in attaining absolute states of being described by the great religious mystics. As the activity of the mystic must end in a *via negativa*, a theology of God's absence, a craving for the cloud of unknowing beyond knowledge and for the silence beyond speech, so art must tend toward anti-art, the elimination of the 'subject', the substitute of chance for intention, and the pursuit of silence.[17]

Sontag saw that this quest for the absolute had the potential to lead to art's annihilation. But at the boundary of annihilation, she envisioned an encounter with the myths of silence in which, as we have seen, she sensed a profound pathos. It could be said that, for her, the search for transcendence became interfused with the pursuit of emptiness, nothingness, silence.

This idea of annihilation brings to the foreground questions about the nature of history. Sontag brought to her role as an American literary critic a strong interest in European literature, almost amounting to a sense that her literary centre of gravity was more European than American; she wrote on the novels of Jean Paul Sartre

---

12   Sontag, 'The Aesthetics of Silence', 11.
13   Sayres, *Susan Sontag*, 91.
14   Sontag, 'The Aesthetics of Silence', 5.
15   Susan Sontag, *Illness as Metaphor* (New York: Farrar, Straus and Giroux, 1978).
16   Ken Wilber, *Grace and Grit* (Boston and London: Shambhala, 1991), 40–47.
17   *Ibid.*, 91–2.

and Albert Camus, evaluated the critical work of Roland Barthes, commented on the films of Ingmar Bergman. But she also looked askew at this European heritage, seeing its potential for being a dead-weight: 'art is foundering in the debilitating tide of what seemed the crowning achievement of European thought: secular historical consciousness'.[18] Her suspicion of many interpretative theories may be seen as an extension of her resistance to this tradition.

For his part, Cage adopted many strategies to ease this historical burden. But in spite of his often-cited determination to move beyond the pervasive perceptual dualisms of Western art-music, a goal that mirrors the wider philosophical tenets of Zen, Cage's American-based views on the European-dominated approach to Western music were often adversarial. Jean-Jacques Nattiez's record of Cage's correspondence with Boulez reveals the gradual recognition by the two men of their often diametrically-opposed viewpoints.[19] What seems surprising, as Nattiez pointed out, is the extent to which they mistakenly believed that they understood each other early in their exchange of ideas; for a while their opposition had all the appearance of similitude.[20] For example, the final section of Cage's 'Lecture on Something' (1959) begins with a provocative assessment of European primacy:

When   going from nothing   towards something,   we have all
the European   history of music   and art   we remember
and there we can see   that this   is well done   but the other is not.
So–and–so contributed   this and that   and criteria.   But now we are
going from   something   towards nothing,   and there is no way
of saying success   or failure   since all things   have equally   their
Buddha nature.[21]

This search for the 'Buddha nature', that is, for the perception of a non-dual essence of things,[22] embodied for Sontag one possible response to the historical estrangement of the artist: 'to compensate for this ignominious enslavement to history, the artist exalts himself with the dream of a wholly ahistorical, and therefore unalienated art ... Art that is "silent" constitutes one approach to this visionary, ahistorical condition'.[23] But – and this in spite of his search for non-duality – Cage asserted more than once that this kind of escape is the prerogative of American, rather than European, music. His assessment of his Darmstadt colleagues is telling:

---

[18]   *Ibid.*, 14.

[19]   For example, Cage and Boulez shared a fascination with the ordering of pitches in their respectively favoured means of chance operations and total serialism. While this broad question was expressed as a shared concern at first, their eventual realization of the oppositional nature of the two processes would lead the composers toward profound aesthetic and philosophical differences. See Jean-Jacques Nattiez, ed., *The Boulez–Cage Correspondence*, trans. Robert Samuels (Cambridge: Cambridge University Press, 1993), 10.

[20]   See Nattiez, ed., *The Boulez–Cage Correspondence*, 24.

[21]   Cage, 'Lecture on Something' (1950 [not 1959]), in *Silence*, 143.

[22]   For a discussion of the idea of the 'Buddha nature', see 'The Mind and the Nature of Mind', in Sogyal Rinpoche, *The Tibetan Book of Living and Dying* (London: Rider Books, 1992), 46–8.

[23]   Sontag, 'The Aesthetics of Silence', 15.

> The vitality that characterizes the current European musical scene follows from the activities of Boulez, Stockhausen, Nono, Maderna, Pousseur, Berio, etc. There is in all of this activity an element of tradition, continuity with the past, which is expressed in each work as an interest in continuity whether in the terms of discourse or organization. … The skills that are required to bring such events about are taught in the academies. However, this scene will change. The silences of American experimental music and even its technical involvements with chance operations are being introduced into new European music. It will not be easy, however, for Europe to give up being Europe.[24]

This is not to say that Cage ever gave up using 'traditional' core material if he felt it would serve him. In 'John Cage and History: Hymns and Variations', William Brooks gave an example in which Cage subjected traditional American hymns to a process of reduction, so that mere vestiges of them remained, surrounded by silence. What this meant for Cage was that 'he included among his endeavours the invention of methods which would accept historical musics, but strip them of exclusionary values'.[25] But there is an irony here in that Cage's silences cannot escape historicization, since, as the Polish musicologist, Zofia Lissa has pointed out, a choice about a silence (or a pause) 'alters according to historical style'.[26] Cage's choices about silence have everything to do with stylistic choices he made in light of his position as a musical thinker in the 1960s, and in reference to some of the historical problems of musical modernity faced at that time. In Sontag's words, 'the value placed on silence doesn't arise by virtue of the *nature* of art, but derives from the contemporary ascription of certain "absolute" qualities to the art object and the activity of the artist'.[27]

Beyond the question of history, we can see through Cage's employment of silences some attempt to deal with temporal issues, since silence is a feature of 'all arts, the products of which develop in time'.[28] In live performance situations, silence may be deemed to be full of potential energy. One concrete illustration of this is how music is heard in the (traditional) concert setting, something that Lissa elucidates with forensic detail as part of her broader project, which can be read as a musicological version of Cage's manifold explorations of music, silence and the way they interrelate:

> The musical work – that is, a given performance of that work – is a process that at a certain moment enters into the silence, then takes its course within it, and with its last sound merges back into it. Thus a specific performance of the musical work and its specific experience by the listener are sandwiched between two silences that are quite different from each other: the silence *before* the performance is full of expectation of the work, the

---

[24]   Cage, 'History of Experimental Music in the United States' (1959), in *Silence*, 74–5.

[25]   William Brooks, 'John Cage and History: Hymns and Variations', in *Perspectives of New Music* 31/2 (Summer 1993), 75.

[26]   'Die Funktionen der Pause ändern sich je nach dem historischen Stil'; Zofia Lissa, 'Die Ästhetischen Funktionen der Stille und Pause in der Musik' (1962), repr. as 'Stille und Pause in der Musik', in Lissa, *Aufsätze zur Musikästhetik: eine Auswahl* (Berlin: Henschel, 1969), 162. English translation assisted by Irene Auerbach.

[27]   Sontag, 'The Aesthetics of Silence', 31 (emphasis from the original).

[28]   'Sie tritt in allen Künsten auf, deren Werke sich in der Zeit entwickein'; Lissa, 'Stille und Pause in der Musik', 160.

silence *after* the performance, in the listener's consciousness, is full of the final structures of the work as they die away.[29]

In light of Cage's writings, Lissa's views are worth considering carefully. She articulates one view of silence – that it may be characterized as an omnipresent factor in a work, but one that advances and retreats from the perceptual surface depending upon the nature of the material that is heard or read over it. In *Silence*, Cage repeatedly works with this approach. The blank, white page becomes a metaphor for silence, with variation in typeface, text density and style of paragraph creating a visual dialectic with this silence. But, remembering Sontag's suspicion of metaphors, we are not surprised to find that an important divergence of view takes place here between her and Cage. Sontag wrote:

> Since the artist can't embrace silence literally and remain an artist, what the rhetoric of silence indicates is a determination to pursue his activity more deviously than before. One way is indicated by Breton's notion of the 'full margin'. The artist is enjoined to devote himself to filling up the periphery of the art space, leaving the central area of usage blank.[30]

In Sontag's view, the final achievement of silence must be to obliterate the work of art and the artist. But Cage's view was diametrically opposed to this. He argued that the achievement of total silence had the potential to imbue one with the awareness that what one might call art (given a world view that does not judge art by Western norms) is omnipresent. Again, this reflects the influence upon Cage of Zen teachings, which posit that the true nature of mind exists beyond obscuring layers of conceptual thought, and that the best means for clearing them is by silent meditation.

Cage's ultimate aim was the realization of an awareness that was beyond the temporal. However, the process of hearing music is irrevocably attached to the passage of real time, so the intrusion of silence, its antithesis, creates questions about the temporal. Cage highlighted this in the text '45' for a Speaker', by noting the passage of time in ten second increments which are read down the left hand margin, implying that the text, including its pauses and silences, must be read with a stopwatch.[31]

Again, the achievement of an 'absolute' silence remains somehow distant. As Sontag wrote:

---

[29] 'Das musikalische Werk, das heißt eine gewisse Aufführung dieses Werkes, ist ein Prozeß, der in einem gewissen Augenblick in die Stille eintritt, sich dann in ihr abspielt und mit den letzten Klängen in sie übergeht. Also eine bestimmte Aufführung des musikalischen Werks und dessen bestimmtes Erlebnis durch den Hörer wird in zwei Stille einmontiert, die sich durch ihren 'Gehalt' stark voneinander unterscheiden: die Stille *vor* der Aufführung ist voller Erwartung auf das Werk, die Stille *nach* der Aufführung voller im Bewußtsein des Hörers verklingender Schlußstrukturen des gehörten Werks'; *ibid.*, 162.

[30] Sontag, 'The Aesthetics of Silence', 12.

[31] Cage, '45' for a Speaker' (1954), in *Silence*, 146–94.

Silence doesn't exist in a literal sense, however, as the *experience* of an audience. It would mean that the spectator was aware of no stimulus or that he was unable to make a response. But this can't happen, nor can it even be induced programmatically …

> Nor can silence, in its literal state, exist as the *property* of an artwork – even of works like Duchamp's readymades or Cage's 4'33", in which the artist has ostentatiously done no more to satisfy any established criteria of art than set the object in a gallery or situate the performance on a concert stage. There is no neutral surface, no neutral discourse, no neutral theme, no neutral form. … Instead of raw or achieved silence, one finds various moves in the direction of an ever receding horizon of silence – moves which, by definition, can never be fully consummated.[32]

Sontag alluded here to a human dilemma that has been discussed in Freudian and, more recently, Lacanian, psychoanalytical theory, namely the force of that which entices yet eludes. Silence is fragile, but the idea of silence is immensely powerful. For human beings, this is a source of frustration, for we may attempt to contemplate silence, yet we carry insuperable obstacles to it within our own bodies, as Cage reminded us in recounting his experiences in an anechoic chamber.[33] There are some potentially challenging conclusions to be drawn from Cage's physical experiments, which make it clear that, in his view, literal silence is somehow incompatible with the condition of being human.

So what is the aim of the questioning? If we cannot experience silence as a literal phenomenon, then our discussions about silence must be about metaphors. And it is this world that Susan Sontag, a probing examiner of metaphor, sought to understand. Instead of remaining entrenched in the aporias of literal silence, she proposed that the varied strategies behind silence be examined and viewed in terms of stylistic variation. (Indeed, her essay is a kind of 'theme and variations'.) Only thus may silence gain its full eloquence, both in terms of transcendent possibility and as signifier of art's tragic relation to consciousness.

Early in her essay, Sontag discussed various styles of silence beginning with the renunciation of vocation, giving the examples of Wittgenstein's school teaching and menial work, and Duchamp's chess-playing as evidence (alongside their own declarations) that these individuals regarded their previous philosophical and artistic endeavours as unimportant. These renunciations carried an enormous charge of moral and ethical strength. Paradoxically, such a choice need not imply a reduction of power. Sontag wrote:

---

[32]   Sontag, 'The Aesthetics of Silence', 9–10.

[33]   See Cage, 'Experimental Music: Doctrine' (1955 [not 1957]), in *Silence*, 13–14. In the essay, Cage described entering an anechoic chamber, a technologically silent space; nevertheless he heard the sounds of his nervous system and blood circulation, when he expected, perhaps, to experience perfect silence (for an excerpt from the original text and further discussion, see Chapter 6 (Brooks). This gap between expectation and realization has counterparts in many of Cage's works, in the linking of musical forms with unorthodox content, generating unexpected sound (or silence) within a specified musical space.

The choice of permanent silence doesn't negate the work. On the contrary, it imparts retroactively an added power and authority to what was broken off – disavowal of the work becoming a new source of its validity, a certificate of unchallengeable seriousness. That seriousness consists in not regarding art ... as something whose seriousness last forever, an 'end', a permanent vehicle for spiritual ambition.[34]

There is another contradiction in store for those who employ silence in this way; it often becomes necessary to become very voluble about the silences! Silence, in any case, has the quality of posing questions, requiring explanations. But since questions and explanations imply articulation, this final contradiction points to silence as having an intrinsically polemical relationship with that which it opposes, namely sound. And if the silence is about an ethical choice, this must be explained. There is often an aim toward transcendence that needs clarification. Later in the essay, Sontag studied those silences associated with 'spiritual ambition' in art. She observed that in such an art, which 'aims to be a total experience, soliciting total attention, the strategies of impoverishment and reduction indicate the most exalted position art can adopt. Underneath modesty is to be discerned an energetic secular blasphemy: the wish to attain the unfettered, unselective, total consciousness of "God"'.[35]

Ironically, such a 'total' consciousness teeters on the brink of its inverse, total nothingness. However, Sontag also seized on the moment of negation as being one of great power:

Committed to the idea that the power of art is located in its power to negate, the ultimate weapon in the artist's inconsistent war with his audience is to verge closer and closer to silence. The sensory or conceptual gap between the artist and his audience, the space of the missing or ruptured dialogue, can also constitute the grounds for an ascetic affirmation.[36]

In this most spare of realms, Sontag found a kaleidoscope of variations. As quoted previously, 'silence is neither experienced, nor is it a property of an artwork'.[37] Consider this extract from Cage's '45' for a Speaker', which is picked up just after 43':

---

[34] Sontag, 'The Aesthetics of Silence', 6.
[35] *Ibid.*, 14.
[36] *Ibid.*, 8.
[37] *Ibid.*, 9.

0"

10"

    There is no

20"

    such thing as silence. Something is al-

    ways happening that makes a sound.

    No one can have an idea

30"

    once he starts really listening.

    It is very simple but extra-urgent

    The Lord knows whether or not

40"

    the next

50"

    (Bang fist).[38]

Cage's obvious statements about silence became like Zen koans, gaining both clarity and obscurity with repetition. His line, 'I have nothing to say and I am saying it',[39] follows ten dense pages of monologue in his lecture–performance, 'Composition as Process'.

As Sontag pointed out, 'the art of our time is noisy with appeals for silence'.[40] Cage tried to demonstrate this in print through several means. As mentioned before, the essays in *Silence* are often deliberately laid out to reveal empty sections and long pauses. In another strategy, he used print so tiny and dense that an effect of silence through obfuscation is created. Cage's account of one of his lectures reveals how challenging his ideas could be.

> So it was that I gave about 1949 my *Lecture on Nothing* at the Artists' Club on Eighth Street in New York City … This *Lecture on Nothing* was written in the same rhythmic structure I employed at the time in my musical compositions (*Sonatas and Interludes*, *Three Dances*, etc.). One of the structural divisions was the repetition, some fourteen times, of a single page in which occurred the refrain, 'If anyone is sleepy, let him go to sleep'. Jeanne Reynal, I remember, stood up part way through, screamed, and then said, while I continued speaking, 'John, I dearly love you, but I can't bear another minute'. She then walked out.[41]

---

[38]   Cage, '45' for a Speaker', 191.
[39]   Cage, 'Composition as Process' (1958), in *Silence*, 51.
[40]   Sontag, 'The Aesthetics of Silence', 12.
[41]   Cage, Forward to *Silence*, ix.

Cage's use of exactly repeated words to the point where the device prompts exasperation is reminiscent of a similar device used by Eric Satie in his piano piece *Vexations* (1893), a theme and variations repeated 840 times and first performed in its entirety in New York in 1963 by a team of pianists organized by and including Cage. In *Silence*, Cage included an essay about Satie in the form of a pastiche of quotations, interspersed with silences. Similarly, in her article, Sontag discussed repetitiveness as a correlate of silence.

> In the era of the widespread advocacy of art's silence, an increasing number of works of art babble. Verbosity and repetitiveness are particularly noticeable in the temporal arts of prose fiction, music, film, and dance, many of which cultivate a kind of ontological stammer – facilitated by their refusal of the incentives for a clean, anti-redundant discourse supplied by linear, beginning-middle-and-end construction.[42]

Another way in which Cage challenged musical utterance was to silence an instrument in its normal function, and then to have it sound in a different way; the works for prepared piano are examples of this. Among Cage's most elegant and most frequently studied use of silence, however, remains *4'33"* (1952). Of all his compositions, this is the one which continues to challenge established musical norms most notoriously, and which is most provocative of debate in academia and among a musically curious public. The work, composed for any instrument or combination of instruments, frames a potentially 'classical' formal space, having three movements (movement I: 30", movement II: 2'23", movement III: 1'40"), but the performance is silent, and physical gestures are made only to indicate the change to a different movement. Through removing all musical content from the piece and leaving only the mute symbol of the opening and closing of the piano lid, or silent bowing of the violin or lifting and falling of the baton to tell us that the piece has started and finished, Cage makes us ask ourselves a number of fundamental questions. These range through the nature of the concert experience, the validity of noise as music, the honesty of experimental composition, to the very nature of silence itself. There is a paradoxical relationship between the highly organized time frame and the chance elements that flow into this space. Though the piece has now existed for decades, it still elicits fresh questions and retains immense value, both as a spur to contemplation (recalling Cage's affiliation with Zen) and as a cultural irritant. This most minimal of works is effective on virtually all the levels of silence which Sontag identified. Cage's own assessment of its value is made clear in an interview with William Duckworth:

> C: I knew that if [*4'33"*] was done it would be the highest form of work. Or this form of work: an art without work. I doubt whether many people understand it yet.
> D: Well, the traditional understanding is that it opens you up to the sounds that exist around you and …
> C: … and to the acceptance of anything … even when you have something as the basis. And that's how it's misunderstood.
> D: What's a better understanding of it?
> C: It opens you up to any possibility only when nothing is taken as the basis.

---

[42]   Sontag, 'The Aesthetics of Silence', 26–7.

D: Is it possible that instead of being taken as too foolish, it's now taken too seriously?

C: No. I don't think it can be taken too seriously.[43]

In a sense, *4'33"* simply places a potentially meditative space into a Westernized musical framework. The resulting level of awareness amongst individual 'listeners' is variable, but potentially very high. Silence becomes the realm of the spirit, with speech losing its enchantment. Sontag captured this in 'The Aesthetics of Silence' in a paragraph about 'bad speech' that could have been written by Roland Barthes:

> Silence undermines 'bad speech', by which I mean dissociated speech – speech dissociated from the body (and, therefore, from feeling), speech not organically informed by the sensuous presence and concrete particularity of the speaker by the individual occasion for using language. Unmoored from the body, speech deteriorates. It becomes false, inane, ignoble, weightless. Silence can inhibit or counteract this tendency, providing a kind of ballast, monitoring and even correcting language when it becomes inauthentic.[44]

The idea present here of a 'physicalization' of language also clarifies the importance of Cage's link with the choreographer, Merce Cunningham. But Sontag was ambivalent about language – 'as the prestige of language falls, that of silence rises'.[45] Much contemporary art has emerged from this inverse relationship. Using language, Sontag had to address herself to the problem of silence in a world of sensory overload and commodification. This leads to another aspect of the stylistic discussion, 'the unstable antithesis of plenum and void'[46] – loud and soft, babble and muteness.[47] One feels that, given her condemnation of the 'false physicality' of dislocated speech noted above, Sontag's view of this 'plenum/void' strategy is likely to be dark: 'the sensuous, ecstatic translinguistic apprehension of the plenum is notoriously fragile. In a terrible, almost instantaneous plunge it can collapse into the void of negative silence'.[48]

Ultimately, Sontag could only find a reconciling counterweight for the ordeals and aporias of silence in the mitigating presence of irony. As she was doubtless aware, it is certainly possible to view many of the projects of Cage in this light. But this seems

---

[43]   William Duckworth, 'Anything I Say will be Misunderstood: an Interview with John Cage', in *John Cage at Seventy Five*, 21.

[44]   Sontag, 'The Aesthetics of Silence', 20.

[45]   *Ibid.*, 21.

[46]   *Ibid.*, 32.

[47]   This brings forward not only the literal auditory overload that is one legacy of technological progress, but also the idea of 'schizophonia', the removal of sound from its source, meaning that 'any sonic environment could, by means of loudspeakers, be substituted for any other'; R. Murray Schafer, *Voices of Tyranny, Temples of Silence* (Indian River, Ont.: Arcana Editions, 1993), 118. While Schafer sees the positive potential in this, especially in terms of the creation of compositional soundscapes, Sontag is negative about disembodied sound and, like Roland Barthes, finds an ethical dimension in the association of 'bad speech' with disembodiment; see Barthes, 'The Grain of the Voice,' in *Image, Music, Text,* essays selected and trans. Stephen Heath (New York: Hill and Wang, 1977), 157.

[48]   Sontag, 'The Aesthetics of Silence', 32.

to me to be a very temporary solution, and Sontag herself, for all her advocacy of camp, comedy and eclecticism, could not see it as a long-term strategy:

> If irony has more positive resources than Nietzsche acknowledged, there still remains a question as to how far the resources of irony can be stretched. It seems unlikely that the possibilities of continually undermining one's assumptions can go on unfolding indefinitely into the future, without being eventually checked by despair or a laugh that leaves one without any breath at all.[49]

Though Sontag leaves us within this rather bleak scenario, she has nevertheless helped us to consider afresh the multi-faceted nature of silence. Her work goes some way in emphasizing its critical nature in various artistic rhetorics. Nonetheless, it is important to emphasize here that her 'elegiac' stance in the late 1960s was very different from Cage's view at that time, as William Brooks suggests:

> During the twenty years after 1950 that Cage had worked through the aesthetic transformations he had described in the 'Lecture on Nothing' and the 'Lecture on Something': first the abnegation of taste, control and even materials in favour of – quite literally – *nothing* ('everybody has a song which is no song at all'); and then ('if one maintains secure possession of nothing') the reacceptance of all that had been discarded ('there is no end to the number of somethings and all of them ... are acceptable'). ... Having reached *nothing* in works like *0'0"* and *Musicircus,* Cage was able to find *something* acceptable in *HPSCHD* and *Cheap Imitation*; the *Song Books* affirmed that acceptance explicitly and joyously.[50]

What a comparative study of Sontag and Cage can effectively reveal is the difference in the polemical stances that they adopted and how this became encoded in the aesthetics of the negative in the 1960s. In Cage's view, the employment of silence as a spur to awareness, the perception of sound, or silence, for its own sake, is affirmative of life in general, and of new directions in music in particular. This is reinforced by changes in his compositional and philosophical approaches, including his rediscovery and engagement with the writings of Thoreau and the computerization of such processes as the generation of *I Ching* hexagrams – something that changed his working practices considerably.[51] In this context, it is important to remember that Cage approached these issues primarily from the standpoint of a creator, albeit one for whom philosophical considerations were intimately bound into the creative process, and sought his answers through fresh creativity, rather than commentary. Sontag's assessment of silence reflected her primary role as a commentator, but also perhaps her greater indebtedness to European culture. It is more existentially oriented and culminates in a bleaker outlook. Her final remarks on irony lead one to conclude that she viewed the employment of silence as a means of achieving artistic freedom

---

[49]   *Ibid.,* 34.

[50]   William Brooks, 'Music II: From the Late 1960s', in *The Cambridge Companion to John Cage,* ed. David Nicholls (Cambridge: Cambridge University Press, 2002), 131–2. The Cage quotations refer to: 'Lecture on Nothing' (1950 [not 1959]), in *Silence*, 126, and 'Lecture on Something' (1950 [not 1959]), in *Silence*, 132.

[51]   *Ibid.,* 131.

as an essentially vain pursuit, since for her, the achievement of a total silence must signify the end of art.

Despite this central difference in outlook, Cage's work remains one of the most exhaustive and inventive explorations of the myriad of possibilities that Sontag discussed. The existence of his works and, perhaps even more so, their continuing success more than a decade after his death suggests that Sontag's *via negativa*, for all the persuasive rigour and seriousness of its articulation, may have been unduly pessimistic. Affirmation can often seem shallower than negation, and a composition such as Cage's *4'33"* has been an easy target for demonization, more often by reputation than by direct experience, as a trite joke in poor taste. In this 'dialogue between two silences' I hope to have shown that Cage's affirmatory approach is no less rigorous and challenging than Sontag's elegiac pessimism.

Chapter 8

Preliminary Thoughts About Silence in Early Western Chant

Emma Hornby

One of the watersheds in the history of Western music is the point in the thirteenth century when notators began to indicate measured silence. Indicating not just silence, but silence that has a precise duration, is what made possible many of the sophisticated uses of silence as an integral part of later Western art music.

But what about the time *before* silence was notated in this way? This essay explores some of the uses of silence in Gregorian chant, a repertory that appears to have been created on Roman models in late-eighth-century Francia.[1] The earliest surviving notated Graduals, containing the Mass Proper chants, date from the end of the ninth century.[2] Two pages (recto and verso of the same leaf) of St Gallen, Stiftsbibliothek, 359, a late-ninth- or early-tenth-century Cantatorium containing the chants sung by the cantor, are reproduced in Appendix 8.1, at the end of this essay.[3] In such manuscripts, notation functions as a memory aid for cantors and choirs who mostly learned the chants by memory.[4] While this kind of notation shows the outline of the melody – the direction of movement up or down and the number of notes to be sung – it does not show precise relative pitch. Since the notation does not indicate whether the singer should rise a 3rd or a 4th, for example, it is not possible to read this notation unless one already knows the tune; it is clearly an aid to memory rather

---

[1]   See David Hiley, *Western Plainchant: a Handbook* (Oxford: Clarendon Press, 1993), 514–20.

[2]   The dates of the invention of neumatic notation and its adoption in the transmission of the Gregorian Mass Proper chants remain fiercely contested, from Kenneth Levy's eighth-century estimate (see *Gregorian Chant and the Carolingians*, Princeton: Princeton University Press, 1998) to Leo Treitler's ninth-century one (see *With Voice and Pen: Coming to Know Medieval Song and How it was Made*, New York: Oxford University Press, 2003). See also Emma Hornby, 'The Transmission of Western Chant in the 8th and 9th Centuries: Evaluating Kenneth Levy's Reading of the Evidence', *Journal of Musicology* 21 (2004), 418–57.

[3]   Facsimile: *Paléographie musicale* series 2: 2 (Solesmes, 1924), 95–6. The example has been reduced to fit on the page; the original dimensions of the manuscript are 28 x 12.5 cm.

[4]   The books were probably library copies for reference rather than for use regularly in performance; the dimensions of a Gradual like the tenth-century Einsiedeln, Benediktinerkloster, Musikbibliothek, 121 (15.3 x 11 cm) make this clear; it would have been difficult to read in poor light, and almost impossible for more than one person to read at one time.

than having the prescriptive function of modern notation. Early neumatic notations have shapes with rhythmic implications,[5] but they do not show precise rhythm or silence; there is no explicit sign for a rest.

In order to discuss the use of silence in Gregorian chant, then, it is necessary to draw on indirect evidence: comments by people writing in the early middle ages about music; and implicit evidence contained within the chants themselves. This article will draw on examples from two performative extremes of monastic life. The second set of examples will be drawn from some of the most complicated and musically-challenging chants sung by a soloist, but first I shall consider silence within the psalms chanted by the whole monastic community.

Silence in Psalm Recitation

Benedictine monasticism was founded in the sixth century, and was the most influential monastic rule in the ninth-century Frankish Empire, from where the earliest notated manuscripts originate. In Benedictine monasteries, the recitation of the entire Psalter each week within the Divine Office was one of the major components of monastic duty.

Psalm performance varied over the centuries. The monastic rules of the fourth to seventh centuries indicate that one monk chanted while the rest responded with short refrains. This changed to choral psalmody, with everyone singing, in the late-eighth century.[6] At this time the missionary fronts needed priests to carry out baptism and eucharist, and this need was met by the ordination of many more monks than had previously been the case. Such ordained monks demanded greater participation in the liturgy, including the singing of psalms in the Office, which shifted in emphasis from being a pious exercise to being an official liturgical occasion.[7] Indeed, one of the first references to the choral singing of the office psalms is in Chrodegang of Metz's Rule for canons, all of whom were priests.[8] In choral psalmody, one half of the community would sing odd verses, and the other would sing even ones.[9]

In the middle of each verse, there was a pause for taking breath, the *media distinctio*. According to the fourteenth-century *Ceremoniae Sublacenses*,[10] this pause was long enough for the singers to exhale and inhale again.[11] Both the Hebrew and

---

[5]   Hiley, *Western Plainchant*, 373–85.

[6]   On this, and the reasons for the shift, see Joseph Dyer, 'Monastic Psalmody of the Middle Ages', *Revue Benedictine* 99 (1989), 41–74.

[7]   *Ibid.*, 72–4.

[8]   *Ibid.*, 72.

[9]   John Harper, *The Forms and Orders of Western Liturgy* (Oxford: Clarendon Press, 1991), 78.

[10]   On the Cistercian influence on this source, see Steven Van Dijk, 'Saint Bernard and the Instituta Patrum of Saint Gall', *Musica disciplina* 4 (1950), 104.

[11]   *Ceremoniae Sublacenses,* in *Corpus consuetudinum monasticarum*, ed. Kassius Hallinger (Siegburg: F. Schmitt, 1963), 2: 27. I am indebted to Fabian Lochner, *Source Readings on the Practice and Spirituality of Chant: New Texts, New Approaches*, <http://www.luc.edu/publications/medieval/vol8/8ch6.html> (accessed 4 April 2005), for this reference.

Greek words for 'spirit' also mean 'breath' or 'wind' and, in Christian teaching, the Holy Spirit is said to have come to the disciples first as a wind (Acts 2). The silence for breathing in the middle of the psalm verse, then, is also an opportunity for the Holy Spirit to visit the faithful; the trope of Holy Spirit as breath of God is also a familiar one, and still current in hymn texts such as Edwin Hatch's 'Breathe on me, breath of God'. There is a theological aspect to this moment of taking breath.[12]

The *media distinctio* was considered to be a ceremonial pause, enhancing the solemnity of the chanting.[13] It sometimes served as an architectural pause, lasting until the echo of the previous pitch had died away; the length of the pause depended on the acoustics of the building. The pause would also have promoted meditation: psalm verses often have two statements that mirror each other, and pausing in the middle gives time for reflecting on the textual structure and doctrinal significance of what is being sung. An important aspect of the *media distinctio* was the unity it embodied: the unity of the monastery breathing and singing together; and the reflection that gave of the unity of the heavenly host.[14]

In the twelfth century, various commentators became incensed about the length of the pause in the psalm verse. While twelfth-century Cistercians still advocated a 'pausa bona' in the middle of the psalm verse, the mendicant orders which sprang up in the later twelfth century – Franciscans and Dominicans, for example – thought that spending hours singing psalms 'destroyed devotion, external activity and study in many monasteries'.[15] The Franciscans replaced the long pause in the middle of the verse with a 'pausa conveniens' that was the same length whatever the day. Dominicans had a short pause on working days and a longer one on Feast days.[16] The presence of the silence is certain, however, as the writer of the *Summa musice* (c. 1200) made clear: singers should 'give careful heed to the middle [of the verse] where [the psalm tone] offers a pause'.[17]

Earlier commentary on the subject of the silence in psalmody is conspicuous by its absence.[18] Early music treatises instead focus on the more abstract, speculative aspects of music theory, such as the ratios of intervals and the divisions of the monochord. While Aurelian of Réôme's *Musica disciplina* (c. 840) is about practical music, it is largely concerned with getting the melodic join between antiphons and

---

[12] This has resonances in Eastern meditation, where exhalation is considered to expel corruption from the body, to be followed by the purity of inhalation. I am grateful to Nicola Lefanu for bringing this to my attention.

[13] Steven Van Dijk, 'Medieval Terminology and Methods of Psalm Singing', *Musica disciplina* 6 (1952), 12.

[14] *Ibid.*

[15] *Ibid.*, 14–15.

[16] *Ibid.*, 15–16.

[17] *Summa musice: a Thirteenth Century Manual for Singers*, ed. Christopher Page (Cambridge: Cambridge University Press, 1991), 113.

[18] As noted by Van Dijk, 'Medieval Terminology', 8. Silence is not mentioned in Anders Ekenberg's study of Carolingian interpretations of chant's meaning; see *Cur Cantatur? Die Funktionen des liturgischen Gesanges nach den Autoren der Karolingerzeit* (Stockholm: Almqvist and Wiksell International, 1987).

psalm recitation consistent and correct, and does not mention the specifics of psalm performance.[19]

The *Commemoratio brevis* (c. 900) is the first theoretical source to concentrate on psalmody.[20] The author mentioned the silence in the middle of the psalm verse in a negative way: he said that there should be no hiatus – no silence – when vowels both precede and follow the half-verse cadence.[21] His series of four examples made the point clearly:

> Ego autem sum vermis et non homo: opprobrium hominum
> Exurge domine in ira tua: et exaltare
> Exurge Domine Deus meus in precepto quod mandasti: et synagoga
> Corripuit me iustus in misericordia et increpavit me: oleum autem

The author followed this with a second set of examples, '*Pro euphonia quoque siue colis*' ('Similarly, for euphony at the half-verse').[22] However, this set of examples does not have vowels before and after the half-verse. Terence Bailey suggested that rather than being another set of pertinent examples, 'this section is, in fact, a supplement containing more examples of medians'.[23] I agree that the set of examples beginning Bailey's edited translation (74–5) may indeed be a supplement, but the rubric 'pro euphonia quoque siue colis' (72) indicates clearly that the four examples immediately following are a set of examples for which silence at the half-verse is not appropriate, although the rationale behind this remains obscure.

The *Commemoratio brevis* stands alone in many ways. For example, its emphasis on proportional rhythm does not seem to be shared by the contemporary musical manuscripts such as the St Gallen Cantatorium, reproduced in Appendix 8.1.[24] *Commemoratio brevis* appears to reflect a local performance practice at least as far as rhythm goes, and one cannot assume that its validity is any wider for the performance of psalms.[25] While the author claimed that he looked afield for information, he acknowledged that the treatise did not reconcile all local practices. Further, the treatise seems to have had a limited distribution.[26]

---

[19] Aurelian of Réôme, *The Discipline of Music (ca. 843)*, trans. Joseph Ponte (Colorado Springs: Colorado College Music Press, 1968).

[20] *Commemoratio brevis de tonis et psalmis modulandis: Introduction, Critical Edition, Translation*, ed. and trans. Terence Bailey (Ottawa: University of Ottawa Press, 1979), vii.

[21] *Item pro euphoniae causa, ut ibi in distinguendo uocales (quae) coeunt hiatus quantum ualet uitetur* ('For the sake of euphony, when articulating juxtaposed vowels as in the following, a hiatus is to be avoided at all costs'); Bailey, *Commemoratio brevis*, 70–71.

[22] *colis* is the singular form of *cola*; psalm verses were divided *per cola et commata* where the *cola* mark the middle of the verses (marked by :) and the *commata* are smaller divisions, marked by a raised dot.

[23] Bailey, *Commemoratio brevis*, 110.

[24] The passages pertaining to proportional rhythm in *Commemoratio brevis* form a central plank of equalist theories of chant performance, as exemplified by Jan Vollaerts, *Rhythmic Proportions in Early Medieval Ecclesiastical Chant* (Leiden: E. J. Brill, 1958).

[25] I am grateful to Óscar Mascareñas for a fruitful discussion of this source and the limited extent to which it appears to reflect wider contemporary practice.

[26] Bailey, *Commemoratio brevis*, 12–15.

Notwithstanding the *Commemoratio brevis* exceptions, it appears that there was normally a silence in the middle of a psalm verse sung by the whole monastic community. The function of this silence is heavily devotional, being ceremonial, meditative and indicative of the unity of the monastic community with the heavenly choir and with the Holy Spirit. There is also a physical aspect beyond the purely practical necessity of breathing in: fifteen or twenty minutes of controlled breathing releases endorphins; it has a calming and uplifting effect. This is primarily ritual rather than musical silence.

Silence in the Second-mode Tracts

While some chants were simple, sung on a regular basis by the entire community, others were highly complex and sung only by the specially trained, and perhaps the most extreme example of this is the second-mode tracts. Angilram (Bishop of Metz, 768–91) made a renowned list of *stipendia*, including the specification of five occasions for which the singer would receive extra payment.[27] No fewer than three of the five chants on the list are second-mode tracts.[28]

Second-mode tracts are sung straight through by a soloist. Each chant was sung in the Mass only once or perhaps twice in a year. And the longest of the second-mode tracts, *Deus deus meus* and *Qui habitat*, take in the region of ten minutes to perform. These still offer a huge challenge to singers.

It is unnecessary to discuss micropauses in these pieces, beyond to state that they exist (see Ex. 8.1 in Appendix 8.1, below). While the performance of apostrophes is still uncertain, many think that they represent re-articulations of the pitch, with a tiny silence in between.[29] However, if this is the case, the silences function rather like staccato, giving character to the notes rather than having musical meaning themselves.

Longer silences certainly occurred in these chants. The second-mode tracts were sung by a single soloist who would have breathed after the stereotyped cadences (assuming good breath control). These cadences generally coincide with a break in the sense of the text, at the end of a clause, a sentence, or a similar textual unit. Second-mode tracts are built up of standardized phrases, so there is rarely if ever any ambiguity about whether a musical gesture is a cadence or not. While the structure of each verse varies depending on the amount of text available and its structure,[30] the four main

---

[27]   James McKinnon, 'Lector Chant versus Scola Chant: a Question of Historical Plausibility', in *Laborare fratres in unum: Festschrift Laszlo Dobszay zum 60. Geburtstag*, ed. David Hiley and Janka Szendrei (Hildesheim and Zurich: Weidmann, 1995), 208. Edited with commentary in Michel Andrieu, 'Règlement d'Angilramme de Metz (768–791) fixant les honoraires de quelques fonctions liturgiques', *Revue des Sciences Religieuses* 10 (1930), 349–69.

[28]   *Qui habitat* twice (on Quadragesima Sunday and Good Friday), *Deus deus meus* (on Palm Sunday) and *Domine exaudi* (on Wednesday of Holy Week).

[29]   Timothy McGee, *The Sound of Medieval Song* (Oxford: Clarendon Press, 1998), 57–8. This interpretation is not consistent with current French practice, as exemplified by performances of the group *Discantus*.

[30]   See James McKinnon, *The Advent Project: the Later-Seventh-Century Creation of the Roman Mass Proper* (Berkeley: University of California Press, 2000), 289.

points of articulation within the verse are one or more weak cadences on D, then a stronger one at the half-verse on C; then a weak cadence on F and a strong one at the end of the verse on D.

While a full exposition of the different cadence shapes and the motivations for using them lies some way beyond the scope of this essay,[31] a summary of some of the cadence shapes will serve to orientate the reader. The pitched examples given here are transcribed from Benevento, Biblioteca capitolare, VI.34, an eleventh-century Gradual.[32] While this manuscript has no special claim to authority, it is representative of the Gregorian tradition,[33] and gives a sense of the melodic outlines beyond what can be inferred from the St Gallen neumes in Appendix 8.1.

Ex. 8.2 is the shape associated with the end of a second-mode tract.[34]

Ex. 8.2   End of Second-mode tract (see also Appendix 8.1)[35]

Several shapes are associated with the end of the verse. Ex. 8.3 shows two of these, associated with different accent patterns at the end of the phrase; /-/- and /---/- respectively:

Ex. 8.3   Second-mode tract, end of the verse

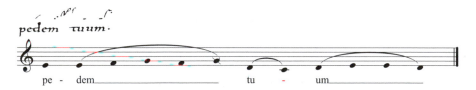

Qui habitat

---

[31]   See Hans Schmidt, 'Untersuchungen zu den Tractus des zweiten Tones', *Kirchenmusikalisches Jahrbuch* 42 (1958), 1–25. My own analytical study of the second-mode tracts, which will explore the structure of the chants in detail, is in progress.

[32]   *Paléographie musicale* 15 (Tournai: Société Saint-Jean l'Evangéliste, Desclée, 1937), 114–15.

[33]   See Emma Hornby, *Gregorian and Old Roman Eighth-Mode Tracts* (Aldershot: Ashgate, 2002), 15–48, especially 47–8.

[34]   The Beneventan manuscript has a scribal error here, copying every note of this phrase one pitch too low (beginning on E and ending on C); all the other pitched manuscripts I have seen have the correct pitches.

[35]   In the transcriptions, a notehead with a diagonal line indicates liquescence (where the final consonant of the syllable is articulated *semi-vocales* on the pitch adjacent to the one transcribed, in the direction indicated by the diagonal line). An x-shaped notehead represents a quilisma, which is an ornament.

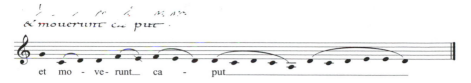

Deus deus meus

The cadence ending on C associated with the end of the first verse-half is almost invariable, and highly recognizable, as in Ex. 8.4:

Ex. 8.4   Second-mode tract, end of the first verse-half (see also Appendix 8.1)

The beginning of the verse cadences weakly on D, once or often twice, depending on the textual circumstances. Although there are several cadence shapes, all are clearly differentiated from those appearing at the ends of verses (see Ex. 8.5):

Ex. 8.5 Second-mode tract, beginnings of the verses (see also Appendix 8.1)
a)

b)

The other weak cadence, at the beginning of the second half-verse, closes on F,

as in Ex. 8.6:

Ex. 8.6   Second-mode tract, beginning of the second half-verse (see also Appendix 8.1)

The clear differentiation of the cadence shapes associated with different formal positions should be evident from these examples.

In his *Micrologus*, Guido d'Arezzo wrote about a hierarchy of cadences in chants, with the last note of what he calls a *pars* slightly lengthened, and the end of a *distinctio* even more lengthened.[36] These might be translated as the end of a phrase and the end of a larger section, such as a verse or verse-half, respectively. Aribo, commenting on Guido, interpreted the word 'morula' as the silence between phrases rather than the closing note itself, and wrote that 'a morula is doubly long or short, if the silence between two pitches is twice as long as the silence between two other pitches'.[37]

Second-mode tracts have different cadences for different formal positions. Based on the comments of Guido and Aribo, the cadences at the ends of *distinctiones* (verses or verse-halves) possibly had longer final notes, or longer silences after the final notes, than the weaker cadences at the ends of *pars* (the cadences on D at the beginning of the verse and on F after the half-verse caesura).

Despite the fact that the silences following these cadences might have had hierarchical lengths, their meaning is still not primarily musical. Instead, the cadences and their associated silences help the listeners to follow the textual form and meaning of the psalm as it unfolds. It is important to note that cadence and silence are inextricably connected in such chants; a silence in the middle of a phrase caused by poor breath control would not have the same impact as one following a cadence. Further, a cadence without a silence does not really function as a cadence. There is an example of this in *Domine exaudi* verse 2, where the half-verse cadence is interpolated into the final phrase of the verse on 'ad me' because of a textual cue; neither the textual syntax nor the broader musical shape would support following the cadence on 'me' with silence (see Ex. 8.7). Cadence and breathing silence complete each other. The silences after cadences have a secondary purpose of giving the singer time to remember what comes next, both musically and textually.

---

[36]   Calvin Bower, 'The Grammatical Model of Musical Understanding in the Middle Ages', in *Hermeneutics and Medieval Cultures*, ed. Patrick Gallacher and Helen Damico (Albany: State University of New York Press, 1989), 140. See also Karen Desmond, '*Sicut in grammatica*: Analogical Discourse in Chapter 15 of Guido's *Micrologus*', *Journal of Musicology* 16 (1998), 417 and 479–80.

[37]   Desmond, '*Sicut in grammatica*', 480–81.

Ex. 8.7 *Domine exaudi,* **end of verse 2 (see also Appendix 8.1)**

Very occasionally, the usual cadential shape is withheld. While the phrase after the half-verse caesura usually ends FEFGGF, it instead ends FEF on three occasions in the repertory. Ex. 8 shows two of these:

Ex. 8.8 *Domine exaudi,* **incomplete cadences (see also Appendix 8.1)**

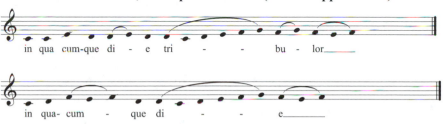

Because there is no full cadence at the end of 'in quacumque die tribulor',[38] the prepositional phrase 'in the day of tribulation' is linked to the main part of the sentence ('turn your ears to me'). The next verse begins with exactly the same music, although one would usually expect completely different melodic movements at the verse beginning, because of the text cue of 'in quacumque die'.[39] As in the previous verse, the prepositional phrase is linked to the rest of the sentence.[40]

Use of the abbreviated cadence is perhaps prompted by a desire to bridge the gap between phrases and link the textual components of these verses, but it also has a rhetorical purpose. Because the usual musical grammar has been overturned, the tension at this point goes beyond a mere silence for taking breath, for assimilating what has passed, and for preparing for what will come next. It might perhaps be likened to an interrupted cadence in common-practice music.

---

[38] The full, normal cadence appears in only two of the approximately twenty-five manuscripts I have consulted so far. These are Paris, Bibliothèque Nationale de France, lat 903, the Gradual from St Yrieix, see *Paléographie musicale* 13 (Tournai: Société Saint-Jean l'Evangéliste, Desclée, 1925), 127; and Oxford, Bodleian Library, Canon liturg. 340, a neumed Gradual from St Moggio, dated c. 1216.

[39] While there is no new psalm verse here, this moment is clearly signalled as being a new verse in the second-mode tract in all the manuscripts I have consulted.

[40] This is consistent in all the manuscripts I have consulted. The third use of the abbreviated phrase is the first verse of *Qui habitat*, where 'in protectione' is joined on to 'dei celi commorabitur' ('[he who lives in the high places] will dwell in the protection of the Lord of the heavens') in all but one of the manuscripts I have consulted. This is Oxford, Bodleian Library, Laud misc. 358 (c. 1160, St Albans Abbey).

My second example is drawn from the Old Roman version of the second-mode tracts. While most areas of Western Europe had the same dialect of liturgical chant, Gregorian chant, Rome maintained its own melodic dialect, which is preserved in three Mass Proper manuscripts.[41] The Roman versions have broadly the same melodic skeleton for the second-mode tracts, but they have different surface melodies.[42] In general, the Roman version has more melodic decoration than the Gregorian one, although this is by no means always the case.

While the second-mode tracts usually have one or even two cadences on D at the beginning of the verse before the cadence on C, the Roman version of the chants occasionally has the usual material for a D-cadence but ends on E instead. In *Deus deus meus* verse 4, 'Tu autem' has a cadence ending on E instead of the expected cadence on D (see Ex. 8.9):[43]

Ex. 8.9   *Deus deus meus,* verse 4

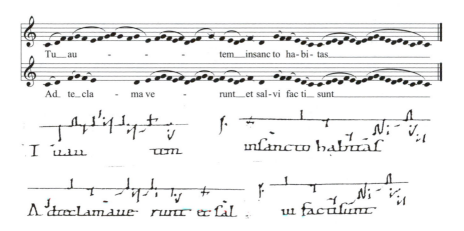

This links the text to the following 'in sancto habitas', and it makes sense to link the subject ('you however') to the rest of the sentence ('live in the holy place'). In *Deus deus meus* verse 6, however, 'ad te clamaverunt' has the same cadence on E, even though the verse-half consists of two separate clauses: 'To you they cried / and you saved them.' There is no syntactical reason to link them together by avoiding the normal cadence. *Deus deus meus* verse 4 might lead one to believe that the Roman

---

[41]   Many studies have been made of the relationship between Old Roman and Gregorian chant since the significance of the Old Roman manuscripts was first realized in the 1950s. For a recent survey, see Hornby, *Gregorian and Old Roman Eighth-Mode Tracts,* 5–7.

[42]   See Schmidt, 'Untersuchungen zu den Tractus'; Theodore Karp, *Aspects of Orality and Formularity in Gregorian Chant* (Evanston, IL: Northwestern University Press, 1998), 315-64. I am preparing a differently focused consideration of the relationship between the Old Roman and Gregorian second-mode tracts.

[43]   *Das Graduale von Santa Cecilia in Trastevere (Cod. Bodmer 74),* ed. Max Lütolf (Cologny-Genève: Fondation Martin Bodmer, 1987), 71r.

cantors cadenced on E rather than D in order to avoid a close and thus to make clear the continuity of the text. But *Deus deus meus* verse 6 makes it clear that this is not the case. In fact, there are several other occasions where the cadence on E is used in the Old Roman tradition despite there being no need to join the text together. The motivation seems to me to be primarily musical. As with the unfinished cadences on F, the silence after the unexpected cadential gesture has extra, and musical, tension. Cadencing on E in D-final chants is more common in Old Roman chants than in Gregorian chants, possibly because they were less concerned with modal propriety than the Frankish cantors.[44] The familiarity of such gestures does not detract from their inherent tension, however.

Modern recordings of second-mode tracts are rare, perhaps because of their virtuosic challenge and their length. In the light of the foregoing observations, Dominique Vellard's recording of *Deus deus meus* is unsatisfying.[45] While Vellard's legendary breath control is astounding (he completes each verse-half in a single breath), the lack of silence after the phrases cadencing on D in the first verse-half and after those cadencing on F in the second verse-half, and the brevity of the pause after the half-verse cadence, makes the performance seem rushed.

Conclusion

This essay has visited two extremes of liturgical chant. In psalm singing, silence is a well-attested part of medieval performance practice, but its meaning is not primarily musical. Instead, the focus is on meditation, unity, ceremony, the visitation of the Holy Spirit, and the release of mood-enhancing endorphins through the controlled breathing of the whole monastic community. The transcendant possibilities, or at least the possibility of a change of mental state, touched on in so many of the chapters in this volume, are clearly present in the silences of medieval monastic psalm singing.

In the second-mode tracts, one can be fairly certain that the singer breathed after the cadences. A breathing space in both the practical and memory-nudging senses, these silences have a primarily textual function, helping to articulate the sense, the syntax, and the textual form. But the silence when the cadence is sidestepped is different. Such silences have tension and rhetorical weight. This is not the precisely-measured silence with which we are familiar in common-practice music, but I consider that these silences, while not specifically notated, *are* calculated and are full of musical meaning.

---

[44]   There are also many examples of passages containing repetitive figures in Gregorian offertories which cadence on a tension-filled sub-semitonal note (B or E). My thanks to Óscar Mascareñas for pointing this out to me. A silence is necessary following such gestures for mental digestion of the preceding musical idea; I am reminded here of the repetitions followed by a long transitional silence in John Cage's 'Lecture on Nothing' (1950) in *Silence* (Middletown, CT: Wesleyan University Press, 1967), 109–29.

[45]   Dominique Vellard and Emmanuel Bonnardot, *Veritas mea: Chant Grégorien dans l'Église romaine de Tavant* (LP, STIL Editions, Stil 2106 SAN 84, 1985).

Afterword

Other considerations that are not directly connected to the matters considered in this essay might be worthy of further study:

- The measurement of time, and of liturgical time, in an era before clocks, when the length of an hour depended on the time of year, might be connected to an exploration of the passing of – and perhaps the measurement of – time communally within psalm singing.
- The relationship between the silences found within the musical items of the liturgy and the other silences that form a part of liturgy and of monastic life might be considered in tandem with the role of Mass Proper chants as alternatives to silence during ritual action. Silence was rare, in fact, within the early medieval Mass. While in the modern Roman Catholic liturgy, there is silence while the priest takes communion, this was not the case in the Middle Ages.[46] The elevation of the host, whether associated with silence as nowadays or, as was often the case in the Middle Ages, with the delayed singing of the Benedictus, was a thirteenth-century development.[47]

---

[46] Hiley, *Western Plainchant*, 24.
[47] *Ibid.*, 24.

Appendix 8.1 **St Gallen, Stiftsbibliothek, 359; late-ninth/
early-tenth-century Cantatorium**[48]

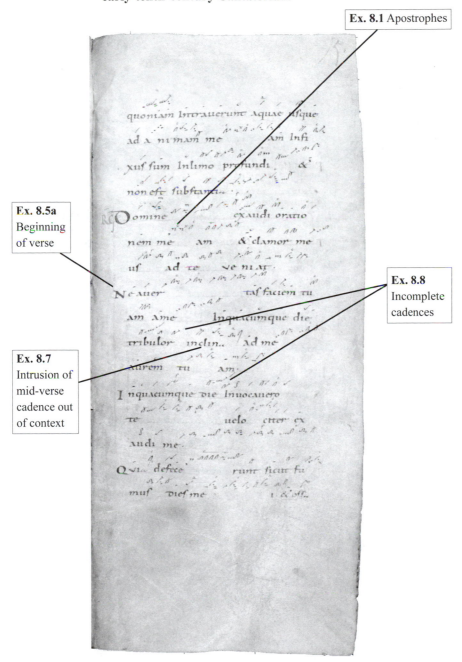

Ex. 8.1 Apostrophes

Ex. 8.5a
Beginning
of verse

Ex. 8.8
Incomplete
cadences

Ex. 8.7
Intrusion of
mid-verse
cadence out
of context

Appendix 8.1 **(continued)**

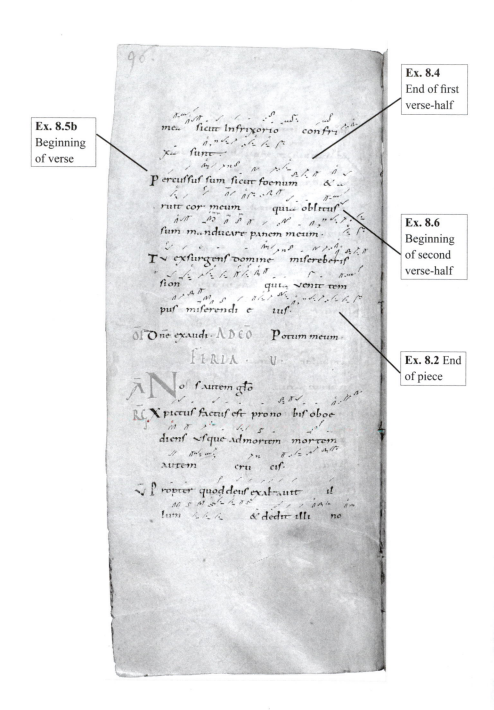

Ex. 8.5b
Beginning
of verse

Ex. 8.4
End of first
verse-half

Ex. 8.6
Beginning
of second
verse-half

Ex. 8.2 End
of piece

Chapter 9

The Communicative Rest

John Potter

For generations, musicians have been used to rests as a metrical measurement of inactivity; they tell you when you stop producing sound and precisely how long it is till you start again. Dictionary definitions tend either to be unnecessarily reductive or to be historical accounts of the evolution of this process, focusing on the quantitative aspects of silence and on how over time increasingly precise ways have been found to express the division of the performer's individual silences.[1] It is now possible to measure silence so accurately that composers are only limited by what performers can take in; beyond a certain point, the complexity of the notation becomes self-defeating. The history of notation is in some sense also a story of composers gaining control of the creative process, often at the expense of the creative performer. The *tenoristae* and *machicotti* who performed Notre Dame polyphony or those who sang twelfth-century *trouvère* songs presumably managed well enough with what seems to us rather basic notational practice, indicating where a rest might occur but not measuring its length.

Performers in general have a complicated attitude to measurement, as the idea of some one or some thing controlling one's actions sits a little uneasily with the ideology of infinite creativity which drives the performance aesthetic. Singers in particular have to communicate words, and although there will usually be a notated rhythm, the composer is often trying to replicate a kind of speech rhythm, so a sophisticated performance may be only notionally rhythmic in a metric sense. The singer's basic task has traditionally been to deliver a text, and this means that as well as answering to the composer, performers have at least an equal responsibility to whoever wrote the words (or, to put it another way, to both the music and the text). Despite the conventions of poetic metre, the performance of words – whether spoken or sung – will normally involve an element of emotional rhetoric which can only be imagined in a silent reading. It is this poetic rhythm which the composer may illuminate, but which the performer has both a duty and an instinct to reveal.

---

[1] A noticeable exception is Ludwig Finscher's 'Pause' in *MGG*, which considers the rhetorical, syntactic and semantic functions of rests; *Die Musik in Geschichte und Gegenwart* (Basel: Bärenreiter, 1997)), 7: 1533–8. The *Harvard Concise Dictionary of Music* gives, 'A silence or notational symbol used to indicate it', which ignores the fact that individual silences will often happen in the context of other musical activity; Don Michael Randel, compiler (Cambridge, MA: Belknapp Press, 1978), 421. Richard Rastall's entry for 'Rest' in *The New Grove Dictionary of Music and Musicians,* 2nd edition, is a purely quantitative history; ed. Stanley Sadie and John Tyrrell (London: Macmillan, 2001), 21: 228–9.

The composer's musical agenda is likely to be far more complex than that of the singer, and precisely accurate word-setting may not be his or her first concern (and some are simply not very good at it). The singer will always instinctively try to make the words work regardless of the appropriateness of the composer's score in this respect.[2] Composers vary enormously in their attitudes to their own scores; for some, the notation may mark a borderline between what may be possible and what it is realistic to expect: Brian Ferneyhough, James Dillon and others have written pieces that have challenged the limits of their chosen performers, whose attempts to realize the notation create a tension essential to the work. Others see the score more as a blueprint, a plan for a construction and not the edifice itself.[3] For many hundreds of years this was inevitably the case, as composer and performer were often one and the same; there was neither the need nor the notational means for composers to be very precise when they wrote things down.

The communicative use of silence has been an essential part of performance rhetoric since Aristotle, Cicero and Quintilian.[4] Communicative silence is in large part about timing and is often a subtle combination of the predictive and the reflective. It is (ironically) often the point at which performer and listener are closest to each other in intent, and audience attention is at its most engaged. We tend to identify the delivery of a piece of music with its notes, and it is perhaps in part because of this that our attention increases when there is an absence of notes. The reflective element is primarily for the benefit of the listener: it has the capacity to enable him or her to make sense of what has gone before, to enter into the creative process of re-constructing the performer's meaning (or indeed, inventing it from scratch). There may only be nanoseconds of time involved and what the listener understands during that period may only be a kind of meta-thought, but at the very least there should be the illusion of something being communicated and the sense that something in the narrative may be about to change, or may have already changed (illusion because performers cannot be sure that they are communicating anything at all: they can express a thought and hope that the listener will be able to make something of it). The predictiveness is fuzzy: the performer may well seek to narrow the interpretative options that may occur to the listener, or might wish to mislead for effect; the listener

---

[2]   To take a simple example: when singing a medieval *contrafactum* (a new text applied to existing music), the original stresses and accents may be displaced. Most modern performers will instinctively go with the word stress rather than the musical one where these two do not agree.

[3]   See Roger Marsh, 'Heroic Motives: Roger Marsh Considers the Relationship Between Sign and Sound in "Complex" Music', *Musical Times* 135 (February 1994), 83–6.

[4]   Classical rhetoric, the art of eloquent persuasion, underpinned the educated Roman's understanding of politics, law and the arts. The study and application of rhetoric survived the Roman eclipse and was incorporated into the three medieval liberal arts of the *Trivium*, together with grammar and logic. Theoretical music (*Musica*) formed part of the scientific *Quadrivium* (with arithmetic, geometry and astronomy); rhetoricians from the first century, Quintilian onwards, also refer to practical musical communication. See George A Kennedy, *Comparative Rhetoric* (Oxford: Oxford University Press, 1998), and Ann E Moyer, *Musica scientia: Musical Scholarship in the Italian Renaissance* (Ithaca: Cornell University Press, 1992).

must have time to question what might be about to happen. For the performer it is a chance to vary the balance between predictability and unpredictability, and getting this equation right is the key to keeping the attention of the audience. It is a crucial part of rhetorical narrative; the audience needs to be both making sense of what has happened and wanting to know what happens next.

The process is at its most obvious in operatic recitative. In Act 2 of Monteverdi's *Orfeo*, Orfeo receives the news of Euridice's death and has to respond with a soliloquy. He begins with the phrase 'tu sei morta' (you are dead).

Ex. 9.1   Monteverdi, *Orfeo*, Act 2

This could have begun on the downbeat, but the composer leaves the chord to settle for almost a whole bar before Orfeo speaks. This is thinking time for Orfeo, and the listener has to be aware that he is thinking, and perhaps speculate on what he might say. It is not measured time but a moment when the singer is silent, so we the listeners can see (and almost hear) him thinking. We become part of the drama ourselves, as Orfeo's response is governed in part by how he judges our reaction to his predicament. When he does enter, it is as a kind of upbeat to the next bar, as though he is still unsure of his thoughts. This doubt is further reinforced by a rhetorical rest before he completes the sentence. We listeners on hearing 'tu …' might think something on the lines of 'you … what?'. And then, 'Why doesn't he know what to say? What is he going to say? When will he say it?'. Then he gets it out: 'you are dead'. Then silence. He has stated the obvious, so presumably he needs more thinking time, and this the composer duly gives him; and in that space he pulls himself together enough to extend the phrase and turn it to his own condition: 'tu sei morta mia vita' – 'you are dead, my life'. Then another rest before he says 'ed io respiro' – 'and I am [still] breathing'. We hear him breathe, and we see and hear him think; by a clever interpolation of rests, Monteverdi allows Orfeo to conflate his own fate with that of Euridice.

In the sixteenth and seventeenth centuries, singers would find themselves performing in church, in the theatre or in a chamber music environment that might be anything from a court to a drawing room. The singing and its associated paralinguistic gestures would be adjusted to suit the circumstances. As musical stage entertainments coalesced into what we now call opera, larger spaces demanded bigger gestures, as did more complex plots. By the eighteenth century, large scale narrative sacred works also required gestures that would impact on big acoustic spaces. Bach's Passion settings are full of sung punctuation, especially the recitatives. In the *Johannes-Passion* at the point where Pilate writes the 'Überschrift' on the cross, the composer marks each phrase with a rest. Some singers de-fragment the narrative here, presumably on the grounds that the rests indicate the sense rather than prescribe the style of delivery, but this glosses over Bach's carefully structured rhetoric. The scene follows the mad scurrying to Golgatha to witness the execution and begins with the announcement of the banal fact of the crucifixion. Bach is tied to the passion text and there is business to get through explaining Pilate's actions. The recitative begins with a rest:

Ex. 9.2   Bach, *Johannes-Passion*, scene 25a [49], bars 1–4

The previous section has ended in G minor, and a rest over the ensuing first inversion of F major gives the singer a chance to get the note, but it also creates a sense of anticipation. Even if we know the story from memory (and Bach's listeners almost certainly did), we need a chance to take in what has happened after the bald statement 'all-da kreuzigten sie ihn'. Bach's rests force the narrative into slow motion, creating an almost visible realisation of the scene. The facts would have been served perfectly adequately without any of the rests in the first sentence, but isolating the individual phrases 'und mit ihm zween andere', 'zu beiden seiten' and 'Jesum aber mitten inne' obliges us to concentrate on the constituent visual elements which gradually come into focus. There is then a longer cadential rest, signifying a new sentence.

Ex. 9.3   Bach, *Johannes-Passion*, scene 25a [49], bars 5–9

The slow motion continues: the creation of the 'Überschrift' takes time, and this is captured in miniature by the rest between 'Überschrift' and 'und satzte', and again by the rest before 'und war geschrieben', dividing the sentence into three symbolic parts. As it is a title, Bach formalizes the vocative space by marking *adagio* for the words themselves. We know what it says, of course, but we need to be reminded of the *significance* of the next phrase 'der Juden König', hence the rest between the two halves of the notice.

Ex. 9.4 Bach, *Johannes-Passion*, scene 25a [49], bars 10–13

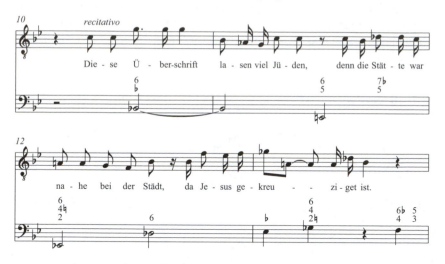

When the recitative sets off again, once more the illusion of time passing is created by using small rests to punctuate the three elements of the next sentence. The Christian symbolism of the ternary units would not be lost on listeners, and this is reinforced as it coincides with the rhetorical 'rule of three', a time-proven formula where lists are presented in the most efficiently digested form. This rule appears once more when enumerating the languages, the longer rests between the elements adding to the sense of horror: writing the notice appears to take longer than killing god:

Ex. 9.5 Bach, *Johannes-Passion*, scene 25a [49], bars 14–16

The non-vocal tropes that were part of any singer's repertoire of communicative devices reached something of a peak in the nineteenth century. We expect more histrionic performances from the more naturalistic plots of Donizetti and his successors, but the evidence from pedagogical writings suggests that singers had been exploiting holes in the music for a long time before the term *verismo* was coined. Manuel Garcia, writing in the 1840s and placing himself firmly in the tradition of his father, associates rests with breathing, where 'they serve, either to better emphasize the distribution of ideas, or to make the performance easier'.[5] In his examples of how arias should be performed we see just what this might mean in practice. The soprano aria from Cimarosa's *Sacrifizio d'Abraham* has the singer interpolating a 'sigh of extreme anguish' in the rest after 'forse' ('perhaps'), as Sara considers the fate of her son:

Ex. 9.6   Garcia, excerpt from Cimarosa, *Sacrifizio d'Abraham* (p. 218)

And later she actually sobs:

Ex. 9.7   Garcia, excerpt from Cimarosa, *Sacrifizio d'Abraham* (p. 221)

---

5   Manuel Garcia, *Traité complet de l'Art du Chant*, part 2 (1847), editions of 1847 and 1872 trans. Donald V. Paschke as *A Complete Treatise on the Art of Singing* (New York: Da Capo Press, 1975), 62–3. Garcia's father, Manuel I, was the tenor for whom Rossini composed the role of Almaviva in *The Barber of Seville*; Garcia *fils* could trace a pedagogical line from his father through his teacher Ansani, to the legendary mid-eighteenth-century teacher Porpora. See James Radomski, *Manuel García (1775–1832): Chronicle of the Life of a Bel Canto Tenor at the Dawn of Romanticism* (Oxford: Oxford University Press, 2000).

These are rests which are far from silent and are very directly communicative of very specific meanings. There is a risk when meanings are unmistakable that the effect will seem tautological. Garcia cautions against exaggeration, but a modern performer is unlikely even to consider adding to the communicative process at this point.

For Verdi, the dramatic imperative operates both on a grand scale and on a micro-level, where the course of the entire narrative can appear to turn on the silence of a rest. In Act 2 of *La traviata* the heroine, the courtesan Violetta, appears finally to be persuaded by Germont to renounce her relationship with his son Alfredo, thus forestalling potential family scandal:

Ex. 9.8   **Verdi, *La traviata*, Act 2, scene 5, bars 290–96**

She knows what she must do but cannot quite bring herself to do it; she tells him to command her, and he says she must tell Alfredo that she no longer loves him. She says he will not believe her, he tells her to leave him. She says he will follow her. Up to this point the dialogue, which is accompanied by strings (and therefore conducted and in time), has a certain predictability, each character making opposing points with almost identical silences between utterances. We get the impression that Violetta still has doubts about which way to go, and the two could have gone on exchanging reasons and excuses until one of them gave way; but Verdi changes the argument rather more subtly: we get to 'allor ...' and everything stops. The orchestra is silent in the next bar, so Germont can replace the predictability of the measured rests with rhetorical time of his own choosing. The notation of 'allor' is the simplest possible (short upbeat and longer downbeat exactly matching the word stress), but it has no rhythmic implications beyond this. The function of this single word, and the rests which precede and follow it, is to enable a decision to be made, and for the audience to feel that it is a part of the decision-making process. The process itself is signalled by the longer rest that the singer can interpolate before 'allor', and the decision is made silently by Violetta in the rest which follows it. We see the process taking place in that silence; no music is necessary. The rests enable this crucial scene to be controlled by the singers, as it would be in real life. When the orchestra stops in bar 294, nothing more can happen until Germont has spoken, and the main event, Violetta's decision, happens when she feels the moment is right.

This is not always reflected in recorded performances, and there is a noticeable divergence between live and studio recordings. The visual dimension is impossible to replicate on record, as singers are wary of introducing 'dead' silence that would be devoid of meaning in a purely aural medium. Rosa Ponselle adds a full beat before replying to Lawrence Tibbett (bar 295) in the 1935 live broadcast recording; Eleanor Steber's 1949 broadcast performance gives the rest its exact value, but adds a beat before the repetition, in effect displacing the action by a bar; in both of these instances what we hear is the singer judging the length of the rest in the knowledge that the audience can see the process happening. In contrast to these live performances, more recent studio recordings with musical drama, but no visible action, often ignore the rests: Cheryl Studer reduces bar 295 by a whole beat in her 1991 version, and Edita Gruberová omits the rest altogether in hers.[6]

These rests are created by and for the drama, but singers also have to communicate with their fellow musicians. One would not expect seventeenth-century recitative to be conducted, so the way the singer manages rests tells the accompanying continuo group where to place their chords. In *a cappella* vocal music this interpersonal communication between singers is essential to group cohesiveness. For a vocal group, silence in any conventional sense can barely be said to exist: for the singers to have a true understanding of their mutual dependency everyone has to be aware of the sharing of information. Communication with each other, even if it happens at a subliminal level, is every bit as important as communication with the audience.[7] There is an important difference between these two sorts of communicative acts: the audience will ultimately construct its own meanings from the information transmitted to them by the singers, and these may or may not coincide with what the singers are trying to say. The communication with fellow performers is full of risk and has to be unambiguous: information not acted upon is redundant, rests which are too long lose their communicative value as the silence becomes not just an absence of sound but an absence of poetic rhythm. There can be no dead silence until the end of the

---

[6]   Naxos Historical 8.110032–33 (1935); Naxos Historical 8.110115–16 (1949); DGG 437 726–2 (1991); and Apex 2564 61511–2 (1992). For details, see the Bibliography.

[7]   For more on how singers communicate within groups, see John Potter, 'Ensemble Singing', in *Cambridge Companion to Singing*, ed. Potter (Cambridge: Cambridge University Press, 2000), 158–64, and Potter, 'Choir as Ensemble: the Debt to Early Music', *Tapiola Choirbook* (forthcoming).

piece, and even then the silence is a rhetorical one in which either performers will be estimating when to start the next piece or the audience will be judging when (or if) they should applaud.

Every piece starts with a breath. Breathing has many functions for singers: it keeps them alive, it enables the voice to be sufficiently powered and controlled, it may communicate to the listener additional emotional information (a sigh or a rapid inhalation, for example), but for a group of musicians performing a madrigal or partsong it will contain crucial information about tempo. If the singers wish to conceal the mechanics of performance from the listener there will be no obvious leading of the start of any given piece. This means that information about tempo has to be exchanged in the silence that precedes the start. The only way this can happen is for everyone to understand that every event, whether a rest or a note, contains essential information which has to be shared. An audience listening to Cipriano de Rore's 'O morte, eterno fin', for example, will probably only be aware that the piece has started when they hear the C major triad that begins the madrigal. By the time the listener hears the first chord, the performers will have been engaged with each other for at least a beat, having agreed a tempo in what the audience will perceive as the silence out of which the piece emerges. This silence is not as quiet as it may seem: the singers' breath acts like an upbeat. Before they breathe the singers will have some idea of the tempo, and in the act of breathing they will negotiate the fine details and confirm where the downbeat should come. This is done by listening to, and matching, the shape of the breath, so that by the time they have all got to the top of their breath (the notional upbeat rest), they will have agreed on only one place where the first chord will start. The success of this strategy (and it will have a 100 per cent success rate in the hands of those who understand the principle) depends on performers trusting each other's information and then acting on it, whatever the consequences.

Ex. 9.9   Rore, 'O morte, eterno fin', bars 1–9

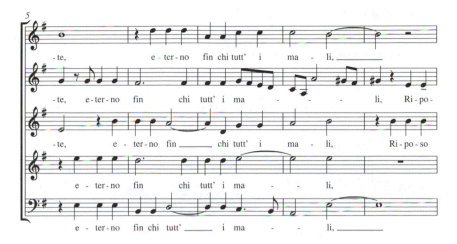

In this particular example, the music does not actually move forward in the tempo suggested by the breath (though it could). The breath has guaranteed that the chord is together – and then the composer has written three beats rest. On the face of it, this seems to undo the communicative strategy which has ensured such a precise start. But these rests form a hugely important communicative function: the audience hears a static C major chord. It may be a surprise – they may know the title, but perhaps do not expect the singers to start dying in C major. Two of the singers are silent. Once they have registered the chord, the listeners are likely to become aware of those who are not actually singing anything. Will one of or both of them begin the narrative? It turns out to be neither, but the second tenor triggers the conversion of the 'O' chord from texture into rhetoric by breaking his silence with an upbeat 'O' immediately before the alto, first tenor and bass sing the first syllable of 'morte'. This is where the piece properly begins, and the end of the beginning is the entry of the soprano, who can luxuriate in her breath, filling it with meaning, as the placing of her note is determined entirely by the placement of the final syllable of 'morte'.

In the Latin or Greek of Ciceronian oration the only clues to the punctuation of an address were to be found in the word order; the skill in delivery came from a practised knowledge of oratorical narration. The understanding of how to punctuate a reading (reading aloud, that is) was a skill that singers would instinctively apply to their own musical performances. They would sing the implied punctuation (implied because a basic knowledge of rhetoric made only minimal help from punctuation marks necessary). Modern editions of renaissance music tend to add punctuation for the benefit of those who may be unfamiliar with the language, but editors invariably ignore the adjustments to the composers' notes that these rhetorical marks imply. In the hands of a great sixteenth-century madrigalist, the music will offer the performers the possibility of a perfect union of words and music, driven by poetic and rhetorical shaping of both. Cipriano de Rore's 1557 setting of Giovanni della Casa's 'O sonno' is almost entirely homophonic, and to sing it strictly in metrical rhythm would be to miss the rich variety of meanings that are revealed as much by the silences as by the notes.

The opening is an address to sleep:

Ex. 9.10 Rore, 'O sonno', bars 1–10

The first phrase, in the vocative so ending with an implied comma, is like a yawn which seems to bring the piece to a full stop as soon as it has begun (the 'sonno' music is reprised almost intact as the two final bars of the piece). The last thing the composer wants is for a performance to be soporific, so Rore inserts a rest immediately after the word 'sleep'. This engages the listener (sleep? So what?), and the piece sets off again with an anticipatory 'O', which might be a repeat of the first word, but turns out to be the conjunction 'either'. Della Casa then inverts the word order, delaying 'placido figlio', the subject of the phrase, until after the quiet, damp, shady night that qualifies it. This is a rhetorical master-stroke that only makes sense if the performers insert some space between 'notte' and 'placido'. This rhetorical rest, unwritten because perfectly obvious to anyone with a background in oratory, comes at the moment the listener is wondering what the subject is going to be, and by delaying the resolution of the grammar, the performer not only completes the sense but makes the listener wait till the last possible moment. But the engagement continues because we know that after 'either' we can eventually expect an 'or'.

Again Rore makes us wait, putting in a rest in top and bottom voices before those voices (at a moment of their choosing) enter with 'o':

Ex. 9.11 Rore, 'O sonno', bars 10–24

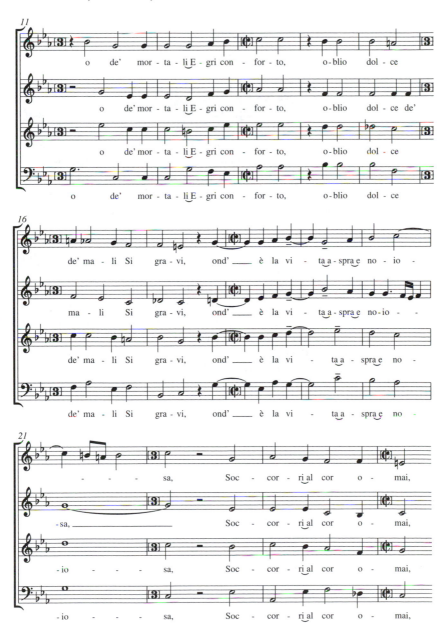

The next phrase is again a perfect match of text and music as Rore follows the poet over the line from 'mali' ('evils') to 'si gravi' ('so grievous') and then stops. The listener is almost being programmed to respond 'so grievous … that what?'. Then we get the answer, having had time to speculate on possible responses of our own. But having had the bitterness of life explained to us, we come to another apparent full stop; only after another rest in which to reflect on what has happened so far, and perhaps to speculate on what the point of all this might be, do we finally (after four lines of text) arrive at the main verb and object in quick succession, 'soccori al cor' ('succour my heart'). Each of these rests, both composed and added by performers, has a reflexive or anticipatory function which is judged by the singers, depending on how well they think the audience is keeping up. They, the performers, negotiate the rests by breathing together. This also adds to the rhetorical function, just as an actor's audible breathing would.

In theory it should be possible to propose a taxonomy of rests, beginning with a number of basic categories such as Predictive, Reflective and Narrative, which might subdivide into Exclamatory, Anticipatory and the like. While this has a certain academic appeal and might also resonate with a composerly control of the music, reducing such powerful communicative devices to simple functions would be to deny the ambiguities involved in the creative performer's role of story-teller. The narrator has to give the impression that he or she is making the story up as they go along, which means also that they should have at least the theoretical possibility of changing the story as it unfolds. This in turn means that the communicative rest almost always has more than one potential function, which the performer is at liberty to reveal or create. The silences implied by these lacunae in the written music are often points where performer and audience are tantalizingly close, almost conspiring together. This is a very personal experience: the performer, and the audience in their response to the performer, effectively own the music at such moments, taking control of the materials away from the composer and his or her score, lifting the music off the page and into the heads of those colluding in the performative act.

Chapter 10

The Air Between Two Hands: Silence, Music and Communication

Julie P. Sutton

Two people have a 'conversation', each person using only one hand. As in real conversation, the partners 'listen' and respond to what the other person is 'saying'. It is not like sign language, or a game of charades, where you try to guess the words. Instead, you try to concentrate your whole existence into that one hand. It is a kind of strange animal, communicating to another equally strange animal. When you find the genuine life of this creature, and it is able to develop a real and varied relationship with the other animal, it is fascinating to watch.

Yoshi Oida[1]

This chapter explores the phenomenon of music and silence as incorporating an unfolding communicative act between people, rather than from a view of music existing as an object for study within a written score. The Japanese actor-director Yoshi Oida's words describe a type of conversation, or what can occur in the space between two people. It is suggested that when we think about and experience music *between* people, we gain further insights into the nature of musical sounds and silences and of music itself.

The initial section of this chapter reflects on general concepts of music and silence as phenomena, and is informed by the author's clinical experience as a UK registered music therapist. This incorporates a stance of music being something that occurs between and in people, within improvisation in the clinical setting. The sounds and silences in the space between people in the therapy room are explored from both interpersonal and musical viewpoints. From their training onwards, music therapists have available a range of theoretical thinking that is informed by literature, including not only music psychology, musicology and music analysis, but also developmental and applied psychology, psychoanalysis and philosophy. This theoretical stance is

Thanks to my colleagues in the UK and Europe and especially those at the Nordoff-Robbins Centre in London for sharing their clinical experiences of silence, to the students in London and Leuven who agreed to improvise and dialogue about the topic, and particularly to Professor Dr Jos De Backer for our ongoing conversation about silence in music therapy. I am grateful to Crispin Bonham Carter for introducing me to the Oida material and to Paul Williams for helping me find much of the psychoanalytic literature. Most importantly of all I thank Ray Hunt for his wisdom, acceptance and quiet support of my research.

[1]   Yoshi Oida, *The Invisible Actor*, trans. Lorna Marshall (London, Methuen, 1997), 76.

embedded within this chapter, with a central section containing two examples from clinical music therapy work. The aim is to offer new perspectives for thinking about the musical silences that pass between human beings during music-making. As the pianist Alfred Brendel noted, 'I am accountable to the composer, but I am also there to communicate something to the listener. I am not delivering a soliloquy, but am somewhere in the middle';[2] in other words, we find part of the music when we study the score, for music is only truly alive in relationship to people.

Although documented sporadically, the topic of silence has often been thought about as a foundation of music, in that what is heard as music comes out of silence. Paradoxically, most music literature has concentrated on sounds rather than what occurs between and behind them. Musicians have tended to neglect long-term study of silence, relying on sounds – phenomena that are easier to capture, describe, talk or write about. Nevertheless, the silence out of which music comes is fundamental, along with the personal, individual connection each of us experiences both with the music that we hear and with the silences sensed and held within and behind sounded music.

This is the framework with which I approach this chapter, beginning with a brief, general contextualization of silence and music, followed by an exploration of time in music. Other perspectives will then be offered, which take the reader into the intersubjective area of human relationships, drawn together within music therapy, the field of the clinical application of music. However, before beginning with the main body of the chapter, it is relevant first to give an introduction to music therapy and a brief outline of the nature of music-making within music therapy sessions.

A Brief Introduction to Music Therapy

In the UK, music therapy is a health profession with registered status and governmental accreditation.[3] Music therapists enter their postgraduate master's training primarily as artists–musicians. The process undertaken in order to qualify for registered status occurs during a recognized theoretical, musical and experiential training, with a focus on the practical application of music in the clinical setting. Music is re-defined within this training process and the student gradually experiences a change to their musician identity, from performing musician to clinician.

In music therapy sessions, a range of musical and psychological applied theory is used by the therapist in order to respond appropriately to the client, central to which is the complexity of a developing therapeutic relationship. In practice, music therapy in the UK – in common with much of Europe – is an active discipline, in that both client and therapist are engaged in clinically improvised music-making.

---

[2] Alfred Brendel, *The Veil of Order*, trans. Richard Stokes (London: Faber & Faber, 2002), 59.

[3] For further information, contact the UK Association of Professional Music Therapists, the Health Professions Council, the British Society for Music Therapy or the European Music Therapy Confederation.

Silence and Music

While musicians have attended to silences within musical works, few have written in detail about the absence of sound in theoretical terms. Clifton, Edgar, Littlefield and Peek are rare examples of authors who chose to focus on silence in music, a task they approached in a variety of ways, showing that there was indeed much that could be gained from such study.[4] Clifton contextualized silences as phenomena in direct relation to what they emerged from and what emerged from them. He found that musical silence did not consist of a single reality, but came in many guises. For instance, 'hard-edged' silences stopped the flow of the music, while other types seemed to be embedded at a deeper level, as if attached to the fabric of the music itself.[5] Clifton's observations stem from two beliefs, relating to the effect of silence upon time perception and the idea that silences are an embodied state in the listener. Edgar chose another approach, citing broader social, cultural and political influences as well as a range of personal factors influencing the individual's response.

Littlefield explored the idea of music being framed by silence, with the frame as part of the art-work, yet paradoxically both separate from and necessary for defining it.

> The beginning silence serves as a call to attention; it focalizes the listener toward what will follow … And yet that silence *is* heard, even empirically. The beginning silence has a propulsive quality, a sense of Doing. It is modalized, or charged with moods, by the audience's expectation of what will follow, even if what follows is unknown to the listener. Out of this silence the music 'officially' begins.[6]

While not sounded externally, silences are nonetheless 'heard' internally and demand response. There is a clear indication that the term 'silence' is not limited to one particular kind of event, nor is it static, but, as Littlefield noted, it is 'charged with moods' and with movement. These are sensed in the listener, who then contributes to what makes up the silence in totality – that is, silence in the score, in the performer, in the listener, as well as in what is held to be its affective and functional significance. While musical sounds are made by musicians to be received by audiences, musical silences are shared equally by the player and the listener. It therefore comes as no surprise, as Peek observed, that some of the most powerful personal and musical experiences occur in silences.[7]

Composers have also neglected writing about the topic of silence, whether consciously or unconsciously. Exceptions are from those who adopted broader philosophical or spiritual perspectives, including thoughts about the necessity for

---

4   Thomas Clifton, 'The Poetics of Musical Silence', *Musical Quarterly* 62/2 (1976), 163–81; Andrew Edgar, 'Music and Silence,' in *Silence: Interdisciplinary Perspectives*, ed. Adam Jaworski (Berlin and New York: Mouton de Gruyter, 1997), 311–27; Richard Littlefield, 'The Silence of the Frames', in *Music/Ideology: Resisting the Aesthetic*, ed. Adam Krims ([Amsterdam]: G&B Arts International, 1998), 213–31; Philip Peek, 'Re-Sounding Silences', in *Sound*, ed. Patricia Kruth and Henry Stobart (Cambridge: Cambridge University Press, 1999), 16–33.

5   Clifton, 'The Poetics of Musical Silence', 164–9.

6   Littlefield, 'The Silence of the Frames', 219.

7   Peek, 'Re-Sounding Silences', 30–32.

silence in relation to the creative process.[8] However, improvising musicians – whose music is formed through composition in the moment – have written in more detail about experiencing silences before, during and after playing. For instance, the free improviser Edwin Prévost states:

> Silence at the beginning means not-knowing, not wanting to know, not wanting the music to move in a pre-ordained direction.
>   Silence within performance marks the pivotal positions the music may reach.
>   Silence at the end of a performance is not an end of a sequence at which there is a resumption of 'normal' activity. The silence is a refined state of musical expression.[9]

Prévost links the creative act of improvising with a state of un-knowingness. Conscious thought processes and desires are let go in order that there is space and freedom for the music that is yet-to-become, embedded in the very experience of hearing silence in relation to sound, as well as in the overall perspective in which we hear improvised music as player and/or listener. Moments emerge from silences that are 'pivotal', suggesting aesthetic and structural functions for musical silence.

My own research provides evidence for this phenomenon. For instance, analysis of free-improvised duets revealed that both musicians made use of silences at structural points as a means of slowing the overall pace of the music, stimulating affective changes in the performing musicians and their listeners. More significantly, although serving a definite role and function in creating tension, silences were not static, with variety in quality, pacing and impetus.[10] Clifton also found this to be true of composed music:

> Silence, since it is not nothingness, is an experienced musical quality which can be pulsed or unpulsed in musical time, attached or detached to the edges of a musically spatial body, and finally, which can often be experienced as being in motion in different dimensions of the musical space-time manifold.[11]

In these ways, musical silences are not mere absences of sounds or finite phenomena relating to structural or temporal features. Instead they are complex within themselves, having the same range of qualities as musical sounds. Musical sounds emerge from silence, and out of silences different phenomena emerge. Like sounded

---

[8]   Composers who have adopted broader perspectives include: Brahms – see J. A. Fuller-Maitland, *Brahms* (London: Methuen, 1911), 69–70; Debussy – see Edward Lockspeiser, ed., *The Literary Clef* (London: John Calder, 1958), p. 110; Brian Ferneyhough – see *Collected Writings*, ed. James Boros and Richard Toop (Amsterdam: Harwood Academic Publishers, 1995), 260; and Jonathan Harvey – see *Music and Inspiration* (London, Faber & Faber, 1999), 166.

[9]   Edwin Prévost, *No Sound is Innocent* (Harlow, Essex: Copula, 1995), 133–4.

[10]   Julie P. Sutton, 'The Pause that Follows: Silence, Improvised Music and Music Therapy', paper presented at the *5th European Music Therapy Congress*, Naples, April 2001; Sutton, '"The Invisible Handshake": an Investigation of Free Musical Improvisation as a Form of Conversation' (PhD diss., University of Ulster, 2001).

[11]   Clifton, 'The Poetics of Musical Silence', 181.

music, silences are in motion, changing over time in quality and function. The subjective experience of time is a core feature of musical silences, and one of the most significant aspects to underlie these phenomena.

Time Out-of-time

It is not possible to discuss musical silence without brief reference to musical time, for silences in music appear to alter time. At the very least, they interrupt our perception of the ongoing flow of musical sounds, ranging from the spaces between individual notes through music's pauses to the overall arching structure of silence framing the beginning and ending of a musical work. The concepts of *chronos* and *kairos* both apply to the passage of time. *Chronos* describes time passing in a linear way (as with the ticking of a clock). In contrast, *kairos* may be said to relate more to silence itself, to a sense of space and a subjective experience of a lack of *chronos* – of a time out-of-time. *Kairos* is also connected to the idea of an endless time out of which the world and its music emerged, along with echoes of the beginnings of this musical world in everyday life. It is this awareness of time that silences open up.

Paradoxically, one's sense of this aspect of the continuity of universal time is also related to its corporeal, lived experience, as the Russian film director Andrey Tarkovsky wrote:

> Time is a condition of our 'I'. It is like a kind of culture medium that is destroyed when it is no longer needed, once the links are severed between the individual personality and the conditions of existence. And the moment of death is also the death of individual time: the life of a human being becomes inaccessible to the feelings of those remaining alive, dead for those around him.[12]

While Tarkovsky treated cinematic silences in terms of *kairos*, he was also interested in holding the paradox of lived, perceived, existential time within as well as outside of chronological time. This same perspective is found in music and other arts, where creativity itself is seen to emerge from silence, requiring stillness within the creator, a sense of separateness from the world and space in which to flourish.[13] Dujka Smoje has noted that this is true in music, within which 'silence creates a sense of atemporality, erasing the sense of movement and with it, rational measurement of time'.[14] Such atemporality links us with much larger questions of existence as noted by Augustine, for whom musical silences and sounds symbolized man's emergence out of an original cosmic nothingness, coming to life and eventually dying back

---

[12]   Tarkovsky, Andrey, *Zapechatlennoe vremia*, trans Kitty Hunter-Blair as *Sculpting in Time: Reflections on the Cinema* (1986), 4th U. of Texas ed. (Austin: University of Texas Press, 1994), 57.

[13]   Sutton, 'Hidden Music: an Exploration of Silence in Music and Music Therapy', in *Musical Creativity: Multidisciplinary Research in Theory and Practice*, ed. Irene Deliège and Geraint Wiggins (Hove: Psychology Press, 2006), 252–72.

[14]   Dujka Smoje, *Silence as Atemporal Music: Tabula rasa, Stille, Silence*, paper presented at the conference *Silence and Music*, University of York, October 2003.

into it.[15] Silences thus bind us both to life and to death, and also to our essential creativity.

Working with the idea of an everlasting silence from which music is born and into which it dies can help to create a sense of endless time within music itself. Composers agreeing with this perspective affirm that their music emerges from spiritual and philosophical discourses; a deep, internal sense of self in connection with a wider, universal collective is held in everlasting silence. Arvo Pärt is one composer holding this mixture of personal motivation and theoretical thinking. During the 1970s, he withdrew from serialism, a formalist approach to Western composition that was so pervasive then that overt rejection can only have been read as highly significant. He began a study of religious, contemplative music, which was integrated into a simplifying and deepening of his work. Pärt developed his thinking about meditative silence, as inextricably linked with an overall concept of creativity: music emerges from an unknown place within the composer, and access to it is dependent on inner quietness and stillness.

Whereas Western traditions have often viewed silence as an entity with negative qualities, Eastern philosophies often offer an opposing view.[16] While an exploration of non-Western philosophies is outside the remit of this chapter, one concept deserves attention, as it relates to an idea of silence that touches on human perceptions of time and timelessness. The Japanese term *ma* combines the ideas of a space, a particular inner state and a sense of illumination. *Ma* is linked with 'spacing and timing ... [implying] a subtle appreciation of the pause or gap'.[17] It is essentially an affective space that exists between things, shown for instance in a process of the attentive, careful timing and placing of a musical tone in relation to all other tones. This concept is also apparent in silences between sounds, in the quality of such silences, in intent listening (to something both outside and inside ourselves), and in the ambiguities that can arise when both presence and absence might be sensed and found. Silences can hold these kinds of paradoxes at levels that are not possible with verbal explanations, and perhaps at which no musical sounds can be made. Finally, *ma* comprises an act of recognizing a space and exploring it, to discover meaning in a context outside chronological time. This idea is closely linked with the possibilities of silences in the musical therapeutic setting, as will be considered later in the chapter.

---

[15]   Catherine Pickstock, 'Soul, City and Cosmos After Augustine', in *Radical Orthodoxy: a New Theology*, ed. John Milbank, Catherine Pickstock and Graham Ward (London and New York, Routledge, 1999), 243–77.

[16]   Sutton, 'Hidden Music – an Exploration of Silences in Music and Music Therapy', *Music Therapy Today* (online) 6/3 (2005), 375–95, available at <http://www.MusicTherapyWorld.net>; *see also* article cited in footnote 14.

[17]   Michael Freeman and Michiko Riko Nose, *The Modern Japanese Garden* (London, Octopus Publishing Group, 2002), 56.

Human Development, Sounds and Silences

To move from pre-composed music to music that is composed in the moment, one may note that what is true of silences in performed composed music is also true of improvised music. Improvisation is by nature interactive – if not between musicians, then between the improvising soloist, the unfolding music and the audience. The interactive aspect of improvisation demands one to move from thinking about the phenomena of musical sounds and silences as experienced by the listener, towards the idea of sounds and silences experienced *between* people. Jeremy Begbie, though coming from a spiritual perspective, nevertheless agrees with music therapy literature, noting that in improvisation 'there would seem to be the growth of personal particularity through musical dialogue'.[18] This growth begins with birth itself, because musical dialogue begins with our first experiences of the world, those experiences carried with us throughout life. It is relevant therefore to consider briefly sounds and silences within early human development.

Developmental theorists have shown that there is a strong inter-communicative aspect to the acquisition of language from the beginning of life.[19] A baby's sense of feeling safe in the world emerges from experiencing his caregivers' attempts to tend to his needs in various ways, including physical holding and the use of the voice. Adults naturally adopt a higher pitch range when talking to babies, unconsciously adapting to what the baby hears best. Furthermore, adults adapt their behaviour to the baby's responses, echoing, matching and reflecting the infant's movements.

Developmental psychology has shown that from around three months after conception we are hearing beings, and that even in the womb we react to sound.[20] As we further develop, we react more specifically to familiar and unfamiliar sounds, entering the world as interactive listeners and as sound-makers, with our first year of life an essentially musical existence. In previous research, Colwyn Trevarthen argued convincingly just how musical the interactions between infant and caregiver are, and Daniel Stern agreed, likening the process to that of a dance.[21] This dance-like flow of sounds and silences between mother and infant prepares the baby for later verbal conversation, described by Trevarthen as 'proto-conversation'.

From the psychoanalytic literature, Hans W. Loewald approached this idea from a different angle, suggesting that while the mother talks to her baby, what is important is not primarily the words themselves or even the conversational nature of the exchange that the mother facilitates, but the quality of the sounds and the

---

[18]   Jeremy S. Begbie, *Theology, Music and Time* (Cambridge: Cambridge University Press, 2000), 206.

[19]   Daniel Stern, *The First Relationship: Infant and Mother* (Cambridge, MA: Harvard University Press, 1977); Colwyn Trevarthen, 'The Foundations of Intersubjectivity: Development of Interpersonal and Co-operative Understanding of Infants', in *The Social Foundations of Language and Thought: Essays in Honor of Jerome S. Bruner*, ed. David R. Olson (New York: W. W. Norton, 1980), 316–42.

[20]   Alessandra Piontelli, *From Fetus to Child: an Observational and Psychoanalytic Study* (London: Tavistock/Routledge, 1992), 34–8.

[21]   See Trevarthen, 'The Foundations of Intersubjectivity', and Stern, *The First Relationship*.

affective characteristics of the ways in which she responds to the baby.[22] This focus on the timbre of the mother's voice supports the view of the musicality of the first relationship. Without these early, essentially musical, life experiences and the flow of movements, feelings, sounds and silences between caregiver and infant, it is difficult for the baby to enter into the cognitive world of talk, and therefore to become an active and integral part of the communicating world.

However, within this world of sounds and silences, too much information presented too quickly can result in an infant or a young child feeling overwhelmed, confused and chaotic inside. Caregivers naturally slow down interaction and offer periods of silence so that the infant has the time and the space in which to digest what has occurred. Developmental psychologists such as Stern have identified this in different ways, for instance in his 'time-out episodes' and his idea of 'retuning' and 'resettling'. As Stern explains:

> The episode of engagement, and the subsequent time-out episode, appear to function as *retaining units* in the *regulation* of the interaction. During each episode of engagement, both mother and infant are trying to stay within the boundaries of the optimal ranges of excitement and affect. The engagement episodes come to an end when an *upper* or *lower* boundary has been exceeded. More often the infant signals this.[23]

Silences serve a regulatory function in the time before cognitive awareness has developed. Linked with this is the concept of 'temporal shapes', a term referring to patterns of human responses that have some connection with the early give-and-take between infant and adult.[24] When this pattern is either not present or unreliable, it has links with a lack of continuity-of-being that is experienced, for instance, by those with Autistic Spectrum Disorder, where the world easily becomes a frightening, traumatic place. In such cases, the careful and delicately applied use of musical intervention during clinical music therapy sessions may be a powerful tool in the discovery and development of new patterns of behaviour or contexts for self-experience.

The nature of our emergence into a world of communicating beings and relationships (along with its sounds and silences) has been explored by a number of authors,[25] but in a recent book Stern draws together the individual's experience

---

[22]   Hans W. Loewald, 'On the Therapeutic Action of Psycho-Analysis', *International Journal of Psychoanalysis* 41 (1960), 19.

[23]   Stern, *The First Relationship*, 81–2 (emphasis from the original).

[24]   Anne Alvarez, *Live Company: Psychoanalytic Psychotherapy with Autistic, Borderline, Deprived and Abused Children* (London: Routledge, 1992), 60–76; Suzanne Maiello, 'The Sound-Object: a Hypothesis about Prenatal Auditory Experience and Memory', *Journal of Child Psychotherapy* 21/1 (1995), 23-41.

[25]   See for instance: John Bowlby, *Attachment and Loss*, 1: *Attachment* (New York: Basic Books, 1969); Stuart Feder, Richard L. Karmel and George H. Pollock, eds, *Psychoanalytic Explorations in Music* (Madison, CT: International Universities Press, 1990); Stuart Feder, Richard L. Karmel and George H. Pollock, eds, *Psychoanalytic Explorations in Music: Second Series* (Madison, CT: International Universities Press, 1993); Stephen N. Malloch, 'Mothers and Infants and Communicative Musicality', *Musicae Scientiae* (1999–2000), 29–58 [special issue: *Rhythm, Musical Narrative, and Origin of Human Communication*]; Piontelli, *From Fetus to Child*; Andrea Sabbadini, 'On Sounds, Children, Identity and a "Quite Unmusical"

and the experience of spaces between the individual and others in time. His thinking combines clinical analytic knowledge with awareness of altered time perception in music, unravelling some of the complex inter-relationships that contribute to our sense of continuity-of-being. As he states, 'the future is implied at each instant of the musical phrase's journey through the present moment'.[26] This statement implies that while we experience ourselves in moments of time, we not only sense these moments as phenomena in the present, but also in the present that is soon to be past and in the present that is soon to be future. As Stern wrote, 'the present moment is never totally eclipsed by the past not fully erased by the future'.[27]

Significantly, Stern notes that the sense of moving forward in music is only possible when two or more musical events are heard within three seconds of each other.[28] If no sounds are heard within that time span the music is felt to stop, halt or pause. While not explicitly differentiating between sounds and silences, Stern gives clear clinical examples in which silences between patient and analyst move toward and past this threshold, and then emerge into new therapeutic areas. This important observation links with early developmental theory and also with the idea that silences are not static, but phenomena during which a movement or shift can emerge and something new appear. Clinical work demonstrates that as a therapist senses and listens to silence from a particular stance and a still inner state, there is potential for movement through or past the natural tendency to lose momentum at this three-second point. The therapist holding this silent threshold potentially enables the patient also to hold or trust the possible shift to a new inner state. The exploration of silence in therapy and in music therapy develops this idea further.

Silence in Therapy and in Music Therapy

A cliché of therapy in general and of psychoanalysis in particular is the amount of time that is spent in silence. An analyst's silence, as she listens to the sounds and silences of her client,[29] can feel powerful, arising as it does between two people in a

---

Man', *British Journal of Psychotherapy* 14/2 (1997), 189–96; Daniel Stern, 'A Micro-analysis of Mother-infant Interaction: Behaviors Regulating Social Contact Between a Mother and her Three-and-a-half Month-old Twins', *Journal of American Academy of Child Psychiatry* 10 (1971), 501–17; Stern, *The Interpersonal World of the Infant: a View from Psychoanalysis and Developmental Psychology* (New York: Basic Books, 1985, 2000); Colwyn Trevarthen, 'Communication and Cooperation in Early Infancy: a Description of Primary Intersubjectivity', in *Before Speech: the Beginning of Interpersonal Communication*, ed. Margaret M. Bullowa (Cambridge and New York: Cambridge University Press, 1979), 231–347; Trevarthen, 'Musicality and the Intrinsic Motive Pulse: Evidence from Human Psychobiology and Infant Communication', *Musicae Scientiae* (1999–2000), 155–211 [special issue: *Rhythm, Musical Narrative, and Origin of Human Communication*].

[26]   Daniel Stern, *The Present Moment in Psychotherapy and Everyday Life* (New York and London: W. W. Norton, 2004), 26.

[27]   *Ibid.*, 31.

[28]   *Ibid.*, 46.

[29]   For clarity, the term 'she' is used throughout to define the therapist and 'he' the client.

situation in which otherwise one would expect words to follow in the improvisation of everyday conversational exchange. In longer silences not only the conversation but the interaction itself may be felt to be under threat. In such instances, anxiety results and ultimately there is danger of the client feeling that the therapist is not present for him; in reality a great deal of the therapist's attention is very much present – sensing, attending to, assimilating and processing the moments that pass. This kind of attentiveness is a complex, internal process, and it includes a dual sense of time, or of 'timeliness'. As Danielle Quinodoz observes, it requires 'attention to the present moment and ... awareness of the [client's personal and also therapeutic] journey as a whole, with its beginning, course, and end'.[30] Therefore, silences in therapy are delicate, complex and many-layered. Although acknowledged in the literature, their complexity is rarely focused on separately or examined in depth. There is a tendency to concentrate instead on the words that come out of silences.

Words, like musical sounds, are more concrete phenomena than silences, and thus less problematic to describe. Like both therapists and musicians, music therapists have tended to focus their writing on musical sounds rather than the silences that occur between these sounds. However, like the two hands that Oida described at the start of this essay, it is because of the air between the sounded notes that we are able to frame what we hear in a musical work. In music therapy the same is true of the air between the notes of a clinical improvisation, of the silence before and after the first note sounds and the last dies away, and of the air between the therapist and client before, during and after these silences. Flower and I were among the first music therapists to focus our writing on silences in music therapy, noting that they opened up different possibilities for reflection within the therapist, as well as potential new experiences in both therapist and client.[31] Jos De Backer, with his theory of *anticipating inner silence*, provides another notable contribution to research in this area.[32] This concept develops new thinking about the silent state of the music therapist at the beginning of the therapy session. It is significant because the material is strongly rooted in the art of music, informed by analytic psychotherapeutic theory. In the *anticipating inner silence*, 'the musician is already present in the music before

[30]   Danielle Quinodoz, *Words that Touch: a Psychoanalyst Learns to Speak*, trans. Philip Slotkin (London, Karnac Books, 2003), 175.

[31]   Claire Flower, 'The Spaces Between the Notes: Silence in Music Therapy', paper presented at the *Association of Professional Music Therapists/British Society for Music Therapy Annual Conference*, London, February 2001; Sutton, 'The Pause that Follows' (2001); Sutton, 'The Invisible Handshake' (2001); Flower and Sutton, 'Silence – "a Refined State of Musical Expression": a Dialogue about Silence in Music Therapy', paper presented at *World Music Therapy Congress*, Oxford, July 2002; Sutton, 'Listening To and Thinking About the Spaces Between the Notes: Silence and Musical Interaction', paper presented at Aalborg University, Denmark, October 2002; Sutton, 'Hidden Music – an Exploration of Silences in Music and Music Therapy' (2005) and version in *Musical Creativity*, ed. Deliège and Wiggins (2006).

[32]   Jos De Backer, 'The Transition from Sensorial Impression into a Musical Form by Psychotic Patients' (PhD thesis, University of Aalborg, Denmark, 2005).

the music sounds'.[33] This idea resonates with composers like Pärt, who broadened his definition of silence to include both the personal and the universal.

De Backer discusses other types of clinical silence, including the therapist's silence when the client is active, with theoretical discussion of therapeutic transference and counter-transference issues. De Backer began to categorize silences, considering the fragmented silences of the client as indications of an inability to sustain musical play, where musical connection with the therapist is broken as a result of an underlying, deep fundamental trauma. This deep thinking about silent spaces between people in the clinical setting is echoed in the psychoanalytic literature, for instance, in the concept of the analyst approaching each analytic encounter without a particular expectation or plan. As Sacha Nacht wrote, 'the analyst must limit himself to a certain way of being present, with an underlying, deeply-felt attitude compounded of acceptance, availability, and the sincere desire to help the patient'.[34]

This stance was exemplified in Wilfred R. Bion's recommendation that the therapist approach each session in a state of openness to tolerate the uncertain and the unknown, without the desire for a particular outcome or understanding.[35] Bion suggested that through the putting-aside or letting-go of the therapist's expectations and needs, there emerged the possibility of a new space to open up within both client and therapist. This therapeutic stance is possible within the inner, silent space created by the therapist, a space that suspends time and opens up possibilities that would otherwise be inaccessible, due to existing desires, expectations and the need to repair.

In considering the therapist's quality of presence in the clinical setting, Mary Jane Markell described this as a state of existence *in the moment*, where different levels of being are possible.[36] Therapeutic change can only take place through deep focus on the moment, yet such focus must be based in a not-knowing stance, where unconscious processes are allowed to unfold. As Markell wrote:

> It does not need to be nameable, explainable, knowable. It is not yet readily available to rational, conceptual thought. Similarly the process of the immediacy of being needs no rational thought.[37]

This embodied state in the therapist of 'immediacy of being' pays full attention to the silent moment, resulting in increased sensitivity to all aspects of the being-state. Linked with the concept of *kairos* and time out-of-time, and also with the idea of *ma* holding possibilities for something new to emerge, this transformed level of awareness, first in the therapist and then in the client, enables new perspectives to be possible. This observation leads the reader into the complex area of spaces between

---

[33]   Jos De Backer, in personal communication with the author, March–September 2005.

[34]   Sacha Nacht, 'Silence as an Integrative Factor', *International Journal of Psychoanalysis* 45 (1964), 300.

[35]   Wilfred R. Bion, *Attention and Interpretation: a Scientific Approach to Insight in Psycho-analysis and Groups* (London: Maresfield Library, 1970), Chapter 3, esp. 26–30.

[36]   Mary Jane Markell, *Sand, Water, Silence – the Embodiment of Spirit: Explorations in Matter and Psyche* (London, Jessica Kingsley, 2002).

[37]   *Ibid.*, 225.

people. How do silences in and between people suggest other ways of listening that can inform what is sounded in words or music?

Hearing Silence and Listening to Silence: Silences in and Between People

Markell's combination of quiet openness, self-awareness, deeply-sensed security and authentic self-possession offered qualities of presence that have been echoed by other practitioners. The sand-play specialist Dora Kalff also referred to the therapist's presence, suggesting that the space inside the therapist should be one of stillness, silence, and – critically – with no movement within their overall state of attentiveness. This composed, held-attentiveness is reflective and introspective, yet with a readiness to be open to something external, to allow it to influence this inner state (i.e. to receive the client). However, in this deep state of attentive-readiness, there has to be more than an openness present in the therapist. An active awareness of what silence may contain is also essential, for if we experience silence at sufficient depth, we are potentially linked not only to presence, but also to absence and loss.

Moving from the phenomena experienced during silences with clients, towards awareness of the autobiographical nature of such moments, Kalff wrote:

> Suddenly it [the silence] is very strong. There is a stillness and nothing moves. After this, there is a movement out of this space. There is also great sadness contained in this process. We are never at the end of the path of becoming more conscious. Every moment may contain that sadness. ... We must never forget what was at the beginning of the story. ... It is vital that we ... understand with our intuitive understanding what is happening for many times it cannot be grasped with language.[38]

Here, Kalff is describing a complex and deep inner process of an experience of silence that is essentially about a profound sense of a self that is paradoxically absent and present. First, the silence holds a space into which anything can or might come. In this held space, there is security of being. Then, there is change, and some movement appears, taking the listener out of the silence. It becomes a movement out of the safe self-state, into something new and unknown. This loss of the secure, holding space is a critical moment. Kalff felt that this pivotal moment had resonance with a universal, deep and profound loss that begins with life itself.

Therefore, as some composers have also suggested, when we experience silence fully, it is a silence into which life itself is born. All subsequent silences carry the echo of this first universal silence, when we are in touch with our first personal experiences of silence, the silence into which our infant needs are not met, the silence of the first separation from the mother, the silences of loss, abandonment, loneliness and, ultimately, of death. In such ways silence may hold what is traumatic about our inner life, as well as what eventually becomes our departure from life. Music, in its sounds and silences, seems perfectly suited to such a process, having within it subtleties of both the heard and the silent presences and absences of being. Therefore, in the therapeutic setting, awareness of the potential depth of the shared experience

---

[38]   Dora Kalff, quoted in Markell, *Sand, Water, Silence*, 158–9.

of silence is essential. This may only come through the therapist's familiarity with and experience of his own silent spaces, as accessed through personal therapeutic work and self-experience.

De Backer notes a complexity of affective experiences within the therapist during shared silences with patients.[39] In a statement surprisingly close to that of Prèvost's 'not-knowing', quoted earlier in the chapter, De Backer has recorded:

> In my therapeutic attitude, all sessions start with silence, and from the silence outwards, the therapeutic space develops. It is not conscious, it's more of an attitude, concerning the therapeutic identity of the therapist. ... Silence makes it possible for the therapist and also the patient to listen to the other and to himself ... the patient can experience from the silence, the silent relationship in this moment, and from this ... the patient can experience 'something can happen now'.

> Two people can be in silence, and something can develop. It appears unexpectedly. It's so difficult to describe. In sounds you can have the illusion that something happened, but only in the therapist & the patient can you experience it, in the intersubjective space.[40]

De Backer's silent, 'intersubjective space' is directly related to Oida's 'air between two hands'. It also resonates with the concept of *ma*, where time and space coincide in a particular way that paradoxically stills onward movement and opens new vistas. These observations contrast dramatically with earlier psychoanalytic literature that identified silences within the consulting room as indications of the presence of defensive structures within the patient (put simply, inability or unwillingness to talk about certain topics at certain times, occurring at levels beyond conscious awareness).

Rather than indicating defensive psychic structures through which the client is not fully present, De Backer's silence-within-the-therapist is one of an open-ended listening, defined as much by space as by time. Within this silence the patient may find a way to become more fully present. The philosopher Heidegger noted that it is only when there is this kind of still space that there may be the possibility of a 'belonging together of being and thinking, i.e. presence and taking-in',[41] a concept that combined or allowed the existence of both presence and absence as an authenticity of 'being'. Linking this thinking with that of the clinical-musical setting re-defines musical silence as more than the absence of notes on the page or sounds made by the musician – or evidence of a universal and eternal music. Such silences are intensely personal, existing within and between people during the act of being-musically-in-the-moment. Furthermore, being-musically-in-the-moment holds presence and absence in tension, in that the present moment also contains absent moments of the recent-past and becoming-future.

---

[39]   De Backer, 'The Transition from Sensorial Impression into a Musical Form by Psychotic Patients', 118–19, 126, 136, 202–6, 283–9.

[40]   De Backer, in personal communication with the author, March–September 2005.

[41]   Martin Heidegger, 'Das Ende der Philosophie und die Aufgabe des Denkens' (1964), in *Zur Sache des Denkens* (Tübingen: Niemeyer, 1969, reissued 1976), 75.

In music therapy, awareness of this paradox enables another possibility, in which silences become vehicles for transforming experiences. Musical silences between people may not only contain what is sensed by the individuals, but may also become a space where something else can happen, as musical sounds lead from one 'now' state to another ('now' being defined as an awareness of the present as it now is, combined with awareness of this present coming into being and moving towards the past). These shared silences open up potential for pause and reflection, holding deeply significant affective states within and between individuals alongside those encompassed by an overall sense of time out-of-time. Such transforming experiences might be possible in other settings, but in music and music therapy they are particularly accessible, as the following examples reveal.

Examples from Music Therapy

From conversations with many music therapists, several identifiable phenomena emerge with respect to silences in the therapy room that occur in and between therapist and client. The awareness of a mutuality or a sharing of silence with the client seems paramount, frequently in conjunction with a dilemma concerning when and how the therapist breaks it through a gesture, a musical sound or a verbal comment. Therapists also note how much easier it is to talk about sounds than silences, commonly defining silence as space within which anticipation, reflection, and an awareness of self are possible.

The following two examples detail descriptions of silences valued as significant in the course of music therapy treatment. The first explains how a six year-old autistic boy was able to begin to become aware of his therapist at the end of his third session. In order to do this he had to slow his natural functioning rate, contain his anxiety about what might happen in an unfamiliar setting, negotiate the musical-emotional exchange between himself and his therapist, and resist the defensive need to fill every space with sounds. This allowed a first silence to unfold. In the second example, the therapist describes how a traumatized young boy was able to hold on to the uncertainty of presence and absence in silences. A combination of slowing the overall pace and the delicate placement of silences enabled the course of the therapy to change. Common to both examples are the qualities of the therapists' listening and reflecting attitudes, and the significance they attributed to the musical-personal silences in the therapy room.

Example 1: A First Silence

The following example occurred at the end of the third 30-minute music therapy session of a six year-old boy with Autistic Spectrum Disorder (ASD). This boy was described as having great difficulty in interacting with anyone. He was a dreamy member of his school group, always alone, and hardly ever spoke. During his three sessions in the therapy room he looked tense, frightened and anxious, running around the room, building a barrier of percussion instruments between himself and the therapist. At times he made the briefest of contributions, touching an instrument for few seconds, emitting a short vocalization or glancing fleetingly at the therapist. In spite of the tentative, tenuous nature of his music, the therapist felt it was positive that he was intrigued enough by what was in the room not to leave.

The therapist describes what took place at the end of this session:

> I create an open, non-threatening musical atmosphere, improvising piano music that is slow-moving, with predictable, repeated chords that sometimes changed in reflection of his short bursts of playing. A sense of continuity is offered in a simple melodic line. Gradually, he becomes able to sustain his music for increasingly longer periods. In doing this he reveals a less heightened state of anxiety and a slowly growing trust in the music making. He then settles for a longer period of time at the metallophone, his music at times tentative, anxious and tenuous. I wait for him, sometimes holding back, sometimes pushing the music forward. I feel I have to provide some musical sense of continuity within which his fragmented responses could sit. After almost ten minutes, the music slowly draws to a close. There is a silence of almost two minutes, during which he gently places his beaters onto the instrument. At the end of the long silence he sighs and breathes out. The quality of this final silence is intense, and impossible to break until he breathes again. It is a silence that holds my presence, and also eventually some of his, in a situation where he had found it very difficult to remain. It marks a passage of time where there is a definite and unfolding sharing of time and space between us, a space that he is just able to hold onto. There is something both delicate and precious about this silence; it marks presence in the face of overwhelming absence. The silence also offers a space where it might be possible to assimilate and begin to process something of what had occurred within the musical sounds.

This silence was highly significant, because it was both within the therapist and also between therapist and child. In terms of this boy's therapy it was essential that it was held and not broken. It spoke silently of the future course of the therapy (i.e. connecting to and then with another person and the emerging growth of a relationship).

Alvarez has warned about ignoring developing psychoanalytic space between the therapist and the ASD client as 'like listening to music while tone-deaf or comparing the scent of two roses without a sense of smell ... [the space between] is a relationship, a duet, not a solo'.[42] Perhaps the nature of this silent space within the therapist and between her and the client was delicate and precious, because it was also beginning to 'be' within him, identifiably so in his need to hold his breath as he began to survive and hold onto what was for him a difficult experience of connectedness.

Example 2: Silences that Become

The client is a young boy with a traumatic history, at a session in which something new emerged in the therapy. The boy plays little finger bells and the therapist, the piano. As the music unfolds, they take turns playing, and a series of short silences occur between the therapist's music and the boy's.

---

[42]   Alvarez, *Live Company*, 202.

The therapist describes his own responses:

> He chooses a new instrument: the small finger cymbals. The beginning was surprising: he sits down quietly beside me at the piano and an 'open silence'[43] appears. Immediately, in the silence, I could come into resonance with him and myself. During this resonance, I am almost guided by something unknown and 'get caught' by something that I did not expect at all, like an atmosphere that comes over me and inspires me. Not knowing what inspires or animates me, spontaneously I slow down my pace. I realise that I enter into a kind of melancholy state. I am surprised to notice how time is being stretched and how I am drawn to a particular musical motif. It is not the music that follows me, but it is I that follow the music. I am surprised by something that pops up in the relationship with him, and, immediately, he reacts.

This is a striking example because of the way in which the therapeutic silences unfolded, its unexpected nature taking the therapist by surprise yet paradoxically seeming natural and inevitable. The quality of tension in the silences is significant: the therapist and the boy are fragile, yet there is an intangible underlying security, in which the therapist holds and contains the client's fragile vulnerability. In addition, the lengths of the silences differ, sometimes obviously, sometimes more subtly. The quality of the silences is not static, it changes from moment to moment, and the pacing differs from silence to silence. There is also a sense of time suspended (*kairos*): a moment could simultaneously be an instant in time, as well as the beginning of a link to something past and therefore a possible continuity. This is reminiscent of Quinodoz's idea that silences could allow both horizontal and vertical perceptions of time. At times, the silence feels unbearable, yet somehow potentially manageable. These are silences containing paradoxes – silences perhaps on the threshold of absence and presence. Given this client's traumatic history, what is most striking is the way that from the beginning the musical silences (owned by therapist, and by client and therapist together) have a sense of overall movement and continuity. The silences made it possible to begin to hold something traumatic, rather than to *become* something traumatic.

What is apparent from these examples is the complexity and depth of material contained in musical silences between people – material that not only has consequence in the clinical music therapy setting, but also significance with respect to our views of music in general. In the two cases, silences allowed the possibility of movement towards and through which new vistas and directions might emerge. Thus the silences became agents of change within therapy. Furthermore, the clinical examples showed that process in and within silence can open up new spaces, through which different experiences of time are contained without any forward-seeking direction to lead the listener onwards. This has direct clinical implications for work with traumatic conditions: a slowing of overall pace can allow the potential space for something else to come into being; rather than repetition of the old, there is a possibility of something new.

In music generally, as in music therapy, silences are not only components indicating the absence of sound. As the two examples revealed, musical silences are

---

43   De Backer, in personal communication with the author, March–September 2005.

not static; just as the movement of dynamic form is heard in musical sounds, so it is also present in musical silences. Silences need not merely be the means of creating a tension of expectation, of catching the attention of the listener, or of marking a work's beginning and end. Silences have a deeper impact within the listener, relating to a complex awareness and deeply held sense of oneself-in-the-moment (*kairos*). Perhaps silences bring the unique combination of personalities involved in musical performance closest together: it is in the silent spaces that composer, performer and listener meet without mediation.

In the clinical setting of music therapy, silence can create a processing space in which time is stretched and the therapist can hold onto a sense of the client in a way that the client may not be able to do alone. In this sense of the therapist's 'being' with the client, silence can mark a presence within the therapist that may prevent an absence within the client. This has implications for the ways in which potential spaces within musical silences may be viewed. However, silences also have the potential to connect us with the most intimate sense of ourselves, whether as a totally present being, or with a deep sense of loss. Such silences may immediately be felt, yet paradoxically also offer a reflective space connecting the creator, the performer and the audience. Musical silences are not an absence of music, but phenomena holding a space within which music itself – and we – exist and are linked together.

The Air between Two Hands

To return to the beginning of this chapter, we are reminded that when we study music, it moves away from the silence of the score and begins to exist within and live between people. Within this space – in all its musical sounds and silences – the art of music has great significance. For in music we feel most powerfully that time is frequently altered and suspended, out of which deeper affective states emerge within and between individuals. Yoshi Oida recognized this when he played with the idea of two actors improvising a conversation, each using only one hand. Watching the actors' hands, Oida directed the reader thus:

> But if we consider what is actually going on here, there is nothing at all. Just two hands twisting, clenching, and wiggling their fingers at each other. What makes it interesting to watch is the relationship between the tiny 'performers'. ... What is interesting is the exchange. The 'acting' doesn't reside in the hand of each actor; it exists in the air between the two hands.[44]

It is not in the hands, but in the space between them that the art resides. Through this deceptively simple acting exercise, Oida revealed a depth that listening to musical silences may also uncover: the possibility of opening the space between people in all its variety and richness, where sounds and words are unnecessary or even inaccessible. It can be hypothesized that it is perhaps silences and not sounds that best hold the paradox of human interaction. But only when silences are allowed to open up within us may this become possible. Not only does the unfolding silence

---

[44] Oida, *The Invisible Actor*, 76.

move in new directions, but a sense develops in which we are freed from time and simultaneously our perceptions change at both temporal and deeply felt, affective levels. This is as important within the therapy room as it is between people in all other settings. Eloquently summarizing what the art of silent and sounded music does, Quinodoz used the words of a patient to put this most simply: 'you have to allow time for time'.[45]

What Oida reminds us, and music therapy teaches, is that if we neglect the hidden and rely on the obvious, we are missing much that relates to who we are, to how we are, and to the inner musical-personal worlds we carry within us. Ultimately, while 'allowing time for time', sounded music is only part of the story, with much to be learned from the silence from which sound comes. Without listening to silences at different levels and without attending to the variety and richness of silences between sounds, we are merely watching the hands of Oida's actors, blind to the exchanges between them. Thus music exists not on the page, nor within the composer or the professional performing musician. In the air, music is made up of sounds and silences, made by and for people. As the art of the actor exists in what occurs between actors and between actor and audience, so, on the purely physical level, music exists in the air. It is perhaps in this aspect of the art of music that we find human intersubjective silence is at its most profound, as it is carried in the air between notes, and in the air between people. It is in such musical silences that we find revealed something rather extraordinary: the range and depth of paradoxes of the human condition.

---

[45]   Quinodoz, *Words that Touch*, 177.

Chapter 11

'Meditation is the Musick of Souls': the Silent Music of Peter Sterry (1613–1672)

Tom Dixon

Music, in the Western tradition, is an art of performance, and its medium is the 'work'. Though we recognize procedures such as improvisation, Western 'classical' convention dictates that the musical work, the fixed creation of the composer, is the unit through which music's existence is most often conceptualized.[1] We grant iconic status to those who have created 'great works', the secondary authority of analysts and commentators being dependent, some might say parasitic, on the existence of such masterpieces. Although we sometimes talk about works as if they were abstract entities, we also take it for granted that their full realization requires musical sound – even a work of four minutes and thirty-three seconds of 'silence' might be said to rely on this assumption to make its point. Those trained to read a score silently from the page are approximating to an auditory experience. Music is something we hear.

In seventeenth-century England, the situation was more fluid. Certainly, the art of composing and performing music flourished, and there were circumstances in which it was preserved with care and even with an eye to posterity.[2] At the same time, those who understood the 'science' of music claimed a level of knowledge far above that of 'the mere Practical Organist' or composer; thus, even given the literary capacity of some professional musicians to produce works on performance technique or compositional theory, it was the university-educated, elite non-professional who was in a position to command the high ground, from which the musical work was scarcely audible. Paradoxically, this ideal of the 'Complete Musitian' combined a

I wish to acknowledge the assistance of the Arts and Humanities Research Council in funding my recently completed PhD on the significance of music in Sterry's work. My thanks are due to the Librarian and staff of Emmanuel College Library, Cambridge, for their kind assistance in making available the Sterry mss; all quotations from this source are included with the permission of the Master and Fellows of Emmanuel College. I would also like to thank Dr Penelope Gouk (University of Manchester) and Dr Frances Dawbarn (Lancaster University) for their help and advice.

[1]   An explanation of the history of this concept is at the heart of Lydia Goehr's study, *The Imaginary Museum of Musical Works* (Oxford: Oxford University Press, 1992).

[2]   An example related to the forms of music to be discussed here is the manuscript compilation of John Jenkins' consort music copied by the composer and annotated by his patron, Sir Nicholas L'Estrange; see Andrew Ashbee, *The Harmonious Musick of John Jenkins*, 1: *The Fantasias for Viols* (Surbiton: Toccata Press, 1992), 54–8.

Baconian focus on the physical properties of musical sound with the silent ratios of mathematics, adding the arcane lore of the natural magician and the versifying skills of the poet for good measure.[3]

Even within this broad spectrum, it is hard to know where to place Peter Sterry as a writer on music. Indeed, in his case the epithet is difficult to justify, in view of the absence from his *oeuvre* not only of any discussion of musical works but of any work written with the express purpose of discussing music.[4] It is thus unsurprising that his contribution to the musical literature of his time has been almost completely overlooked.[5] Nor can this omission be blamed simply on a modern misunderstanding of earlier categories, since it is doubtful whether many of his contemporaries would have associated Sterry with music – certainly no surviving assessments of him do so. To reconstruct Sterry's universal musical 'model', one has to search for scattered references among the pages of his religious prose. Yet the model is there to be found, repeatedly supplying a medium for his irenic vision of spiritual fulfilment on both individual and societal levels: the resolution of the discord of human imperfection into the perfect harmony of the Divine purpose. In this way, Sterry the Platonist philosopher rejuvenates for his times the supposedly obsolescent tradition of *musica universalis*, while Sterry the Cromwellian and Nonconformist divine gives silent musical expression, first to millennial anticipation, then to 'the experience of defeat'.

---

[3]   The terms, and the categories they describe, are taken from the preface to the English translation, attributed to Lord Brouncker, of *Renatus Descartes Excellent Compendium of Musick: With Necessary and Judicious Animadversions Thereupon, by a Person of Honour* (London, 1653). For a full discussion of the classification of music in schemes of knowledge at this time, see Penelope Gouk, *Music, Science and Natural Magic in Seventeenth-Century England* (New Haven and London: Yale University Press, 1999), Chapter 3.

[4]   The promise of a treatise on the subject is heralded by the title of one of Sterry's manuscript works, 'The Consort of Musicke'; see Peter Sterry, *Select Writings*, ed. N. I. Matar (New York: Peter Lang, 1994), 168–76. However, in its evocation of the music of creation and of Christ as instrumentalist, this short item does not differ in kind from many other passages in Sterry's *oeuvre*.

[5]   Modern scholarship on Sterry to date has failed to address the place of music in his work in any detail, although the subject is touched on very briefly in the following: Vivian de Sola Pinto, *Peter Sterry, Platonist and Puritan: a Biographical and Critical Study with Passages Selected from his Writings* (1934; New York: Greenwood Press, 1968), 73–5; N. I. Matar, Introduction to Peter Sterry, *Select Writings*, 12–13 (see also Matar's notes on pp. 91 and 175–6); Matar, '"Alone in Our Eden": a Puritan Utopia in Restoration England', *Seventeenth Century* 2 (1987), 195–6; Matar, '"Oyle of Joy": the Early Prose of Peter Sterry', *Philological Quarterly* 71/1 (1992), 35–6; Mary Nevins, 'Peter Sterry, a Platonic Independent' (PhD diss., Columbia University, 1954), 59 and 101–*n*; Alison Teply, 'The Mystical Theology of Peter Sterry: a Study in Neoplatonist Puritanism' (PhD diss., University of Cambridge, 2004), 183–4. There is also a brief discussion of Sterry in this context in Graham Strahle, 'Fantasy and Music in Sixteenth- and Seventeenth-Century England' (PhD diss., University of Adelaide, 1987), 201. The place of music in Sterry's work is the subject of my PhD dissertation, '"Spiritual Musick": the Model of Divine Harmony in the Work of Peter Sterry (1613–1672)' (University of Manchester, 2005).

Sterry was born into a London merchant family prosperous enough to give him an education at the 'Puritan seminary' of Emmanuel College, Cambridge.[6] His contemporaries there in the 1630s included the mathematician John Wallis, later an authority on the science of music, as well as the Platonist theologians and philosophers Benjamin Whichcote, Ralph Cudworth, Nathaniel Culverwel and John Smith.[7] Though no direct evidence linking him with musical practice survives, Sterry is likely to have absorbed the thriving culture of instrumental music in the university environment, perhaps even the controversial polyphonic services of the Laudian chapels.[8] Diverted from a promising academic career by the prospect of serving the rising star of Parliamentarian opposition, Robert Greville (Lord Brooke), at the onset of the Civil War, he gained a reputation in the 1640s for his charismatic if somewhat obscure preaching. He also became involved in the plans for a Protestant reform of knowledge facilitated by the London-based 'intelligencer', Samuel Hartlib, in which music played an important role in preparing for the anticipated millennium, the thousand-year rule of the Saints foretold in *Revelation*.[9] Attracting the attention of Cromwell, he was made official preacher to the Council of State and, later, household chaplain in the Protectorate establishment. The Restoration brought with it the challenges of ministering to the London Nonconformist 'underground', but also apparently some leisure for writing, as well as the advent of the 'Lovely Society', Sterry's informal religious and educational community at West Sheen, Surrey.

Significantly, both Sterry's late patron, Lord Lisle, and his earlier employer, Greville, provide links to the intellectual legacy of Sir Philip Sidney.[10] The iconic Elizabethan court poet's international cultural milieu had itself been informed by Italian and French interpretations of a musical syncretism – a blending of Christian and ancient pagan sources privileging music as a macrocosmic/microcosmic structural principle – initially indebted to the work of the seminal Florentine Neoplatonist, Marsilio Ficino (1433–1499). (This diachronic perspective was reinforced by the intensified interest in Neoplatonic philosophy in Sterry's 1630s Cambridge environment.) Sterry himself owned copies of Ficino's works, often citing or

---

[6]   For the most detailed account of Sterry's life, see Pinto, *Peter Sterry*, 3–63.

[7]   Henry More, another leading Cambridge Platonist, was educated at nearby Christ's College. For Emmanuel College in Sterry's time, see the appropriate sections of Sarah Bendall, Christopher Brooke and Patrick Collinson, *A History of Emmanuel College, Cambridge* (Woodbridge: Boydell Press, 1999).

[8]   It is known that some Emmanuel students attended these services, against the rules of their college; Bendall, Brooke and Collinson, *A History of Emmanuel College*, 207.

[9]   There are numerous references to music in Hartlib's private journals; see *The Hartlib Papers: a Complete Text and Image Database of the Papers of Samuel Hartlib (ca. 1600–1662)*, CD-ROM (Ann Arbor: University of Michigan Press, 1995).

[10]   Philip Sidney, Lord Lisle (afterwards 3rd Earl of Leicester) was the great-nephew of the poet, while Robert Greville was the adopted son and heir of Sir Fulke Greville, Sir Philip's lifelong friend and biographer. For an exploration of the Sidney tradition in the context of Sterry's work, see my unpublished MA dissertation, '"Or Rather in an Heavenly Paradise": Peter Sterry, Philip Sidney (Lord Lisle) and the Philosophy of a Restoration Community' (MA diss., Lancaster University, 2002).

paraphrasing him, and the West Sheen community's ethos of spiritual healing owed much to the 'music therapy of the soul' offered by the Florentine philosopher.

These ideas, whose origins were attributed to Pythagoras, received their classic formulation in the works of Plato, translated by Ficino for his Medici patron. But one was obliged to read neither Ficino nor his ancient sources to be aware of the concept of a musically empowered universe: it was part of the common currency. The harmony of the spheres is surely the most familiar emblem of silent music, or at any rate music inaccessible to our earthly senses: 'But while this muddy vesture of decay/Doth grossly close it in, we cannot hear it.' As we move into the seventeenth century, the fact that such notions had long since merged with traditional Aristotelian-Ptolemaic cosmology has encouraged, among historians, an uncritical acceptance of their demise in the face of newer ways of understanding the universe. Yet we should be wary of directly associating the spread of changes in natural knowledge with the disappearance of world harmony, 'the untuning of the sky', even if empiricist histories of seventeenth-century English music theory persist in emphasizing this supposed disjuncture.[11] Certainly, it is not difficult to find seventeenth-century English writers who parodied the audible existence of cosmic harmony, dismissed it as 'prodigiously silly', explained it away on rational grounds, or explicitly stated that the idea was outdated.[12] Nevertheless, that the universal music was eminently adaptable to a revised cosmology had already been demonstrated, in a European context, in the work of Johannes Kepler, and the concept of a musical universe continued to exert its influence on the finest of minds at least up to the time of Isaac Newton.[13]

In the musical dimension of Sterry's thought, the emphasis moved away from the physical properties of the cosmos to the relationship between God and the soul, although this distinction itself has an earlier history. In Renaissance Christian Neoplatonism, indeed, planetary harmony represented only one dimension of the idea of supra-sensual music. A clear differentiation was made between the cosmic harmony of the spheres and *musica divina* (music in the mind of God), voiced

---

[11]   For example, Rebecca Herissone, *Music Theory in Seventeenth-Century England* (Oxford: Oxford University Press, 2000), 2–3.

[12]   Convinced that 'the world would have no great losse in being deprived of this Musick, unlesse at sometimes we had the priviledge to heare it', John Wilkins insisted that 'it is not now, I think, affirmed by any'; *A Discourse Concerning a New World & Another Planet* (London, 1640), 56. See also Seth Ward, in Allen G. Debus, *Science and Education in the Seventeenth Century: the Webster-Ward Debate* (London: Macdonald, 1970), 45; Samuel Parker, *A Free and Impartial Censure of the Platonick Philosophie* (Oxford, 1666), 42–3; [John Wallis], *Truth Tried: or, Animadversions on a Treatise Published by the Right Honourable Robert Lord Brook* (London, 1642), 74.

[13]   On Kepler, see Jamie James, *The Music of the Spheres: Music, Science, and the Natural Order of the Universe* (1993; London: Abacus, 1995), 140ff. The significance of a musical cosmos in Newton's thought was established some decades ago, in P. M. Rattansi and J. E. McGuire, 'Newton and the Pipes of Pan', *Notes and Records of the Royal Society of London* 21 (1966), 108–43; it has been consolidated in more recent work, including Gouk, *Music, Science and Natural Magic*, Chapter 7; Ayval Leshem, *Newton on Mathematics and Spiritual Purity* (Dordrecht: Kluwer, 2003).

explicitly by Ficino: 'According to the Platonists, divine music is twofold. They think that the one certainly exists in the eternal mind of God, and that the other in truth exists in the order and motions of the heavens.'[14] Ficino made a secondary distinction, too, between the strictly mathematical ratios of the cosmos and the universal music's less quantifiable attributes: its spiritual beauty, its 'natural force', its place in an integrated, organic universe.[15] These are the aspects of heavenly harmony that informed the music of Sterry's Christian Platonism. Too great an emphasis on the threat posed to the universal music by seventeenth-century 'scientific advances' diverts attention from this rich and continuing vein.[16] Sterry had little to say about a planetary music, the literal existence of which it was becoming increasingly difficult to uphold. Rather it is the link between *musica divina* – the mystical, musical spirit, at once the '*Spire-top* of Things' and the 'Unfathom'd Depth of Glorious Life' – and the music of human life, through the mediation of Christ, 'the *Chiefe Musician*', which informed his explicitly Christian context.[17]

Musica divina was beyond all earthly notions of time, space and sense perception, although it necessarily encompassed all of these. As the manifestation in time and space of God's eternal harmony, planetary music – interchangeable, for some writers, with the music of the angels – was in principle audible, if only our senses (like Pythagoras') could be sufficiently purified and correctly attuned. This was felt to be brought within the realms of possibility through the microcosmic replication of this music within the human soul, which, as Sterry wrote, 'figureth it self ... as a Divine Musick [that] soundeth through all the parts and changes of the Coelestial, the Elementary Sphears'.[18] This was 'the *Angelical Musick* in the mind', to be experienced through the 'internal' or 'spiritual' senses 'in one simple and undivided Unity'.[19] Was it 'silent'? Certainly it was inaccessible to the outward sense of hearing. In Sterry's prose, though, the intensity with which the experience of 'hearing' this inward music is expressed, often in terms of 'real' vocal and instrumental media, blurs any precise distinction between music and silence.

We can glimpse through Sterry's work the capacity of Puritanism's more elevated and enlightened manifestations to encourage a spiritual concept of music, capable

---

[14]   Ficino, quoted in William R. Bowen, 'Ficino's Analysis of Musical *Harmonia*', in *Ficino and Renaissance Neoplatonism*, ed. Konrad Eisenbichler and Olga Zorzi Pugliese (Ottawa: Dovehouse Editions, 1986), 17–18. See also Gary Tomlinson, *Music in Renaissance Magic: Toward a Historiography of Others* (Chicago and London: University of Chicago Press, 1993), 120; Edward A. Lippman, *A History of Western Musical Aesthetics* (Lincoln and London: University of Nebraska Press, 1992), 8.

[15]   Brenno Boccadoro, 'Marsilio Ficino: the Soul and the Body of Counterpoint', in *Number to Sound: the Musical Way to the Scientific Revolution*, ed. Paolo Gozza (Dordrecht: Kluwer, 2000), 121–2; Claude V. Palisca, *Humanism in Italian Renaissance Musical Thought* (New Haven and London: Yale University Press, 1985), 170.

[16]   Joscelyn Godwin, *Harmonies of Heaven and Earth: the Spiritual Dimension of Music from Antiquity to the Avant-Garde* (London: Thames & Hudson, 1987), 60.

[17]   Peter Sterry, *The Rise, Race, and Royalty of the Kingdom of God* (London, 1683), 24.

[18]   Peter Sterry, *A Discourse of the Freedom of the Will* (London, 1675), 94.

[19]   *Ibid.*, 51; Sterry, 'The Consort of Musicke', 168.

of rising above controversial issues of the day such as its place in worship or the use of instruments in church.[20] It would be a mistake, though, to think of his musical model as a disembodied spiritual or philosophical construct entirely divorced from the music of the physical world. In fact it encompassed facets of current secular practice, notably the media of the lute and the viol consort to which Sterry had ample access both at Cambridge and London, providing a sound underpinning for an 'absolute' music unfettered by verbal constraint, a concept we more readily associate with the idealist philosophies of later ages.[21] It was the already obsolescent style of the balanced, equal-voiced instrumental fantasia which provided the closest model for Sterry's thought; music in which, as he himself expressed it, 'All the sweet proportions of all the parts would be discorded ... if any one, the least, and least considered part, were taken out of the whole'.[22] Though it continued to be a challenging medium, from the perspective implicit in Sterry's model the increasingly fragmentary tendency of the consort in his time toward florid virtuosic writing and the polarization of parts diminished its appropriateness. For example, although arguably supplying welcome variety, the practice of writing elaborate divisions (variations in which the melodic line was broken up into shorter note values) over a simple ground bass can be seen as the antithesis of Sterry's consort ideal: 'if you will pourtray a *Devil*', he obliquely observed, '*Darkness* must be the *Ground*, *Division* the *Work* upon it'.[23] On the other hand, that the ideal of balanced instrumental polyphony could continue to exercise willing hands and creative minds even after Sterry's death is suggested by the continuing production of manuscript copies of such music, as well as by the late appearance of Purcell's enigmatic fantasias, changes in harmonic idiom notwithstanding.

As well as providing a vehicle for admired professional *virtuosi*, both the lute and viol were cultivated on an amateur basis among the gentry and the academic fraternity: the Cambridge Platonists Henry More and John Smith are known to have been players.[24] Both More and Smith were among the writers, educated at Cambridge

---

[20]   The terms 'Puritan' and 'Puritanism' are used in this paper with caution, firstly because the emphasis in relatively recent historiography on the shared religious beliefs and priorities of the majority of English Protestants has rendered them problematic; secondly, because it is difficult to reconcile Sterry's significant doctrinal departures from Calvinism – for example, his espousal of a belief in universal salvation, and his somewhat free adaptation of strict Calvinist determinism – with the traditional image of a 'Puritan'. In the present context, the terms are intended to indicate Sterry's 'godly' background – his association with Emmanuel College, his place in the Cromwellian regime, his adherence to post-Restoration Nonconformity. For detailed discussion of Sterry's theology, see Nevins, 'Peter Sterry'; D. P. Walker, *The Decline of Hell: Seventeenth-Century Discussions of Eternal Torment* (Chicago: University of Chicago Press, 1964), 104–21.

[21]   See Mark Evan Bonds, 'Idealism and the Aesthetics of Instrumental Music at the Turn of the Nineteenth Century', *Journal of the American Musicological Society* 50/2 (1997), 387–420.

[22]   Sterry, *A Discourse of the Freedom of the Will*, 30.

[23]   Sterry, *The Rise, Race, and Royalty of the Kingdom of God*, 9.

[24]   Marjorie Hope Nicholson and Sarah Hutton, eds, *The Conway Letters: the Correspondence of Anne, Viscountess Conway, Henry More and their Friends, 1642–1684* (1930; Oxford:

in the 1630s, who were able to utilize for their own purposes an existing discourse in which music's spiritual and universal aspects were explored. From Cudworth's analogies linking the Divine mind in creation with the musical understanding which harmonized the separate parts of a composition, to Culverwel's image of the 'moral musick' of the Divine laws playing in consort, the frequency with which music enters into Cambridge Platonist writing suggests that, at the very least, the 'Puritan' colleges of the time did not wholly discourage this mode of thought.[25] From his own practical perspective, the Cambridge musician Thomas Mace, a lay clerk at Trinity from the 1630s onwards, also interpreted music as an expression of the universal order, an approach linking him intellectually with his more academic contemporaries.[26] Indeed, he shared their goal of assimilating music to divinity as a means through which the Christian mystery could be '*Contemplated*, and made perceptible'.[27] In stressing music's powers of communication and sympathy with the soul, and expounding the symbolic significance of the octave, Mace clearly echoed the spirit of Sterry's model, an impression reinforced by the nature of his own professional musical involvement with the lute and the viol.

It was in Sterry's musical model, though, that the venerable Platonic tradition of cosmic harmony was adapted most fully and most sympathetically, as a spiritually therapeutic response to the bitter conflicts of his time. Echoing Plotinus' concept of the emanation of the Divine principle from its source in 'the One' to inform all creation, and its return to is source, Sterry's silent consort celebrated the interconnection of all being, the interdependence of its individual parts. The more specifically Christian implications of this universal music encompassed the incarnation and ascension of Christ as well as the symbolism of Jacob's ladder. In keeping with this theme of spiritual interconnection, the structure of the remainder of this essay reflects music's place in the journey of the soul from her Divine source to her union with the body, and her corresponding re-ascent. The ontological levels of the soul's progress will be evoked by means of seven short extracts from Sterry's work.

Clarendon, 1992), 306–7. Inventory relating to the will of John Smith, dated 3 August, 1652 (Cambridge, Vice Chancellor's Probate Court, 111/302). Andrew Ashbee notes that 'church and university can be set alongside family as institutions where like-minded persons could and did meet to perform consort music'; 'The Transmission of Consort Music in Some Seventeenth-Century English Manuscripts', in *John Jenkins and his Time: Studies in English Consort Music*, ed. Andrew Ashbee and Peter Holman (Oxford: Clarendon, 1996), 244.

[25] See, for example, Ralph Cudworth, *The True Intellectual System of the Universe* (London, 1678), 676; Nathaniel Culverwel, *An Elegant and Learned Discourse of the Light of Nature, with Several Other Treatises* (London, 1652), 21.

[26] Thomas Mace, *Musick's Monument* (London, 1676), 265ff.

[27] *Ibid.*, Preface and 268.

1. [God is] the first harmony, the most perfect, the most exalted, the universal Harmony; the fountain of all Harmonies.[28]

Musica divina, music in the Divine mind. This is the truly silent music, inaccessible to any of our faculties, yet the source of the music we know in all its manifestations. Sir Thomas Browne conceptualizes this most aesthetic of mysteries as 'that harmony, which intellectually sounds in the eares of God'.[29] For Sterry, Browne's fellow seventeenth-century English Platonist, the Divine music is 'one simple and undivided Act of Harmony', beyond but inclusive of every possible facet of the successive unfolding of the music we hear, just as Eternity is beyond but inclusive of all time.[30] What adds interest to Sterry's approach from a musical perspective is that he does not treat the musical qualities of the Absolute as a theoretical philosophical concept. Music, rather, is for him a mercurial entity fluctuating between ineffable silence and the edge of audible existence, a medium for approaching the unknowable. At one remove, as it were, from the silence of *musica divina* is Christ the mediator, simultaneously 'the first image of God' and 'the first image of the creation'.[31]

2. [The 'chiefe musitian', Jesus Christ, is] the Mediator uniting all things created, and uncreated ... The Harmony dwelling in this Person, forming itselfe in transcendent Loves, Beauties and Delights upon his Spirit, Imagination, and whole shape, is the Eternall Word in Union with the first Draught, and Life Picture of the Angellicall Nature, and Invisible Part of the Creation in Christ the Heade of Angells. The golden Lute in his hand with many strings, on which he plays with delicate, lively and immortall Touches, the heavenly Musicke in all parts of It at once, is the whole Frame of Caelestiall, *or Heavenly Bodies in the visible part of Things, pure, shining and high* ... [32]

As we have already seen, ideas of cosmic harmony exerted a continuing influence throughout the seventeenth century. Following Ficino and the early-sixteenth-century Venetian writer Francesco Giorgi – the works of both were available to him in the library of Emmanuel College in the 1630s – Sterry equated the intellectual soul of the Platonists with the angelic music and the cosmic dance engendered by Christ's universal instrument.[33] As Christ the mediator joins Heaven and Earth, so in the microcosm of the individual the music symbolized by Christ's lute mediates between spiritual and corporeal dimensions.

---

[28]   Sterry, *A Discourse of the Freedom of the Will*, 13.

[29]   Sir Thomas Browne, *Religio Medici* (London, 1642), 142.

[30]   Sterry, *A Discourse of the Freedom of the Will*, 22.

[31]   *Ibid.*, 51.

[32]   Sterry, 'The Consort of Musicke', 171–2.

[33]   For Giorgi, see his *De Harmonia Mundi Totius* (Venice, 1525); also, D. P. Walker, *Spiritual and Demonic Magic from Ficino to Campanella* (London: The Warburg Institute, 1958), 114; Cesare Vasoli, *Profezia e ragione: studi sulla cultura del Cinquecento e del Seicento* (Naples: Morano, 1974), 258, 263–5, 279. For the contents of Emmanuel College Library in the 1630s, see Sargent Bush, Jr. and Carl J. Rasmussen, *The Library of Emmanuel College, Cambridge, 1584–1637* (Cambridge: Cambridge University Press, 1986), 133.

The lute, for Sterry a recurrent symbol of the undefined territory where music shades into silence, the nexus between the Divine musical universe and human musical practice, was a particularly prominent feature of musical life in Cambridge.[34] It was here in the 1630s that he took a pioneering role in an intellectual movement that was to have a profound and far-reaching influence on English thought: one source reports Sterry and his Emmanuel colleague John Sadler as 'the first ... to make a public profession of Platonism in the university'.[35] The main reason for these first stirrings of Cambridge Platonism being treated as an innovation was that Sterry and his colleagues were challenging accepted views in their willingness to extend significantly the range of theology's non-Christian content.[36] At the heart of their theology was a *Neo*-Platonism based on the 'rational mysticism' of Plotinus – 'Plato without politics', and with a more whole-hearted acceptance of music.[37] We can get an idea of how *risqué* this was considered to be at the time from the later correspondence of Sterry's one-time Cambridge neighbour, Henry More, in which he recalls that 'I bought one [i.e. a copy of Plotinus' works] when I was Junior Master for 16 shillings and I think that I was the first that had either the luck or the courage to buy him'.[38] If More was indeed the first, Sterry, who still owned a copy after the Restoration, is unlikely to have been far behind, since it is the specifically Plotinian concept of emanation (or derivation) from the One through Intellect and Soul to the shadowy world of matter, and the return to the One, which gives shape to Sterry's musical thought (and incidentally to the present essay).[39]

---

[34] For the lute at Cambridge, see N[icholas] H[ookes], 'To Mr. Lilly, Musick-Master in Cambridge', in *Amanda, a Sacrifice to an Unknown Goddesse, or, A Free-will Offering of a Loving Heart to a Sweet-heart* (London, 1653), 56–8; Mace, *Musick's Monument*; Matthew Spring, *The Lute in Britain: a History of the Instrument and its Music* (Oxford: Oxford University Press, 2001), 430–31.

[35] Thomas Baker, quoted in Pinto, *Peter Sterry*, 10.

[36] Ernst Cassirer, *The Platonic Renaissance in England* (Austin: University of Texas Press, 1953), 25.

[37] For the extent of Plotinus' influence on the Cambridge Platonists, see Alexander Jacob, 'The Neoplatonic Conception of Nature in More, Cudworth and Berkeley', in *The Uses of Antiquity: the Scientific Revolution and the Classical Tradition*, ed. Stephen Gaukroger (Dordrecht: Kluwer, 1991), 101 and 103; Alexander Jacob, Introduction to Henry More, *A Platonick Song of the Soul* (Lewisburg, PA, and London: Bucknell University Press, 1998), xii; Cassirer, *The Platonic Renaissance in England*, 50. For the aspects of Plotinus' philosophy under discussion, see Dominic J. O'Meara, *Plotinus: an Introduction to the 'Enneads'* (Oxford: Clarendon, 1993), 108; John Rist, 'Plotinus and Christian Philosophy', in *The Cambridge Companion to Plotinus*, ed. Lloyd P. Gerson (Cambridge: Cambridge University Press, 1996), 389; C. A. Patrides, 'The High And Aiery Hills of Platonisme: an Introduction to the Cambridge Platonists', in *The Cambridge Platonists*, ed. Patrides (London: Edward Arnold, 1969), 17; Cassirer, *The Platonic Renaissance in England*, 154.

[38] Henry More, quoted in Jacob, Introduction to *A Platonick Song of the Soul*, xii.

[39] For Sterry's book collections, see Pinto, *Peter Sterry*, 57. My present focus on Plotinus, and his undoubted importance for the Cambridge thinkers, should not obscure two considerations. Firstly, it was not in the nature of late-Renaissance thought to recognize the strict distinctions between Plato and his later followers and interpreters characteristic of modern scholarship, so that for the most part all of this work was considered simply as

3. The Soul, from its Divine Unity … descendeth into its Angelick Image, or
    Intellectual Form. … From thence she passeth into her rational Form, in which
    she is a contexture of universal and particular Images mutually infolding each
    other … in a beautiful Harmony. … The Changes of the Soul through all these
    Diversities of forms, are all most orderly and harmonious, all together make
    up one most ravishing Harmony of Divine Beauty and Musick.[40]

Where does music come from? The question has exercised minds from the earliest
times to the present, and shows no sign of having been definitively resolved. Indeed,
there are present-day thinkers who are unwilling to discount the possibility that
music 'provides access to another separate layer of existence or order of reality', or
that through it 'we are vouchsafed some sort of vision'.[41] A vision of what, and from
where? In the context of Platonism, the answer necessarily involves a higher, inner
or truer realm of being. For Plotinus in particular, the ultimate source of heard music
is clear, music's ontological status losing at least some of its Platonic ambivalence,
with reduced emphasis on its propensity to deceive and mislead, and commensurately
more on its capacity to reflect the Ideal realm itself.[42] 'Harmonies unheard in sound',
he claimed, 'create the harmonies we hear';[43] 'who that truly perceives the harmony
of the Intellectual Realm could fail, if he has any bent towards music, to answer to
the harmony in sensible sounds?'[44] The *Corpus Hermeticum*, of Plotinus' era, though
once thought to be a direct survival of a pristine 'ancient theology', tells us that
mankind was born from 'the wisdom of understanding in silence', and that to know
music is to be 'versed in the correct sequence of all things'.[45] Ficino, who translated
both Plotinus and the *Hermetica*, conceived of music as a part of this sequence, a
means of communication between levels or states of being and of bringing the soul
into contact with the Divine. He valued musical practice, provided that it was of a
suitably enlightened kind, for its capacity to impart to the soul a 'desire to fly back
to its rightful home, so that it may enjoy that true music again'.[46] Moreover, the

---

'Platonism'. Secondly, subsequent Christian thinkers from Augustine onward incorporated
Neoplatonic traits into their contributions, exercising in their turn a great influence on thinkers
of the succeeding centuries, Sterry not excepted.

[40]   Sterry, *A Discourse of the Freedom of the Will*, 82–3.
[41]   Bruce Naughton, quoted in Nicholas Cook, *Music, Imagination and Culture* (Oxford:
Clarendon, 1990), 153; Jerrold Levinson, 'Musical Profundity Misplaced', *Journal of
Aesthetics and Art Criticism* 50/1 (1992), 60.
[42]   Wayne D. Bowman, *Philosophical Perspectives on Music* (New York and Oxford:
Oxford University Press, 1998), 57; O'Meara, *Plotinus*, 94–5.
[43]   Plotinus, *The Enneads*, trans. Stephen MacKenna, 4th ed., rev. B. S. Page (London:
Faber and Faber, 1969), 59 (I.vi.3).
[44]   Plotinus, *Enneads*, 149 (II.ix.16); Cassirer, *The Platonic Renaissance in England*,
99–100.
[45]   Anon., *Hermetica: the Greek* Corpus Hermeticum *and the Latin* Asclepius, trans.,
with Notes and Introduction, Brian P. Copenhaver (Cambridge: Cambridge University Press,
1992), 49, 74.
[46]   Marsilio Ficino, *The Letters of Marsilio Ficino*, trans. by members of the Language
Department of the School of Economic Science, London (London: Shepheard-Walwyn,
1975), 1: 45.

connection could operate in either direction; 'When [music] imitates the celestials', Ficino wrote, 'it also wonderfully arouses our spirit upwards to the celestial influence and the celestial influence downward to our spirit.'[47]

For the Cambridge Platonists, more circumspect than Ficino on the overt manipulation of celestial influence, 'hearing' the Divine music required an inner state induced through contemplation. 'Meditation is the Musick of Souls', affirmed Sterry, 'in which God delights to descend and shew himself.'[48] It should not be concluded, however, that the appeal to magical forces had by now entirely receded from the Platonist worldview. We are familiar with the category of natural magic largely from the work of historians of science; among them, there is still a tendency to treat natural magic exclusively as a practice, a set of procedures that eventually became ousted by or merged with the scientific method.[49] For the Cambridge Platonists, however, it represented an internalized spiritual procedure, functioning 'to elevate the soul to deiformity'.[50] For Sterry in particular, natural magic was intimately bound up with the musical model. Indeed music, as a typological manifestation of Divine love, *was* the magic: 'all things move by a *divinely natural Magick*; that is, by the force of Harmony'.[51] The universal world-soul, a Platonic concept widely employed by the Cambridge thinkers, was invoked by Sterry to explain our intuitive response: it plants a 'hidden seed of Harmony' in each of its outward manifestations in the process of emanation from the Divine centre, as the 'Essential Image' of the spirit 'passeth through all perticular fformes'.[52] The process was sometimes conceptualized by means of the infinite renewal of the octave, in which literal pitch-change was transformed into an expression of the Divine mystery both at the centre of creation and enclosing it, a notion clearly implying Plotinian emanation.[53] Sterry captured the relation of the unheard music to its physical counterpart by means of a compositional conceit: Divine unity is the ground of the music, its emanative outflowings the divisions.[54] If we aspire to 'hear' the utter simplicity at the source of this music we must listen with the 'Spiritual Ear'; any attempt to exemplify it outwardly cannot but be inadequate.[55] The paradox is that the stillness of the centre encompasses all the diversities and complexities of musical creation. Translated into present-day

---

[47]   Marsilio Ficino, *De Vita Libri Tres*, trans. C. V. Kaske and J. R. Clark as *Three Books on Life* (Binghamton, NY: The Renaissance Society of America, 1989), 359.

[48]   Peter Sterry, *The Appearance of God to Man in the Gospel* (London, 1710), 199.

[49]   Gouk, *Music, Science and Natural Magic*, 15.

[50]   Daniel Fouke, *The Enthusiasticall Concerns of Dr. Henry More: Religious Meaning and the Psychology of Delusion* (Leiden: Brill, 1997), 35.

[51]   Sterry, *A Discourse of the Freedom of the Will*, 90; see also Gretschen Ludke Finney, *Musical Backgrounds for English Literature, 1580–1650* (1962; repr. Westport, CT: Greenwood Press, 1976), 80: 'As controlling forces in the universe, music and love might be two aspects of one reality'.

[52]   Sterry, *A Discourse of the Freedom of the Will*, 91; Sterry, 'Of the Sun', Cambridge, Emmanuel College Library MS 294, fol. 84.

[53]   See, for example, the diagram used by Mace in *Musick's Monument*, 269.

[54]   Peter Sterry, 'What is God?', Cambridge, Emmanuel College Library MS 292, fol. 320.

[55]   Sterry, *The Rise, Race, and Royalty of the Kingdom of God*, 510.

philosophical discourse, this equates to the idea that all music is 'discovered' rather than 'created'. Even from an empiricist standpoint, it is possible to recognize that the 'sonic elements' of music pre-exist the use to which they are put in a particular composition or performance.[56]

4. Being it self, in its universal Nature, from its purest heighth, by beautiful, harmonious, just degrees and steps, descendeth into every Being, even to the lowest shades. All ranks and degrees of Being, so become like the mystical steps in that scale of Divine Harmony and Proportions, Jacobs Ladder. Every form of Being to the lowest step, seen and understood according to its order and proportions in its descent upon this Ladder, seemeth as an Angel, or as a Troop of Angels in one, full of all Angelick Musick and Beauty. Every thing as it lieth in the whole piece, beareth its part in the Universal Consort.[57]

That the silence of *musica divina* necessarily contains within itself all possible musics explains Plotinus' belief that, however shadowy and unreal is physical existence, the world of Becoming, it is not utterly cut off from the world of true Being. In the phrase attributed to the dying Sir Philip Sidney, heard music is a 'terrestrial echo' of its heavenly prototype.[58] The 'hidden seed' of Divine harmony informs 'all particular harmonies, all sorts of music'. The implication is that, just as even the 'lowest step' on the 'ladder' of life retains its resonance with Divinity, no form of earthly music, however humble or superficial, is entirely excluded from the universality of the Divine harmony. As, for Plotinus, there is 'a beauty ... in all kinds of music', so for Sir Thomas Browne even 'vulgar and Taverne Musick' can induce 'a deepe fit of devotion'.[59]

In the densely packed social milieu of pre-Civil War Cambridge, where the distinctly un-Puritan student misdemeanours recorded at Emmanuel included 'staying out ... all night ... frequenting suspicious or scandalous houses, drinking wine and [engaging in] clamorous singing',[60] there was no shortage of 'vulgar and Taverne Musick'. On the other hand, the university environment did offer musical genres that helped to cultivate the kind of refined aesthetic taste felt to be more attuned to the silent music of contemplation. Nathaniel Culverwel contrasted the 'noyse and crackling' of 'sensitive pleasure' (i.e. the pleasure of the senses) with the 'mental and noëtical delight' of the lute, an instrument capable of producing 'the sweetest and yet the stillest and softest musick of all'.[61] Similarly, for Sterry, 'the softest, sweetest ... Delights' of the lute were fundamental to his conception of the intimate relation of music to silence.[62] Not even the hushed tones of the lute,

---

[56]   Renee Cox, 'Are Musical Works Discovered?', *Journal of Aesthetics and Art Criticism* 43/4 (1985), 369.

[57]   Sterry, *A Discourse of the Freedom of the Will*, 30.

[58]   Finney, *Musical Backgrounds for English Literature*, 27; Bowman, *Philosophical Perspectives on Music*, 57; Cassirer, *The Platonic Renaissance in England*, 99–100.

[59]   Plotinus, *Enneads*, 56 (I.vi.1); Browne, *Religio Medici*, 141.

[60]   Bendall, Brooke and Collinson, *A History of Emmanuel College*, 58.

[61]   Culverwel, *An Elegant and Learned Discourse of the Light of Nature*, 190.

[62]   Sterry, *The Rise, Race, and Royalty of the Kingdom of God*, 40.

however, could hope to emulate Divine perfection: the artefact, Plotinus warned, must never be confused with its ultimate source.[63] The limitation of heard music, for Sterry, was in its inability fully to escape its physical dimension; the world of Becoming would always be dependent on the world of Being.

> 5. As musick is conveyed sweetest, and furthest upon a river in ye Night: so is ye Musick of ye heavenly voice carried most clearly, pleasantly to ye understanding, when all ye outward senses ly wrapt up in darkness, and ye depth of night.[64]

We have followed the emanations of the spirit from the centre of the One to the outermost reaches of shadow, the physical world. But the Protean nature of the human soul allows a return, the first step being to turn away from the senses to the inner life – 'leave the senses idle, and the birth of divinity will begin', the *Corpus Hermeticum* tells us, whilst Plotinus claims that, in order to be its true self, the soul must detach itself from consciousness.[65] On a macrocosmic level, Sterry's Christian vision expresses the process in terms of Crucifixion and Redemption: 'The death of Jesus Christ is as the *midnight* of things. The *Sun* of the eternal Image and Glory, having by its *course*, in the shadowy Image, touched the *utmost bound* of *distance* from it self, now begins its *return* to it self again.'[66] He is equally inclined to couch the concept in terms of expert lute technique, since

> Nothing is more apt among Natural things to delight, and ravish our Souls, than the Musick of an excellent hand carried down in just degrees by soft, and melting strains to the lowest, and there, as it were, quite silenced; then on a sudden carried up again to a Sprightly and Triumphant height.[67]

In its physical dimension, Sterry's image of the strains of music carried over the night air (to which he returns on more than one occasion) recalls the interest of some of his more Baconian contemporaries in the measurable properties of sound, even if his own concern is with the mystical or aesthetic aspects of the phenomenon.[68] It is an image epitomizing the ambivalence of his attitude to the senses. In fact,

---

[63]   Jean-Marc Narbonne, 'Action, Contemplation and Interiority in the Thinking of Beauty in Plotinus', in *Neoplatonism and Western Aesthetics*, ed. Aphrodite Alexandrakis (Albany: State University of New York Press, 2002), 9.

[64]   Letter to Peter Sterry, jnr., quoted in Pinto, *Peter Sterry*, 184.

[65]   O'Meara, *Plotinus*, 103; Angela Voss, 'Marsilio Ficino, the Second Orpheus', in *Music as Medicine: the History of Music Therapy since Antiquity*, ed. Pergrine Horden (Aldershot: Ashgate, 2000), 168; *Hermetica*, 50; Narbonne, 'Action, Contemplation and Interiority', 14.

[66]   Sterry, *A Discourse of the Freedom of the Will*, 130.

[67]   Sterry, *The Rise, Race, and Royalty of the Kingdom of God*, 205.

[68]   For example, one of the 'Quaeres' posed and discussed by the natural philosopher and musician, Edmund Chilmead, was, 'Why sounds are heard further in the Night, than in the Day?'. The issue had been raised in the pseudo-Aristotelian *Problemata*, and Bacon himself had investigated the question of why '*Sounds* are better heard, and further off in an Evening, or in the Night, than at the Noon or in the Day'; see Mordechai Feingold and Penelope M. Gouk, 'An Early Critique of Bacon's *Sylva Sylvarum*: Edmund Chilmead's Treatise on Sound',

he often seems torn between the utter negation of sense – the music of the soul – and the experience of a music heard in rarefied, enhanced circumstances; after all, Boethius had taught that *musica instrumentalis* was instrumental in the sense of initiating a return to the level of unheard music.[69] It seems that, for Sterry, the ethereal semi-silence of distant music represented a kind of half-way stage, retaining the transcendent quality of exquisite musical performance whilst shaking off its distracting associations with matter: 'Musicke is sweetest at a distance; because it is strained in the passage, and freed from the jarring of the instruments.'[70] Like many of Sterry's musical concepts, though, the phenomenon of distant music defies easy categorization, for it is this same music of the heavenly voice, heard from afar, which in his controversial interpretation is the instrument of universal salvation, the souls of sinners after death submitting to the irresistible, purifying force of 'the Divine Harmony'.[71]

> 6. Nay thus all this musick in a full consort soundeth from every part of your life, is plaid by angells, sung by this sweet quire in every Moment. Open[,] open your ears to hear it, let it sing all your thoughts to a divine Calme, and rest, yea let all y^t is within you[,] your Body, Soul and Spirit dance to it. This wisdome, this Musick is of Eternall Spirit.[72]

Despite the difficulties involved in dating much of Sterry's extant output with any precision – we have most of it in the form of posthumous publications or undated manuscripts – there is little doubt that the last decade or so of his life, the period immediately following the Restoration of the monarchy in 1660, was a time in which he was able to attend more closely to the production and revision of his work. He spent these years as a spokesman for religious dissent, dividing his time between the London Nonconformist groups made up of his friends and former Cromwellian colleagues, and the community he had founded on the estate of his patron, Lord Lisle. These were sections of society that had seen their political power, their millennial aspirations to build God's kingdom in the here and now, crumble to dust. On the evidence of his writings, Sterry saw his role in part as that of a Pythagorean musical healer, preparing now for a second coming of the spirit, creating hope out of despair, individual fulfilment from collective failure. He likened his followers to those of Pythagoras, who 'compos'd and calm'd their Spirits' by music, and taught them to value it as a haven of tranquillity amid the difficulties of everyday life.[73] In his surviving letters from this period, catastrophic external events – the

---

Annals of Science 40/2 (1983), 151; Francis Bacon, *Sylva Sylvarum: or, A Naturall History in Ten Centuries* (London, 1651), 38.

[69]   Bowman, *Philosophical Perspectives on Music*, 63.

[70]   Sterry, *Select Writings*, 128.

[71]   Sterry, 'That the State of Wicked Men after this Life is Mixt of Evill, and Good Things', Cambridge, Emmanuel College Library MS 291, fol.102.

[72]   Sterry, letter to Peter Sterry, jnr., Cambridge, Emmanuel College Library MS 292, fol. 155–6.

[73]   'By this as Musick arm your Souls with a peaceful Complacency, when you are to go into the Tumults of Action: By this as Musick, charm your Souls to a Peacefull Repose, when

executions of his regicide friends, the ravages of the plague, London's conflagration
– elicited no comment.[74] Instead, he emphasized the need to acknowledge God's
greater purpose, to resolve the discord of earthly distractions into the harmony of the
celestial consort. When viewed from the unchanging perspective of the eternal, 'our
Groans themselves' were transformed into 'a sweet Harmony, *Divine Breathings*,
the *Musick* of Heaven'.[75]

This same resolution of the dissonance of life's trials into the soothing concord
of the Divine harmony was applied, too, on an even more intensely personal level.
A particularly moving example is provided by an incomplete manuscript in the style
of an allegorical romance which Sterry addressed to his daughter, apparently on the
loss of her baby son.[76] It is entirely typical of the close relationship between *musica
divina* and musical practice in Sterry's thought that his images have an underlying
flavour of real experience. Now assuming 'a godlike form', the dead infant appears
to Gratiana (Sterry's daughter) in a dream, his approach signalled by 'Melodious
sounds' issuing from

> unseen musitians, which with so powerfull a delicacy toucht her soule, not only through
> her ears, but through every part, that, as her soule a golden harpe, so her body a silver case
> to ye harp seemed rapt, & changed into one harmony with that, wch moved upon it.[77]

The surprise and sheer joy of their meeting is suggested by the *cori spezzati* idiom
of alternating choirs:

> A person spake, & Gratiana answered, as if all ye angells, & Spheares in two Quires had
> plaid, & sung in parts to each other.[78]

Heavenly celebration is transformed into intimacy, as their subsequent conversation
is evoked by analogy to the lute duet,

> like ye sweet sound of two lutes which tuned to one leason, & one part melt their soft
> notes, & harmony into an undistinguish[ed] musicke.[79]

Without underestimating the devastating nature of the external event in its own
terms, Sterry emphasizes the need for even so personal a tragedy to be harmonized

---

they withdraw from Noise and Action'; quoted in Pinto, *Peter Sterry*, 176. On Iamblichus'
account of Pythagoras' use of music to cure bodies and souls, see S. K. Heninger, Jr, *Touches
of Sweet Harmony: Pythagorean Cosmology and Renaissance Poetics* (San Marino, CA:
Huntington Library, 1974), 103.

[74]   N. I. Matar, 'Peter Sterry and the "Paradise Within": a Study of the Emmanuel College
Letters', *Restoration* 13 (1989), 79–80; Matar, 'Alone in our Eden', 191.

[75]   Sterry, *The Appearance of God to Man in the Gospel*, 95.

[76]   Sterry, untitled romance fragment to incomplete spiritual romance, untitled, Cambridge,
Emmanuel College Library MS 292, fols. 129–140.

[77]   *Ibid.*, fols. 131–2.

[78]   *Ibid.*, fol. 136.

[79]   *Ibid.*, fol. 137.

with the Divine music, making Gratiana's heart 'joys throne', as the identities of child and saviour become imperceptibly merged.

Sterry's task of adapting this musical healing of the spirit to the circumstances of his time and place was one for which his philosophical inheritance had provided ample preparation. Augustine may have been the first to articulate the distinction between the 'inner' working of the soul and the 'outer' sphere of 'worldly action', but Plotinus has been credited with the first philosophy of the self, and one which used aesthetic experience as a means to inner development.[80] In the early Renaissance, the specifically musical implications of this philosophy had been pursued by Ficino, whose musico-magical invocations were aimed principally not at the external manipulation of nature but at the goal of 'rais[ing] the mind to the highest considerations and to God'.[81] Ficino and others of his persuasion taught that music acts on the psyche through the *pneuma psychicon*, the animal or psychical spirit, an entity drawing credibility from Galenic medicine's theory of the spirits.[82] Moreover, these spirits drew their power from the *spiritus mundanus*, corresponding to the Cambridge Platonists' world-soul.[83] Through the force of magical sympathy, the individual soul could thus respond to higher levels of reality, just as an untouched lute-string would vibrate at the sound of another. And, for Sterry, it was Christ the mediator – 'tuned' to the soul of the believer 'by mutuall Love, each to other' – who could convert these sounding notes into 'spirituall musicke'.

7.   [All music, even that of the angels], is infinitely surmounted by those unexpressible, incomprehensible Harmonies of the Divine Essence, which it is not possible for any created sense to take in.[84]

For Plotinus, returning to the One was to be 'awakened to myself away from the body, becoming outside all else and within myself ... having become one with the divine'.[85] Musically, this represented the ultimate perfection, above anything conceivable by unaided reason, to be glimpsed rarely and no more than intermittently by intuitive

---

[80]   Charles Taylor, *Sources of the Self: the Making of the Modern Identity* (Cambridge, MA: Harvard University Press, 1989), 121; O'Meara, *Plotinus*, 97 and 118.

[81]   Angela Voss, '*Orpheus Redivivus*: the Musical Magic of Marsilio Ficino', in *Marsilio Ficino: his Theology, his Philosophy, his Legacy*, ed. Michael J. B. Allen and Valery Rees (Leiden: Brill, 2002), 234; see also Walker, *Spiritual and Demonic Magic from Ficino to Campanella*, 105; Tomlinson, *Music in Renaissance Magic*, 131.

[82]   Claude V. Palisca, 'Moving the Affections through Music: Pre-Cartesian Psycho-Physiological Theories', in *Number to Sound*, 293. Tommaso Campanella, one of Sterry's favourite authors, linked spirit theory directly to musical taste: 'Men prefer grave or light melodies, rugged or soft ones, according as their vital spirits are gross or tenuous, robust or weak'; quoted in Clarence de Witt Thorpe, *The Aesthetic Theory of Thomas Hobbes, with Special Reference to his Contribution to the Psychological Approach in English Literary Criticism* (Ann Arbor: University of Michigan Press, 1940), 61.

[83]   Ficino, *De Vita*, 361.

[84]   Sterry, *A Discourse of the Freedom of the Will*, 92.

[85]   O'Meara, *Plotinus*, 104.

intellect.[86] Sterry's 'disciple' and posthumous editor, Jeremiah White, tells us that it is as if we were to experience and understand *in one instant* 'all those Notes both *open* and *stopt*, both *Sharps* and *Flats*, both *Concords* and *Discords*, both *Trebles*, *Bases* and *Means*, or whatsoever else Varieties of Contrarieties might be Instanced' – in other words, all possible created music.[87] An understanding of the One can be approached only in terms of the distinction between time and eternity. All heard music, of course, happens in time; in fact, one way of defining music is as the audible expression of time. Even cosmic music was supposed to take place in time: Plotinus wrote that 'the stars exist, we are told, for the display and delimitation of time and that there may be a manifest measure'.[88] Time can imitate eternity, as the writer of the *Hermetica* asserted, but eternity cannot be fully accessible to our time-driven existence.[89]

Through the purification of the spirit we can, however, begin to approach it. Given its power to initiate this process, Sterry's express or implied attitude to heard music in his writings is generally one of affirmation. The recurrent use of musical imagery, especially – and unusually for his time – according prominence to instrumental genres, is characteristic of his idiom, and indeed there are occasions when it is difficult to tell whether he is writing about sounding or silent music, or both. There is no suggestion in his work of that intransigent opposition to the practice of music that sometimes surfaces in religious responses of the period. One might instance Sterry's contemporary, the professional musician Solomon Eccles, who on his conversion to Quakerism made a bonfire of his instruments on Tower Hill, adjudging all heard music to be 'babylon's music', even though he continued to approve of a silent music 'that pleaseth God'.[90] By contrast, Sterry's view was in line with that of his Cambridge contemporary, John Smith: 'wherever [true religion] finds *Beauty* [and] *Harmony* … it is ready to say, *Here*, and *There is God*'.[91] At the same time, Sterry left us in no doubt about the true function, and limitation, of earthly music as a reminder of and gateway to the ultimate reality of the music of silence. When it has done its work of preparation, and we have taken flight with the spirit, the 'spire top of all things', then we are truly silent: 'We seem to touch [the infinity of God]', he says, 'with the … simplest *Unity* of *Spirits*, by a *silence* and *cessation* of all created powers or faculties in us.'[92]

---

[86]   Michael J. B. Allen, 'The Absent Angel in Ficino's Philosophy', *Journal of the History of Ideas* 36/2 (1975), 236.

[87]   Jeremiah White, *The Restoration of All Things: or, A Vindication of the Goodness and Grace of God* (London, 1712), 103.

[88]   Plotinus, *Enneads*, 236 (III.vii.12).

[89]   *Hermetica*, 86.

[90]   Solomon Eccles, *A Musick-Lector: or, The Art of Musick* (London, 1667), 7.

[91]   John Smith, *Select Discourses* (London, 1660), 433.

[92]   Sterry, *A Discourse of the Freedom of the Will*, 40; also Henry More: 'Eternal rest, joy without passing sound; what sound is made without collision?'; quoted in Cassirer, *The Platonic Renaissance in England*, 65.

Chapter 12

Silent Music and the Eternal Silence

Nicky Losseff

The two main themes that are explored in this chapter concern the apparently paradoxical concept of 'silent music'. The first part of the chapter centres around poetry of the sixteenth-century Spanish Carmelite St John of the Cross and concerns human, mystical perceptions of 'silent music'. The second follows parallel to this and discusses whether St John's experience of 'silent music' was veridical. I cannot, as a musician, resist being fascinated by the possible 'existence' of a type of music which is silent – not merely unheard, but unhearable, and experienced cognitively as a form of silence. Could 'silent music' be more than a linguistic paradox? Could it be as much a musical as a mystical experience? Is one of music's multiple and slippery ontologies one of silence?

Silent Music

Mi Amado, las montañas,	My beloved, [is] the mountains,
Los valles solitarios nemorosos,	The solitary, wooded valley,
Las ínsulas extrañas, los ríos sonorosos,	The strange islands, the sonorous rivers,
El silbo de los aires amorosos,	The whisper of the amorous breezes,
La noche sosegada	The tranquil night
En par de los levantes de la aurora,	At the time of the rising of the dawn,
La música callada, la soledad Sonora,	The silent music, the sonorous solitude,
La cena, que recrea y enamora.	The supper that recreates and enkindles love.

St John of the Cross (1542–91), 'Song between the Soul and the Beloved'
From *Spiritual Canticles,* Stanzas 13–14[1]

During St John of the Cross's darkest night of the soul, he fell in love with God. Some sense of that mystic union comes down to us through the richly pastoral imagery of the *Spiritual Canticles,* a dialogue between the Soul – the Bride of Christ

---

This chapter is dedicated to Gentian Rahtz.

[1]   San Juan de la Cruz, *Obras de San Juan de la Cruz*, ed. Padre Silverio de Santa Teresa, 3rd ed. (Burgos: Tipografía de 'El Monte Carmelo', 1943), 447; for an English version, see St John of the Cross, *The Complete Works of St John of the Cross, Doctor of the Church*, trans. and ed. E. Allison Peers (Wheathampstead, Herts.: Anthony Clarke, 1964), 2: 27.

– who struggles to speak about the identity of the Beloved – Christ the Spouse – through language which articulates an ultimate mystery and a transcendence of ordinary categories of experience by defying what language itself can realistically express.[2] After all, music is normally sonorous, and solitude, silent. In theological terms, St John uses an inherent paradox to communicate a sense of the numinous and the ineffable: 'silent music' can only be a *conceptual* audition, perceived not through the fleshly senses but directly through the soul's inner ear, and as a concept it serves to demonstrate a religious truth in a way that cannot be grasped at all – and yet cannot be grasped in any other way.

St John places the ideas 'silent music' and 'sonorous solitude' not among other paradoxes, however, but straightforward natural images: valleys, islands, rivers, breezes, the night, even food. The reason for this might seem rather prosaic: the first seventeen stanzas of the *Spiritual Canticles* were composed during his long period of solitary confinement in a filthy dungeon, where he suffered appalling physical deprivations,[3] and while his body was breaking down, his mind reached the greatest heights of spiritual ecstasy. In his prison of sensual denial, it is no surprise that images of natural beauty and other forms of nourishment, both remembered and constructed, came closest to representing what seemed most marvellous in the world, acting in effect as a form of sustenance.

The *Spiritual Canticles* express an awareness of the divine in a way not atypical for those for whom religious experience has its own evidential force. Working in the field of Psychology of Religion, Caroline Franks Davis has suggested that such people may spend the rest of their lives struggling to spell out what they have experienced. These experiences, Davis proposed, will characteristically be expressed through a mixture of images rooted strongly in the host culture, though even so, those images will indicate attempts to transcend the limitations of human experience.[4] Thus, it is typical for revelations to combine the ineffable with that which is more readily understood.[5] Yet the musical equivalent of St John's pastoral images would be angelic

---

[2]   Colin P. Thompson, *The Poet and Mystic: a Study of the Canto espiritual of San Juan de la Cruz* (Oxford: Oxford University Press, 1977), 113. Thompson considers that through the use of paradox here, St John is 'making language itself the servant of the encounter with the Beloved' (*ibid.*).

[3]   The full story of the imprisonment can be found in Richard P. Hardy, *The Life of St John of the Cross: Search for Nothing* (London: Darton, Longmann and Todd, 1982), 61–78.

[4]   Caroline Franks Davis also suggests that religious experiences tend to be described using heavily theory-laden terms and culturally influenced imagery; see *The Evidential Force of Religious Experience* (Oxford: Clarendon, 1989), 85.

[5]   Davis, *The Evidential Force of Religious Experience*, 38–9. Knowledge of such concepts may seem inaccessible to normal routes of enquiry and thus unconvincing as experiences to be taken seriously – in this case, either of God or of music – but other 'real' non-cognitive experiences such as emotion and pain are equally non-referential, inexpressible and contain meaning beyond the self-authenticating, Davis argues. Pain, Elaine Scarry has argued, 'shatters language'; its resistance to language 'is not simply one of its incidental or accidental attributes but is essential to what it is'. Non-cognitive experiences other than pain may also be veridical, even if their comprehension requires the assent of faith. See Elaine Scarry, *The Body in Pain: the Making and Unmaking of the World* (Oxford and New York:

voices, or heavenly harmonies – concepts that have no place in the saint's imagery. Unlike other mystics who use this kind of musical metaphor, St John's 'silent music' does not communicate a 'vision' – or rather, an audition – of actual music. This is made absolutely clear by his own commentary to the *Spiritual Canticles*, in which 'silent music' is said to surpass any music we can know or imagine, but even so tastes something of a musical condition:

> In the aforesaid tranquillity and silence of the night, and in that knowledge of the Divine light, the soul is able to see a marvellous fitness and disposition of Wisdom in the diversities of all its creatures and works, all and each of which are endowed with a certain response to God, whereby each after its manner testifies to that which God is in it, so that it seems to hear a harmony of sublimest music surpassing all that concerts and melodies of the world. The Bride calls this music silent because, as we have said, it is a tranquil and quiet intelligence, without the sound of voices; and in it are thus enjoyed both the sweetness of the music and the quiet of the silence. And so she says that her Beloved is this silent music, because the harmony of spiritual music is known and experienced in him.[6]

We might explore what 'silent music' can mean by looking at what both 'music' and 'silence' evoke over and above their usual sense. For St John, 'music' is overtly equated here with 'sweetness' and a 'tranquil and quiet intelligence'. But in his time, music was also *musica mundana*, the Platonic, inaudible music that embodies number in a transcendent sense, and *musica humana*, the 'music' which unites body and soul, and which can be perceived, as Boethius articulated, by 'whoever penetrates into his own self. ... For what unites the incorporeal nature of reason with the body if not a certain harmony ...? What other than this unites the parts of the soul ...?'[7] In imagining a music which 'surpasses all the concerts and melodies of the world', St John seems at first sight to be hinting at the Music of the Spheres, or so Colin Thompson has suggested.[8] However, what St John experienced is separate from this type of speculative music by its nature as spiritual revelation. The Music of the Spheres is a Pythagorean expression of the structured, harmonic perfection of the cosmic order: the planets dancing their divinely-ordered and inexorable course – a music perceived by the intellect, as Joscelyn Godwin has made clear.[9] Even though it cannot reach human ears, and even though it may exist whether or not it is expressed, this music takes place in time (notionally at least) and 'sounds' of the

---

Oxford University Press, 1985), 5. It is debatable, however, if any of these experiences are non-cognitive in the medical sense; we can only understand them through the mechanisms at our disposal, after all.

[6]   From *Spiritual Canticles*, Chapter 25, in John of the Cross, *Complete Works*, 2: 84–5. For the original Spanish text, see *Obras de San Juan de la Cruz*, 522.

[7]   Ancius Manlius Severinus Boethius, *Fundamentals of Music*, trans., with Introduction and Notes, Calvin M. Bower, ed. Claude V. Palisca (New Haven and London: Yale University Press, 1989), 10; this translation was prepared from Gottfried Friedlein, *De institutione musica* (Leipzig, 1867).

[8]   Thompson, *The Poet and Mystic*, 113–14.

[9]   The fullest study of speculative music is Joscelyn Godwin's *Harmonies of Heaven and Earth: the Spiritual Dimension of Music from Antiquity to the Avant-Garde* (London: Thames and Hudson, 1987).

planets turning. It is unheard by humans, but not literally unhearable or silent. Some theorists even assigned musical tones to these conceptual harmonies of the universe, as Godwin has discussed.[10] St John's 'silent music', however, is both infinite and complete in itself. Unlike either heard or inaudible music, it does not require the passing of time to be grasped but is comprehended by the soul instantaneously.

If 'music' is a loaded term, then so equally is 'silent', which invites comparison between 'absence' or 'nullity' and 'a Nothingness beyond Being that, unlike the *néant* of the existentialists, is paradoxically its sole support and origin'.[11] Such Nothingness or 'lack of utterance' has a long history of been perceived as 'utterance itself'. As Stan Link has pointed out, 'ideas like absence, nothingness and negation inform a great deal of artistic and philosophical achievement which, in turn, indicates their sway over human imagination, perception and cognition'.[12] René Guénon, using silence as a simile for positive Nothingness, considered that

> as Non-Being, or the nonmanifested, comprehends or envelops Being, or the principle of manifestation, so silence contains within itself the principle of the word. In other words, just as Unity is nothing but the metaphysical Zero affirmed, the word is silence expressed.[13]

St John's 'silent music' was primarily a religious experience, but one which offered the possibility of a music disassociated from the flesh. We will turn later to those musical aspects; but first, does such an experience have value as a support for religious claims? Davis, in particular, has offered a sympathetic approach to arguments which others have perceived as largely unconvincing, or too rare and obscure to be accessible to ordinary routes of enquiry.[14] Perceptions of 'silent music' resemble other religious experiences and may be felt as non-cognitive. Norbert Schedler has pointed out that the meaning of religious experience cannot be determined simply by verifying the observations of mystics and visionaries; language is too loaded to communicate without the association of emotions and other meanings. In particular, statements involving the idea of God may primarily have an emotive function – to arouse in the religious hearer a sense of awe and wonder at 'creation'.[15] But as Davis pointed out, if these are considered the *only* functions of religious language, then statements of religious experience are denied any factual significance.[16] Then again, for T. R. Miles, religion is 'silence qualified by parables', and religious experiences

---

[10]   *Ibid.*, 124–89.

[11]   *Ibid.*, 193.

[12]   Stanley Boyd Link, 'Essays towards Musical Negation' (PhD diss., Princeton University, 1995), 69. Link's dissertation was published in a shortened and extensively revised form as Stan Link, 'Much Ado about Nothing', *Perspectives of New Music* 33/1–2 (Winter/ Summer 1995), 216–72. In this chapter, I refer always to the original, fuller version.

[13]   René Guénon, *The Multiple States of Being*, trans. Joscelyn Godwin (New York: Larson, 1984). Quoted in Godwin, *Harmonies of Heaven and Earth*, 193.

[14]   Davis, *The Evidential Force of Religious Experience*, 1.

[15]   Norbert O. Schedler, 'Talk about God-Talk: a Historical Introduction', in *Philosophy of Religion: Contemporary Perspectives*, ed. Schedler (New York: Macmillan, 1974), 221–50.

[16]   Davis, *The Evidential Force of Religious Experience*, 6–7.

are those experiences that occur when the subject 'tries to come to terms with cosmic issues'. When such experiences are expressed through the use of religious imagery, they should be 'radically demythologized', to be properly assessed, even to the extent of omitting references to 'God'. For Miles, these types of experience are certainly not those of mystic access to other worlds, but rather obtain value from their illumination of self-understanding and human relationships. Therefore, to experience God is really an experience of love or a sense of 'holiness' in the world.[17] Again, Davis offered an explanation as to why such a view is unsatisfactory: because 'people do take their experiences to give them access to something beyond the material world. Reports of experiences can usually be "demythologized" to some extent, but often a "sense of presence" remains which Miles would not be able to get rid of without classifying the experience as illusory in some way'.[18]

It would seem that Davis, at least, might accept St John's 'silent music' as a 'veridical perceptual experience' and one whose expression could not be further stripped down without removing a 'subtle and potentially vast network of associations'.[19] Further, St John's term, though puzzling and oxymoronic, is precise enough for others to be able to recognize that they have had 'the same sort of experience'. 'Silent music' has certainly become well-known enough as a concept among students of mysticism and religious experience, even having been adopted by William Johnston as the title of a book on the 'science of meditation'.[20] In any case, 'there is a view that mystical experiences are described as ineffable because they are inherently paradoxical. The mystic seems to experience the dissolution of the subject-object distinction, see God as both personal and impersonal, and so on – apparent contradictions'.[21] It could be argued, however, that mystical experiences are not paradoxical in themselves, but only appear so when expressed through language. Furthermore, mystic experiences can seem alien and inconceivable to non-believers, who naturally home in on the way they are expressed rather than identifying with the experience. 'Belief' in this case means that the leap of faith has been made, and knowledge of the divine fully internalized. It is easy enough to explain St John's mystic visions as reflecting his highly charged psychological state; indeed, all mystics lay themselves open to such an indictment[22] – but we should not rule out the possibility that his experience was veridical, reconciling as it does the human and the divine. Here, the borderline between the cognitive (that can be expressed in language) and the non-cognitive (which cannot be expressed at all) blurs.

For St John, music was usually a doubly loathsome art of the body, flesh being central both to its realization and its reception. But a new type of music, 'silent music' could be received in a way that did not require degeneration into the body in

---

[17]   T. R. Miles, *Religious Experience* (London: Macmillan, 1972), 229–52.

[18]   Davis, *The Evidential Force of Religious Experience*, 9.

[19]   *Ibid.*, 11.

[20]   William Johnston, *Silent Music: the Science of Meditation* ([London]: Collins, 1974).

[21]   Davis, *The Evidential Force of Religious Experience*, 16–17.

[22]   As has been suggested by Laurie A. Finke, in 'Mystical Bodies and the Dialogics of Vision', in *Maps of Flesh and Light: the Religious Experience of Medieval Women Mystics*, ed. Ulricke Wiethaus (New York: Syracuse University Press, 1993), 35.

order to be expressed – a need which, for the true ascetic, is beyond tolerance. We can see that St John's encounter with the divine through 'silent music' could also be wholly satisfying as a musical experience. For musicians, though, the idea of 'silent music' invites speculation less about what St John was trying to express as a mystic, but instead, whether, and how, we can understand 'silent music' to belong among music's own ontologies. Since musicians cannot resist contemplating what meaning can be derived from musical experience of all types, it is perhaps not surprising that descriptions of 'silent music' that bear some resemblance to St John's experiences do exist in music theory, thus suggesting the existence of 'silent music' as a category of music as well as a type of spiritual experience.

The most immediate knowledge of theoretical, non-heard music that St John could have claimed is the neo-Platonic, tri-partite division of music into *mundana*, *humana* and *instrumentalis*. If he was familiar with Marsilio Ficino, then he would also have been familiar with *musica divina*: not only planetary harmony but also music in the mind of God.[23] None of these seems to serve adequately as a model; but there are some precedents for his descriptions in the musical and spiritual philosophies of other cultures. The fact that St John could not have known of the existence of these is irrelevant if we grant his experience the status of veridicality. Three centuries earlier in the Indian treatise *Sangîtaratnâkara*, the Kashmiri scholar Sârngadeva had described both sounding and non-sounding forms of music. *Âhata nâda* – 'struck', or sounding music – was the manifested form of music. This manifested form did not exist for the purposes of entertainment, but because it was connected with *anâhata nâda* – 'unstruck', or *non-sounding* music. The identity of unstruck music was inextricably linked with the creative principle of the Universe, and acted as the channel via which humans could be brought into contact with the divine; by this means, the soul could achieve liberation.[24] All creation comes from a single soundless world note, the *Nâda-Brahman*:[25] the primordial, silent source of all sound and the primary cause of the phenomenal world. All sound comes from *Nâda-brahman* – indeed, is a manifested aspect of this silent source – and thus is to be equated with the absolute itself, since the manifest refers to the unmanifest through implication:

---

[23]   For details about Ficino's ideas, see Chapter 11 (Dixon).

[24]   Sârngadeva, *Sangîtaratnâkara of Sârngadeva: Sanskrit Text and English Translation With Comments and Notes*, trans. R. K. Shringy (New Delhi: Munshiram Manoharlal, 1999), vol. 1.

[25]   Here, Sârngadeva's echoes the Upanishads. Joachim-Ernst Berendt's *The World is Sound: Nâda Brahma, Music and the Landscape of Consciousness* (Rochester, VT: Destiny, 1983) appears to be the only study to address the question of *Nâda Brahma*'s identity. It contains thought-provoking discussion as to the connections between sound and creation, but was not intended as an academic study; the concepts discussed are less theorized or carefully critiqued than would be considered ideal in academic writing.

[N]âda has two forms, the created and the uncreated, the former being an object of sense perception and the latter a matter of mystic experience ... in which sound and light are fused together and there is direct perception [of the Divine].[26]

The human duty of the musician is to 'manifest' the music that connects the individual with the eternal. This suggests at first sight that the same music can be both of the body in its manifested form (*âhata nâda*), and of the Divine in its unmanifested form (*anâhata nâda*). By finding the connection between unmanifested and manifested sound, the individual can be brought into contact with the divine creative principle of the universe, which has two aspects: the transcendental, and that which dwells in the heart. By implication, the musician is somehow to 'hear' and realize a music that already has a recoverable identity. However, this is complicated by the fact that the entire concept of *anâhata nâda* is contained within a single, silent world note, the *Nâda-Brahman*. Finding a link to *anâhata nâda* is primarily for liberation from the cycle of existence, not for the musician's enjoyment, though it can also serve for enjoyment when manifested in the world.[27] Thus, it is through *Nâda-Brahman,* as Arnold Bake recognized, that the individual self merges with the creative principle of the universe.[28] For our discussions here, the most important characteristic of *anâhata nâda* ontologically is that it is the unfractured totality of music, the creative principle of the universe in its transcendental form. Mani Sahukar has provided an evocative suggestion about the relationship of heard music to a fractured *Nâda-Brahman*:

In India ... music has held this unique value, as being an all-embracing principle that evolves order out of chaos, that pulsates in every form of life, so that the whole phenomenal world becomes just an outpouring of music emanating from Brahma's *Nâd*, – the soundless word. ... The white ray of the sun can be spread out into the colours of the rainbow, and these very colours can be gathered together again into the pristine white ray. May it not be that the myriad sounds of music are the result of the disintegration of a single world note, the *Nâd* of Brahma?[29]

When Sahukar went on to ask, 'Is it impossible for these disintegrated notes to combine again to produce the original world note?' – we are again invited to consider human music's relationship with the divine, unmanifested form, since all human music becomes in effect an eternal offering to the celestial silence. St John might have avoided the problem of the human body as vehicle for the manifestation of what is mystically perceived; but for Sârngadeva, self-aware intelligence or, in other terms, the individual soul, 'can never keep an identity without a physical vehicle'. Sahukar's imagery is highly evocative. Just as we cannot 'see' light itself but only the colours into which it divides, nor can we 'hear' the soundless primordial note that is the source of all heard music.[30]

---

[26] Sârngadeva, *Sangîtaratnâkara*, 1: 21.

[27] *Ibid.*, 1: 104–5.

[28] Arnold Bake, 'The Music of India', in *New Oxford History of Music*, 1: *Ancient and Oriental Music*, ed. Egon Wellesz (London: Oxford University Press, 1957), 198.

[29] Mani Sahukar, *Indian Classical Music* (New Delhi: Reliance, 1986), 16–17.

[30] Hildegard almost prefigures this understanding of the nature of light when she said she cannot see the living light but only 'the reflection of the living light'. See Barbara Newman,

Then again, the idea of a 'silent music' also occurs in the Zen koan *Tetteki Tosui*, attributed to the Zen master Hsüeh-Tou (980–1052). Normally a flute is made from bamboo, but *tetteki* is made of solid iron and has neither fingerholes nor mouthpiece. *Tosui* means 'to blow it upside down'. As 'the sound of one hand clapping' functions as a subject for contemplation, so *tetteki tosui* cannot be handled by the musician 'who wanders among the lines of the grand staff ... but one who plays the stringless harp can also play this flute with no mouthpiece'.[31] It is through contemplation of such paradoxes that the clear tones of enlightenment may sound: in Zen, logic and intellection do not bring answers. These 'clear tones' are equated with 'Great Sound', which for Hsüeh-Tou is the sound that transcends ordinary sound:

> The moon floats above the pines,
> And the night veranda is cold
> As the ancient, clear sound comes from your fingertips.
> The old melody usually makes listeners weep,
> But Zen music is beyond sentiment.
> Do not play again unless the Great Sound of Lao-tsu accompanies you.[32]

Sister of Wisdom: St Hildegard's Theology of the Feminine (Aldershot: Scolar, 1987), 6–8.

[31]   Nyogen Senzsaki and Ruth Strout McCandless, trans. and ed., *The Iron Flute: 100 Zen Koans* (Boston, Rutland and Tokyo: Tuttle Publishing, 2000), 5.

[32]   *Ibid.*, 6.

For Lao-tsu (6th century BCE), 'the name that can be named is not the eternal name'.[33] Might the unnameable name be the eternal name; the unhearable music, the eternal music?

These two examples suggest that the idea of 'silent music' has been a potent symbol for spiritual contemplative experience as well as an identifiably musical phenomenon. No wonder it is coveted by those for whom the body, as a site of filth and decay, can be no more than a purveyor of the sensuous: a kidnapper of the mind and soul away from God. Hearing outwardly the sounds of the world can only distract, but hearing the inner, 'silent music', is granted as a form of grace, ignored at the individual's peril. 'Silent music' as a coveted experience gives us a key to the words of another Jesuit, the nineteenth-century poet Gerard Manley Hopkins. In 'The Habit of Perfection' (1866, originally subtitled 'The Novice'), the subject seems to be participating in the same tradition as St John as he implores:

> Elected silence, sing to me
> And beat upon my whorlèd ear. ...[34]

Here, silence has been chosen – elected – as a way of life, but in this silent state, the Novice also invokes the body in begging for 'sung silence' to be mediated, metaphorically, through the physical organ of hearing. Silence already surrounds the Novice by choice, but it is also required to penetrate inwardly. Indeed, throughout the poem, by focusing on each of the senses in turn (hearing, speech, sight, taste, smell, touch), Hopkins brings into focus the time-honoured struggle of the mystic, for whom the human, in contemplation of meeting the divine, pleads for numinous experience to bypass the body altogether: a struggle famously articulated by St Augustine, who could never quite decide whether the direct mystic access 'without the mediation of any text' which music could bring militated against the visceral disturbances which sweet-sounding voices stirred up in him.[35] Sometimes music could filter the soul past sensations of the flesh into a realm of blissful contemplation free in itself of carnality, but ultimately its vivifying beauty surpasses its uses for transcending the material realm. Holsinger traces a chronological move in St Augustine's writings away from an early period of vilifying the body – moving from the corporeal to the incorporeal – towards a reclamation of music as a practice of the flesh.[36] It would

---

[33] Lao-tsu [Lao Tzu], *The Tao Te Ching*, intro. Martin Palmer and Jay Ramsay, trans. Man-Ho Kwok, Martin Palmer and Jay Ramsay (Rockport, Shaftesbury and Brisbane: Element, 1997), 43.

[34] Gerard Manley Hopkins, 'The Habit of Perfection', in *The Poetical Works of Gerard Manley Hopkins*, ed. Norman H. MacKenzie (Oxford: Clarendon, 1990), 89.

[35] See Bruce W. Holsinger, *Music, Body, and Desire in Medieval Culture: Hildegard of Bingen to Chaucer* (Stanford: Stanford University Press, 2001), 61–83.

[36] Holsinger, *Music, Body, and Desire in Medieval Culture*, 75. I imagine things were easier for Mechtild of Hackeborn, to whom highly visual revelations resulted apparently directly from the sung liturgy and who remained untroubled by the clear corporeality of her experiences. Mechtild is discussed by Mary Jeremy Finnegan; see 'Saint Mechtild of Hackeborn: *Nemo Communior*', in *Peaceweavers: Medieval Religious Women*, ed. J. A. Nichols and L. T. Shank (Kalamazoo: Cistercian Publications, 1991), 2: 213–21. My attention was drawn to Mechtild through the postgraduate work of Anna Sander, Centre for Medieval

appear that Augustine's sympathies naturally lay with Democritus in distinguishing true-born knowledge from the bastard products of sight, hearing, smell, taste, touch.[37] Hopkins, though, is able to express the *opposite* of this turmoil, since his Novice knows enough of mystic experience to beg for a type of *silent* music.

Had St Augustine been granted the privilege of this experience, no doubt his inner torture and unrest would have been resolved at a stroke. For the Novice, uncloistered existence results in bodily turbulence; 'sung silence' is desired as a respite from this. Music's sweetness normally has to be reconciled with the sensuous experience it evokes, but now the unstill body's ache of physical existence can be massaged away by the sung *silence* of God's presence. Like St John, who could know 'silent music' in a way that bypassed the taint of the body's physicality – the traditional site of danger for the mystic – the Novice invokes all the simultaneous sweetnesses possible in the absence of the body: the pure intelligence and bliss of musical experience without its corporeal hazards. Hopkins knew St John's work for sure: he invoked the Spanish mystic's ideas again, later in the poem, by an allusion to 'double dark' (line 9), which refers to the twofold Dark Night of the Soul: the first, the Night of Sense, in which the senses are purged and subdued to the spirit, and the Night of the Spirit, 'wherein the soul is purged and laid bare', being prepared 'for the union of love with God'.[38]

The Novice's 'elected silence' has been likened by Norman Mackenzie to Keats's 'unheard melodies' in 'Ode on a Grecian Urn' (1820) – 'ditties of no tone' which are piped to the spirit:

> Heard melodies are sweet, but those unheard
> Are sweeter still; therefore, ye soft pipes, play on;
> Not to the sensual ear, but, more endeared,
> Pipe to the spirit ditties of no tone … .[39]

Here, again, there is a confusion between music that is silent and music that is unheard. Hopkins seemed to be invoking a 'silent music' that we can recognize from St John of the Cross; but Keats's melodies are merely frozen, permanently, to a single moment. The portrayal of music-making on the urn is similar to any other pictorial representation of action: given infinite time, the characters would move and their music would be heard.[40] The silence of these melodies stems partly from

---

Studies, University of York. I thank Anna for discussions about Mechtild's visions and about 'silent music'.

[37]   See Norman H. Mackenzie, 'Commentary', in Hopkins, *Poetical Works*, 286.

[38]   Mackenzie, 'Commentary', in Hopkins, *Poetical Works*, 287. For explorations of Hopkins' relationship with his religion, see Donald Walhout, *Send My Roots Rain: a Study of Religious Experience in the Poetry of Gerard Manley Hopkins* (Athens and London, OH: Ohio University Press, 1981), and Anthony Kenny, *God and Two Poets: Arthur Hugh Clough and Gerard Manley Hopkins* (London: Sidgwick and Jackson, 1988).

[39]   John Keats, 'Ode on a Grecian Urn' (1820), in *Complete Poems*, ed. Jack Stillinger (Cambridge, MA: Harvard University Press, 1982), 372–3.

[40]   I have borrowed here from ideas expressed by Reinhard Strohm in *Music in Late Medieval Bruges* (Oxford: Clarendon, 1990), 1, who characterizes the soundscape of late

the fact that they are historically unrecoverable; Keats could never know how that music sounded, since that of ancient Greece is lost to us, but even so, it was a type of music that did, notionally, have a historical existence. It has even been suggested that Keats's 'still urn' and 'soft pipes' refer to the 'still music' that appears in Shakespeare and Milton to mean soft, low, gentle music, especially that of the recorder. Indeed, Keats's copy of *A Midsummer Night's Dream* contains marginalia surrounding the stage direction which calls for 'still music', evidencing without question his knowledge of that particular sense of the phrase. Thus, George and Judy Cheatham have argued, Keats 'first boldly states the paradox of unheard melodies, then immediately weakens it, modulating "unheard music" – literally still – into merely "soft music" – idiomatically so. In doing so, he makes the paradox believable'.[41] For Cleanth Brooks, 'the pipes ... are playing very softly; if we listen carefully, we can hear them; their music is just below the threshold of normal sound'.[42] Actually, though, there is no real paradox. We *cannot* hear the pipes: that is the point. Besides, Keats showed no sign that he had experienced a type of 'silent music' in a religious sense.

However, it is interesting that Hopkins' Novice uses the same combination of pastoral and paradoxical imagery, pleading:

Pipe to me pastures *still* and be
The *music* that I care to hear.[43]

In this case, Norman Mackenzie is surely correct in suggesting that the 'pastures still' represent a combination of the 'green pastures' and 'still waters' of Psalm 23.[44] Nevertheless, the juxtaposition of 'pipe', 'still' and 'music' are noteworthy, and further feed George Steiner's speculation that Keats's ascription of beauty to truth might, as well as a rhetorical flourish, have been 'a piece of theology'[45] (at least, if not to Keats, it may have read as a piece of theology to Hopkins – since Keats coupled two concepts, a type of natural beauty the senses can know and 'ditties of

---

medieval Bruges in terms of its townscape, as represented in pictures.

[41]   George and Judy Cheatham, 'Soft Pipes, Still Music, and Keats's "Ode"', *American Notes and Queries* 21/7–8 (1983), 102.

[42]   Cleanth Brooks, *The Well Wrought Urn: Studies in the Structure of Poetry* (London: Dennis Dobson, 1947), 157. Literary criticism has now of course moved well beyond such questions as whether or not the 'ditties of no tone' are or are not hearable. Brooks was one of most influential of the 'new critics' whose close reading of this *Ode* concerned itself with contemplating the enigmas of the images in the poem in a way that was revolutionary in the 1940s. Though this type of criticism has been superseded in current scholarship by literary-theoretical approaches, the questions posed by Brooks about specific details of the poem are relevant for this study. For discussion on critical approaches to the poem, see James O'Rourke, ed., *Ode on a Grecian Urn: Hypercanonicity and Pedagogy,* Romantic Circles Praxis Series (Electronic edition: University of Maryland: 2003), accessed at <http://www.rc.umd.edu/ praxis/grecianurn> (accessed on 19 July 2005).

[43]   Hopkins, *Poetical Works*, 89 (emphasis added).

[44]   Mackenzie, 'Commentary', in Hopkins, *Poetical Works*, 286.

[45]   George Steiner, *Real Presences: Is there Anything in What We Say?* (London and Boston: Faber and Faber, 1989), 216.

no tone' knowable only to the spirit, which both Jesuits, St John and Hopkins, would readily have understood).

It is tempting to liken 'silent music' to the angelic songs which are heard inwardly, even though literally silent to the ear. As Evelyn Underhill has documented, St Francis of Assisi, St Catherine of Sienna, Richard Rolle, Henry Suso and Hildegard of Bingen all experienced auditions of this type.[46] Hildegard, the best-known of medieval 'auditionaries', was even able to transmit through notation the music that was revealed to her by God.[47] In their cases, it has been suggested that this form of perception 'probably corresponds with the temperamental bias of the self, the ordered sweetness of Divine Harmony striking responsive chords in the music-loving soul'.[48] There can be no doubt, however, that all these mystics 'heard' identifiable music, albeit of such sweetness that the body was strained to the utmost in bearing the weight of the bliss that followed; as Sabina Flanagan has detailed, Hildegard's body frequently broke down under the strain of divine agency.[49] Henry Suso's mystic auditions seem to have been closely related to plainchant – he mentioned specific texts, sung by angels, that made his soul so overflow with joy that his feeble body was unable to support such happiness.[50] St Teresa of Ávila described her auditions as 'perfectly formed, but they are not heard with the physical ear. Yet they are received much more clearly than if they were so heard'.[51] Interestingly, St John of the Cross was prone to treat this kind of auditions with suspicion, declaring

> I am appalled at what happens these days – namely when some soul with the very smallest experience of meditation, if it be conscious of certain locutions of this kind in some state of recollection, at once christens them all as coming from God … whereas it is not so at all, but as we have said, it is for the most part they who are saying these things to themselves …[52]

The coupling of God's revelation with music has other resonances with corporeality, since the human voice has occupied such a special position as mediator between the body and the Word incarnate. The history of this specific interaction extends over millennia and across many different religions. Hindus think of the manifested soul in terms of a mediating force, *prana*, which is not breath itself but rides

---

[46]   See Evelyn Underhill, *Mysticism: a Study in the Nature and Development of Man's Spiritual Consciousness* (1912), University Paperbacks (London: Methuen, 1960), 77–9.

[47]   See Sabina Flanagan, *Hildegard of Bingen: a Visionary Life* (London and New York: Routledge, 1989).

[48]   Underhill, *Mysticism*, 277.

[49]   Flanagan, *Hildegard of Bingen*, 4–9.

[50]   Underhill, *Mysticism*, 277; original from *Heinrich Suso's, genannt Amandus, Leben und Schriften*, ed. Melchior Diepenbrock (Regensburg: Pustet 1829), Chapter 6.

[51]   St Teresa of Ávila, *The Life of Teresa of Ávila by Herself*, trans. with an introduction by J. M. Cohen (Harmondsworth: Penguin, 1957), 74.

[52]   St John of the Cross, *Ascent of Mount Carmel*, Book 2, Stanza 2, Chapter 29, paragraph 4; in *Complete Works*, 1: 197. For the original Spanish text, see *Obras de San Juan de la Cruz*, 209.

upon it.[53] Sufic thought also makes reference to life itself riding on the breath.[54] For Christians reading directly from early Western Aramaic gospels, the meanings 'spirit' and 'breath' both reside in the same word, *ruha*.[55] The scriptures provide other examples of manifestations of the silent divine through the mediation of the voice: descriptions of moments at which the 'silent music' of divine utterance is realized through the human form, such as the Word that existed 'with God' before its manifestation in human form. For Muslims, since the Qur'an was already in a silent (in human terms), divine existence, it only needed articulation through a musical, human voice to become heard to all through the medium of the Prophet Muhammad. As Philip Bohlman has suggested, 'the concept of the human as vessel for the voice of God provides a common ontological moment – indeed, a remarkable metaphysical coupling of God and humans through voice and music'.[56] This type of revelation appears to be the *opposite* of 'silent music'; the one experience evidences the essence of Divine as public knowledge, the other, the most private.

'Silent Music' and the Eternal Silence

'Silent music' is, we have seen, 'more' than music and more than silence – more even than the most pregnant of silences. However, the concept does inevitably invite consideration of music's many different relationships with phenomenal silence,

---

[53]   The term itself indeed comes from the Sanskrit *pra* (before) *ana* (breath): see Sri Nisargadatta, *I am That* (1976; Bombay: Chetana, 1991), App. 3; see also Ayetra, *Prana: the Secret of Yogic Healing* (Maine: Samuel Weiser, 1996), 3.

[54]   Hazrat Inayat Khan, perhaps the best known musician-turned-Sufi, and a prolific writer and teacher, drew a distinction between the perceptible breath, felt by the nostrils as it goes in and out, and mystic breath: the current which carries the air out and brings the air in. 'This is what the mystic calls nafs, which means "the self" [also often translated as "the soul"] … breath … runs from the physical plane into the innermost plane; a current that runs through the body, mind, and soul, touching the innermost part of life and also coming back'. See his *The Music of Life* (1983; New Lebanon, NY: Omega, 1988), 203–4. More recently, the Sufi writer, Reshad Feild, writing on the science and art of the breath, maintained that 'the secret of eternal life is hidden in the moisture on the breath. Both the past and the future are transformed through the present moment, without a conscious human being'; see his *The Last Barrier* (Shaftsbury, Rockport MA, and Brisbane: Element, 1976), opening bio-data.

[55]   Neil Douglas-Klotz, *The Hidden Gospel: Decoding the Spiritual Message of the Aramaic Jesus* (Wheaton, IL, and Madras: Quest, 1999), 41–2. Douglas-Klotz pointed out that whenever a saying of Jesus refers to spirit, we must remember that he would have used an Aramaic or Hebrew word. In both these languages, the same words stand for spirit, breath, air and wind. So 'Holy Spirit' must also be 'Holy Breath'. The duality of spirit and body, which we often take for granted in our Western languages, falls away (p. 1). Douglas-Klotz pointed out that translations of the Bible from the Greek – i.e. those in common use – obscure these meanings.

[56]   Philip Bohlman, 'Ontologies of Music', in *Rethinking Music*, ed. Nicholas Cook and Mark Everist (Oxford and New York: Oxford University Press, 1999), 27.

one of its Others.[57] In everyday circumstances, music encounters its Other in the silences within musical performance, where, Stan Link has suggested, 'malignant' as a description 'is too negative and entirely too strong, but [where] the absence of sound should be seen neither as benign nor even inert'.[58] Music also encounters its Other in the 'silences of the frame' which mark the thresholds of musical works.[59] The more powerful these silences, that of frame and that which is musically contextual, the more they invite us to ponder on what music lacks that makes them so important: which makes the presence of silence so profound that to define it as any kind of absence is untenable. It remains a matter for individual perception to decide if the *silence eternel* that may be glimpsed in musical performance is an idea drawn from actual silences – those of the frame and those that are musically contextual – or whether contextual silences in musical works partake of the larger 'eternal silence', operating as a pointer to something more significant.[60] In other words, perhaps musical silences can be so meaningful that they resist the appeal of the purely aesthetic altogether, instead operating as windows to mystic perception. Within music, it is tempting to imagine silence as being more meaningful the more it is bound to its immediate context; but as Link went on to suggest, 'silence is where *we are*, not where it is. … Our impression of the input and meaning of silence in a musical context is therefore heightened by a sense of transcendence: the ideal silence banishing the real'.[61] The problem with 'ideal' silences glimpsed in musical contexts is that they are still temporally bounded by music, however. There is never enough time to transcend the moment before music interrupts us.

Such issues take us back to the idea of manifested and unmanifested music – *âhata nâda* and *anâhata nâda*. They invite us to consider the extent to which silence might be the noumenal – a 'thing in itself' – to heard music as the phenomenal – that which is knowable by the senses. As Link has suggested, there is a relationship between musical silence as 'a metaphor, eternity, nothingness' and 'the effect of silence'. Perhaps, however, this elevates music to a hegemonic position in the hierarchy of silence and sound which it does not deserve. Silence is certainly a primary requirement if 'silent music' is to be experienced, as St John made clear ('In the aforesaid tranquillity and silence of the night …'). The poet José Bergamín pointed out that for St Paul, '"Faith comes from hearing and hearing from the word of God". Music also comes "from the sense of hearing". Be careful that it is not the thief come

---

[57]   Another of music's Others is (unstructured) noise, according to Jacques Attali; see *Noise: the Political Economy of Music*, trans. Brian Massumi, forward by Frederic Jameson, afterword by Susan McClary (Minneapolis: University of Minnesota Press, 1985), Chapter 1.

[58]   Link, 'Essays towards Musical Negation', 25.

[59]   This phrase is taken from Richard Littlefield, 'The Silences of the Frames', in *Music/Ideology: Resisting the Aesthetic*, ed. and intro. Adam Krims, commentary Henry Klumpenhouwer (Amsterdam: Overseas Publishers Association, 1998), 213–31; Littlefield, in turn, borrows from Edward T. Cone.

[60]   Link, 'Essays towards Musical Negation', 12–13.

[61]   *Ibid.*, 5–6.

to steal the divine word from you'.[62] Bergamín seems to be suggesting that music is incompatible with faith because the word of God only needs silence and nothing else to be heard – an idea extended by Yves Roullière, who has gone even further in his search for what separates sounded music from the serene and calm intelligence of 'silent music'. Roullière proposed that the full weight of thought, 'fear-induced by the bitter and raw reality of the eternal silences of the infinite spaces', can eventually only melt into 'music' which offers it a sweet opening of relief.[63] Far from being something sweet, though, music under those circumstances can only be a ghastly form of saccharin. We are back to the fleshly abhorrence of the mystic, who craves an entirely different experience from any that the loathsome body can offer. The most important concession Bergamín made was to concede that music can *create* silence in such a way as to underline the very importance of silence – reflecting Link's statement that silence is 'where *we are*'. This is a highly significant admission, since otherwise, for Bergamín, music was a particularly intense form of sensual evil. Music can be theophany – a visible manifestation of God – but not if it be received through the body in a form that causes disturbance and takes the soul away from union with God. If silence is music's Other, then, as St John recognized, music is immanent in silence for those who hear God to be given voice in all creation.[64]

The idea that silence is not defined by surrounding sounds is also familiar through the Japanese concept of *ma*: silence whose ontology is not determined by what it is framed by, but by its own emptiness, existing outside time. If silence's relationship with time is uncertain, then even so is music's. As Philip Bohlman has suggested,

> Music may be ontologically dependent on time, but time is ontologically dependent on music. ... More than any other aesthetic-spiritual practice, music passes between myth and history, between the worlds before time and the worlds of historical time. ... The ontological presence of music in time and outside of time makes it possible to remember the past and imagine the future, to cross the boundaries between narratives experienced and those transposed onto other beings, and to embed music in cognitive and spiritual processes of knowing experiences and worlds other than one's own.[65]

Here, Bohlman is addressing issues of music as an act of remembrance and memory, but in speaking of its embeddedness in 'spiritual processes of experiences and worlds other than our own', one is inevitably drawn to speculate about its Other's (silence's)

---

[62]   Yves Roullière, 'La musique tacite', *La nouvelle revue française* nos 462–3 (1991), 27, commenting on Bergamín's work, *Head in the Clouds*, in which music is rejected in favour of silence (Romans, 10:17). The original reads: '"La foi vient par l'ouïe et l'ouïe par la parole de Dieu", disait saint Paul. La musique aussi vient "par l'ouïe". Prends garde qu'elle ne soit le voleur venant te dérober la parole divine'. I am extremely grateful to Neil and Martin Sorrell for providing me with a translation of Roullière's article.

[63]   'Aussi est-elle l'idéal "pont d'or *de la pensée*". Effrayé par "le silence éternel des espaces infinis", les profondeurs souterraines et sous-marines, bref par la vertigineuse, âpre et amère réalité, la pensée incline à peser de tout son poids pour se fondre dans la musique et se livrer corps et âme à sa merci dans l'attente de voir s'offrir d'inouïes ouvertures.' Roullière, 'La musique tacite', 28.

[64]   *Ibid.*, 30.

[65]   Bohlman, 'Ontologies of Music', 29–30.

relationship with the present and its ability to act as a connecting thread between other spiritual worlds. For there can be no possibility that silence, unlike music, can ever disappoint us in the matter of mystery. Thus, silence can act as a fulcrum between worlds of the flesh and the spirit, whether this be in the guise of 'silent music', as a thing-in-itself, as infinity, or as nullity – or even as an alternative dimension on the 'other side' of sound in which speculative musics can turn their course. In this way, the eternal silence can be conceptually present during the silences of music, and 'silent music' is immanent in the silence of contemplation.

Joscelyn Godwin has discussed in depth the conceptual and theoretical world of possibilities which lie beyond the point where heard music stops.[66] He has followed Kayser in positing that there is a reality for the Pythagorean 'subharmonic series' which does not necessarily need to be objective or audible to be appreciated as symbolic. However, reviewing Godwin's sources reveals limitations to the extent to which the concepts of 'silent music' and speculative music can be conflated. It might appear that the 'silent music' of St John of the Cross, a solid iron flute played upside down, and *âhata* and *anâhata nâda* might function as the final links in a chain of thought that reaches beyond characterizing this phenomenon as a 'silence of heaven'[67] or as a 'Nothingness beyond being that, unlike the *néant* of the existentialists, is paradoxically its sole support positive origin',[68] and instead, towards characterizing this silent *source* of music as music's conceptual inverse. (One is reminded of Lewis Carroll's Alice, who stepped through the looking glass to find beyond it a parallel world, back to front, with its own set of realities; like Plato's cave, the reflection claims a greater reality than the physical world.) For the ancient Greeks, an overtone and 'undertone' series had been expressed, in both the Pythagorean Table and in the 'lambdoma': a lambda-shaped diagram which starts from 'unity' (or in other words, the tone, expressed as $1/1$), with harmonic overtones proceeding down the right leg, and conceptual 'undertones' down the left. Whatever the origin of the lambdoma, it is, as Godwin has rightly pointed out,

> an incomparable aid to speculative music, as a means towards symbolic explanation a possible illumination concerning cosmic and metaphysical realities. … One might say [of the Pythagorean table] that whenever the two forces of contraction and expansion meet and are held in some sort of proportional balance, a being arises – and a tone is sounded. Every being is both number and tone; both quantity and quality; both existence and value. All have the same root: the originating $1/1$ tone that represents God the Creator.[69]

Hans Kayser went so far as to suggest that beyond the point $1/1$, there lies the point $0/0$, 'which sounds no tone but is the silence towards which all tones tend' – a point which, mathematically, contains all impossible fractions which equal zero or infinity, and which, in religious traditions, are characterized in various ways as the

---

[66]   Godwin, *Harmonies of Heaven and Earth*, 188–93.
[67]   Bishop Synesius, quoted in Godwin, *ibid.*, 193.
[68]   *Ibid.*, 193.
[69]   *Ibid.*, 190–91.

Unmanifest. For Guénon, 'metaphysical Zero, while being Unity unaffirmed, is also something more than that, and infinitely more'.[70]

But the Pythagorean lambdoma cannot effectively function as an aid to conceptualizing both the Music of the Spheres *and* 'silent music'. As I have already suggested, there would seem to be a basic difference between a world tone, *Nâda-brahman*, that contains within its pregnant silence the possibility for all creation, and the ordered structures of the Music of the Spheres. Unlike St John's 'silent music', the Music of the Spheres is not essentially allied to a philosophical concept of Nothingness. The Music of the Spheres is not silent, and nor is it the same as 'silent music'. Joscelyn Godwin asserted that 'there is no musical equivalent for 0/0', and he is probably correct: Kayser was perhaps over-enthusiastic in proposing a concept within the lambdoma that actually belongs in another taxonomical scheme.

§

From our starting point, we have perhaps gained little towards understanding how, in a physiological sense,[71] St John could have knowledge of music in the form of silence, though we have at least traced experiences similar to his in other cultures and suggested a basis in musical taxonomy for the type of music he experienced. We have also allowed worldly silences within manifested music to claim some kinship with their eternal counterparts. It is beyond the scope of this chapter to look deeply into the psychology of such experiences – though when we come face to face with ourselves during contextual musical silences, our sense of fullness or discomfort might reveal something about our own psychological states that could well benefit from further investigation. If so, we might approach those for whom the concept of 'silent music' is real with at least a modicum of sympathy. It is too easy to suggest 'silent music' to be an experience born of, or even an expression of, spiritual desperation. After all, there is no way of knowing except through the body, which is, at least, for the moment, our only interface between inner and outer reality. Every mystic who is filled with fleshly loathing, and whose idea of reality might exist on the margins of the body, must surely have knowledge of this paradox even while longing for the release from the body that death brings.

---

[70]   Guénon, *Multiple States of Being*, 48; quoted in Godwin, *ibid.*, 193.

[71]   However, even if we currently cannot measure such experiences, there is certainly some common ground between St John's experience of 'unmanifested' music and experiences of faith healing – Aubrey T. Westlake discusses experiences of this in *The Pattern of Health: a Search for a Greater Understanding of the Life Force in Health and Disease* (Boulder, CO: Shambhala, 1973); see especially 76–88. In both cases, what can seem miraculously instantaneous is usually experienced over time. The time element is eliminated: a vast truth is comprehended, a body is healed, in a single flash. Both could be said to take place through types of parallel vibrational experience which confound traditional forms of measurement, and perhaps the characterizations of states of the body that are familiar to practitioners of alternative healing might be a useful way to comprehend St John's highly altered state of perception.

Ultimately, whether we accept 'silent music' as a category of music or not, it is only a musical experience to those able to receive it as spiritual experience. For some musicians it has informed both performance and composition,[72] but phenomenal music and the silence contained within it can only be a meagre echo of the noumenal Great Sound, the unmanifested melody. George Steiner has suggested that our capacities 'to respond to musical form and sense directly implicate the human condition'. If this is so, and if we can relate this to the concept of 'silent music', then this suggests that the human condition can aspire towards a state of openness to knowledge of the unknowable – the 'tides of infinity'. Such a condition need serve no purpose other than a striving for individual self-actualization. But if there can be a return from this transcendence to full awareness of the body – or, put another way, a condition of social rehabilitation – then in having reached identification with the infinite, openness without limit, the experiential knowledge of unknowing and even, if we are lucky, of 'silent music', one can return to the human condition replete with the knowledge of a source of human existence, and of human music, on which the soul can draw infinitely. No further experience of human silence – that which is rooted in the body – can ever be the same. Unfortunately, no further experience of human music can be the same either. Given that mystical revelations often manifest themselves through the medium most beloved and familiar to the recipient, this is an unspeakable loss for the musician. Heard music can never again contain enough mystery. The best that can subsequently be done is to offer up our human music in full knowledge of its fractured state.

But when music is made in this full knowledge, it is not pointless; Sârngadeva surely knew this when he described the body as 'a heap of filth surrounded by impurities; and yet intelligent people utilize it as a means for worldly enjoyment and for salvation'.[73] And should we, like Susan Sontag, be misguided enough to think that the activity of the mystic must always 'end in a *via negativa*, a theology of God's absence, a craving for the cloud of unknowing beyond knowledge and for the silence beyond speech',[74] then let us remember that even so, activity only accompanies the journey, never its destination.

---

[72] See Chapter 2 (Hill). See also Kudsi Erguner, 'A Mystic Journey', *Unesco Courier* (May 1996), 22–5 [issue title: *Silence*]; and John Tavener, *The Music of Silence: a Composer's Testament* (London and New York: Faber and Faber, 1999).

[73] Sârngadeva, *Sangîtaratnâkara*, 103.

[74] Susan Sontag, 'The Aesthetics of Silence', in *Styles of Radical Will* (1969; London: Vintage, 1994), 4–5.

Selected Bibliography

General Sources

Adorno, Theodor Wiesengrund. 'Memorandum: Music in Radio'. Unpublished essay, June 1938. Paul F. Lazarsfeld papers, Columbia University, New York. Quoted in Richard Leppert, 'Commentary', in Theodor W. Adorno, *Essays on Music*, selected, with introduction commentary and notes by Richard Leppert, trans. Susan H. Gillespie. Berkeley, Los Angeles and London: University of California Press, 2002. 213–50.

[Adorno, Theodor Wiesengrund and] Hanns Eisler. *Composing for the Films*. New York: Oxford University Press, 1947.

Allen, Michael J. B. 'The Absent Angel in Ficino's Philosophy', *Journal of the History of Ideas* 36/2 (1975), 219–40.

Altman, Rick. 'Four and a Half Film Fallacies', in *Sound Theory, Sound Practice*, ed. Rick Altman. New York: Routledge, 1992. 35–45.

_____. 'The Silence of the Silents', *Musical Quarterly* 80/4 (1996), 648–718. Later expanded in *Silent Film Sound.* New York: Columbia University Press, 2004.

Alvarez, Anne. *Live Company: Psychoanalytic Psychotherapy with Autistic, Borderline, Deprived and Abused Children*. London: Routledge, 1992.

Ames, Van Meter. 'Zen and Pragmatism', *Philosophy East and West* 4/1 (April 1954), 19–33.

Andrieu, Michel. 'Règlement d'Angilramme de Metz (768–791) fixant les honoraires de quelques fonctions liturgiques', *Revue des Sciences Religieuses* 10 (1930), 349–69.

Apollinaire, Guillaume. 'La victoire', in *Calligrammes: poémes de la paix et de la guerre, 1913–1916*. Paris: Éditions Gallimard, 1925. 179–182.

Ashbee, Andrew. *The Harmonious Musick of John Jenkins*, 1: *The Fantasias for Viols*. Surbiton: Toccata Press, 1992.

_____. 'The Transmission of Consort Music in Some Seventeenth-Century English Manuscripts', in *John Jenkins and his Time: Studies in English Consort Music*, ed. Ashbee and Peter Holman. Oxford: Clarendon, 1996. 243–70.

Attali, Jacques. *Bruits: essai sur l'économie politique de la musique* (1977), trans. Brian Massumi as *Noise: the Political Economy of Music*. Minneapolis: University of Minnesota Press, 1985.

Aurelian of Réôme. *The Discipline of Music (ca. 843)*, trans. Joseph Ponte. Colorado Springs: Colorado College Music Press, 1968.

Ayetra. *Prana: the Secret of Yogic Healing*. Maine: Samuel Weiser, 1996.

Bacon, Francis. *Sylva Sylvarum: or, A Naturall History in Ten Centuries*. London, 1651.

Bailey, Kathryn. *The Life of Webern*. Cambridge: Cambridge University Press, 1998.

Bailey, Terence, ed. and trans. *Commemoratio brevis de tonis et psalmis modulandis: Introduction, Critical Edition, Translation*. Ottawa: University of Ottawa Press, 1979.

Bake, Arnold. 'The Music of India', in *New Oxford History of Music*, 1: *Ancient and Oriental Music*, ed. Egon Wellesz. London: Oxford University Press, 1957. 195–227.

Barthes, Roland. 'The Grain of the Voice', in *Image, Music, Text*, essays selected and trans. Stephen Heath. New York: Hill and Wang, 1977. 179–89.

Barzun, Jacques. *A Stroll with William James*. Chicago: The University of Chicago Press, 1983.

Beckett, Samuel. *The Complete Dramatic Works*. London: Faber and Faber, 1986; paperback ed. 1990. Including: *Rough for Radio I* (1961 in French; first pubd in English, 1976), 265–71; *Words and Music: a Piece for Radio* (1961; BBC Third Programme, 13 November 1962), 285–94.

Begbie, Jeremy S. *Theology, Music and Time*. Cambridge: Cambridge University Press, 2000.

Bendall, Sarah, Christopher Brooke and Patrick Collinson. *A History of Emmanuel College, Cambridge*. Woodbridge: Boydell Press, 1999.

Berendt, Joachim-Ernst. *The Third Ear: on Listening to the World*, trans. Tim Nevill. Shaftesbury: Element Books, 1988.

————. *The World is Sound: Nâda Brahma, Music and the Landscape of Consciousness*. Rochester, VT: Destiny, 1983.

Bergson, Henri. *Essai sur les données immédiates de la conscience* (1889), 6th ed. Paris: Quadrige, 1997.

Bernard, Jonathan. 'Colour', in *The Messiaen Companion*, ed. Peter Hill. London: Faber and Faber, 1994. 203–19.

————. 'Messiaen's Synaesthesia: the Correspondence Between Color and Sound Structure in his Music', *Music Perception* 4 (1986), 41–68.

Betts, Ernest. 'Why "Talkies" are Unsound', *Close Up* 4 (April 1929), 22–4. Repr. in *Close Up, 1927–1933: Cinema and Modernism*, ed. James Donald, Anne Friedberg and Laura Marcus. London: Cassell, 1998. 89–90.

Bion, Wilfred R. *Attention and Interpretation: a Scientific Approach to Insight in Psycho-analysis and Groups*. London: Maresfield Library, 1970.

Blos, Peter Jr. 'Silence: a Clinical Exploration', *Psychoanalytic Quarterly* 41 (1972), 348–63.

Boccadoro, Brenno. 'Marsilio Ficino: the Soul and the Body of Counterpoint', in *Number to Sound: the Musical Way to the Scientific Revolution*, ed. Paolo Gozza. Dordrecht: Kluwer, 2000. 99–134.

Boethius, Ancius Manlius Severinus. *Fundamentals of Music*, trans., with Introduction and Notes, Calvin M. Bower, ed. Claude V. Palisca. New Haven and London: Yale University Press, 1989. Trans. prepared from: Gottfried Friedlein, *De institutione musica*, Leipzig, 1867.

Bohlman, Philip. 'Ontologies of Music', in *Rethinking Music*, ed. Nicholas Cook and Mark Everist. Oxford and New York: Oxford University Press, 1999. 17–34.

Bonds, Mark Evan. 'Idealism and the Aesthetics of Instrumental Music at the Turn of the Nineteenth Century', *Journal of the American Musicological Society* 50/2 (1997), 387–420.

Boretz, Benjamin. 'Regretting John Cage and Kenneth Gabora; a Gathering of Texts', in *Perspectives of New Music*, 31/2 (Summer 1993), 118–26.

Bowen, William R. 'Ficino's Analysis of Musical *Harmonia*', in *Ficino and Renaissance Neoplatonism*, ed. Konrad Eisenbichler and Olga Zorzi Pugliese. (University of Toronto Italian Studies, No. 1.) Ottawa: Dovehouse Editions, 1986. 17–27.

Bower, Calvin. 'The Grammatical Model of Musical Understanding in the Middle Ages', in *Hermeneutics and Medieval Cultures*, ed. Patrick Gallacher and Helen Damico. Albany: State University of New York Press, 1989. 133–45.

Bowlby, John. *Attachment and Loss*, 1: *Attachment*. New York: Basic Books, 1969.

Bowman, Wayne D. *Philosophical Perspectives on Music*. New York and Oxford: Oxford University Press, 1998.

Brendel, Alfred. *The Veil of Order*, trans. Richard Stokes. London: Faber & Faber, 2002.

Brett, Philip. Review of *Letters from a Life: Selected Letters of Benjamin Britten*, vols. 1–2, *Journal of the Royal Musical Association* 119/1 (1994), 144–51.

Brooks, Cleanth. *The Well Wrought Urn: Studies in the Structure of Poetry*. London: Dennis Dobson, 1947.

Brooks, William. 'Choice and Change in Cage's Recent Music', in *TriQuarterly 54* (Spring 1982), 148–66. Repr. in *A John Cage Reader*. New York: C. F. Peters Corporation, 1982. 82–100.

_____. 'John Cage and History: Hymns and Variations', in *Perspectives of New Music* 31/2 (Summer 1993), 74–103.

_____. 'Music II: From the Late 1960s', in *The Cambridge Companion to John Cage,* ed. David Nicholls. Cambridge: Cambridge University Press, 2002. 128–147.

_____. 'Music in America: an Overview', in *The Cambridge History of American Music*, ed. David Nicholls. Cambridge: Cambridge University Press, 1998. 30–48, 257–75.

Browne, Sir Thomas. *Religio Medici*. London, 1642.

Brummer, Vincent. 'Philosophy, Theology, and the Reading of Texts', *Religious Studies* 27/3 (1991), 451–62.

Bryson, Norman. *Vision and Painting: the Logic of the Gaze*. New Haven: Yale University Press, 1983.

Bush, Sargent, Jr., and Carl J. Rasmussen. *The Library of Emmanuel College, Cambridge, 1584–1637*. Cambridge: Cambridge University Press, 1986.

Cage, John. *A Year from Monday*. Middletown, CT: Wesleyan University Press, 1967; London: Calder and Boyars, 1968. Including: 'Two Statements on Ives', 36–42; 'How to Pass, Kick, Fall, and Run' (1965), 133–40.

[_____]. *John Cage*, ed. Richard Kostelanetz. New York: Praeger Publishers, 1970. Including: 'Defense of Satie' (1948), 77–84.

[_____]. *John Cage, Writer: Previously Uncollected Pieces*, ed. Richard Kostelanetz. New York: Limelight Editions, 1993. Including: 'Listening to

Music (1937)', 15–19; 'A Composer's Confessions' (1948), 27–44; 'Preface to *Indeterminacy*' (1959), 75–9; 'An Autobiographical Statement' (1989), 237–47.

————. *Silence: Lectures and Writings*. Middletown, CT: Wesleyan University Press, 1961; reissued London: Marion Boyars, 1978. Including: 'The Future of Music: Credo' (1940 [not 1937]), 3–6; 'Experimental Music' (1955 [not 1957]), 7–12; 'Experimental Music: Doctrine' (1957), 13–17; 'Composition as Process' (1958), 18–56; 'History of Experimental Music in the United States' (1959), 67–75; 'Edgard Varèse' (1958), 83–4; 'Goal: New Music, New Dance' (1939), 87–8; 'Lecture on Nothing' (1950 [not 1959]), 109–27; 'Lecture on Something' (1950 [not 1959]), 128–45; '45' for a Speaker' (1954), 146–94.

Cage, John with Robert Dunn. *Catalogue*. New York: C. F. Peters Corp., 1962.

Cassirer, Ernst. *The Platonic Renaissance in England*. Austin: University of Texas Press, 1953.

Cavell, Stanley. *The World Viewed: Reflections on the Ontology of Film* (1974), enlarged ed. Cambridge, MA, and London: Harvard University Press, 1979.

Cheatham, George and Judy Cheatham. 'Soft Pipes, Still Music, and Keats's "Ode"', *American Notes and Queries* 21/7–8 (1983), 101–3.

Chion, Michel. *L'audio-vision: son et image au cinéma* (1990), ed. and trans. Claudia Gorbman as *Audio-vision: Sound on Screen*. New York: Columbia University Press, 1994.

Clarkson, Austin. 'The Intent of the Musical Moment', in *Writings Through John Cage's Music, Poetry, and Art*, ed. David W. Bernstein and Christopher Hatch. Chicago: University of Chicago Press, 2001. 62–112.

Clifton, Thomas. 'The Poetics of Musical Silence', *Musical Quarterly* 62/2 (1976), 163–81.

Cook, Nicholas. *Music, Imagination and Culture*. Oxford: Clarendon, 1990.

Cooke, Mervyn. 'Film Music', in *Grove Music Online*, ed. Laura Macy. <http://www.grovemusic.com>, accessed 4 January 2006.

Cox, Renee. 'Are Musical Works Discovered?', *Journal of Aesthetics and Art Criticism* 43/4 (1985), 367–74.

Crooks, Ed. 'The Cageian Sublime'. Unpublished paper presented at *Hung Up on the Number 64: International Conference on John Cage*, Huddersfield University, 4 February 2006.

Cudworth, Ralph. *The True Intellectual System of the Universe*. London, 1678.

Culverwel, Nathaniel. *An Elegant and Learned Discourse of the Light of Nature, with Several Other Treatises*. London, 1652.

Cuvillier, Armand. *Précis de philosophie: classe de philosophie*. Paris: Armand Colin, 1953.

Darbyshire, Ian. 'Messiaen and the Representation of the Theological Illusion of Time', in *Messiaen's Language of Mystical Love*, ed. Siglind Bruhn. New York: Garland, 1998. 33–51.

Davis, Caroline Franks. *The Evidential Force of Religious Experience*. Oxford: Clarendon, 1989.

De Backer, Jos, 'A Collage of Silence'. Unpublished paper presented at the National Conference of Music Therapy, *Music and Psychiatry: De Stilte*. UC St-Jozef Kortenberg, Belgium, 15 October 2003.

_____. 'The Transition from Sensorial Impression into a Musical Form by Psychotic Patients'. PhD thesis, University of Aalborg, Denmark, 2005.

Debus, Allen G. *Science and Education in the Seventeenth Century: the Webster-Ward Debate*. London: Macdonald, 1970.

Descartes, René. *Renatus Descartes Excellent Compendium of Musick: With Necessary and Judicious Animadversions Thereupon, by a Person of Honour* [trans. William Brouncker, Viscount Brouncker]. London, 1653.

Deschênes, Bruno. *Aesthetics in Japanese Arts*. <http://www.thingsasian.com/goto_article/article.2121.html>, accessed 24 March 2006.

Desmond, Karen. '*Sicut in grammatica*: Analogical Discourse in Chapter 15 of Guido's *Micrologus*', *Journal of Musicology* 16 (1998), 467–93.

Dickinson, Peter, ed. *CageTalk: Dialogues With and About John Cage*. (*Eastman Studies in Music*, 38.) Rochester, N.Y.: University of Rochester Press; Woodbridge: Boydell & Brewer, 2006.

Dilworth, David A. 'Suzuki Daisetz as Regional Ontologist: Critical Remarks on Reading Suzuki's *Japanese Spirituality*', in *Philosophy East and West* 28/1 (January 1978), 99–110.

Dixon, Thomas. '"Or Rather in an Heavenly Paradise": Peter Sterry, Philip Sidney (Lord Lisle) and the Philosophy of a Restoration Community'. MA diss., Lancaster University, 2002.

_____. '"Spiritual Musick": the Model of Divine Harmony in the Work of Peter Sterry (1613–1672)'. PhD diss., University of Manchester, 2005.

Donne, John. Sermon 'Preached at the Funeral of Sir William Cokayne, December 12, 1626', repr. as Sermon No. 10 in *John Donne's Sermons on the Psalms and Gospels,* ed. Evelyn M. Simpson. Berkeley: University of California Press, 1991. 219–40.

Douglas-Klotz, Neil. *The Hidden Gospel: Decoding the Spiritual Message of the Aramaic Jesus*. Wheaton, IL, and Madras: Quest, 1999.

Duckworth, William. 'Anything I Say will be Misunderstood: an Interview with John Cage', in *John Cage at Seventy Five*, ed. Richard Fleming and William Duckworth. (*The Bucknell Review* 32/2.) Lewisburg: Bucknell University Press; London: Associated University Presses, 1989. [15-33]

Dulac, Germaine. [Article in] *Monde* (12 January 1929); reported as 'Holland and the Visual Ideal' by André Stufkens, in *European Foundation Joris Ivens Newsletter* No. 6 (November 2000), <http://www.ivens.nl/newslet6.htm#rain>, accessed 25 March 2006.

Dyer, Joseph. 'Monastic Psalmody of the Middle Ages', *Revue Benedictine* 99 (1989), 41–74.

Eccles, Solomon. *A Musick-Lector: or, The Art of Musick*. London, 1667.

Edgar, Andrew. 'Music and Silence,' in *Silence: Interdisciplinary Perspectives*, ed. Adam Jaworski. Berlin and New York: Mouton de Gruyter, 1997. 311–27.

Ekenberg, Anders. *Cur Cantatur? Die Funktionen des liturgischen Gesanges nach den Autoren der Karolingerzeit*. Stockholm: Almqvist and Wiksell International, 1987.

Eliade, Mircea. *The Sacred and the Profane: the Nature of Religion* (1957), trans. Willard R. Trask. New York: Harcourt Brace Jovanovich, 1959, 1987.

Emerson, Ralph Waldo. 'Intellect', in *Complete Works*, 2: *Essays, Series 1*, new and rev. ed. Boston: Houghton, Mifflin, 1894.

Emmerig, Thomas. 'Stille in der Musik und der "leere Raum" in der Zeichnung', *Musiktheorie* 19/3 (2004), 212–30.

Erguner, Kudsi. 'A Mystic Journey', *Unesco Courier* (May 1996), 22–5 [issue title: *Silence*].

Feder, Stuart, Richard L. Karmel and George H. Pollock, eds. *Psychoanalytic Explorations in Music*. Madison, CT: International Universities Press, 1990.

_____, eds. *Psychoanalytic Explorations in Music: Second Series*. Madison, CT: International Universities Press, 1993.

Feild, Reshad. *The Last Barrier*. Shaftsbury, Rockport MA, and Brisbane: Element, 1976.

Feingold, Mordechai and Penelope M. Gouk. 'An Early Critique of Bacon's *Sylva Sylvarum*: Edmund Chilmead's Treatise on Sound', *Annals of Science* 40 (1983), 139–57.

Ferneyhough, Brian. *Collected Writings*, ed. James Boros and Richard Toop. Amsterdam: Harwood Academic Publishers, 1995.

Ficino, Marsilio. *De Vita Libri Tres*, trans. C. V. Kaske and J. R. Clark as *Three Books on Life*. (Medieval and Renaissance Texts and Studies, 57). Binghamton, NY: The Renaissance Society of America, 1989.

_____. *The Letters of Marsilio Ficino*, trans. by members of the Language Department of the School of Economic Science, London. 7 vols. London: Shepheard-Walwyn, 1975–81.

Finke, Laurie A. 'Mystical Bodies and the Dialogics of Vision', in *Maps of Flesh and Light: the Religious Experience of Medieval Women Mystics*, ed. Ulricke Wiethaus. New York: Syracuse University Press, 1993. 28–44.

Finnegan, Mary Jeremy. 'Saint Mechtild of Hackeborn: *Nemo Communior*', in *Peaceweavers: Medieval Religious Women*, ed. J. A. Nichols and L. T. Shank. Kalamazoo: Cistercian Publications, 1991. 2: 213–21.

Finney, Gretschen Ludke. *Musical Backgrounds for English Literature, 1580–1650*. 1962; repr. Westport, CT: Greenwood Press, 1976.

Finscher, Ludwig. 'Pause', in *Die Musik in Geschichte und Gegenwart*. Basel: Bärenreiter, 1997. 7: 1533–8.

Flanagan, Sabina. *Hildegard of Bingen: a Visionary Life*. London and New York: Routledge, 1989.

Floros, Constantin. *Gustav Mahler*, 3: *Die Symphonien* (1985), trans. Vernon and Jutta Wicker as *Gustav Mahler: the Symphonies*. Portland: Amadeus Press, 1993.

Flower, Claire. 'The Spaces Between the Notes: Silence in Music Therapy'. Unpublished paper presented at the *Association of Professional Music Therapists/ British Society for Music Therapy Annual Conference*, London, February 2001.

Flower, Claire and Julie P. Sutton. 'Silence – "a Refined State of Musical Expression": a Dialogue about Silence in Music Therapy'. Unpublished paper presented at *World Music Therapy Congress*, Oxford, July 2002.

Forte, Allen. 'An Octatonic Essay by Webern: No. 1 of the "Six Bagatelles for String Quartet", Op. 9', *Music Theory Spectrum* 16/2 (Autumn 1994), 171–95.

Fouke, Daniel. *The Enthusiasticall Concerns of Dr. Henry More: Religious Meaning and the Psychology of Delusion*. Leiden: Brill, 1997.

Freeman, Michael and Michiko Riko Nose. *The Modern Japanese Garden*. London, Octopus Publishing Group, 2002.

Fuller-Maitland, J. A. *Brahms*. London: Methuen, 1911.

Garcia, Manuel. *Traité complet de l'Art du Chant*, part 2 (1847), edns of 1847 and 1872 trans. Donald V. Paschke as *A Complete Treatise on the Art of Singing*. New York: Da Capo Press, 1975.

Giorgi, Francesco. *De Harmonia Mundi Totius*. Venice, 1525.

Godwin, Joscelyn. *Harmonies of Heaven and Earth: the Spiritual Dimension of Music from Antiquity to the Avant-Garde*. London: Thames & Hudson, 1987.

Goehr, Lydia. *The Imaginary Museum of Musical Works*. Oxford: Oxford University Press, 1992.

Goléa, Antoine. *Rencontres avec Olivier Messiaen*. Paris: Slatkine, 1984.

Gorbman, Claudia. *Unheard Melodies: Narrative Film Music*. Bloomington: Indiana University Press; London: British Film Institute, 1987.

Gouk, Penelope. *Music, Science and Natural Magic in Seventeenth-Century England*. New Haven and London: Yale University Press, 1999.

Grant, Stefan-Brook. 'Samuel Beckett's Radio Plays: Music of the Absurd'. Cand. Philol. degree, University of Oslo, 2000. <http://www.samuel-beckett.net/ch1.html>, accessed 30 March 2006.

Griffiths, Paul. *Olivier Messiaen and the Music of Time*. London: Faber and Faber; Ithaca: Cornell University Press, 1985.

Guénon, René. *The Multiple States of Being*, trans. Joscelyn Godwin. New York: Larson, 1984.

Hallinger, Kassius, ed. *Corpus consuetudinum monasticarum*, 12 vols. Siegburg: F. Schmitt, 1963–87. *Ceremoniae Sublacense*, in vol. 2, 1963.

Hardy, Richard P. *The Life of St John of the Cross: Search for Nothing*. London: Darton, Longmann and Todd, 1982.

Harper, John. *The Forms and Orders of Western Liturgy*. Oxford: Clarendon Press, 1991.

Hartlib, Samuel. *The Hartlib Papers: a Complete Text and Image Database of the Papers of Samuel Hartlib (ca. 1600–1662)*, CD-ROM. Ann Arbor: University of Michigan Press, 1995.

Harvey, Jonathan. *In Quest of Spirit: Thoughts on Music*. Berkeley and Los Angeles: University of California Press, 1999.

———. *Music and Inspiration*. London, Faber & Faber, 1999.

Heidegger, Martin. 'Das Ende der Philosophie und die Aufgabe des Denkens' (1964), in *Zur Sache des Denkens*. Tübingen: Niemeyer, 1969, reissued 1976.

Heller, Berndt. 'The Reconstruction of Eisler's Film Music', *Historical Journal of Film, Radio and Television* 18/4 (1998), 541–59.

Henderson, Harold. *Catalyst for Controversy: Paul Carus of Open Court*. Carbondale: Southern Illinois Press, 1993.

Heninger, S. K., Jr. *Touches of Sweet Harmony: Pythagorean Cosmology and Renaissance Poetics*. San Marino, CA: Huntington Library, 1974.

Herissone, Rebecca. *Music Theory in Seventeenth-Century England*. Oxford: Oxford University Press, 2000.

Hermetica: the Greek Corpus Hermeticum *and the Latin* Asclepius, trans., with Notes and Introduction, by Brian P. Copenhaver. Cambridge: Cambridge University Press, 1992.

Hiley, David. *Western Plainchant: a Handbook*. Oxford: Clarendon Press, 1993.

Hill, Matthew. 'Messiaen's *Regard du silence* as an Expression of Catholic Faith'. DMA diss., University of Wisconsin–Madison, 1995.

Hill, Peter. 'Piano Music I', in *The Messiaen Companion*, ed. Peter Hill. Oregon: Amadeus Press, 1995. 72–104.

Holsinger, Bruce W. *Music, Body, and Desire in Medieval Culture: Hildegard of Bingen to Chaucer*. Stanford: Stanford University Press, 2001.

H[ookes], N[icholas]. 'To Mr. Lilly, Musick-Master in Cambridge', in *Amanda, a Sacrifice to an Unknown Goddesse, or, A Free-will Offering of a Loving Heart to a Sweet-heart*. London, 1653. 56–8.

Hopkins, Gerard Manley. *The Poetical Works of Gerard Manley Hopkins*, ed. Norman H. MacKenzie. Oxford: Clarendon, 1990. Including 'The Habit of Perfection', 89–90; also, by MacKenzie: Introduction, xxv–lxxv; Commentary, 215–513.

Hornby, Emma. *Gregorian and Old Roman Eighth-Mode Tracts*. Aldershot: Ashgate, 2002.

_____. 'The Transmission of Western Chant in the 8th and 9th Centuries: Evaluating Kenneth Levy's Reading of the Evidence', *Journal of Musicology* 21 (2004), 418–57.

Hughes, Ed. 'Scoring "Rain": A Contemporary British Composer's Perspective', in *European Foundation Joris Ivens Newsmagazine* No. 11 (November 2005), 26.

Ives, Charles. *Essays Before a Sonata, The Majority, and Other Writings*, ed. Howard Boatwright. New York: W. W. Norton, 1961. Including: *Essays Before a Sonata* (1921), 3–102: 'Emerson', 10–36; 'The Alcotts',44–8; 'Epilogue', 70–102; 'Postface to *114 Songs*' (1922), 120–31.

Jacob, Alexander. 'The Neoplatonic Conception of Nature in More, Cudworth and Berkeley', in *The Uses of Antiquity: the Scientific Revolution and the Classical Tradition*, ed. Stephen Gaukroger. Dordrecht: Kluwer, 1991. 101–21.

James, Jamie. *The Music of the Spheres: Music, Science, and the Natural Order of the Universe*. 1993; London: Abacus, 1995.

James, William. *Essays in Radical Empiricism; A Pluralistic Universe*. New York: Longmans, Green and Co., 1912 and 1909 respectively; repr. together, New York: Longmans, Green and Co., 1943.

_____. *The Meaning of Truth: a Sequel to 'Pragmatism'*. New York: Longmans, Green, and Co., 1909. xii–xiii. Excerpted in *The Writings of William James: a Comprehensive Edition*, ed. John J. McDermott, rev. ed. Chicago: The University of Chicago Press, 1977.

_____. *Pragmatism*. New York: Longmans, Green and Co., 1907; repr. Amherst, NY: Prometheus Books, 1991.

_____. *The Principles of Psychology*. New York: Henry Holt, 1890; repr. New York: Dover, 1950.

_____. *The Writings of William James: a Comprehensive Edition*, ed. John J. McDermott, rev. ed. Chicago: The University of Chicago Press, 1977.

Jankélévitch, Vladimir. *La musique et l'ineffable*. Paris: Seuil, 1983. Trans. Carolyn Abbate as *Music and the Ineffable*. Princeton: Princeton University Press, 2003.

John of the Cross, St. *The Collected Works of St John of the Cross*, trans. Kieran Kavanaugh and Otilio Rodgriguez. Washington DC: ICS Publications, 1991.

_____. *The Complete Works of St John of the Cross, Doctor of the Church*, trans. and ed. E. Allison Peers. Wheathampstead, Herts.: Anthony Clarke, 1964.

John of the Cross, St [San Juan de la Cruz]. *Obras de San Juan de la Cruz*, ed. Padre Silverio de Santa Teresa, 3rd ed. Burgos: Tipografia de 'El Monte Carmelo', 1943.

Johnson, Robert Sherlaw. *Messiaen*. Berkeley: University of California Press, 1975.

Johnston, William. *Silent Music: the Science of Meditation*. [London]: Collins, 1974.

Joyce, James. *Finnegan's Wake* (1939). 3rd edn, London: Faber and Faber, 1966.

_____. *Ulysses* (1936); The Corrected Text, ed. Hans Walter Gabler with Wolfhard Steppe and Claus Melchior. London: The Bodley Head, 1986.

Kant, Immanuel. *Critique of Pure Reason* (1781), trans. Norman Kemp Smith, rev. 2nd ed. Basingstoke: Palgrave Macmillan, 2003.

Kaplinsky, Catherine. 'Emerging Mind from Matter', in *Contemporary Jungian Analysis*, ed. Ian Alister and Christopher Hauke. London, Routledge 1998.

Karp, Theodore. *Aspects of Orality and Formularity in Gregorian Chant*. Evanston, IL: Northwestern University Press, 1998.

Keats, John. 'Ode on a Grecian Urn' (1820), in *Complete Poems*, ed. Jack Stillinger. Cambridge, MA: Harvard University Press, 1982. 372–3.

Kennedy, George A. *Comparative Rhetoric*. Oxford: Oxford University Press, 1998.

Kenny, Anthony. *God and Two Poets: Arthur Hugh Clough and Gerard Manley Hopkins*. London: Sidgwick and Jackson, 1988.

Khan, Hazrat Inayat. *The Music of Life*. 1983; New Lebanon, NY: Omega, 1988.

Lao-tsu [Lao Tzu]. *The Tao Te Ching,* intro. Martin Palmer and Jay Ramsay, trans. Man-Ho Kwok, Martin Palmer and Jay Ramsay. Rockport, Shaftesbury and Brisbane: Element, 1997.

Leppert, Richard. *The Sight of Sound: Music, Representation and the History of the Body*. Berkeley: University of California Press, 1993.

Leshem, Ayval. *Newton on Mathematics and Spiritual Purity*. Dordrecht: Kluwer, 2003.

Levinson, Jerrold. 'Musical Profundity Misplaced', *Journal of Aesthetics and Art Criticism* 50/1 (1992), 58–60.

Levy, Kenneth. *Gregorian Chant and the Carolingians*. Princeton: Princeton University Press, 1998.

Link, Stan. 'Much Ado About Nothing', *Perspectives of New Music* 33/1–2 (Winter/ Summer 1995), 216–72.

_____ [Stanley Boyd Link]. 'Essays towards Musical Negation'. PhD diss., Princeton University, 1995.

Lippman, Edward. *A History of Western Musical Aesthetics*. Lincoln and London: University of Nebraska Press, 1992.

Lissa, Zofia. 'Die Ästhetischen Funktionen der Stille und Pause in der Musik' (1962). Repr. as 'Stille und Pause in der Musik', in Lissa, *Aufsätze zur Musikästhetik: eine Auswahl*. Berlin: Henschel, 1969.

Littlefield, Richard. 'The Silence of the Frames', in *Music/Ideology: Resisting the Aesthetic*, ed. and intro. Adam Krims, commentary Henry Klumpenhouwer. [Amsterdam]: G&B Arts International, 1998. 213–31.

Lochner, Fabian. *Source Readings on the Practice and Spirituality of Chant: New Texts, New Approaches*. <http://www.luc.edu/publications/medieval/vol8/8ch6. html>, accessed 4 April 2005.

Lockspeiser, Edward, ed. *The Literary Clef*. London: John Calder, 1958.

Loewald, Hans W. 'On the Therapeutic Action of Psycho-Analysis', *International Journal of Psychoanalysis* 41 (1960), 16–33.

London, Kurt. *Film Music: a Summary of the Characteristic Features of its History, Aesthetics, Technique, and Possible Developments*, trans. Eric S. Bensinger. London: Faber & Faber, 1936.

McClary, Susan. *Conventional Wisdom: the Content of Musical Form*. Berkeley and Los Angeles: University of California Press, 2001.

Mace, Thomas. *Musick's Monument*. London, 1676.

McGee, Timothy. *The Sound of Medieval Song*. Oxford: Clarendon Press, 1998.

McKinnon, James. *The Advent Project: the Later-Seventh-Century Creation of the Roman Mass Proper*. Berkeley: University of California Press, 2000.

_____. 'The Early Christian Period and the Latin Middle Ages: Introduction', in *Strunk's Source Readings in Music History*, rev. ed. Leo Treitler. New York: W. W. Norton, 1998. 113–18.

_____. 'Lector Chant versus Scola Chant: a Question of Historical Plausibility', in *Laborare fratres in unum: Festschrift Laszlo Dobszay zum 60. Geburtstag*, ed. David Hiley and Janka Szendrei. Hildesheim and Zurich: Weidmann, 1995. 201–11.

Maconchy, Elizabeth. 'String Quartet No. 6'. Unpublished talk, Oxford, 3 February 1952. Manuscript held at St Hilda's College Library, Oxford.

_____. 'What is Modern Music'. Unpublished talk, Dublin Music Society, 1940. Manuscript held at St Hilda's College Library, Oxford.

Maiello, Suzanne. 'The Sound-Object: a Hypothesis about Prenatal Auditory Experience and Memory', *Journal of Child Psychotherapy* 21/1 (1995), 23-41.

Malloch, Stephen N. 'Mothers and Infants and Communicative Musicality', *Musicae Scientiae* (1999–2000), 29–58. Special issue: *Rhythm, Musical Narrative, and Origin of Human Communication*.

Maltz, Daniel N. 'Joyful Noise and Reverent Silence: the Significance of Noise in Pentecostal Worship', in *Perspectives on Silence*, ed. Deborah Tannen and Muriel Saville-Troike. Norwood, NJ: Ablex Publishing, 1985. 113–37.

Markell, Mary Jane. *Sand, Water, Silence – the Embodiment of Spirit: Explorations in Matter and Psyche*. London, Jessica Kingsley, 2002.

Marks, Martin Miller. *Music and the Silent Film*. New York: Oxford University Press, 1997.

Marmion, Columba. *Le Christ dans ses mystères* (1919*)*, trans. Mother M. St Thomas as *Christ in His Mysteries*. St Louis: B. Herder Book Co., 1939.

Marsh, Roger. 'Heroic Motives: Roger Marsh Considers the Relationship Between Sign and Sound in "Complex" Music', *Musical Times* 135 (February 1994), 83–6.

Mars-Jones, Adam. 'Quiet, Please', *Granta* 86 (Summer 2004), 244–9.

Matar, N. I. '"Alone in Our Eden": a Puritan Utopia in Restoration England', *Seventeenth Century* 2 (1987), 189–98.

_____. '"Oyle of Joy": the Early Prose of Peter Sterry', *Philological Quarterly* 71/1 (1992), 31–46.

_____. Forward to Peter Sterry, *Select Writings*, ed. Matar. New York: Peter Lang, 1994.

_____. 'Peter Sterry and the "Paradise Within": a Study of the Emmanuel College Letters', *Restoration* 13 (1989), 76–85.

Messiaen, Olivier. *Music and Color: Conversations with Claude Samuel*, trans. E. Thomas Glasgow. Oregon: Amadeus Press, 1994.

_____. Foreword to *Quatuor pour la fin du temps*. Paris: Durand, 1941. 1–4.

_____. *Technique de mon language musical*. Paris: Alphonse Leduc, 1944; English trans. John Satterfield, Paris: Leduc, 1956.

_____. *Traité de rythme, de couleur et d'ornithologie*. Paris: Alphonse Leduc, 1996.

_____. General introduction to *Vingt regards sur L'Enfant-Jèsus*. Paris: S. A. Durand Editions Musicales, 1944. Also Preface to 'Regard du silence', 128–37.

_____. Liner notes to *Vingt regards sur L'Enfant-Jésus*. Yvonne Loriod (Messiaen's wife), piano. Recorded 1973. CD, Erato 4509-91705, 1993 (digitally re-mastered from original analogue recording).

Michaely, Aloyse. *Die Musik Olivier Messiaens: Untersuchungen zum Gesamtschaffen*. Hamburg: Karl Dieter Wagner, 1987.

Miles, T. R. *Religious Experience*. London: Macmillan, 1972.

Miller, Leta E. 'Cultural Intersections: John Cage in Seattle (1938–1940)', in *John Cage: Music, Philosophy and Intention, 1933–1950*, ed. David W. Patterson. New York and London: Routledge, 2002. 45–82.

Milson, John. 'Organ Music I', in *The Messiaen Companion*, ed. Peter Hill. Oregon: Amadeus Press, 1995. 51–71.

Moldenhauer, Hans, in collaboration with Rosaleen Moldenhauer. *Anton von Webern: a Chronicle of his Life and Work*. London: Victor Gollancz, 1978.

Mompou, Federico. *Discurso leido en la solemne recepción pública de D. Federico Mompou: Dencausse el día 17 de mayo de 1952*. Barcelone: Real Academia de Bellas Artes de San Jorge, n.d.

More, Henry. *A Platonick Song of the Soul*, ed. and with an introductory study by Alexander Jacob. Lewisburg, PA, and London: Bucknell University Press, 1998.

Moyer, Ann E. *Musica scientia: Musical Scholarship in the Italian Renaissance*. Ithaca: Cornell University Press, 1992.

Mulvey, Laura. *Death 24x a Second: Stillness and the Moving Image*. London: Reaktion Books, 2006.

Nacht, Sacha. 'Silence as an Integrative Factor', *International Journal of Psychoanalysis* 45 (1964), 299-303.

Nadeau, Maurice. *Histoire du surréalisme*. Paris: Éditions du Seuil 1964.

Narbonne, Jean-Marc. 'Action, Contemplation and Interiority in the Thinking of Beauty in Plotinus', in *Neoplatonism and Western Aesthetics*, ed. Aphrodite Alexandrakis. Albany: State University of New York Press, 2002. 3–18.

Nattiez, Jean-Jacques, ed. *The Boulez–Cage Correspondence*, trans. Robert Samuels. Cambridge: Cambridge University Press, 1993.

Nettl, Bruno. 'Music', in *The New Grove Dictionary of Music and Musicians*, 2nd ed., ed. Stanley Sadie and John Tyrrell. London: Macmillan, 2001. 17: 425–37.

Nevins, Mary. 'Peter Sterry, a Platonic Independent'. PhD diss., Columbia University, 1954.

Newman, Barbara. *Sister of Wisdom: St Hildegard's Theology of the Feminine*. Aldershot: Scolar, 1987.

Nicholls, David. *American Experimental Music, 1890–1940*. Cambridge: Cambridge University Press, 1990.

Nichols, Roger. *Messiaen*. London: Oxford University Press, 1975.

Nicholson, Marjorie Hope and Sarah Hutton, eds. *The Conway Letters: the Correspondence of Anne, Viscountess Conway, Henry More and their Friends, 1642-1684*. 1930; Oxford: Clarendon, 1992.

Nieto, José C. *Mystic, Rebel, Saint: a Study of St John of the Cross*. Geneva: Librairie Droz, 1979.

Nisargadatta, Sri. *I am That*. 1976; Bombay: Chetana, 1991.

Noda, Matao. 'East-West Synthesis in Kitaro Nishida', *Philosophy East and West* 4/4 (January 1955), 345–59.

Nwoye, Gregory O. 'Eloquent Silence among the Igbo of Nigeria', in *Perspectives on Silence*, ed. Deborah Tannen and Muriel Saville-Troike. Norwood, NJ: Ablex Publishing, 1985. 185–91.

Ohtake, Noriko. *Creative Sources for the Music of Toru Takemitsu*. Aldershot: Scolar Press, 1993.

Oida, Yoshi. *The Invisible Actor*, trans. Lorna Marshall. London, Methuen, 1997.

O'Meara, Dominic J. *Plotinus: an Introduction to the 'Enneads'*. Oxford: Clarendon, 1993.

O'Rourke, James, ed. *Ode on a Grecian Urn: Hypercanonicity and Pedagogy*. (Romantic Circles Praxis Series). Electronic edition: University of Maryland, 2003. <http://www.rc.umd.edu/praxis/grecianurn>, accessed 19 July 2005.

Page, Christopher. *Summa musice: a Thirteenth Century Manual for Singers* Cambridge: Cambridge University Press, 1991.

Palisca, Claude V. *Humanism in Italian Renaissance Musical Thought*. New Haven and London: Yale University Press, 1985.

_____. 'Moving the Affections through Music: Pre-Cartesian Psycho-Physiological Theories', in *Number to Sound: the Musical Way to the Scientific Revolution*, ed. Paolo Gozza. Dordrecht: Kluwer, 2000. 289–308.

Parker, Samuel. *A Free and Impartial Censure of the Platonick Philosophie*. Oxford, 1666.

Pascal, Blaise. *Pensées sur la religion et sur quelques autres sujets* (1665), trans A. J. Krailsheimer as *Pensées*. Harmondsworth: Penguin, 1966.

Patrides, C. A. 'The High And Aiery Hills of Platonisme: an Introduction to the Cambridge Platonists', in *The Cambridge Platonists*, ed. Patrides. London: Edward Arnold, 1969. 1–41.

Patterson, David. 'Appraising the Catchwords, c. 1942–1959: John Cage's Asian-Derived Rhetoric and the Historical Reference of Black Mountain College'. PhD diss., Columbia University, 1996.

————. 'The Picture That Is Not in the Colors: Cage, Coomaraswamy, and the Impact of India', in *John Cage: Music, Philosophy and Intention, 1933–1950*, ed. David W. Patterson. New York and London: Routledge, 2002. 177–215.

Peek, Philip. 'Re-Sounding Silences', in *Sound*, ed. Patricia Kruth and Henry Stobart. Cambridge: Cambridge University Press, 1999. 16–33.

Perry, Ralph Barton. *The Thought and Character of William James*, 2 vols. Boston: Little, Brown, 1935.

Peyser, Joan. *Boulez*. New York: Schirmer Books, 1976.

Picard, Max. *Die Welt des Schweigens*. Erlenbach: Eugen Rentsch Verlag, 1948. Trans. Stanley Goodman as *The World of Silence*. London: Harvill, 1948; repr. Chicago: Regnery Gateway, 1952; facs. repr. Wichita, KS: Eighth Day Press, 2002.

Pickstock, Catherine. 'Soul, City and Cosmos After Augustine', in *Radical Orthodoxy: a New Theology*, ed. John Milbank, Catherine Pickstock and Graham Ward. London and New York, Routledge, 1999. 243–77.

Pinto, Vivian de Sola. *Peter Sterry, Platonist and Puritan: a Biographical and Critical Study with Passages Selected from his Writings*. 1934; New York: Greenwood Press, 1968.

Piontelli, Alessandra. *From Fetus to Child: an Observational and Psychoanalytic Study*. London: Tavistock/Routledge, 1992.

Plotinus. *The Enneads*, trans. Stephen MacKenna, 4th ed., rev. B. S. Page. London: Faber and Faber, 1969.

Poggioli, Renato. *Teoria dell'arte d'avanguardia*, trans. Gerald Fitzgerald as *The Theory of the Avant-Garde*. Cambridge, MA: Belknap Press of Harvard University Press, 1968.

Pople, Antony. 'Messiaen's Musical Language: an Introduction', in *The Messiaen Companion*, ed. Peter Hill. Oregon: Amadeus Press, 1995. 17–31.

Potter, John. 'Choir as Ensemble: the Debt to Early Music', in *Tapiola Choirbook*. Forthcoming.

————. 'Ensemble Singing', in *Cambridge Companion to Singing*, ed. John Potter. Cambridge: Cambridge University Press, 2000. 158–64.

Prévost, Edwin. *No Sound is Innocent*. Harlow, Essex: Copula, 1995.

Prince, Stephen. 'Guns and Cameras: From the PCA to the Passion of the Christ'. Unpublished talk given at Vanderbilt University, 30 September 2005.

Quinodoz, Danielle. *Words that Touch: a Psychoanalyst Learns to Speak*, trans. Philip Slotkin. London, Karnac Books, 2003.

Radomski, James. *Manuel García (1775–1832): Chronicle of the Life of a Bel Canto Tenor at the Dawn of Romanticism*. Oxford: Oxford University Press, 2000.

Randel, Don Michael, comp. 'Rest', in *Harvard Concise Dictionary of Music*. Cambridge, MA: Belknapp Press, 1978. 421.

Rastall, Richard. 'Rest' in *The New Grove Dictionary of Music and Musicians*, 2nd ed., ed. Stanley Sadie and John Tyrrell. London: Macmillan, 2001. 21: 228–9.

Rattansi, P. M. and J. E. McGuire. 'Newton and the Pipes of Pan', *Notes and Records of the Royal Society of London* 21 (1966), 108–43.

Rée, Jonathan. *I See a Voice: a Philosophical History*. London: Flamingo, 2000.

Retallack, Joan. 'Introduction: Conversations in Retrospect', in John Cage, *MusiCage: Cage Muses on Words, Art and Music*. Hanover and London: University Press of New England, 1996. xiii–xliii.

_____. 'Poethics of a Complex Realism', in *John Cage: Composed In America*, ed. Marjorie Perloff and Charles Junkerman. Chicago: University of Chicago Press, 1994. 242–73.

Richardson, Dorothy. 'Continuous Performance 4: a Thousand Pities', *Close Up* 1 (October 1927), 60–64. Repr. in *Close Up, 1927–1933: Cinema and Modernism*, ed. James Donald, Anne Friedberg and Laura Marcus. London: Cassell, 1998. 166–8.

Rinpoche, Sogyal. 'The Mind and the Nature of Mind', in *The Tibetan Book of Living and Dying*. London: Rider Books, 1992. 46–8.

Rist, John. 'Plotinus and Christian Philosophy', in *The Cambridge Companion to Plotinus*, ed. Lloyd P. Gerson. Cambridge: Cambridge University Press, 1996. 386–413.

Rössler, Almut. *Contributions to the Spiritual World of Olivier Messiaen*, trans. Barabara Dagg and Nancy Poland. Duisburg: Gilles and Francke, 1986.

Roullière, Yves. 'La musique tacite', *La nouvelle revue française* nos 462–3 (1991), 27–31.

Sabatini, Arthur J. 'Silent Performances: On Reading John Cage', in *John Cage at Seventy Five*, ed. Richard Fleming and William Duckworth. (*The Bucknell Review* 32/2.) Lewisburg: Bucknell University Press; London: Associated University Presses, 1989. 74–96.

Sabbadini, Andrea. 'Listening to Silence', *Scandinavian Psychoanalytic Review* 15 (1992), 27–36.

_____. 'On Sounds, Children, Identity and a "Quite Unmusical" Man', *British Journal of Psychotherapy* 14/2 (1997), 189–196.

Sahukar, Mani. *Indian Classical Music*. New Delhi: Reliance, 1986.

Sandbothe, Mike. *Die Verzeitlichung der Zeit: Grundtendenzen der modernen Zeitdebatte in Philosophie und Wissenschaft*. Darmstadt: Wissenschaftliche Buchgesellschaft, 1998.

Sârngadeva. *Sangîtaratnâkara of Sârngadeva: Sanskrit Text and English Translation With Comments and Notes*, trans. R. K. Shringy. New Delhi: Munshiram Manoharlal, 1999. Vol. 1.

Sayres, Sohnya. *Susan Sontag: the Elegiac Modernist*. London: Routledge, 1990.

Scarry, Elaine. *The Body in Pain: the Making and Unmaking of the World*. Oxford and New York: Oxford University Press, 1985.

Schafer, R. Murray. *Voices of Tyranny, Temples of Silence*. Indian River, Ont.: Arcana Editions, 1993.

Schedler, Norbert O. 'Talk about God-Talk: a Historical Introduction', in *Philosophy of Religion: Contemporary Perspectives*, ed. Schedler. New York: Macmillan, 1974. 221–50.

Schmidt, Hans. 'Untersuchungen zu den Tractus des zweiten Tones', *Kirchenmusikalisches Jahrbuch* 42 (1958), 1–25.

Schoenberg, Arnold. Foreword to Webern's *Six Bagatelles for String Quartet, Op. 9*. Vienna: Universal, 1924. [2].

Schopenhauer, Arthur. *Die Welt als Wille und Vorstellung* (1819, rev. 1844), trans. E. F. J. Payne *The World as Will and Representation*. Indian Hills, CO: Falcon's Wing Press, 1958; repr. with minor corrections, New York: Dover, 1966.

Scott, David. 'William James and Buddhism: American Pragmatism and the Orient', *Religion* 30 (2000), 333–52.

Seidel, Wilhelm. 'Stille', in *Die Musik in Geschichte und Gegenwart*, 2nd ed., ed. Ludwig Finscher. Kassel: Bärenreiter, 1998. 8: 1760–65.

Senzsaki, Nyogen and Ruth Strout McCandless, trans. and ed. *The Iron Flute: 100 Zen Koans*. Boston, Rutland and Tokyo: Tuttle Publishing, 2000.

Shultis, Chris. *Silencing the Sounded Self: John Cage and the American Experimental Tradition*. Boston: Northeastern University Press, 1998.

'Silence *noun*', in *The Oxford Dictionary of English*, rev. ed., ed. Catherine Soanes and Angus Stevenson. Oxford: Oxford University Press, 2005. Accessed in *Oxford Reference Online*, <http://www.oxfordreference.com>, accessed 24 March 2006.

Sinclair, James B. *A Descriptive Catalogue of The Music of Charles Ives*. New Haven: Yale University Press, 1999.

Smith, Barbara Herrnstein. *Poetic Closure: a Study of How Poems End*. Chicago and London: Chicago University Press, 1968.

Smith, John. *Select Discourses*. London, 1660.

Smoje, Dujka. *Silence as Atemporal Music: Tabula rasa, Stille, Silence*. Unpublished paper presented at the conference *Silence and Music*, University of York, October 2003.

Solomon, Larry. 'The Sounds of Silence'. Accessed at <http://solomonmusic.net/4min33se.htm>, on 29 March 2007.

Sontag, Susan. 'The Aesthetics of Silence', in *Styles of Radical Will*. New York: Farrar, Straus and Giroux, 1969; reissued London: Vintage, 1994. 3–34.

_____. *Against Interpretation and Other Essays*. New York: Farrar, Strauss & Giroux, 1967; reissued London: Vintage, 1994.

_____. *Illness as Metaphor*. New York: Farrar, Straus and Giroux, 1978.

_____. 'In Memory of their Feelings', in *Cage–Cunningham–Johns: Dancers on a Plane*, ed. Judy Adam. London: Anthony d'Offay Gallery, 1989; reissued London: Thames and Hudson in association with Anthony d'Offay Gallery, 1990. 13–23.

_____. *On Photography*. New York: Farrar, Straus and Giroux, 1977; reissued London: Penguin Books, 1978.

Souris, André. 'Notes sur le rythme concret', *Polyphonie* 2 (1948), 4–11. Repr. in Souris, *Conditions de la musique et autres écrits*. Bruxelles and Paris: Editions de l'Université de Bruxelles, 1977. 241–7.

Spring, Matthew. *The Lute in Britain: a History of the Instrument and its Music*. Oxford: Oxford University Press, 2001.

Stein, Gertrude. *Selected Writings of Gertrude Stein*, ed. Carl Van Vechten. New York: The Modern Library, 1962. Including: *The Autobiography of Alice B. Toklas* (1932), 3–237; 'The Gradual Making of the Making of Americans' (1934), 241–58.

Steiner, George. *Real Presences: Is there Anything in What We Say?* London and Boston: Faber and Faber, 1989. As *Real Presences*, Chicago: University of Chicago Press, 1989.

Stern, Daniel. *The First Relationship: Infant and Mother*. Cambridge, MA: Harvard University Press, 1977.

_____. *The Interpersonal World of the Infant: a View from Psychoanalysis and Developmental Psychology*. New York: Basic Books, 1985, 2000.

_____. 'A Micro-analysis of Mother-infant Interaction: Behaviors Regulating Social Contact Between a Mother and her Three-and-a-half Month-old Twins', *Journal of American Academy of Child Psychiatry* 10 (1971), 501–17.

_____. *The Present Moment in Psychotherapy and Everyday Life*. New York and London: W. W. Norton, 2004.

Sterry, Peter. *The Appearance of God to Man in the Gospel*. London, 1710.

_____. 'The Consort of Musicke', in *Select Writings*, ed. N. I. Matar. New York: Peter Lang, 1994. 168–76.

_____. *A Discourse of the Freedom of the Will*. London, 1675.

_____. Letter to Peter Sterry, jnr. Cambridge, Emmanuel College Library MS 292. Fols. 155–6.

_____. 'Of the Sun'. Cambridge, Emmanuel College Library MS 294. Fol. 84.

_____. *The Rise, Race, and Royalty of the Kingdom of God*. London, 1683.

_____. 'That the State of Wicked Men after this Life is Mixt of Evill, and Good Things'. Cambridge, Emmanuel College Library MS 291. Fol. 102.

_____. [Untitled romance fragment to incomplete spiritual romance]. Cambridge, Emmanuel College Library MS 292. Fols. 129–40.

_____. 'What is God?'. Cambridge, Emmanuel College Library MS 292. Fol. 320.

Strahle, Graham. 'Fantasy and Music in Sixteenth- and Seventeenth-Century England'. PhD diss., University of Adelaide, 1987.

Strohm Reinhard. *Music in Late Medieval Bruges*. Oxford: Clarendon, 1990.

Suso, Henry. *Heinrich Suso's, genannt Amandus, Leben und Schriften*, ed. Melchior Diepenbrock. Regensburg: Pustet 1829.

Sutton, Julie P. 'Hidden Music: an Exploration of Silence in Music and Music Therapy', in *Musical Creativity: Multidisciplinary Research in Theory and Practice*, ed. Irene Deliège and Geraint Wiggins. Hove: Psychology Press, 2006. 252–72.

_____. 'Hidden Music – an Exploration of Silences in Music and Music Therapy', *Music Therapy Today (online)* 6/3 (2005), 375–95, available at <http://www.MusicTherapyWorld.net>.

_____. 'The Invisible Handshake": an Investigation of Free Musical Improvisation as a Form of Conversation'. PhD diss., University of Ulster, 2001.

_____. 'Listening To and Thinking About the Spaces Between the Notes: Silence and Musical Interaction'. Unpublished paper presented at Aalborg University, Denmark, October 2002.

_____. 'The Pause that Follows: Silence, Improvised Music and Music Therapy'. Unpublished paper presented at the *5th European Music Therapy Congress*, Naples, April 2001.

Sutton, Julie P., ed. *Music, Music Therapy and Trauma: International Perspectives*. London, Jessica Kingsley, 2002.

Suzuki, Daisetz Teitaro. *Mysticism: Christian and Buddhist*. London: George Allen & Unwin, 1957.

_____. 'Zen and Pragmatism – A Reply', *Philosophy East and West*, 4/2 (July 1954), 167–74.

Takemitsu, Tōru. *Confronting Silence: Selected Writings*, trans. and ed. Yoshiko Kakudo and Glenn Glasow, with a foreword by Seiji Ozawa. Berkeley: Fallen Leaf Press, 1995.

Tarkovsky, Andrey. *Zapechatlennoe vremia*, trans Kitty Hunter-Blair as *Sculpting in Time: Reflections on the Cinema* (1986). 4th U. of Texas ed., Austin: University of Texas Press, 1994.

Tavener, John. *The Music of Silence: a Composer's Testament*. London and New York: Faber and Faber, 1999.

Taylor, Charles. *Sources of the Self: the Making of the Modern Identity*. Cambridge, MA: Harvard University Press, 1989.

Teahan, John F. 'The Place of Silence in Thomas Merton's Life and Thought', in *The Message of Thomas Merton*, ed. Brother Patrick Hart. Kalamazoo, MI: Cistercian Publications, 1981. 91–114.

Teply, Alison. 'The Mystical Theology of Peter Sterry: a Study in Neoplatonist Puritanism'. PhD diss., University of Cambridge, 2004.

Teresa of Ávila, St. *The Life of Teresa of Ávila by Herself*, trans. with an introduction by J. M. Cohen. Harmondsworth: Penguin, 1957.

Thompson, Colin P. *The Poet and Mystic: a Study of the Canto espiritual of San Juan de la Cruz*. Oxford: Oxford University Press, 1977.

Thorpe, Clarence de Witt. *The Aesthetic Theory of Thomas Hobbes, with Special Reference to his Contribution to the Psychological Approach in English Literary Criticism*. Ann Arbor: University of Michigan Press, 1940.

Toesca, Maurice. *Les douze regards* (1944), pubd as *La Nativité* in Michel Ciry, *La Nativité: eaux-fortes originales*. Paris: Marcel Sautier, [1952].

Tomkins, Calvin. *The Bride and the Bachelors: the Heretical Courtship in Modern Art*. New York: Viking Press, 1965.

Tomlinson, Gary. *Music in Renaissance Magic: Toward a Historiography of Others*. Chicago and London: University of Chicago Press, 1993.

Treitler, Leo. *With Voice and Pen: Coming to Know Medieval Song and How it was Made*. New York: Oxford University Press, 2003.

Trevarthen, Colwyn. 'Communication and Cooperation in Early Infancy: a Description of Primary Intersubjectivity', in *Before Speech: the Beginning of Interpersonal Communication*, ed. Margaret M. Bullowa. Cambridge and New York: Cambridge University Press, 1979. 231–347.

_____. 'The Foundations of Intersubjectivity: Development of Interpersonal and Co-operative Understanding of Infants', in *The Social Foundations of Language and Thought: Essays in Honor of Jerome S. Bruner*, ed. David R. Olson. New York: W. W. Norton, 1980. 316–42.

_____. 'Musicality and the Intrinsic Motive Pulse: Evidence from Human Psychobiology and Infant Communication', *Musicae Scientiae* (1999–2000), 155–211. Special issue: *Rhythm, Musical Narrative, and Origin of Human Communication*.

Underhill, Evelyn. *Mysticism: a Study in the Nature and Development of Man's Spiritual Consciousness* (1912). (University Paperbacks.) London: Methuen, 1960.

Van Dijk, Steven. 'Medieval Terminology and Methods of Psalm Singing', *Musica disciplina* 6 (1952), 7–26.

_____. 'Saint Bernard and the Instituta Patrum of Saint Gall', *Musica disciplina* 4 (1950), 99–109.

Van Emmerik, Paul. 'An Imaginary Grid: Rhythmic Structure in Cage's Music up to circa 1950', in *John Cage: Music, Philosophy , and Intention, 1933–1950*, ed. David W. Patterson. New York and London: Routledge, 2002. 217–38.

Vasoli, Cesare. *Profezia e ragione: studi sulla cultura del Cinquecento e del Seicento*. Naples: Morano, 1974.

Vattimo, Gianni. *La fine della modernità*, trans. and with introduction by Jon R. Snyder as *The End of Modernity: Nihilism and Hermeneutics in Post-Modern Culture*. Baltimore: Johns Hopkins University Press; Cambridge: Polity Press, 1988; reissued Cambridge: Polity Press, 1994.

Vollaerts, Jan. *Rhythmic Proportions in Early Medieval Ecclesiastical Chant*. Leiden: E. J. Brill, 1958.

Voss, Angela. 'Marsilio Ficino, the Second Orpheus', in *Music as Medicine: the History of Music Therapy since Antiquity*, ed. Pergrine Horden. Aldershot: Ashgate, 2000. 154–72.

_____. '*Orpheus Redivivus*: the Musical Magic of Marsilio Ficino', in *Marsilio Ficino: his Theology, his Philosophy, his Legacy*, ed. Michael J. B. Allen and Valery Rees. Leiden: Brill, 2002. 227–41.

Walhout, Donald. *Send My Roots Rain: a Study of Religious Experience in the Poetry of Gerard Manley Hopkins*. Athens and London, OH: Ohio University Press, 1981.

Walker, D. P. *The Decline of Hell: Seventeenth-Century Discussions of Eternal Torment*. Chicago: University of Chicago Press, 1964.

_____. *Spiritual and Demonic Magic from Ficino to Campanella*. London: The Warburg Institute, 1958.

[Wallis, John.] *Truth Tried: or, Animadversions on a Treatise Published by the Right Honourable Robert Lord Brook*. London, 1642.

Westlake, Aubrey T. *The Pattern of Health: a Search for a Greater Understanding of the Life Force in Health and Disease*. Boulder, CO: Shambhala, 1973.

White, Jeremiah. *The Restoration of All Things: or, A Vindication of the Goodness and Grace of God*. London, 1712.

Wilber, Ken. *Grace and Grit*. Boston and London: Shambhala, 1991.

Wilkins, John. *A Discourse Concerning a New World & Another Planet*. London, 1640.

Williams, Alan. 'Historical and Theoretical Issues in the Coming of Recorded Sound to the Cinema', in *Sound Theory, Sound Practice*, ed. Rick Altman. New York: Routledge, 1992. 126–37.

Wojtyla, Karol. *Faith According to St John of the Cross* (1948), trans. Jordan Aumann. San Francisco: Ignatius Press, 1981.

Music Sources

Manuscript Sources

Benevento, Biblioteca capitolare, VI.34. Facsimile: *Paléographie musicale* 15. Tournai: Société Saint-Jean l'Evangéliste, Desclée, 1937.

Einsiedeln, Benediktinerkloster, Musikbibliothek, 121.

Paris, Bibliothèque Nationale de France, lat. 903. Facsimile: *Paléographie musicale* 13. Tournai: Société Saint-Jean l'Evangéliste, Desclée, 1925.

Oxford, Bodleian Library, Canon. liturg. 340.

Oxford, Bodleian Library, Laud misc. 358.

St Gallen, Stiftsbibliothek, 359. Facsimile: *Paléographie musicale* series 2: 2. Solesmes, 1924. 95–6.

Published Scores

Cage, John. *Experiences II* (1948). New York: Henmar Press, 1961.

_____. *Sonatas and Interludes* (1946–8). New York: Henmar Press, 1960.

Eisler, Hanns. *Vierzehn Arten, den Regen zu beschreibe: Variationen für Flöte, Klarinette, Violine, Viola, Violoncello and Klavier, opus 70* (1941), new ed., ed. Manfred Grabs. Leipzig: Edition Peters, 1976.

Hughes, Ed. *Light Cuts Through Dark Skies*. York: University of York Music Press, 2001.

Ives, Charles. *Central Park in the Dark* (1906), ed. John Kirkpatrick and Jacques-Louis Monod. Hillsdale, NY: Mobart Music Publications, Inc., 1973.

_____. *The Unanswered Question* (1906), ed. Paul C. Echols and Noel Zahler. New York: Peer International, 1984.

Lütolf, Max, ed. *Das Graduale von Santa Cecilia in Trastevere (Cod. Bodmer 74)*. Cologny-Genève: Fondation Martin Bodmer, 1987.

Maconchy, Elizabeth. *String Quartet No. 2* (1936). London: Alfred Legnick, 1959.

Messiaen, Olivier. *Le banquet céleste: pour orgue*. Paris: Alphonse Leduc, 1934; nouvelle éd., Paris: Leduc, 1960.

_____. *Vingt regards sur L'Enfant-Jèsus*. Paris: S. A. Durand Editions Musicales, 1944.

Takemitsu, Tōru. *A Way A Lone: for String Quartet*. Mainz and New York: Schott, 1982.

_____. *A Way A Lone: for String Orchestra*. Mainz and New York: Schott, 1981.
Webern, Anton. *Six Bagatelles for String Quartet, Op. 9*. Vienna: Universal, 1924.

Sound Recordings

Beckett, Samuel. *Words and Music*. Dir. Everett C. Frost. Music by Morton Feldman.
    With Alvin Epstein, David Warrilow and the Bowery Ensemble. (Part of *The
    Beckett Festival of Radio Plays*.) CD, Everett Review, 1987.
Joyce, James. *Finnegan's Wake*, Part I, Chapter 8, excerpts read by Joyce. Recorded
    August 1929. Accessed at <http://www.finneganswake.org/joycereading.htm>,
    accessed on 11 March 2006.
_____. *Ulysses*. Dir. Roger Marsh. Produced by Nicolas Soames. Recorded and ed.
    by Jez Wells. With Jim Norton and Marcella Riordan. 22 CDs, Naxos Audiobooks
    NAX30912, 2004.
Maconchy, Elizabeth. *String Quartets Nos. 1–4*. (*The Complete String Quartets*,
    vol. 1.) Hanson String Quartet. CD, Unicorn-Kanchana DKP(CD) 9080, 1989.
    Reissued in *Complete String Quartets*, CD, Forum FRC9301, 2003.
Messiaen, Olivier. *Vingt regards sur L'Enfant-Jésus*. Yvonne Loriod (Messiaen's
    wife), piano. Recorded 1973. CD, Erato 4509-91705, 1993 (digitally re-mastered
    from original analogue recording).
Verdi, Giuseppe. *La traviata*. With Rosa Ponselle, Frederick Jagel and Lawrence
    Tibbett. The Metropolitan Opera Chorus and Orchestra, cond. Ettore Panizza.
    Recorded: New York, 5 January 1935. Naxos Historical 8.110032–33, 1998.
_____. *La traviata*. With Giuseppi di Steffano, Eleanor Steber and Robert Merrill.
    The Metropolitan Opera Chorus and Orchestra, cond. Giuseppi Antonicelli.
    Recorded: New York, 22 January 1949. Naxos Historical 8.110115–16, 2001.
_____. *La traviata*. With Cheryl Studer, Luciano Pavarotti and Juan Pons. The
    Metropolitan Opera Orchestra and Chorus, cond. James Levine. Recorded: New
    York, June 1991. Deutsche Grammophon, DGG 437 726–2, 1992.
_____. *La traviata*. With Edita Gruberová, Neil Shicoff and Giogio Zancanaro.
    The Ambrosian singers and London Symphony Orchestra, cond. Carlo Rizzi.
    Recorded: London, Abbey Road Studios, February 1992. Warner, Apex 2564
    61511–2, c. 1993.
Veritas mea: Chant Grégorien dans l'Église romaine de Tavant. With Dominique
    Vellard and Emmanuel Bonnardot. LP, STIL Editions, Stil 2106 SAN 84, 1985.

Films

Apocalypse Now. Dir. Francis Ford Coppola. Screenplay by John Milius and F. F.
    Coppola after Joseph Conrad's *Heart of Darkness*. Cinematography by Vittorio
    Storaro. Music by Carmine Coppola and F. F. Coppola, also by The Doors ('The
    End') and from Richard Wagner's *Die Walküre*. With Marlon Brando, Martin
    Sheen, Robert Duvall, Dennis Hopper and Harrison Ford. Zoetrope/United
    Artists, 1979.

C'era una volta il West / Once Upon a Time in the West. Dir. Sergio Leone. Written by Dario Argento, Bernardo Bertolucci and Leone. Cinematography by Tonino Delli Colli. Film score by Ennio Morricone. With Henry Fonda, Charles Bronson, Claudia Cardinale, Jason Robards and Gabriele Ferzetti. 165 minutes, mono. Rafran–San Marco, 1968; (USA) Paramount, 1969.

Il buono, il brutto, il cattivo / The Good, the Bad, and the Ugly. Dir. Sergio Leone. Produced by Alberto Grimaldi. Written by Luciano Vincenzoni and Leone. Cinematography by Tonino Delli Colli. Music by Ennio Morricone. With Clint Eastwood, Lee van Cleef, Eli Wallach and Aldo Giuffrè. PEA/Gonzales/ Constantin, 1966.

Entr'acte. Dir. René Clair. Screenplay by Francis Picabia adapted by Clair. Cinematography by Jimmy Berliet. With Francis Picabia, Marcel Douchamp, Man Ray, Jean Börlin, Inge Frïss, Darius Milhaud, Erik Satie, Georges Auric etc. 22 minutes, silent, black and white. 1924. Originally shown with music by Erik Satie, at the Théâtre des Champs Elyseés, Paris.

The Jazz Singer. Dir. Alan Crosland. Screenplay by Samson Raphaelson. Vitaphone sound. With Al Jolson and May McAvoy. 88 minutes. Warner Bros., 1927.

Lola rennt / Run Lola Run. Dir. and written by Tom Tykwer. Soundtrack by Tom Tykwer, John Klimek and Rynhold Heil. With Franka Potente and Moritz Bleibtreu. 81 minutes. X-Filme Creative Pool, 1998.

Nosferatu: Phantom der Nacht / Nosferatu the Vampyre. Dir. Werner Herzog. Screenplay by Herzog after Bram Stoker's *Dracula*. Cinematography by Jorg Schmidt-Reitwein. Music by Popol Vuh. With Klaus Kinski, Isabelle Adjani, Bruno Ganz and Roland Topor. Two versions filmed simultaneously, in German 107 minutes, in English 124 minutes. Werner Herzog Filmproduktion, Gaumont S.A., Paris, and Zweiten Deutschen Fernsehen, 1979.

Regen / Rain. Dir. and written by Joris Ivens and Mannus Franken. 12 minutes, silent, black and white. CAPI Amsterdam, 1929.

Rififi / Du rififi chez les hommes. Dir. and written by Jules Dassin, after a novel by Auguste Le Breton. Cinematography by Philippe Agostini. Film score by Georges Auric. With Jean Servais, Carl Möhner, Robert Manuel, Jules Dassin, Marie Sabouret and Janine Darcey. 115 minutes, mono, Western Electric Sound System, black and white. Indusfilms/Prima/Société Nouvelle Pathé Cinéma, 1955.

Road to Perdition. Dir. Sam Mendes. Cinematography by Conrad Hall. Screenplay by David Self after the novel by Max Allan Collins and Richard Piers Rayner. Film score by Thomas Newman, supervising sound editor Scott Hecker, foley mixer Lane Birch. With Tom Hanks, Paul Newman, Jude Law, Tyler Hoechlin and Jennifer Jason Leigh. 117 minutes. Dreamworks Pictures, 2002.

The Silence of the Lambs. Dir. Jonathan Demme, screenplay by Ted Tally, after the novel by Thomas Harris. Cinematography by Tak Fujimoto. Film score by Howard Shore, sound designer Skip Lievsay, production sound mixer Christopher Newman. With Anthony Hopkins, Jodie Foster, Scott Glenn and Ted Levine. 118 minutes, Dolby Surround sound. Orion Pictures, 1991.

Index